D1378736

Women and Politics

Paths to Power and Political Influence

Second Edition

JULIE **DOLAN**

Macalester College

MELISSA **DECKMAN**

Washington College

MICHELE L. **SWERS**

Georgetown University

Longman

Boston   Columbus   Indianapolis   New York   San Francisco   Upper Saddle River
Amsterdam   Cape Town   Dubai   London   Madrid   Milan   Munich   Paris   Montreal   Toronto
Delhi   Mexico City   São Paulo   Sydney   Hong Kong   Seoul   Singapore   Taipei   Tokyo

Editor-in-Chief: Eric Stano
Supplements Editor: Donna Garnier
Marketing Manager: Lindsey Prudhomme
Production Manager: Jacqueline A. Martin
Project Coordination and Electronic Page Makeup: PreMediaGlobal
Cover Designer/Manager: Nancy Danahy
Cover Illustration/Photo: Gerald Herbert/AP Photo/AP Associated Press
Senior Manufacturing Buyer: Dennis J. Para

For permission to use copyrighted material, grateful acknowledgment is made to the copyright
holders on p.363, which are hereby made part of this copyright page.

Library of Congress Cataloging-in-Publication Data

Dolan, Julie.
Women and politics : paths to power and political influence / Julie Dolan, Melissa Deckman,
Michele L. Swers. —2nd ed.
    p. cm.
Includes bibliographical references and index.
ISBN-13: 978-0-205-82715-2
ISBN-10: 0-205-82715-2
    1. Women—Political activity—United States.   I. Deckman, Melissa M. (Melissa Marie),
1971—II. Swers, Michele L.   III. Title.
HQ1236.5.U6D635 2010
320.973082—dc22

                                                                          2010019449

Longman
is an imprint of

www.pearsonhighered.com

ISBN-13: 978-0-205-82715-2
ISBN-10:   0-205-82715-2

CONTENTS

CHAPTER 7

Women in Congress and the State Legislatures 227

CHAPTER 8

Women in the Executive Branch 263

CHAPTER 9

Women in the Judiciary 304

PREFACE

INTRODUCTION

As graduate students in the mid-1990s, all three of us began studying women and politics. At that point, there was much excellent scholarship to guide us but certainly a manageable and seemingly finite amount. What we could not have known then is just how tremendously the field would grow in a relatively short period of time. In the past twenty years, the field has witnessed a virtual explosion of scholarship. Since the historic "Year of the Woman" in 1992, women have increased their presence in the U.S. House of Representatives from 6 percent to 17 percent and in the Senate from 2 percent to 17 percent. These historic gains have spurred a great deal of new and innovative scholarly research that has been both exhilarating and exhausting—whereas the field was manageable at one point in time, it is now becoming increasingly difficult, if not impossible, to keep apace of all the emerging published and unpublished work.

One of our primary aims in writing this book is to synthesize and make accessible to a wider audience the vast amount of new scholarly research on women as political actors and especially as political elites in the United States.

NEW TO THE SECOND EDITION

Women have made enormous strides in politics since the first edition of this text went to press. In the summer of 2006, Nancy Pelosi was serving as the Minority Leader in the Democratic party, Hillary Clinton was running for re-election for a second term as the junior Senator from the state of New York, and Sarah Palin was seeking the Republican party nomination for Governor of Alaska, challenging sitting Governor Frank Murkowski in the process. On the United States Supreme Court, Sandra Day O'Connor had retired months earlier, leaving Ruth Bader Ginsburg as the sole female voice on the court.

As the second edition goes to press, clearly much has changed. Nancy Pelosi is the current and first female Speaker of the United States House of Representatives, a position she has held since the Democrats took control of Congress following the midterm elections in 2006. Hillary Clinton is the Secretary of State in President Barack Obama's administration, an appointment she received after first squaring off against Senator Obama in an enormously competitive campaign for the Democratic nomination to the presidency. Sarah Palin has returned to private life, resigning as Governor of Alaska almost a year after she made history as the first Republican woman nominated as vice president of the United States. And Sonia Sotomayor has recently joined

Ruth Bader Ginsburg on the Supreme Court, becoming the first Hispanic and third female Justice of the Court. This edition provides new in-depth coverage of all of these women and their paths to power and political influence. In addition, we update the text to reflect new gains women have made at all levels of government, as citizens, in the media, and in the parties and interest groups.

Recognizing the historic nature of the 2008 presidential elections, the second edition includes numerous updates related to the election.

- Chapter 3 includes discussion of the Obama and McCain campaigns' attempts to woo women voters on the campaign trail. While President Obama ultimately benefited from a seven-point gender gap, clearly many women voted for the McCain and Palin ticket. As such, we include a new analysis of female voters in the 2008 elections, looking more closely at different subgroups of women and their ultimate vote choices. We also examine the gender gap in the Democratic primary elections, paying special attention to the role women voters played in delivering many states to Hillary Clinton. Hillary Clinton benefited from a gender gap in almost every state she carried, while Barack Obama almost never did.

- Chapter 4, The Impact of the Media on Political Women, has been updated in a number of places. First, we include a new profile of CBS anchor Katie Couric, the first woman to solo anchor one of the major three evening news broadcasts. Couric was one of three journalists to land high-profile interviews with Governor Sarah Palin during the 2008 elections, ultimately receiving the Walter Cronkite award for excellence in television journalism for her efforts. Second, the chapter includes new discussion and analysis of the media coverage received by First Lady Michele Obama and Speaker Nancy Pelosi.

- Our chapter on female candidates for political office, Chapter 5, has been updated with entirely new sections devoted to the candidacies of both Hillary Clinton and Sarah Palin. Even though Clinton and Palin were both running at the top of the ticket, they faced challenges common for female candidates at all levels of office: damaging voter stereotypes and sexist media treatment. We detail the types of media coverage each woman received on the campaign trail, voters' perceptions of both women, and their own campaigns' strategies for overcoming voter stereotypes about their abilities and fitness for the job.

- Chapter 6, Women in Local Government, includes a new profile of The Gender and Multicultural Leadership Project, an organization actively increasing our knowledge about women of color elected at all levels of government in the United States.

- In Chapter 7, we detail Pelosi's rise to power, her commitment to women's and children's issues as part of her legislative agenda, and her overall leadership style. We also update this chapter to reflect new gains women are making in leadership roles in the U.S. Congress and in state legislatures.

- In Chapter 8, Women in the Executive Branch, we provide further analysis of the historic candidacies of Hillary Clinton and Sarah Palin, doing so with an eye toward comparing and contrasting them with the women who preceded them in their own pursuit of the White House. Besides beginning her campaign as the frontrunner for the Democratic nomination, an historic first, Clinton's candidacy was extraordinary for a number of reasons. This chapter recounts the various ways in which Clinton made history on the campaign trail.

- Chapter 8 also includes new discussion of Sarah Palin's vice presidential candidacy. Like Geraldine Ferraro, the first Democratic woman nominated on a vice presidential ticket, Palin was chosen by McCain, in part, to appeal to women voters. A relative unknown when she joined the ticket, Sarah Palin quickly energized many female and Republican voters. We recount her various contributions to the campaign in this chapter. We also update the chapter to reflect gains women are making in the Obama administration, including details about Valerie Jarrett, who is said to be one of the most powerful players in the Obama White House.

- Chapter 9 is updated to include new information about Justice Sonia Sotomayor, the third woman to sit on the Supreme Court of the United States. We devote special attention to her confirmation hearings and the ways in which both race and gender influenced the conversation.

- Finally, we update all of the chapters to incorporate new scholarship published since the first edition went to press.

ACKNOWLEDGMENTS

We owe a tremendous debt of gratitude to the extraordinary community of women and politics scholars. In fact, the idea for this book was born over the period of a few years at the Midwest Political Science Association's annual conference, where, for many years, the women and politics panels have been both inspiring and excellent. The three of us have religiously attended the spring meetings for the past decade, sought out the women and politics panels, and found ourselves together at dinner engaged in discussions about the state of the field and what we thought was missing. The most glaring omission, we thought, was the lack of in-depth coverage of women as political elites. How did they arrive at their positions in Congress and the state legislatures, governor's mansions, presidential and gubernatorial cabinets, executive branch agencies and departments, state and federal judicial posts, interest groups and the parties, city councils and school boards? What impact have women officials had on the conduct of politics and the nature of policy outcomes? While teaching women and politics courses at our respective institutions, we all had difficulties finding enough accessible material to assign our students to sufficiently convey the state of scholarship on women as political elites. How could we best communicate the substance and excitement of the field to our undergraduate and graduate students?

We found ourselves cobbling together readings from websites, journals, and books, but wishing that someone would bring all of the literature together in one place to make it more accessible and user friendly for our students. After a few years had passed, we decided to do it ourselves.

Despite the gains that women have made in recent years, women remain woefully underrepresented in just about every single body politic in the United States. Although women make up more than half of the U.S. population, why is it that so few of them enter politics? The vast majority of women in the United States work outside the home, but remarkably few choose politics as a vocation. Why might this be the case? Our book examines these questions in detail, looking at women's diverse experiences in the world of politics. We profile a variety of political women along the way and draw from most recent research completed at the national, state, and local levels. We also strive to provide ideological balance, covering women in both the Democratic and Republican parties, as well as conservative, moderate, and liberal women.

We have many people to thank for their support and assistance. As we mentioned earlier, this book draws on years of inspiration coming out of the Midwest and other political science conferences. Without this incredible community of scholars presenting papers, writing books and articles, and otherwise advancing the state of knowledge in the field, this book simply would not be possible. The study of women and politics has grown terrifically in the past decade and we are grateful to be part of the discussion.

Furthermore, there are a number of individuals who have gone above and beyond to help us along the way. We would especially like to thank three senior scholars and pioneers in the field: Peggy Conway, Karen O'Connor, and Marian Lief Palley. All three of these women have written extensively about women and politics, and each of us has used their texts in preparing and teaching our own women and politics courses. We admire them as scholars, mentors, and teachers. We have all benefited from their guidance, advice, support, and friendship along the way. In fact, we owe special thanks to Karen O'Connor for bringing the three of us together and for introducing us to Peggy and Marian. We cannot express how grateful we are to be able to work with such extraordinary women.

Thanks also go to Barbara Palmer for sharing her cutting-edge research, data, advice, and sense of humor with us over the years. We would also like to thank Alana Jeydel, who provided much appreciated advice at the start of the project and David H. Rosenbloom who was always ready and willing to listen, strategize, and generously share his time and advice.

A number of additional people agreed to be interviewed for the book or to otherwise share their time and expertise with us. The book is much richer because of their contributions and we would like to acknowledge them here: Peter Fenn (Fenn Communications Group), Christine Sierra (Gender and Multicultural Leadership Project), Margaret Moore (National Center for Women and Policing), Gregory S. Hurley and Joan Cochet (National Center for State Courts), Amy Sullivan (author of Political Aims blog), Stefanie Lindquist (former federal law clerk), Mayor Margo Bailey, Bonnie Watkins (Minnesota Women's Consortium),

Drucilla Stender Ramey (National Association Women Judges), Ann Wagner (Republican National Committee), and Ann Lewis (Democratic National Committee).

Likewise, we are grateful to a number of individuals and organizations that greatly facilitated our data collection efforts. Barbara Palmer and Dennis Simon provided data about the 2008 congressional elections and James King and James Riddlesperger shared their federal appointees data with us. Their generosity saved us many hours of additional work! In addition, we drew heavily on the Federal Judicial Center, the National Center for State Courts, the Public Information Office of the Supreme Court, the International City/County Management Association, the National League of Cities, and the Center for American Women and Politics for additional data reported in this book.

Each of us also would also like to extend warmest thanks to a number of people at our respective institutions. We would like to thank our colleagues in the Departments of Political Science at Macalester College and Washington College and in the Department of Government at Georgetown University. We are very grateful for the supportive and collegial environments they provide. In writing the first edition of this text, all three of us also benefited from sabbatical leaves at our respective institutions and owe thanks to Provost Dan Hornbach (Macalester College), Dean Joachim Scholz (Washington College), and Dean Gerald Mara (Graduate School at Georgetown University). We could not have completed the project without such support and are grateful to have had the opportunity. We also benefited from the assistance of a number of highly talented, dedicated, and capable research assistants. Thanks go to Alix Heard, Kate Henningsen, Laura Dziorny, Erin O'Connor, Waffiyah Mian, Michele Parvinsky, Carin Larson and Shauna Shames at Georgetown University; Jonathan Kropf, Elizabeth Durney, Kara Bovee, Kellan Anfinson, Egle Tamosaityte, Andy Haug, Patrick McGarrity and Ben Garnett at Macalester College; and Christy Rowan, Tracy Stewart, Becky Binns, and Martin Dunphy at Washington College.

At Pearson Longman, we would like to thank our executive editor, Eric Stano, for his support for the project, and his assistant Elizabeth Alimena, for keeping track of all the pieces of the project. We would also like to thank production manager Jacqueline Martin and project editor Aparna Yellai for expertly coordinating and managing the entire production process. Additional thanks go to Linda Sykes for devoting untold hours to hunting down obscure photos, securing the permission to use them, and otherwise making sure all of the photos in the book look great.

We wish to thank the following reviewers for their valuable insights and suggestions: Barbara Burrell, Northern Illinois University; Stephen J. Stambough, California State University at Fullerton; Joan Thompson, Arcadia University; and Nikki R. Van Hightower, Texas A&M University.

Finally, we all three have amazing families to thank for their love and support. Each of us is blessed with a wonderful husband (Bill Lee, Sean Fallon, and Andrew Todd Swers) and two amazing children (Oliver Lake Lee, Easton Sylvester Lee, Mason Wesley Fallon, Gavin Christopher Fallon, Alexander

Evan Swers, and Lisa Danielle Swers), and we cannot thank them enough for the constant joy and meaning they bring to our lives. Likewise, our extended families have provided years of support and love and we want to let them know just how much we appreciate all they do for us: Dennis, Glenys, Scott and Sara Dolan, TC Lee and Lucy Wang, Lloyd and Diann Deckman, Andrew and Lesley Fallon, Theodore and Belle Probst, Arlene and Marvin Birnbaum, Ronald and Gwen Swers, and Jeffrey and Shana Swers.

JULIE DOLAN
MELISSA DECKMAN
MICHELE L. SWERS

Introduction and Theoretical Framework

2 008 was an historic year for women in politics in the United States. Senator Hillary Clinton began the year running strong for the Democratic nomination for the presidency, Governor Sarah Palin breathed new excitement into the presidential election when she was selected as John McCain's running mate in August, and voters were more receptive than ever before to the idea of electing a female president.

In fact, to many it seemed like women had finally broken the highest, hardest glass ceiling. Hillary Clinton launched her presidential candidacy in January 2007 as the frontrunner for the Democratic nomination, making history as the first woman to do so. Many suggested that she was the inevitable nominee, noting that she had raised significantly more money than her male competitors, that public opinion numbers strongly tilted in her favor, and that she was a formidable candidate who rarely made mistakes on the campaign trail. After 18 months in the running, she came closer to winning the nomination than any other woman in U.S. history. She ultimately conceded the nomination to fellow Senator Barack Obama, the first African American to win his party's nomination and soon thereafter, the presidency.

Only two months after Clinton conceded to Obama, Governor Sarah Palin arrived on the scene, running as the first Republican woman nominated to the office of the vice presidency. Before selecting Palin as his running mate, Senator John McCain was running behind Barack Obama in most public opinion polls. Her candidacy immediately energized the campaign and appeared to attract new voters to the ticket. In fact, following the Republican national convention, many polls showed McCain and Palin running slightly ahead of Obama and Joe Biden, and many voters indicated that the addition of Palin made them more likely to vote for McCain (Newport 2008).

At the same time, voters in the United States were becoming more receptive to the idea of electing a female president. When pollsters first began asking the question in the 1930s, only one-third of Americans said they would vote for a qualified woman for president. When Clinton kicked off her campaign in January 2007, nearly 90 percent of individuals agreed that they would vote for a woman nominated by their own political party (Polling Report 2009).

Besides Clinton and Palin, other women served in highly visible and influential government positions in 2008. Nancy Pelosi was serving in her second year as the first female Speaker of the House of Representatives, and Condoleezza Rice was finishing up her term as George W. Bush's second Secretary of State. Thus, an outsider watching politics unfold in 2008 might assume that women had arrived—that women were finally competing on a level playing field in the masculine realm of American politics.

For all the attention Clinton, Palin, Pelosi, and Rice received in 2008, the fact remains that women are still vastly outnumbered in American politics today. For high-ranking political offices, such as the United States Congress and state governorships, the vast majority of candidates are still male. Further, although women continue to make inroads into political office across all three branches of government, men still outnumber women by large margins. Men hold approximately eight out of ten congressional and state legislative seats, governor's positions, and judicial posts in both state and federal courts and only three women have ever served on the Supreme Court of the United States.

Outside of the bright lights of a presidential campaign, there are many more opportunities to participate in politics at the state and local levels, and women have been contributing and participating in these other arenas for decades. Although these women are more invisible to the general public, many women "do politics" in local political party organizations and advocacy groups, statewide elected executive positions such as lieutenant governor and attorney general, on school boards, city councils, and in mayoral offices. In fact, far more women serve on city councils than in the state legislatures or the United States Congress. Darcy, Welch, and Clark (1994) estimate that 20 times more women serve on city councils than in state and federal offices combined! Although neither Clinton nor Palin emerged victorious in 2008, both women's candidacies tell us a fair bit about the strides women have made in their pursuit of political office and highlight the types of challenges that remain for women in American politics. This book examines not only their stories, but the stories of many more women across the political spectrum in the United States.

Two themes run through the book to help organize our thinking about the role of women in American politics today. One is that political women are a very diverse lot, engaged in politics in many different ways. Since the suffrage movement, women have repeatedly lined up on different sides of the aisle, fighting for their own conception of the ideal world. Yet much research on women and men in politics highlights the ways in which women differ from men, inadvertently suggesting that political women have more in common with one another than they do with political men. Although the temptation is to think of women as a monolithic bloc, the reality is much more complex.

The candidacies of Hillary Clinton and Sarah Palin nicely illustrate this point. There were clear ideological differences between the two women, as Hillary Clinton pointed out when McCain selected Palin as his running mate. After congratulating Palin on the nomination, Clinton affirmed that "Governor Palin will add an important new voice to the debate," but also argued that Palin's policies would take the country in the wrong direction (Nichols 2008). Female voters lined up for both women, but their supporters were, for the most part, not cut from the same cloth. Conservative women embraced Palin's candidacy and her positions, while liberal women were attracted to Clinton's candidacy.

We argue throughout the book that although women share many common interests, they bring a diversity of viewpoints to the table. Women do not always see eye to eye on what is best for women, and it is not uncommon for opposing women's groups to claim that they both speak for women and have women's best interests at heart. For example, women's groups do battle on both sides of the abortion wars and both sides sincerely believe that they are fighting to make women's lives better. On the pro-choice side, organizations such as NARAL Pro-Choice America and the National Organization for Women (NOW) see abortion rights as absolutely essential to securing women's full equality. Women's pro-life groups, such as Feminists for Life, on the other hand, oppose abortion on the grounds that it "validate[s] the patriarchical worldview . . . that women, encumbered as they are by their reproductive capacity, are inferior to men" (quoted in Burkett 1998). Thus, both sides appear to agree that women should not be defined by their reproductive capacities, but they disagree as to how to ensure that this does not happen.

Similarly, as Chapter 2 describes, the variety of women's organizations fighting for female suffrage in the late 1800s and early 1900s were hardly a monolithic bloc. Early on, two different organizations with different goals, strategies, and tactics emerged. The American Woman Suffrage Association (AWSA) was the more conservative of the two organizations, focusing its efforts solely on women's suffrage and pursuing a state-by-state approach through fairly conventional means (Strom 1975). The National Woman Suffrage Association (NWSA), by contrast, advocated female suffrage as one of many social reforms that would move women toward greater equality in American society. It also adopted more unconventional tactics than did AWSA, staging protests and using civil disobedience in its efforts to secure a women's suffrage amendment to the U.S. Constitution.

On the other side, some women organized in opposition to female suffrage (Camhi 1994). Most of these women were of high social standing and believed wholeheartedly that suffrage would place too great a burden on women and, consequently, wreak havoc on families (Flexner 1975; Camhi 1994). As they saw it, women's place was in the home, and the burdens of suffrage would divorce women, in part, from their roles as wives and mothers.

As these stories and many more in the following pages will illustrate, political women often have different ideas about what is best for women and how to achieve progress for women. Throughout the book, we strive to cover the diversity of women's experiences and viewpoints, regardless of whether these women identify themselves as feminists. We aim to provide a balanced account of women in politics by highlighting women on both sides of the political aisle and demonstrating the diversity of ideological perspectives embraced by today's political women.

Our second theme throughout the book is the importance of gender roles for understanding and categorizing women's experiences and contributions to politics and governance in the United States. Historically, men and women have occupied different spheres in society. While men's contributions typically have been in the public sphere, where they work outside of the home to provide for the family, women's contributions have been within the private sphere, where they are responsible for running the household, raising and educating children, and attending to the religious and moral health of the family.

In fact, it was fairly common in the nineteenth and early twentieth centuries to exclude women from the public sphere because of expectations about the separate spheres for the sexes as well as assumptions about their different "natures." One accomplished paleontologist from the nineteenth century argued against female suffrage for the reason that "woman is physically incapable of carrying into execution any law she may enact . . . [As such] the sexes cannot take an equal share of governmental responsibilities even if they should desire to do so" (Cope 1888). Besides natural differences in physical strength, he also drew distinctions between what he perceived to be natural differences in the mental capacities of the sexes: "We find in man a greater *capacity* for rational processes . . . In women we find that the deficiency of endurance of the rational faculty is associated with a general incapacity for mental strain, and, as her emotional nature is stronger, that strain is more severe than it is in man under similar circumstances" (emphasis in original, Cope 1888). Similar reasoning was used to keep women out of public schools, fearing that they would become too overwhelmed by the strains and rigors of education, endangering their abilities to bear healthy children and take care of the home in the future (Clarke 1873; Camhi 1994).

The United States Supreme Court employed just this sort of reasoning in 1908 in the case of *Muller v. Oregon*, arguing that women's special role in the family, combined with their weaker physical nature, provided a societal justification for limiting their role in the workplace. As the opinion stated,

> That woman's physical structure and the performance of maternal functions place her at a disadvantage in the struggle for subsistence is obvious. This is especially true when the burdens of motherhood are upon her. Even when they are not, by abundant testimony of the medical fraternity continuance for a long time on her feet at work, repeating this from day to day, tends to injurious effects upon the body, and as healthy mothers are essential to vigorous offspring, the physical well-being of woman becomes an object of public interest and care in order to preserve the strength and vigor of the race. (*Mueller v. Oregon*, 208 U.S. 421)

These are just a few examples of the ways in which gender roles were historically used to keep women contained within the private sphere and out of the public sphere. Times have certainly changed since the Supreme Court ruled that separate spheres justified treating women differently under the law, and today few scholars rely on biological differences to interpret and understand how the sexes participate in politics or in public and social life more generally. Society now accepts that women are no longer necessarily bound by their roles as mothers, as most women—with or without children—are active in the workplace outside of the home and have made great progress not just in politics but also in other fields, such as law, medicine, education, and business.

Despite women's great advancements, however, we maintain that gender roles still matter today and help us to interpret and understand women's paths to public office and the types of work they do in the public sphere once they arrive. That is, even after laws and customs change to grant women equal political rights, women continue to follow slightly different paths than do political men, and these paths are quite often consistent with stereotypical gender roles. Some go so far as to say that "the political system . . . endorses and practices masculinism" (Borrelli 2002; 22), with unfortunate consequences for women. MaryAnne Borrelli (2002) argues that "gender role traditions systematically privilege masculinity and deprecate femininity," such that women are routinely placed in less powerful political positions and have fewer opportunities to access the levers of power even when they hold virtually the same positions as do men in politics and government.

The following chapters provide plenty of examples of the ways in which gender roles still structure and influence American politics. For one, women often become involved in politics as a natural extension of their roles as wives and mothers. In the battle for suffrage, many women's organizations advocated extending the vote to women because they would use it to reform society and improve conditions for the family and home. In fighting against the Equal Rights Amendment (ERA), some women's organizations claimed that it would upset traditional gender roles and ultimately lead to the destruction of the family (see Chapter 2). Women on the campaign trail often lament that voters and the media treat them first as women and second as candidates, suggesting that gender roles are still deeply engrained in the American psyche (see Chapter 5). Women officeholders typically hold different types of positions once in office, and these positions are more often than not consistent with stereotypical gender roles. For example, legislative and executive women are more likely to be found on committees and in departments dealing with education, health care, and other social service issues (see Chapters 7 and 8). Some of this can be explained by women's occupational training, which also tends to be consistent with gender roles. Sexual segregation in the workplace is so pervasive that we can easily attach gender labels to most occupations. For example, women are much more likely than men to be nurses and teachers, whereas men are more likely to be found working as firefighters, mechanics, and plumbers. Gender roles continue to structure American society today, and so it is not particularly surprising that gender roles influence women's practice of politics.

Part I of the book, **Women's Paths to Power**, focuses on women's engagement in politics from outside of the system. Although women did not gain the right to vote until 1920, when the Nineteenth Amendment was added to the U.S. Constitution, women have been active in the political life of the country from quite early on. Without the right to vote, women in the early twentieth century joined clubs and organizations of all sorts. Although not explicitly political in nature, many of these organizations joined together to fight for female suffrage and later on turned their attentions to other political issues. Today women continue to organize, advocate, and petition the government through organized interest groups. **Chapter 2, Women in Social Movements, Interest Groups, and the Political Parties**, details the rich history of women's civic involvement, focusing especially on the Seneca Falls Convention in 1848, the battle for suffrage, and the fights for and against the Equal Rights Amendment. The chapter also traces women's involvement in present-day interest groups and political parties in the United States.

Since women won the right to vote, the political parties have waxed and waned in their devotion to courting a potential "women's vote." As detailed in **Chapter 3, The Gender Gap in Elections and Public Opinion**, both the Democratic and Republican parties were deliberate in their appeals to female voters in the presidential elections of 2008 and 2004, both strategizing about how to appeal to women and secure their votes. With women voters outnumbering male voters by nearly 8 million and making up the majority of undecided and independent voters, both Obama and McCain developed strategies for appealing to women and getting them to turn out to vote on Election Day. Even so, both campaigns realized that women do not form a monolithic bloc when it comes to their attitudes, political ideology, voting behavior, or partisan identification. Slightly more women identify as Democrats and vote for the Democratic Party, but there is great diversity in the viewpoints and policy preferences of women in the U.S. population. Chapter 3 examines the diversity of women's voting behavior and policy preferences across time, adding new analysis of women's votes in the 2008 elections.

Chapter 4, The Impact of the Media on Political Women, focuses on women and the media. Outside of government, the news media work alongside politicians, report their doings to the public, and provide access to power. Yet journalism today, especially in the most prestigious positions, remains a male-dominated field. This chapter includes a new profile of CBS anchor Katie Couric, the first woman to anchor one of the major networks' evening newscasts. We also look at the roles women play as journalists, talking heads, and television reporters as well as the ways in which women's organizations have tried to use the media to promote their causes, both successfully and unsuccessfully. Some women's groups have molded media coverage to their advantage, while others have not been so adept. Finally, the chapter discusses media coverage of first ladies and female politicians. On the heels of the 2008 elections, we include details about Michelle Obama and Nancy Pelosi's media coverage.

Chapter 5, Women as Candidates for Elective Office, covers the experiences of women running for elective office. Despite the presence of Clinton and Palin at the top of the ticket in 2008, women have always been far less likely than men to run for political office in the United States. We explore some of the reasons for women's reluctance to run in this chapter. We also devote special attention to the candidacies of Hillary Clinton and Sarah Palin, focusing on the media coverage they received and their own attempts to persuade voters that they were the best woman for the job. Finally, we discuss some of the challenges common for female candidates on the campaign trail, including voter stereotypes about their qualifications, sexist media coverage, and subtle discrimination from the political parties.

Part II, Women in Power, focuses on women who occupy formal positions of power. Specifically, we examine elite women in the following areas: in local political institutions (such as city councils, school boards, and county commissions), in Congress and the state legislatures, in the state and federal executive branches, in the White House and governor's mansions, and in the judiciary. Each chapter includes a discussion of the different types of players involved in each level and branch of government, their roles and responsibilities, the paths women travel in order to arrive at these positions, and the ways in which they influence policy once they arrive.

All of the chapters in Part II get at the question of women's representation. Although women continue to lag behind men in just about all elected and appointed government positions, we examine the types of contributions they make while in office. Does it matter that women are vastly underrepresented in political office in the United States? Do women and men have different political interests? Does the presence of women in government and advocacy groups substantively alter the nature and quality of government outputs? Is political life qualitatively different with greater numbers of women serving in high places? We draw from the wealth of scholarly research that has been published in the last decade to address some of these questions.

In addition, we pay special attention to the leadership styles embraced by women in positions of political power. Many scholars find evidence that women employ a consensus-oriented leadership style rather than a command-and-control style, adopting styles that are more inclusive than those used by their male colleagues (Rosenthal 1998; Rosener 1990). We examine these questions throughout Part II of the book.

Because most women begin their political careers at the local level, **Chapter 6, Women in Local Politics and Government**, details women's involvement in arenas such as school boards, city and county councils, and as local executives. As local governments have become increasingly relevant policy venues in their own right, women's involvement at this level of politics has become important, especially as many decisions made by such government actors affect the day-to-day lives of average citizens. However, policy influence is not limited to elected officials in local politics, so we examine the role of women in local government as bureaucrats, which we define broadly to cover a range of positions from city managers to school administrators to police officers. We also take a look at women's involvement in grassroots movements, which often form to fight for economic, environmental, and other rights.

Finally, we examine women as local business leaders, with the acknowledgment that such leaders often work closely with elected officials in helping to shape and develop economic policy.

Chapter 7, Women in Congress and the State Legislatures, highlights the historical progress women have made in the state legislatures and the United States Congress. Nancy Pelosi became the first female Speaker of the House following the 2006 elections, and we highlight her rise to power in this chapter. We then turn to investigating the impact women have had on the policy agenda and the institutional norms of legislative bodies. For example, research conducted at the state level indicates that women are more likely to view other women as a distinct portion of their constituency, and they are more likely to feel a responsibility to represent women's interests than do their male colleagues. Additionally, the plethora of research conducted at the state and national levels reveals that women are more likely to sponsor legislation concerning women's issues such as education, welfare, and reproductive rights, and they are more likely to view these issues as a high priority. The chapter also considers the ideological differences among women and how these differences impact their interpretation of women's interests and their ability to work together across party lines.

Chapter 8, Women in the Executive Branch, examines women's contributions to governance from the executive branch. No woman has ever served as president or vice president of the United States, but many have thrown their hat into the ring over the years. We pay particular attention to Hillary Clinton and Sarah Palin's historic candidacies in 2008, comparing and contrasting them with the women who preceded them in their pursuit of the White House. We also look at some of the women who have served as governors and other statewide elected officials before turning to a discussion of women in presidential and gubernatorial cabinets. Finally, we address whether or not executive women bring unique perspectives and leadership styles to their roles and entertain the possibility that a female president would govern differently than a male president.

Finally, **Chapter 9, Women in the Judiciary,** provides a historical glimpse at women's roles in the judiciary, including details about some of the first women to serve as judges in the United States. We add new information about the third woman to serve on the United States' Supreme Court, Justice Sonia Sotomayor. We also discuss the implications of an increased female presence on the bench: Do women decide cases differently than men, particularly in cases that more directly affect women, such as sex discrimination? Do they use a "different voice" in their legal reasoning?

After reading this text, readers should have an excellent grasp of women's status as political actors in the United States, their paths to higher office, their behavior in office, the diversity of viewpoints and goals among political women, and the difference they make. We showcase political women across the ideological spectrum and in all sorts of venues, not only because their stories are fascinating but also because we hope to inspire a new generation of women to become politically engaged. As we demonstrate throughout the book, women from all walks of life have stood up to make their voices heard. They did not start out as professional politicians but as women who thought they could make a difference and improve their communities by getting involved. The United States is a much richer place because of their efforts.

REFERENCES

Borrelli, MaryAnne. 2002. *The President's Cabinet: Gender, Power, and Representation*. Boulder: Lynne Rienner.

Burkett, Elinor. 1998. *The Right Women*. New York: Touchstone.

Camhi, Jane Jerome. 1994. *Women Against Women: American Anti-Suffragism: 1880–1920*. Brooklyn: Carlson Publishing Inc.

Clarke, Edward H. 1972 [1873]. *Sex in Education: A Fair Chance for the Girls*. New York: Arno Press.

Cope, Edward D. 1888. "The Relation of the Two Sexes to Government." pp. 166–169 in *Women's Rights in the United States: A Documentary History*, ed. Winston E. Langley and Vivian C. Fox. Westport, CT: Praeger Publishers.

Darcy, R., Susan Welch, and Janet Clark. 1994. *Women, Elections and Representation*. Lincoln, NE: University of Nebraska Press.

Flexner, Eleanor. 1975. *Century of Struggle: The Women's Rights Movement in the United States*. Cambridge, MA: Belknap Press of Harvard University Press.

Newport, Frank. 2008. "Republicans' Enthusiasm Jumps After Convention." Gallup Poll, September 8th. Accessed online at http://www.gallup.com/poll/110107/Republicans-Enthusiasm-Jumps-After-Convention.aspx

Nichols, John. 2008. "Clinton Praises Palin Pick." *The Nation* (30 August). Accessed online at www.thenation.com/blogs/thebeat/351275/clinton_praises_palin_pick.

Polling Report. 2009. "Government and Politics." Accessed online at www.pollingreport.com/politics.htm.

Rosener, Judy. 1990. "Ways Women Lead." *Harvard Business Review* 68, no. 6: 119–125.

Rosenthal, Cindy Simon. 1998. *When Women Lead: Integrative Leadership in State Legislatures*. New York: Oxford University Press.

Strom, Sharon Hartman. 1975. "Leadership and Tactics in the American Woman Suffrage Association: A New Perspective from Massachusetts." *Journal of American History* 62, no. 2:296–315.

Women in Social Movements, Interest Groups, and the Political Parties

Today we take for granted women's political rights and responsibilities. But for much of American history, politics in the United States was a "man's world" from which women were excluded on legal, moral, and social grounds. During the nineteenth and early twentieth centuries, women lost most of their legal rights upon marriage and were considered the property of their husbands. Married women had no right to own property, no right to an education, no right to their children in cases of divorce, no access to most professions, and no right to the wages they earned. Gender relations were guided by the principle of separate spheres in which men were the breadwinners for their families and represented their households in the public sphere. Women were expected to take care of the home, raise and educate the children, and conduct themselves on a higher moral plane.

Despite being largely excluded from the political world, including being denied the right to vote, some women still managed to participate and shape public life. One early example of such political activism is in the abolitionist movement, in which many women worked alongside men to stop slavery. Elizabeth Cady Stanton and Lucretia Mott were two such women. They met one another at the 1840 World Anti-Slavery Convention in London. Skilled organizers in their own right, both were infuriated when they were denied seats at the convention and relegated to the balcony because they were women. Many female abolitionists began to realize that their lot in life was little better than slaves in that they shared few legal rights. As a result, Stanton and Mott organized the first women's rights convention in Seneca Falls, New York, in 1848, which marks the beginning of the American feminist movement. Issuing the Declaration of Rights and Sentiments modeled on the Declaration of Independence, these women called for a complete overhaul of the laws and traditions guiding relationships between the sexes (see Appendix A for the full text of the Declaration of Rights and Sentiments). The women who gathered at Seneca Falls passed resolutions seeking to overhaul laws and achieve a more equitable social and legal standing for women, including the right to vote (Baker 1984; Hartmann 1989; Flexner and Fitzpatrick 1996).

The organizers at Seneca Falls, however, were far ahead of their time in terms of their conceptions about women's rights and had little real chance in the mid-nineteenth century of changing either discriminatory laws against women or social views about women's place in public affairs. Conference organizers, however, began to see that crucial to any changes in women's status would be their ability to participate in elections. As a result, the first widespread movement involving women was the fight for women's suffrage, which lasted more than 70 years. This chapter takes a closer look at women's struggle to attain the right to vote during this period.

The chapter then examines the "second wave" of feminism that developed several decades after women gained suffrage rights in 1920, as a response to larger societal shifts in women's roles in the 1960s, including the increasing number of women in the workforce, the expansion of women's access to higher education, and rising divorce rates. Women also became active in numerous political movements at the time, including antiwar and civil rights causes. These activist women suffered a similar fate as female abolitionists in that the male leaders of those organizations undervalued their contributions. Women organized in their own right to fight against the discriminatory behavior they faced at the workplace, in state and federal legislation, and in society. This chapter closely examines these struggles and how such battles culminated in the failed bid for an Equal Rights Amendment (ERA) to the U.S. Constitution (Hartman 1989; Mansbridge 1986; Costain 1992).

The unsuccessful battle over the ERA revealed that women were not monolithic in their political views, as it sparked an intense backlash among more socially conservative women and men. These individuals believed that the second-wave feminist movement challenged women's traditional place in the home and undermined the American social fabric (Mansbridge 1986; Klatch 1987; Schreiber 2008). Today debate about women's role in society continues, and women (and men) are of diverse opinions regarding numerous political issues relevant to women such as reproductive rights, child care, and education. This chapter examines women's participation in current political organizations geared at women's issues, ranging from liberal to conservative in nature. The chapter concludes by looking at women's historical involvement in the Democratic and Republican parties as well as their current place in both parties.

THE FIGHT FOR SUFFRAGE

The 72-year fight (1848–1920) for suffrage reflects the evolution of different types of feminism. The women who organized the convention at Seneca Falls were feminists who sought a more radical restructuring of women's place in society, and many suffragists, such as Susan B. Anthony, would follow this rationale for attaining women's right to vote. Later other women joined the battle for women's suffrage who were less interested in changing women's status but instead used their moral authority as mothers to justify their participation in the movement. These women, such as temperance women who were opposed to the sale of alcohol, believed that the female vote would allow for the passage of legislation that would "clean up" corrupt government regimes along with society at large (see *Paths to Power: Women in the Progressive Movement*). The battle for suffrage also illustrates the conflicts that emerged among women as they confronted issues of race, region, and class (Kraditor 1981; Flexner and Fitzpatrick 1996).

PATHS TO POWER

Women in the Progressive Movement

Although early feminists such as Elizabeth Cady Stanton and Lucretia Mott based their calls for social change on the grounds of human rights, many activists of the Progressive Era subscribed to a vision of civic motherhood. These activists embraced the view of women as selfless, moral agents and used it to justify an increasing level of participation in the public realm, expanding from the home to the school, the local community, the state, and the national government (Baker 1984). As Rheta Childe Dorr, journalist and member of the General Federation of Women's Clubs, explained:

> Woman's place is in the home . . . But Home is not contained within the four walls of an individual home. Home is the community. The city full of people is the Family. The public school is the real Nursery. And badly do the Home and the Family and the Nursery need their mother. (Dorr 1910, 327)

Many women such as Jane Addams, the founder of Hull House, and Florence Kelly, a leader of the National Consumers League, served in settlement houses offering health and welfare services and education to immigrants living in the overcrowded city tenement houses. Women of the National Consumers League and the Women's Trade Union League focused on the problems of working conditions for women and children. The Women's Christian Temperance Union worked for temperance legislation and ultimately sought an amendment to the Constitution that prohibited the sale of alcohol. The National Congress of Mothers and the General Federation of Women's Clubs participated in a range of reform activities from public sanitation to the establishment of kindergartens and the creation of mothers' pensions (an early form of welfare for widowed mothers). The National American Woman's Suffrage Association fought for the ballot, believing that women voters would eventually elect reform-minded politicians who would make progressive changes in public policy.

Women often held memberships in several of these groups and these national organizations and their local affiliates participated in various and overlapping reform causes (Skocpol 1992; Flexner and Fitzpatrick 1996; Norton et al. 1986). ■

The early suffragists who forged their political consciousness in the abolitionist movement based their calls for the ballot on human rights, the equality of citizens, and the rights of all humans to achieve self-actualization. The Declaration of Rights and Sentiments adopted at the Seneca Falls convention included the first formal demand for women's suffrage based on the equality of humankind and the right to the pursuit of life, liberty, and happiness laid out by Thomas Jefferson in the Declaration of Independence. Men including Horace Greeley, Henry Blackwell, and Frederick Douglass and women leaders such as Elizabeth Cady Stanton, Susan B. Anthony, and Lucy Stone worked to abolish slavery and gave speeches, organized petition drives, and lobbied legislatures on behalf of rights for African Americans and women.

To aid their cause, abolitionist leaders formed the American Equal Rights Association. After a successful campaign for the Thirteenth Amendment to abolish slavery, ratified in 1865, many believed that full citizenship rights for African Americans and women would soon be a reality. However, the introduction of the Fourteenth Amendment, which protects the privileges and immunities of citizens from infringement by the states and guarantees due process for citizens, created a major split in the movement for equal rights because for the first time the word *male* was used in the Constitution. It appeared in Section 2, which dealt explicitly with voting rights (Kraditor 1981; Flexner and Fitzpatrick 1996). Supporters of the amendment argued that since the Civil War was fought to abolish slavery and there was no public outcry in support of women's rights commensurate to the call for redressing the wrongs against former slaves, this was the "Negro's Hour." They believed that voting reform must be achieved incrementally. Tying women's suffrage to this already controversial proposal—which was geared at establishing full citizenship for the freed slaves and other African Americans—could doom the amendment. Those suffragists who opposed the amendment, including Susan B. Anthony and Elizabeth Cady Stanton, feared that including the word *male* in the Constitution would undermine women's claims to citizenship and the accompanying rights and privileges. Moreover, they believed that passage of the Fourteenth Amendment as written would require an act of Congress or even a constitutional amendment to grant women the right to vote in federal elections. Indeed, more than ten years later in *Minor v. Happersett* (1875), the Supreme Court ruled that by refusing to register Virginia Minor, the president of the Missouri Woman Suffrage Association, to vote, the state of Missouri was not denying her the privileges and immunities of citizenship because voting was not a right of citizenship but a privilege granted by the states. Additional attempts to win the ballot by illegally registering women to vote and pursuing a citizenship claim through the courts were equally unsuccessful (Kraditor 1981; Flexner and Fitzpatrick 1996; Cushman 2001).

As a result of the conflict over the Fourteenth Amendment and the exclusion of sex from the Fifteenth Amendment, which bars denial of the right to vote based on "race, color, or previous condition of servitude," two competing organizations organized to fight for women's suffrage in 1869. The more radical group, the National Woman's Suffrage Association (NWSA) led by

Anthony and Stanton, was dedicated to winning a federal amendment for women's suffrage. They restricted membership to women only and were active in a range of causes including working conditions for women, divorce reform, and elevating the position of women in the church. The more conservative organization, the American Woman Suffrage Association (AWSA), led by Lucy Stone and Henry Ward Beecher, both notable abolitionists, concentrated only on the right to vote and avoided other causes that could alienate important members of the political community. Rather than working for a federal amendment, they focused their energy on a state-by-state campaign for the ballot. After more than 20 years with little to show for their efforts, the two organizations finally merged to form the National American Woman's Suffrage Association (NAWSA) in 1890, concentrating its efforts on obtaining the right to vote within individual states (Flexner and Fitzpatrick 1996; Kraditor 1981).

By 1890 the Progressive movement was in full swing, and many of the white middle-class women who adopted the fight for the vote claimed the ballot was necessary to achieve the goals of civic motherhood and their chosen reform causes. Thus, Aileen Kraditor (1981) notes that the arguments made by suffragists in these years moved away from calls for the ballot based on simple

Woman Suffrage Headquarters in Cleveland, Ohio, in 1912. Pictured at far right is Miss Belle Sherwin, president of the National League of Women Voters.

justice and toward arguments based on expediency including why women deserved the vote and what women would do with the ballot.

The Women's Christian Temperance Union (WCTU) was one of the first reform groups to adopt the fight for suffrage. Under the leadership of Frances Willard, in 1881, the group called for the vote as a "Home Protection Ballot." Willard and other temperance leaders believed that women voters would pass local and state laws banning the manufacture and sale of liquor—an important goal that they believed would stop the impoverishment of families and the abuse of women and children who were harmed by husbands and fathers who succumbed to alcoholism. Thus, union literature disassociated itself from the natural rights arguments of suffragist organizations by pointing out that "The WCTU seeks the ballot for no selfish ends. Asking for it only in the interest of the home, which has been and is woman's divinely appointed province, there is no clamor for 'rights,' only a prayerful, persistent plea for the opportunities of Duty" (quoted in Bordin 1981, 119).

Through the WCTU, numerous conservative women who would eschew a rights-based movement that challenged traditional gender roles were drawn to the cause of suffrage. During many state initiative fights to grant women the vote, it was these temperance women who provided the majority of the activists in the campaigns. However, the prominence of the temperance movement in the suffrage cause also provoked the opposition of liquor manufacturers to suffrage and the industry utilized its considerable resources to finance campaigns against suffrage whenever states held a referendum on the question (Bordin 1981; Tyler 1949; Flexner and Fitzpatrick 1996).

Like the women of the WCTU, the white upper middle and middle class club women of the General Federation of Women's Clubs (GFWC) also took up the cause of suffrage in the 1900s in order to achieve their reform goals. The GFWC grew out of the numerous local literary women's clubs established in urban areas in the late 1860s. Seeking to continue their education after marriage, club women studied literature, art, and music. They presented papers and critiqued each other's works. By 1890, many of these clubs were involving themselves in social reform. The largest and most publicly active clubs included Sorosis, a club of career women in New York City, and the New England Federation of Women's Clubs, a group of elite reformers in Boston. Seeking to have a wider impact on public affairs, Jane Cunningham Croly, a journalist and leader of Sorosis, invited 97 clubs to attend its twenty-first anniversary convention and to form a national organization. The GFWC grew to 500,000 members in 1910 and 1 million by 1914. These women viewed the ballot as a necessary tool to achieve their plethora of reform goals including the establishment of kindergartens and traveling libraries, improvement of the working conditions of women and children, public sanitation, and natural resource conservation (Blair 1980; Wood 1912; Wells 1953).

Although the incorporation of club women and temperance crusaders expanded the ranks of those fighting for suffrage and united women across regions, the need to maintain the support of such a wide-ranging constituency also led to the adoption of tactics and policies antithetical to the cause of equal rights that suffrage represented. Reacting to the expansion of immigration in northern cities and racial relations in the South, many suffragists began to argue that women needed the vote in order to counteract the influence of the "undesirable" elements of society: the uneducated immigrants in the North who sold their votes to the political machines and black men in the South. Thus, speakers at suffrage conventions provided statistics to demonstrate that if granted the vote, the nativist educated white women would far outnumber the population of immigrant and black men who they believed contributed to the corruption of public affairs. To support the goal of limiting the vote to the more "deserving" elements of society, many suffragists advocated the adoption of education requirements for the vote (Kraditor 1981; Flexner and Fitzpatrick 1996). Thus, Elizabeth Cady Stanton advocated an educational qualification for voters because:

1. It would limit the foreign vote
2. It would decrease the ignorant native vote by stimulating the rising generation to learning . . .
3. It would dignify the right of suffrage in the eyes of our people to know that some preparation was necessary . . .

One of the most potent objections to woman suffrage is the added ignorant and depraved vote that would still further corrupt and embarrass the administration of our Government . . . It is the interest of the educating working-men, as it is of the women, that this ignorant, worthless class of voters should be speedily diminished. With free schools and compulsory education, there is no excuse in this country for ignorance of the elements of learning. (quoted in Kraditor 1981, 133)

To win the suffrage referendum in southern states, the movement needed the support of southern women. Therefore, the leaders of NAWSA adopted a state's rights position that allowed local suffrage groups to exclude black women from their organizations and did not repudiate the racist arguments used in favor of the suffrage cause. Still the suffrage movement endured years of defeats before the adoption of the Nineteenth Amendment to the U.S. Constitution that granted women the right to vote federally. In 1890, Wyoming became the first state to enter the union with full suffrage for women, and Colorado adopted female suffrage in 1893. A few states adopted laws allowing women to vote in school board or municipal elections. However, after the 1896 state referendum in which Utah and Idaho became the third and fourth states to adopt women's suffrage, no other state voted to give women full suffrage until Washington in 1910 (Kraditor 1981; Flexner and Fitzpatrick 1996).

In campaign after campaign suffragists were stymied by poor organization and a lack of resources as they faced opponents backed by business interests, the liquor industry, and political machines. These party machines feared that armed with the vote women would seek to ban child labor, reform working conditions for women, pass prohibition, and support civil service reform. These antisuffrage groups had the support of important political figures, ranging from state legislators, members of Congress, and former President Grover

Cleveland, who pointed to the destabilizing impact women's suffrage would have on the home, the family, and the nation. Additionally, antisuffragist women who came from wealthy families (and were often politically well-connected) spoke out against suffrage as an unnecessary burden on women who did not want or need it because their men represented them and cared for their interests (Flexner and Fitzpatrick 1996).

Frustrated by the continued slow expansion of suffrage at the state level, in 1916 NAWSA leader Carrie Chapman Catt formulated a "winning plan." The plan called for abandoning the state-by-state campaigns that had yielded limited success in favor of a single-minded focus on a federal constitutional amendment. The crusade for a federal suffrage amendment was also championed by the women of the Congressional Union for Woman Suffrage. Led by Alice Paul, these women had left the NAWSA because they believed the tactics of NAWSA leaders were too timid. Moreover, they rejected NAWSA's nonpartisan advocacy, and building on Paul's experience with the militants in the British suffrage movement, the Congressional Union women advocated a policy of holding the party in power responsible for the lack of suffrage. They also picketed the White House, as the current president, Woodrow Wilson—a Democrat—shared the same party affiliation as the majority party in Congress. Therefore, they actively worked to defeat Democratic congressional candidates and to hold the Wilson administration responsible for women's exclusion from the vote, particularly in those states where women had already been granted the right to vote and could be galvanized as a potential voting bloc to punish politicians who did not support suffrage.

Ultimately, Wilson changed his mind and supported the suffrage cause, and what became known as the Susan B. Anthony amendment passed through Congress and was moved to the states for ratification. After 56 state referendum campaigns, 480 efforts to get state legislatures to allow state referenda, 47 campaigns for suffrage at state constitutional conventions, 277 attempts to include votes for women in state party platforms, and 19 campaigns to get a federal amendment through Congress and then ratified by three-quarters of state legislatures, this goal was finally achieved when Tennessee became the thirty-sixth state to adopt the women's suffrage amendment in 1920 (Kraditor 1981; Klein 1984; Flexner and Fitzpatrick 1996).

FEMINISM, THE SECOND WAVE (1960s–PRESENT)

After achieving the goal of suffrage, the women's movement lost its grassroots base. The country was recovering from World War I and desired a "return to normalcy" under President Warren G. Harding. Individual women leaders gravitated to new causes and became active in organizations promoting the interests of working-class women, peace, birth control, and equal rights. The leaders of NAWSA formed the League of Women Voters, a nonpartisan group dedicated to educating women about issues and their new responsibilities as voters so women could cast intelligent ballots and participate effectively in politics. The more radical members of the Congressional Union established the

National Woman's Party and promoted a new Equal Rights Amendment (ERA), authored by Alice Paul, to eliminate sex discrimination in all areas of society. Other women began to move into the male-dominated major political parties. There were some efforts to coordinate the demands of women reformers, particularly through the Women's Joint Congressional Committee. Established in 1919, the group brought together women's groups including the League of Women Voters, the Business and Professional Women's Clubs, the American Association of University Women, the National Consumers League, the Women's Trade Union League, and the National Council of Jewish Women to lobby the state and national governments for legislation dealing with education, child labor, peace, maternal health, and a range of other issues. However, after a few legislative victories, particularly the passage of the Sheppard-Towner Act providing federal funds for prenatal and maternal health care education, the failure to deliver a unified women's vote nationally and a dispute over the ERA quickly eviscerated the power of this union (Hartmann 1989; Andersen 1996).

The Rebirth of the Feminist Movement

The 1960s provided the confluence of factors that initiated the rebirth of the feminist movement. With regard to social conditions, the participation of women in the job market grew to 35 percent of the national workforce, birthrates declined, the introduction of the birth control pill allowed more women to control their fertility, and more women were enrolled in college. Additionally an increased divorce rate and the decision of many women to marry later in life increased the number of unmarried women.

However, women's increased presence in the job market and higher education did not translate into a transformation of attitudes concerning women's proper place among most Americans. After World War II, American society sent "Rosie the Riveter" and her female counterparts who worked in the war industries back home, and the country celebrated the ideal of female domesticity, taking care of home and children. Working women were concentrated in low-paying jobs and many college-educated women felt stifled by the routine of domesticity.

In 1963, Betty Friedan published *The Feminine Mystique*. Interviewing members of her class of 1942 at Smith College, Friedan found that these women were deeply dissatisfied with their lives as housewives and could not reconcile the intellectual and social stimulation of their college years with the isolation and routine of housework and child care. The book ignored the plight of minority and working-class women; however, it raised the consciousness of educated middle-class housewives who now realized that their feelings of powerlessness were shared, and they could use the political process to make changes (Hartmann 1989; Costain 1992).

While *The Feminine Mystique* raised the consciousness of older educated middle-class women, younger college-aged women were coming to the conclusion that gender discrimination was pervasive in society rather than a consequence

PATHS TO POWER

Black Women in the Civil Rights Movement

Most students have heard the story of Rosa Parks and the Montgomery bus boycott. A secretary of the local National Association for the Advancement of Colored People (NAACP), Parks' arrest for refusing to give up her seat on the bus to a white man sparked a protest movement that led to the end of Jim Crow segregation laws in the United States.

Ms. Parks was just one of many black women who played a pivotal role in the struggle for civil rights. Another key player in the Montgomery bus boycott was Jo Ann Robinson, an English teacher at Alabama State College. Robinson led the Women's Political Council (WPC), an organization founded by local professional black women in 1946 to register black women to vote. Robinson and the WPC promoted the bus boycott by organizing WPC members and recruiting students and faculty at Alabama State College to prepare information sheets and distribute them throughout the black community.

Robinson also helped found the Montgomery Improvement Association. With Martin Luther King, Jr. as president, Robinson served on its executive board and edited its newsletter. She was a member of the team that negotiated with local and state officials and helped organize alternative transportation and worked to sustain support in the black community for the bus boycott, which lasted almost a year (Hartmann 1989).

Ella Baker was another key civil rights leader who often goes unmentioned. Baker was a founder of the Southern Christian Leadership Conference (SCLC) led by Martin Luther King, Jr. Baker was a community organizer who had developed NAACP chapters throughout the country as the NAACP field secretary and director of branches in the early 1940s. At great risk to her own life, Baker traveled the South enrolling blacks in the NAACP and helped to identify ways local leaders could combat segregation despite the fact that the NAACP was an outlawed organization in the South and its members were routinely tortured, killed, or run out of town (Omolade 2004). Although male ministers controlled the SCLC, in the 1950s Baker set up its office in Atlanta, was its first associate director, and temporarily served as executive director. Baker helped organize student protests and sit-ins and, through her position at SCLC, she provided the leadership and organizational support that led to the formation of Student Non-Violent Coordinating Committee (SNCC)—a group committed to decentralized leadership and local control (Omolade 2004). She was involved in SNCC's major projects and decisions throughout its lifetime despite being significantly older than its membership. SNCC leader John Lewis proclaimed, "in terms of ideas and philosophy and commitment, she was one of the youngest persons in the movement" (Hartmann 1989).

Baker and Robinson represent just two of the many black women who participated in the civil rights movement. Many women provided leadership in organizing marches, sit-ins, and voter registration drives and countless others were brutalized and jailed as they participated in the nonviolent protests that were the hallmark of the civil rights movement (Hartmann 1989; Omolade 2004). ■

of personal failings. Moreover, these younger activists believed that this discrimination should be attacked through political action. Many college-aged women participated in the civil rights, student, and antiwar movements (see *Paths to Power: Black Women in the Civil Rights Movement* for more information). Within these movements women learned how to gain attention to a cause and organize and mobilize a grassroots base. However, the younger women also found that their contributions were not equally valued, and they were inhibited from advancing to leadership roles in their respective movements. When the civil rights movement increasingly turned toward "black power," white activists were pushed out of the movement and new more radical leaders like Stokely Carmichael emphasized that black men needed to regain their manhood. In the antiwar movement, women found themselves in supporting roles as only men could burn their draft cards. Women who participated in the student movement and organizations such as Students for a Democratic Society were shut out of leadership roles and their concerns for women's rights were largely dismissed. In 1967 the National Conference for a New Politics gathered 200 civil rights, antiwar, and radical organizations. When women tried to raise their concerns about sex discrimination, the conference rejected these demands as trivial compared to the needs of other oppressed groups. This led women activists to start their own women's groups in cities across the country (Freeman 1975; Hartmann 1989).

The Emergence of the Older and Younger Branches of the Feminist Movement

Organizationally, scholars note that the feminist movement developed along two tracks. These two branches of the movement have been referred to as the older and younger branches or the liberal and radical feminists. Liberal feminists utilized political action to achieve social and political changes that would eliminate sex discrimination and allow women to achieve equal rights whereas radical feminists eschewed traditional methods of politics and attacked the ingrained sexism of society in order to raise feminist consciousness and achieve women's liberation (Freeman 1975; Hartmann 1989; Costain 1992; Ferree and Hess 1994). Both branches of the women's movement were mobilized at a time when the political system was open to the influence of new groups.

The younger branch focused its efforts on local activism and community building. Utilizing skills built in the protest politics of the civil rights, antiwar, and New Left movements, the activists in the younger branch devoted themselves to consciousness raising, which involved getting women to recognize that what they believed were personal problems actually stemmed from inherent sex discrimination in the institutions of society and through socialization processes. The consciousness-raising sessions and writings that came out of participation in the movement advanced the theoretical and ideological foundations of feminism. These women formed groups that emphasized equality and participatory democracy in both action and structure. Therefore, they did not have hierarchical structures with recognized leaders. Instead they rotated leadership positions and made decisions based on consensus.

The younger branch feminists sought to create new institutions devoted to women's needs. They established women's health clinics, feminist bookstores, child care centers, and rape crisis centers. Many younger branch groups also gained notoriety for employing radical shock protest techniques. Group names like SCUM (the Society to Cut Up Men) and WITCH (Women's International Conspiracy from Hell) were designed to shock mainstream America. WITCH staged hexing events such as the hexing of the New York Stock Exchange and Mrs. Pat Nixon during the first lady's trip to Portland, Oregon, in 1968. Other younger branch feminists staged a protest at the 1968 Miss America Contest in which they threw underwear, cosmetics, and false eyelashes into a "freedom trashcan" and crowned a sheep Miss America. The groups also held protests at bridal fairs and staged hairy legs demonstrations. These techniques often embarrassed the older branch of the movement, which preferred to focus on traditional lobbying methods, and feared the impact of these protests on public support for the larger movement (Freeman 1975; Hartmann 1989; Costain 1992; Ryan 1992).

The older branch grew out of women's involvement with President Kennedy's Commission on the Status of Women. Victorious in the extremely close presidential election of 1960, President Kennedy recognized that the New Deal coalition of voters forged by President Roosevelt was declining and both Republicans and Democrats were looking for ways to mobilize new groups of voters to create a governing majority. Viewing women as a potentially emerging voting force, Kennedy agreed to the suggestion of Esther Peterson, Assistant Secretary of Labor and the director of the Women's Bureau of the Department of Labor, that he appoint a Commission on the Status of Women (CSW) to recommend proposals to combat sex discrimination in government and the private sector. The CSW would have the added benefit of deflecting attention away from the demand for an ERA put forth by women's groups such as the National Woman's Party, the National Association of Colored Women, and the Business and Professional Women's Clubs. The ERA could potentially split the Democratic Party since organized labor vehemently opposed its adoption, fearing that it would lead to the elimination of the protective legislation that Progressive era reformers had fought for in order to improve the working conditions of women (Freeman 1975; Hartmann 1989; Costain 1992; Ryan 1992; Ferree and Hess 1994).

Chaired by Eleanor Roosevelt, the report issued by the CSW in 1963 documented social, economic, and legal discrimination against women across the country and led to the creation of a Citizen's Advisory Council on the Status of Women and an Interdepartmental Committee on the Status of Women. In response to the findings of the CSW and the pressure of women's groups, governors across the country created state-level Commissions on the Status of Women. These state commissions continued the work of documenting discrimination against women and met together in annual conferences to share their findings. Thus, the work of the federal and state commissions helped create the organizational capacity for a renewed feminist movement. With the support of the federal and state governments, commission members developed the data necessary to demonstrate pervasive discrimination against women. The national conferences brought women together from across the country to share their findings, network with fellow commission members, and develop contacts inside the federal government (Freeman 1975; Hartmann 1989; Costain 1992; Ryan 1992; Ferree and Hess 1994).

In addition to the creation of the State Commissions on the Status of Women, Congress passed two important pieces of legislation to advance women's rights. In response to the lobbying efforts of labor unions and women's groups organized by Esther Peterson, Congress passed the Equal Pay Act in 1963. Although the act would not address the fact of a sex-segregated workforce in which occupations predominantly composed of women pay less than occupations of similar skill level that are predominantly composed of men, the act did mandate that employers could no longer pay women less than men who perform the same job and established a precedent of government action on behalf of economic equity for women (Hartmann 1989; Costain 1992).

The inclusion of sex in Title VII of the Civil Rights Act of 1964 constituted the second important legislative advancement for women. The act prohibits discrimination based on race, color, religion, sex, or national origin in public accommodations and employment. The law also created an Equal Employment Opportunity Commission (EEOC) to investigate job discrimination complaints. One of the crowning achievements of the civil rights movement, the inclusion of sex in Title VII was a contentious proposition (Freeman 1975; Hartmann 1989; Costain 1992; Ferree and Hess 1994; Gelb and Palley 1996). Although sincerely supported by some legislators, particularly Martha Griffiths (D-MI), who originally intended to introduce the addition of sex as her own amendment, other liberal members of Congress including Edith Green (D-OR), who sponsored the Equal Pay Act, opposed the addition of sex to the act for fear that it would doom the bill and its efforts to curtail racial discrimination. In fact, the incorporation of sex was added as an amendment in the House Judiciary Committee by an ardent opponent of the Civil Rights Act, Representative Howard Smith (D-VA), the chair of the House Rules Committee—who hoped to doom the entire bill. Numerous southern legislators voted in favor of the addition of sex and against the entire bill. During the House floor debate over the amendment, some liberal male members treated it as a joke. In response, Martha Griffiths (D-MI) scolded her colleagues asserting that "if there had been any necessity to have pointed out that women were a second-class sex, the laughter would have proved it" (quoted in Hartmann 1989, 55; Costain 1992, 38). Representative Edith Green (D-OR), who opposed the amendment, nonetheless sought to reinforce the legitimacy of claims of sex discrimination by stating "Any woman who wants to have a career, who wants to go into the professions, who wants to work, I feel, cannot possibly reach maturity without being very keenly and very painfully made aware of all the discrimination placed against her because of her sex" (quoted in Costain 1992, 39). Despite its inauspicious start, the Civil Rights Act of 1964 with the Title VII inclusion ultimately passed.

The controversy surrounding the inclusion of sex in Title VII impacted the calculations of the EEOC concerning how heavily to focus on enforcement of the sex provision. With limited resources and a belief that race was the major focus of their mission, EEOC commissioners did not devote much attention to the task of rooting out sex discrimination in employment. Two of the EEOC commissioners, Richard Graham and Sonia Pressman, as well as other women serving inside the government, encouraged Betty Friedan to form an interest group outside of government—an NAACP for women—to put pressure on the EEOC. When the EEOC refused to address the problem of sex-segregated want ads, in which newspapers listed positions by sex, the delegates to the national conference of the State Commissions on the Status of Women drafted resolutions urging the EEOC to enforce the Title VII provisions concerning sex discrimination. However, the delegates were barred from introducing these resolutions, as they would be construed as a criticism of the Johnson administration. Recognizing the need for a pressure group that was independent of the government, Betty Friedan and others formed the National Organization for Women (NOW) in 1966. Among the group's 126 charter members were former EEOC commissioners Richard Graham and Aileen Hernandez and seven former and current members of State Commissions on the Status of Women. Thus, the group began as an elite Washington-based network that later developed a grassroots base of chapters throughout the nation (Freeman 1975; Hartmann 1989; Costain 1992).

The newly created NOW devoted itself to attacking sex discrimination by adopting a strategy that combined direct executive and legislative lobbying with mass protest and the litigation of test cases that had been perfected by the civil rights movement. Utilizing these multiple political tools, NOW convinced President Lyndon Johnson to expand the executive order that is the basis for federal affirmative action programs to include sex. They also forced newspapers to eliminate sex-segregated want ads after intensive lobbying and a protest campaign that included picketing the headquarters of the *New York Times* and a national day of demonstrations in five cities targeted at the EEOC. In addition to reversing its earlier ruling on sex-segregated job ads, NOW activities also contributed to the decision of the EEOC to withdraw its support for state protective laws that restricted women's access to employment (Freeman 1975; Hartmann 1989; Costain 1992; Ryan 1992; Carabillo et al. 1993; Ferree and Hess 1994).

The litigation activities of NOW's Legal Defense and Education Fund (LDEF) also helped break down discriminatory barriers in all areas of society. For example, *Weeks v. Southern Bell* established the precedent that an employer must open all jobs to women who wish to apply by ruling that barring women from jobs that involve lifting more than 30 pounds constitutes a violation of Title VII of the Civil Rights Act of 1964. By 1974, NOW's LDEF had participated in more than 50 major legal cases concerning issues including family law, property rights, civil rights, and employment discrimination. Mass marches brought media attention to the movement and new members and supporters. For example, the 1970 "Women's Strike for Equality" held on the fiftieth anniversary of suffrage in favor of legalized abortion, government-sponsored child care, and equal educational and employment opportunities attracted 500,000 women in New York City and 20,000 women to demonstrations and rallies in 90 cities across 42 states. These mass protests often brought together women from the older and younger branches of the movement (Freeman 1975; Hartmann 1989; Costain 1992; Ryan 1992; Carabillo et al. 1993; Ferree and Hess 1994).

Although NOW enjoyed numerous successes, it also experienced internal and external conflicts concerning its goals, tactics, and methods of organization. Soon after its formation, Betty Friedan drafted a NOW Bill of Rights to present to the parties and candidates in the 1968 election and to create a plan for political action (see Box 2.1.) The inclusion of demands for an ERA and support for abortion rights drove some activists out of the organization. In particular, support for the ERA drove away women associated with organized labor whose unions opposed the elimination of protective legislation for women, such as laws regulating women's hours (for example, preventing businesses from making women work night shifts) and the types of jobs they could perform. Other women objected to the inclusion of abortion rights. Some of these women formed the Women's Equity Action League, which devoted itself solely to issues regarding employment, education, and taxes. Other activists objected to the

---

BOX 2.1

The Older and Younger Branches of Feminism

NOW's Bill of Rights and the Redstockings Manifesto illustrate the differences in the goals and membership of the older and younger branches of the feminist movement. The NOW Bill of Rights reflects the older branch's commitment to achieve gender equality through legal reform. It emphasizes changes in law and adoption of public policies such as expansion of education and child care services and enforcement of antidiscrimination laws to allow women to achieve equality in society and the workplace.

In contrast, the younger branch viewed legal reform and women's rights advocacy as inadequate. They devoted themselves to the pursuit of women's liberation, a goal that would require profound social change in gender relations. They established consciousness-raising groups to allow women to share their experiences, provide mutual support, and explore the societal and political foundations of discrimination. Members of the Redstockings Collective in Boston issued the Redstockings Manifesto. Just as the NOW Bill of Rights is meant to draw on the American liberal tradition of equal rights, the Redstockings Manifesto draws on the ideas of the Communist Manifesto to characterize women as an oppressed social class that must rise up in revolution against its oppressors (Shanley 1988; Freeman 1975) (see Appendix B for the full text of the NOW Bill of Rights and the Redstockings Manifesto). ∎

hierarchical decision-making structure of NOW that limited opportunities for local initiatives and sharing of power (Freeman 1975; Hartmann 1989; Ryan 1992). Women like Ti-Grace Atkinson of the New York chapter of NOW left the group to form the Feminists, which adopted an organizational structure conducive to equal participation of all members. Over time, NOW and other feminist groups have also received criticism as being organizations of middle-class white women that neglect the interests of working-class and minority women (Hartmann 1989; Costain 1992; Barakso 2004; Strolovitch 2007).

In addition to these internal movement struggles, the women's movement began to face new barriers in the political system. The election of President Nixon in 1968 as an advocate for the conservative "Silent Majority" that was upset by the turmoil of the civil rights, New Left, antiwar, and women's rights movements closed the executive branch to women's influence. However, Congress was increasingly open to their demands. The civil rights movement—and the passage of the Civil Rights Act of 1964 and the Voting Rights Act of 1965—created a coalition of members of Congress that was responsive to initiatives framed as demands for equal rights. Between 1972 and 1974 Congress passed Title IX to the Educational Amendments Act barring gender discrimination in education, the Women's Educational Equity Act, the Equal Credit Opportunity Act, and the ERA.

Although members of Congress embraced these initiatives that were designed to achieve what Gelb and Palley call "role equity" for women, they would not address legislation that embraced "role change" (Gelb and Palley 1996). In fact, movement historian Anne Costain (1992) claims that the agenda of the women's movement was co-opted by Congress as the groups focused on the equal rights agenda and set aside the special needs demands such as maternity leave rights in employment, establishment of government-funded child care centers, and tax deductions for home and child care expenses for working parents that were all included in the 1968 NOW Bill of Rights (see Appendix B).

THE EQUAL RIGHTS AMENDMENT (ERA)

Section 1. Equality of rights under the law shall not be denied or abridged by the United States or by any state on account of sex.

Section 2. The Congress shall have the power to enforce, by appropriate legislation, the provisions of this article.

Section 3. This amendment shall take effect two years after the date of ratification.

(Text of the Equal Rights Amendment)

After women won the vote, Alice Paul, leader of the National Woman's Party, believed that women needed an amendment to ban all discrimination based on sex in order for women to achieve full equality. To achieve this end she drafted an ERA. First introduced in Congress in 1923, the amendment was reintroduced in various forms every year through 1971. Both major parties adopted platforms proclaiming their support: Republicans in 1940 and Democrats in 1944, despite facing strong opposition from labor unions that feared its impact on protective legislation for women workers. Despite the difficulty of passing constitutional amendments, which requires ratification by two-thirds of the members of both houses of Congress and three-quarters of state legislatures (38 states), the ERA fell only three states short of ratification in 1982 (see Table 2.1). This represents a much stronger performance than other recent popular amendments that have failed to make it out of Congress, including amendments requiring a balanced budget and amendments banning flag burning and abortion. Additionally, public opinion polls spanning from congressional passage in 1972 to its failure in 1982 indicated that a majority of the public supported the amendment (Mansbridge 1986).

The ERA was finally passed by Congress after successful lobbying efforts by women's groups including NOW and Business and Professional Women's Clubs. These groups coordinated their actions with sympathetic members of Congress, who forced the ERA out of committee in order to achieve hearings

TABLE 2.1

States and the Ratification of the ERA

35 of 38 Needed States Ratified the ERA		15 States Failed to Ratify the ERA
Alaska	New Hampshire	Alabama
California	New Jersey	Arizona
Colorado	New Mexico	Arkansas
Connecticut	New York	Florida
Delaware	North Dakota	Georgia
Hawaii	Ohio	Illinois
Idaho	Oregon	Louisiana
Indiana	Pennsylvania	Mississippi
Iowa	Rhode Island	Nevada
Kansas	South Dakota	North Carolina
Kentucky	Tennessee	Oklahoma
Maine	Texas	South Carolina
Maryland	Vermont	Utah
Massachusetts	Washington	Virginia
Michigan	West Virginia	
Minnesota	Wisconsin	
Montana	Wyoming	
Nebraska		

Source: National Council of Women's Organizations ERA Task Force, www.equalrightsamendment.org/ratified.htm.

on the issue and moved the amendment toward a vote by the full House and Senate. In 1972, the ERA was finally granted a floor vote and passed the House and Senate by wide margins: 354 to 23 in the House and 84 to 8 in the Senate.

During the House and Senate debates, women's groups and their allies defeated unfriendly amendments, such as exceptions for state protective legislation for women workers (such as laws regulating the types of jobs they could perform) and the exclusion of women in combat that sought to weaken the ERA. Thirty states had ratified the amendment by early 1973 (Mansbridge 1986; Hartmann 1989).

However, the controversial 1973 Supreme Court decision *Roe v. Wade* activated a strong antifeminist movement that opposed the goals of feminists who supported abortion rights and the ERA. Led by conservative women like Phyllis Schlafly, founder of STOP ERA and Eagle Forum, and Beverly LaHaye, founder of Concerned Women for America, the women who participated in the anti-ERA effort and the larger New Right movement were often socially conservative Christians. Many of these women were from the middle and lower-middle classes, and a large proportion were homemakers (Schreiber 2008; Klatch 1987; Conover and Gray 1983). Often mobilized through activism in their churches, the opposition forces excelled at grassroots organization and lobbying at the state level. The women involved in the anti-ERA movement wrote notes by hand to their state legislators and engaged in daily lobbying of individual state legislators in key states. Just as the pro-ERA forces utilized mass marches and protest techniques to highlight the connection between the ERA and American ideals of equality and the women's suffrage movement, anti-ERA activists engaged in their own symbolic politics as they sought to play on the American public's attachment to the ideals of motherhood, home, and family. Thus, STOP ERA activists handed out apple pies to state legislators with poems that read, "My heart and my hand went into this dough. For the sake of my family please vote no" (Mansbridge 1986; Ferree and Hess 1994; Ryan 1992).

Feminist groups countered with national economic boycotts against states that had not ratified the ERA, hundreds of letters mailed to legislators, and protest marches on state capitols. However, women's groups did not have grassroots organizations in specific states that had not ratified the amendment, particularly the conservative strongholds in the South. Additionally, it was difficult for the pro-ERA forces to point to concrete policy changes impacting gender roles that would result from the passage of the ERA. For example, many ERA activists used 59 cents, the wage gap between men and women, as an argument in favor of ERA. However, since the ERA had passed Congress in 1972, several Supreme Court decisions and the actions of the EEOC had eliminated some of the most egregious examples of sex discrimination, such as the protective labor laws that prevented women from being hired for jobs in specific fields and regulated their hours. As an amendment to the federal constitution, the ERA's language was vague and would only apply to actions of the federal government. Therefore, it would provide limited authority to act on issues of sex discrimination by states or private employers (Mansbridge 1986).

Although the impact of the ERA on sex discrimination in the workplace was a source of conflict, the one substantive impact that was not disputed by either the pro-or anti-ERA forces was that the ERA would require women to be drafted into the military if the country was to institute another draft during wartime. Drafting women was widely unpopular. In fact, one of the most effective strategies of anti-ERA activists in battleground states involved bringing baby girls wearing signs saying "please don't draft me" to rallies at state capitols. Although most Americans support the concept of equal rights, there is less agreement regarding appropriate gender roles in the realms of employment, family, and the military. As shown in Table 2.2, Americans both support the idea of equality for women in the workplace and value the ideal of women as mothers and primary caregivers of children.

TABLE 2.2

Public Opinion and Gender Roles

It is much better for everyone involved if the man is the achiever outside the home and the woman takes care of the home and family.

	1972–1982	1998	2002	2006
Agree	65%	34%	38%	35%
Disagree	34%	63%	61%	63%
Don't Know	1.5%	2%	1%	1%

It is more important for a wife to help her husband's career than to have one herself.

	1972–1982	1998
Agree	55%	18%
Disagree	41%	78%
Don't Know	3%	3%

Note: This question was not asked in 2002 or 2006.

A working mother can establish just as warm and secure a relationship with her children as a mother who does not work.

	1972–1982	1998	2002	2006
Agree	48%	67%	63%	67%
Disagree	50%	32%	36%	33%
Don't Know	1%	1%	0%	1%

A preschool child is likely to suffer if his or her mother works.

	1972–1982	1998	2002	2006
Agree	66%	41%	45%	40%
Disagree	32%	56%	54%	59%
Don't Know	2%	3%	0%	1%

Source: General Social Surveys 1972–2006.

Opponents of the ERA capitalized on fears concerning the impact of the ERA and the larger feminist movement on the status of homemakers, the welfare of the nuclear family, the obligation of the husband to support his wife and children in marriage and in cases of divorce, and the moral fabric of society. Such fears contributed to the mobilization of a strong antifeminist backlash (Mansbridge 1986; Gelb and Palley 1996).

Despite the activism of the opposition groups, the national lobbying efforts by pro-ERA women's groups, which sponsored a large mass march on Washington to renew efforts to pass the amendment, convinced Congress to pass an extension of the original seven-year deadline that had been set when the ERA initially passed Congress in 1972. However, only five more states had ratified by 1977 and anti-ERA forces successfully persuaded some states that ratified the amendment to vote to rescind their ratification. Although these votes were nonbinding, they had a detrimental impact on the movement. The amendment went down to defeat in June 1982, the new deadline set by Congress (Mansbridge 1986).

The fight for the ERA mobilized a new generation of activists on both the feminist and antifeminist sides and the political landscape became increasingly polarized regarding issues concerning the place of women in American society. With the election of Ronald Reagan in 1980, social conservatives gained a strong ally in the executive branch. Reagan openly opposed the ERA and the Republican Party eliminated support for the amendment from its party platform. Reagan used his executive authority to curtail affirmative action programs geared at hiring more women and minorities in government and to scale back the investigation and enforcement activities of the EEOC concerning racial and sex discrimination claims. He also used his nomination power to appoint conservative judges to the federal courts. Antifeminist groups utilized their increased access to the press for policy initiatives that would reinforce traditional family values and limit access to abortion and the expansion of sex discrimination laws (Mansbridge 1986; Costain 1992; Conway et al. 1999; Schreiber 2008). Meanwhile, feminist organizations aligned themselves with the Democratic Party and focused on electoral politics. Recognizing that more female than male state legislators voted for the ERA, feminist groups worked to increase the number of women elected to political office by recruiting, training, and raising funds for women candidates. In 1984, feminist activists were able to convince the Democratic presidential nominee Walter Mondale to choose the first female vice presidential candidate, Geraldine Ferraro (Mansbridge 1986; Costain 1992).

The conservative movement and social conservatives continued to gain power throughout the 1980s and 1990s. In 1994, Republicans gained the majority in Congress for the first time in forty years and feminists no longer had access to the congressional agenda. The 2000 election and 2004 re-election of President George W. Bush meant that feminists had no allies among the ruling party in either the executive or legislative branches of the national government. Although feminist groups helped elect more women to public office and continued to lobby Congress for legislation addressing reproductive rights, family leave, and sexual harassment, feminist groups found themselves on the defensive trying to prevent the passage of policy changes that would restrict women's rights, particularly in the area of reproductive freedom. The Democratic takeover of Congress in 2006 and the election of a Democratic President, Barack Obama, in the 2008 election means that feminists now have more access to policymakers. It remains to be seen whether they will be able to translate that access into concrete policy changes to benefit women's rights.

WOMEN AND INTEREST GROUPS

As a social movement, the first and second waves of the feminist movement sought to dramatically change American society by altering the accepted view of women's proper role in the public and private spheres. Social movements are both a cause and consequence of dramatic social upheaval. By contrast, interest groups are more enduring factors of the American political landscape. Their narrower purpose seeks to effect policy change on a specific issue or set of issues (Costain 1992; Gelb and Palley 1996; McAdam 1982). Even before women won the right to vote, women joined and formed groups to persuade local, state, and national officeholders to change the law on issues ranging from abolition to temperance. Women's groups including the National Congress of Mothers, the Women's Christian Temperance Union, the National Consumers League, the National Association of Colored Women, and the General Federation of Women's Clubs contributed heavily to the development of government responsibility for social welfare programs in the Progressive era (Skocpol 1992; Andersen 1996).

Advocating the philosophy of civic motherhood in which political activism was not a violation of the principle of separate spheres but a natural extension of women's duty to protect children and the home, these women lobbied the state and national governments for laws and programs addressing a wide range of issues, including maximum-hour laws for women and children, abolition of child labor, forestry and natural resource conservation, mothers' pensions (the precursor to modern-day welfare), public sanitation, civil service reform, and the creation of juvenile courts.

These women's groups gained legitimacy by claiming to represent the interests and views of women, and they utilized their exclusion from traditional politics and the doctrine of separate spheres to claim authority as they sought reforms for moral and not political ends. Lacking the ability to vote politicians out of office, these groups were still able to sway officeholders because they had strong grassroots organizations in which local and state groups were connected to a national organization and could be mobilized to publicize issues and lobby government officials.

In her detailed study of the General Federation of Women's Clubs' involvement in the development of mothers' pensions, Theda Skocpol (1992) noted that for each issue engaged, club women consulted experts, undertook detailed investigations of current state practices, and studied the laws of other states. The clubs designed public education campaigns to gain support through moral exhortation and created model programs. Local and state legislatures were then lobbied to pass laws, establish regulatory commissions, and appoint women to these commissions. As a result of the activism of women's groups, women were appointed as factory inspectors, members of labor bureaus, truancy officers, police matrons, school board members, library commissioners, and members of social welfare agencies (Skocpol 1992; Baker 1984). Upon reviewing the efforts of the Harrisburg (PA) Women's Civic Club, a member reported that:

> It is no longer necessary for us to continue at our own cost, the practical experiment we began in street cleaning . . . nor is it necessary longer to strive for a pure water supply, a healthier sewage system, or the construction of playgrounds. This work is now being done by the City Council, by the Department of Public Works, and by the Park Commission. (quoted in Door 1910, 37)

As a demonstration of the power of the activism of Progressive Era women's groups, surveying the development of state labor laws regarding women's working conditions, Skocpol found that state federations of women's clubs were active in lobbying for 13 of the 19 women's hour laws that were passed from 1909 to 1917. Additionally, state federations actively lobbied for mothers' pensions to provide a source of financial support to widowed women with children in 24 states between 1912 and 1920. In those states where federations did not endorse pensions, the state legislature either failed to adopt pensions at all or adopted them much later than other states (Skocpol 1992). At the national level, the GFWC and other women's groups lobbied heavily for the Pure Food and Drug Act and the Sheppard-Towner Infancy and Maternity Protection Act.[1] They also worked for the establishment of the Children's Bureau and the reorganization of the Women's Division of the Bureau of Labor Statistics into a separate Women's Bureau to investigate the conditions of women workers and advocate for their welfare (Skocpol 1992; Baker 1984).

Like their Progressive Era counterparts, modern-day women's interest groups gain legitimacy by proclaiming to represent women's interests. However, groups have different and often opposing definitions of what constitutes women's interests and what women want. Many of the contemporary women's interest groups grew out of the feminist movement and the antifeminist countermovement.

Additionally, there was an explosion in the number of national-oriented interest groups in the late 1960s and early 1970s. This interest group expansion stems from important changes that made the political system more open to interest group influence and from technological innovations that made it easier to contact and mobilize supporters (Berry 1997; Davidson, Oleszek, and Lee 2009). The increasing activism of the federal government during Lyndon Johnson's Great Society increased the number of government programs resulting in the creation of groups devoted to protecting and expanding their benefits and groups advocating for (or against) increased regulations on business

---

[1] The Sheppard-Towner Act was officially known as the Federal Act for the Promotion of the Welfare and Hygiene of Maternity and Infancy.

and the environment, for example. In response to the Watergate scandal in the Nixon administration, Congress passed "sunshine laws" designed to open government activities to public scrutiny. As congressional hearings, committee meetings, and floor debate became open to the public, and information on the activities of the president and bureaucracy could be attained through requests under the Freedom of Information Act, groups gained easier access to information impacting their interests.

Interest groups involved in elections also flourished as a result of the decline of the power of the political parties. Parties were weaker because of the expansion of direct primary laws (state parties had less control over nominees to represent them in the general campaign), candidate-centered campaigns (in which parties became less important in terms of running campaign organizations), and campaign finance reform laws in the 1970s that decreased the power of the party to raise campaign money. Following passage of the Federal Election Campaign Act (FECA) in 1971 and its amendments in 1974, interest groups began establishing political action committees (PACs) to donate money to candidates, which in turn expanded their access to policymakers.[2] Finally, the advancement of technology, particularly the recent development of the internet, has reduced the costs associated with establishing a group and mobilizing activists (Berry 1997; Davidson, Oleszek, and Lee 2009; Hall and Wayman 1990).

NOW remains the most widely known women's group. As mentioned earlier, the group grew out of the President's Commission on the Status of Women and was created in 1966 with the intention of creating a "NAACP for women" to eliminate discrimination against women (Carabillo et al. 1993). Today NOW claims to be the largest grassroots-based feminist organization in the United States with over 500,000 members and more than 550 chapters in all 50 states (National Organization for Women 2010a). The group has a broad-based agenda advocating for policies to eliminate discrimination against women in the workplace, schools, the justice system, and all other sectors of society. Reproductive rights and other women's health issues, violence against women, the ERA, pay equity, family friendly workplaces, and eliminating discrimination based on race and sexual orientation are also among the group's top priorities (National Organization for Women 2010b).

From the early years, NOW committed itself to being an action-oriented group committed to the mobilization of women at the grassroots level and to the pursuit of fundamental social change rather than to the more limited goal of legal equality with men. To that end NOW combines traditional lobbying

---

[2]Political action committees or PACs were established by the federal government as part of the 1974 Federal Election Campaign Act in order to monitor and limit campaign spending by businesses and interest groups. Any corporation, union, or other interest group can form a PAC and register it with the Federal Election Commission, which monitors its spending on federal candidates. PACs are allowed to spend up to $5,000 on a federal campaign per election for each election cycle (meaning they can spend $10,000 if a candidate runs in a primary and in the general election).

and education activities with more radical forms of political engagement such as mass marches and protests (Freeman 1975; Barakso 2004). Former NOW President Patricia Ireland describes the benefits of marches and other mass actions as follows:

> We use them to organize and to inspire. A mass action builds our strength and our momentum—and shows that strength to politicians and to ourselves. Successful mass actions also have positive "hangover effects": the tremendous individual and group efforts needed to organize a big march expands our lists of contributors and supporters and provides an opportunity to develop skills and activism at the grass roots. These new community organizers can continue to expand that network and use it to turn out the vote or bring constituent pressure for an issue. (Ireland 1996, 249)

In April 2004 NOW joined with other women's groups including Planned Parenthood, National Abortion Rights Action League, and the Feminist Majority to organize the March for Women's Lives. According to group leaders, this mass protest brought over 1.15 million marchers to Washington, D.C., to advocate for reproductive rights and to protest policies of the Bush administration concerning abortion, family planning, and other women's

Aerial view of the crowd gathered for the NOW 2004 March for Women's Lives. Protesters gathered to support reproductive rights.

health issues (Barr and Williamson 2004).[3] More recently, after the California Supreme Court upheld Proposition 8, a voter initiative that banned gay marriage in California, NOW joined with other groups to organize protests against the decision in cities across the nation (National Organization for Women 2009).

In addition, NOW Foundation, the educational and legal arm of NOW, often uses the courts to pursue legal cases. For example, in its ongoing effort to protect women's reproductive rights, NOW has sought to apply RICO statutes or racketeering laws to prevent Operation Rescue and other aggressive anti-abortion protestors from blocking access to abortion clinics (*NOW v. Scheidler*). The safety of women and providers at abortion clinics gained renewed attention in 2009 after the murder of Dr. George Tiller, an abortion provider in Kansas, by an anti-abortion activist (Slevin 2009).

Finally, NOW, like many other organizations, has consistently been involved in presidential and congressional elections, conducting voter registration drives, endorsing candidates, and seeking to publicize its issues with the public and the major candidates. In 2008 the group endorsed Senator Hillary Clinton (D-NY) in her run for the presidency and the group actively campaigned for her throughout the primary season (National Organization for Women 2007).

Although NOW continues to be the most widely known feminist organization, there are numerous other active feminist women's groups. These groups vary in the breadth of their agendas and the range of activities in which they participate. For example, groups like the Feminist Majority Foundation and the American Association of University Women are similar to NOW in their devotion to a broad range of issues and their focus on political activism utilizing a broad range of techniques from lobbying to litigation, issue research, and mass protest. There is also an increasing trend toward specialization in the feminist community in which groups concentrate their activism and research on one specific issue such as abortion, gay rights, domestic violence, or pacifism. The National Abortion Rights Action League (NARAL), the National Coalition Against Domestic Violence, and CODEPINK: Women for Peace are all groups that participate in grassroots activism for a particular cause. Still other organizations are brought together by a shared identity based on professional status or demographics such as age or race. Examples of these organizations include the Older Women's League, the Black Women's Health Imperative, and Business and Professional Women.

Finally, there are numerous women's think tanks, which conduct public policy research on issues that impact women and families, and legal advocacy groups, which focus their energy on activities such as providing legal representation for women in discrimination cases. For example, the Institute for Women's Policy Research publishes annual reports on the Status of Women in

---

[3]The United States Park Police no longer provides crowd estimates because these estimates have become politicized as competing interest groups contest the figures.

the States that rank each state based on women's status in political participation, employment and earnings, social and economic autonomy, reproductive rights, and women's health and well-being. These reports are used to garner attention to these issues and spur legislation and policy change to address women's concerns. Similarly, the National Women's Law Center and the Center for Women's Policy Studies also focus on legal aid and public policy research rather than grassroots activism (see Appendix C for information on contemporary women's organizations).

Although there is great diversity in the activities and goals of organizations associated with the feminist movement, there is also a burgeoning conservative women's movement. In her book, *Women of the New Right*, Rebecca Klatch (1987) describes two archetypes of conservative women: the socially conservative woman and the laissez-faire conservative. The political activism of the social conservative woman is strongly influenced by her religious beliefs and a desire to protect the traditional family, particularly regarding woman's role in the home and the care of children. Whereas the social conservative is motivated to activism by her moral code, the laissez-faire conservative is devoted to the ideals of individual rights, free market principles, and limited government. Thus, these women tend to eschew debates on social issues such as abortion and focus their efforts on economic concerns such as workplace issues. For example, laissez-faire conservative women oppose programs such as affirmative action as an unconstitutional preference and government intrusion that violates free market principles without improving the position of women and minorities (Klatch 1987; Schreiber 2002b, 2008).

Concerned Women for America is the largest group representing socially conservative women. Just as the awakening of a feminist consciousness in the early 1960s spurred the formation of NOW, Concerned Women for America grew out of the antifeminist countermovement. These women were mobilized in response to their opposition to the ERA, the *Roe v. Wade* decision on abortion, and the International Women's Year conferences and celebrations that elevated feminist principles concerning women's rights. Founded in 1979 in San Diego, California, by Beverly LaHaye, the group reaches out to Christian women as wives and mothers in an effort to protect the traditional family and reassert biblical principles as a foundation of public policy. LaHaye was at the center of the New Right movement in the 1970s and 1980s, traveling the country and giving speeches on family values and the moral decay of the nation, writing books, and conducting her own radio show. Her husband, the Reverend Tim LaHaye, was a founding member of Jerry Falwell's Moral Majority, one of the leading organizations in the mobilization of the New Right in the 1980s (Marshall 1995; Schreiber 2002a, 2002b, 2008). According to the group's mission statement, "The mission of CWA is to protect and promote Biblical values among all citizens—first through prayer, then education, and finally by influencing our society—thereby reversing the decline in moral values in our nation" (Concerned Women for America 2010).

In her memoir, *Who But a Woman?*, Beverly LaHaye maintains that she founded CWA to "combat the goals of the feminist movement" after witnessing what she and other Christian women viewed as an attack on traditional families that occurred at the National Women's Convention in Houston, Texas, in 1977 to celebrate International Women's Year. LaHaye opposed the adoption of resolutions by the convention including "the ratification of the Equal Rights Amendment; the 'right' of homosexuals and lesbians to teach in public schools and to have custody of children; federally funded abortion on demand; approval of abortion for teenagers without parental knowledge or consent; federal government involvement in twenty-four-hour-a-day child care centers, and more" (LaHaye 1984, 27). The group built its membership through church networks attracting the support of ministers, distributing literature to recruit evangelical Protestant women, and holding coffees with like-minded women.

Today CWA represents a national network of over 500 prayer/action chapters connected to a professional staff at the national headquarters, which opened in 1985 (www.cwfa.org/history.asp). The prayer/action chapters mobilize grassroots women by meeting to learn and pray about issues and then take action on them, such as writing letters to Congress or newspaper editorial boards (www.states.cwfa.org/states). In order to promote the return to biblical values, the group focuses on issues including opposition to abortion, homosexuality, and pornography. It also opposes the United Nations as undermining American sovereignty, advocates for the expansion of religious liberty meaning the ability to bring religion back into the public square, and seeks to restore Judeo-Christian values and parental authority in the public school system.

Like their feminist counterparts such as NOW and AAUW, CWA conducts lobbying efforts and prepares voter guides to draw the attention of its members and legislators to its key issues. The group is also particularly aggressive in exposing what it considers the excesses of the feminist movement in order to demonstrate that they are the "true" representatives of mainstream women's opinion (Schreiber 2002a, 2002b, 2008). For example, in the early 1990s, CWA's magazine, *Family Voice*, ran a monthly series of "Feminist Follies" featuring radical quotes by feminist leaders as they appeared in their group's own publications and a cartoon of a disheveled woman wearing a large NOW button with her fist in the air (Marshall 1995, 324–326).

In contrast to the social issue focus of Concerned Women for America, the Independent Women's Forum (IWF) concentrates on the economic and limited government issues that concern laissez-faire conservatives. Angered by the media coverage of the Clarence Thomas–Anita Hill hearings,[4] in which the feminist view was equated with the perspective of all women, this group was founded in 1992 by a group of women who worked for the George H. W. Bush administration. They decided to create an organization to counter the feminist

---

[4]The hearings involved the confirmation of Clarence Thomas to be an Associate Justice on the U.S. Supreme Court in 1991. The all-male Senate Judiciary Committee heard testimony from Anita Hill, who had accused Thomas of sexual harassment when she worked for him at the Equal Employment Opportunity Commission. Liberal women's organizations believed that Hill was mistreated and her allegations were not taken seriously by many of the senators during questioning. Thomas, who denied the charges, was eventually appointed to the bench.

establishment by providing a voice for conservative women who believe in individual freedom, self-government, and personal responsibility. IWF eschews moral debates and does not take a position on abortion. Instead it focuses on economic issues and reducing government regulation (Schreiber 2002a, 2002b, 2008).

The group believes that government programs designed to help women in fact disrespect women and limit their choices. For example, IWF opposes the Title IX program as it applies to athletics. Title IX is federal legislation that mandates that public schools that receive federal funds, both at the secondary and collegiate levels, must ensure that women's sports programs receive equal treatment and the same funding as men's programs. The IWF views Title IX as a quota system that demeans the legitimate athletic accomplishments of women and denies opportunities to men by requiring a strict measure of proportionality in participation in college athletics when women are relatively less interested in athletics than men (Schreiber 2002a, 2008).

IWF leaders are well connected to, or are themselves, key policy and opinion makers. Many of the women associated with IWF held positions in the administration of George W. Bush and served as advisors to the McCain campaign. Thus, IWF leaders focus their efforts on providing research and gaining media attention to a conservative viewpoint on women's issues.

WOMEN'S GROUPS AND ELECTORAL POLITICS

One of the most effective ways to influence policymaking is to get involved in electoral politics to make sure like-minded candidates are elected to office. In a political system where parties are relatively weak and campaigns are candidate centered, numerous women's groups have entered the business of candidate recruitment, fund-raising, voter mobilization, and provision of campaign-related service.

One of the first groups to get involved in electoral politics was the National Women's Political Caucus (NWPC). Founded in 1971, the group was organized to move women into decision-making positions at all levels of political power including elected positions in Congress and the state legislatures, appointed positions in the executive branch, and positions of influence in the political parties. Early leaders included well-known feminist activists such as Gloria Steinem, founder of *Ms. Magazine*; Betty Freidan, author of *The Feminine Mystique* and first president of NOW; congresswoman and antiwar activist, Bella Abzug; and the first black congresswoman, Representative Shirley Chisholm (D-NY).

To spread feminist goals as widely as possible, the NWPC took care to present itself as a multiethnic and bipartisan organization. The presidency rotated between a Republican and a Democrat. The group's first leadership board included Indian rights leader, LaDonna Harris; head of the National Council of Negro Women, Dorothy Height; and Chicana activist, Lupe Anguiano (Hartmann 1989). Later the group organized separate Republican and Democratic task forces.

NWPC achieved some of its greatest victories in the 1970s and 1980s. The group was pivotal in convincing the Democratic Party to require equal representation of women in state delegations to the presidential nominating conventions. NWPC has helped identify qualified women nominees and lobbied presidential administrations to nominate women for cabinet posts. It has provided campaign training and financial support to many women candidates. In the 1990s, the group experienced a decline in membership as other organizations with similar goals proliferated (Hartmann 1989; McGlen et al. 2002).

Campaign finance reform changes adopted in 1974 in response to the Watergate scandal encouraged the formation of PACs to donate funds to parties and to individual candidates. In addition, the failure of the ERA provided increased urgency to the goal of increasing the number of women in office as many women's groups realized that female state legislators had voted for the ERA in greater numbers than did their male counterparts. Therefore, with more women in office the ERA might have passed and issues important to women's groups would have received more attention. This led NOW and other major women's organizations to focus more of their efforts on electing women and changing the face of power rather than simply lobbying the current slate of leaders (see Chapter 5 for more information on women's PACs) (Hartmann 1989; Burrell 2009). As a result, numerous new women's PACs joined NWPC in the effort to elect more women to office, including the Women's Campaign Forum, the oldest bipartisan women's PAC; NOW PAC, which donates to federal candidates; and NOW Equality PAC, which supports feminist candidates at the state and local levels.

As women's groups have increased their involvement in all phases of electoral politics, they have faced conflicts concerning whether and how closely to align themselves with the political parties and whether to limit their endorsements to women or to support like-minded men. For feminist organizations like NOW the decision to get involved in electoral politics itself was controversial. Although national leaders such as Eleanor Smeal, NOW president during the fight for the ERA, viewed electoral involvement as essential to the advancement of feminist goals, many activists felt involvement in mainstream electoral politics would undermine NOW's ability to build a grassroots action-oriented organization and remain on the vanguard of feminism (Barakso 2004; Young 2000).

Beyond the decision to commit to an electoral strategy, organizations have had to decide whether to align themselves with one party or to support women candidates from either party, or to support any like-minded male or female candidates (Young 2000). NOW endorses both men and women who support the feminist agenda. Two of the oldest organizations, the National Women's Political Caucus and the Women's Campaign Forum, both founded in the early 1970s, continue to support women candidates from both the Democratic and Republican parties who support their goals. For example the Women's Campaign Forum donates to and provides campaign support for pro-choice candidates without regard to party affiliation. Conversely, EMILY's List supports only pro-choice

Democratic women and WISH List (Women in the Senate and House) was founded in 1992 to help pro-choice Republican women (Burrell 1994, 2009). Even though these groups are strongly identified with one of the political parties, their goals can still come into conflict with the national parties. For example, EMILY's List has been criticized by some Democratic leaders for actively campaigning for women candidates in Democratic primary races against Democratic men who had supported feminist goals in the past (Raasch 2002; Burrell 2009).

The active involvement of women's groups in providing early funding and endorsements for women candidates has proven particularly important in the primary stage when the parties are loathe to take an active role in the contest, preferring to let a winner emerge before they plunge resources into a campaign. Women candidates, particularly Democratic women, who have the active backing of women's groups like EMILY's list are more likely to command the resources needed to make them credible candidates and emerge as the winner of the nomination in the important primary contests (Burrell 1994, 2009; Day, Hadley, and Brown 2001).

Our discussion of interest groups demonstrates that women have a long history of coming together to engage in political activism for a variety of causes. However, although all these groups claim to represent women's interests, there is no one "women's point of view." Today women's organizations are involved in a broad range of issues and they represent women from all demographic groups and across the ideological spectrum. These groups utilize a variety of techniques to influence the policy process from grassroots mass protest to litigation and public policy research. The political skills women have learned through participation in interest groups have helped them shape the policy agenda and have provided many women with the skills necessary to run their own successful campaigns for office.

WOMEN AND THE POLITICAL PARTIES

Throughout American history, women have participated in social movements and created interest groups to influence government and advocate for policy change. Conversely, political parties were historically part of the male/public sphere and women have struggled to gain entry into these organizations in the same way that women had to fight for the right to vote and hold public office. The rise of the modern political party dates back to the late 1820s—and the election of Andrew Jackson as president. Jackson's election ushered in a period of widespread mass participation in politics where white male citizens, regardless of class and property ownership, voted in elections and engaged in politics. Political parties took on their modern-day role of seeking to win elections by selecting candidates, mobilizing voters, and conducting campaigns (Aldrich 1995).

Throughout the 1800s and early 1900s, party politics was also a major part of male social life. According to Paula Baker (1984), parties united all white men across the social classes by providing entertainment, a definition of manhood, and the basis for a male ritual. Men advertised their partisanship by taking part in rallies, joining local organizations, reading party newspapers, and wearing campaign paraphernalia. In the cities men participated in military-style parades in support of their candidates and in rural areas the parties sponsored picnics. In an effort to combat the idea that women were too emotional to participate in politics, speaking in the late 1890s, the suffragist Anna Howard Shaw described male partisan gatherings this way:

> Women are supposed to be unfit to vote because they are hysterical and emotional . . . I had heard so much about our emotionalism that I went to the last Democratic National Convention held at Baltimore, to observe the repose of the male contingent. I saw some men take a picture of one gentleman whom they wanted elected, and it was so big they had to walk sideways as they carried it forward; they were followed by hundreds of other men yelling, shouting, and singing the "Hown Dawg" song; then, when there was a lull, another set of men would start forward under another man's picture, not to be outdone by the "Hown Dawg" melody, screaming, yelling, and shouting at their people. I saw men jump upon the seats and throw their hats in the air and shout: "What's the matter with Champ Clark?" Then, when those hats came down, other men would kick them back into the air, shouting at the top of their voices: "He's all right!!!" Then I heard others screaming and shouting and yelling for "Underwood!! Underwood, first last and all the time!!!" No hysteria about it—just patriotic loyalty, splendid manly devotion to principle. And so they went on and went on until 5 o'clock in the morning—the whole night long, I saw men jump in their seats, and jump down again, and run around in a ring . . .
>
> I have been to a lot of women's conventions in my day, but I never saw a woman knock another woman's bonnet off her head as she shouted: "She's all right!". . . . (Quoted in Kraditor 1981, 108–109)

Given the centrality of political parties in the life of the male citizen, it is not surprising that the major parties, the Democrats and the Republicans, opposed suffrage and any role for women in the parties beyond the supporting role of helping to canvass for candidates and mobilize voters. Women first gained meaningful influence in third parties. Associated with reform movements such as temperance, cleaning up government, and social welfare reform, third parties including the Prohibition Party, the Populists, and the Progressives gave women leadership positions on party committees, allowed them to serve as delegates to party conventions, and even supported their candidacies for office on their tickets. Women gained support from these parties both because of their devotion to the party's reform causes and because the parties hoped that the mobilization of women as a new voting block could help them build the majority coalition that would lead them to become a major force in American politics (Andersen 1996; Freeman 2000).

However, throughout the long fight for suffrage, women's relationship to the major parties remained tense. The major parties were suspicious of the reform movements with which suffragist women associated themselves. Reformers wanted to clean up politics and take away power from the political machines by promoting secret ballots and direct democracy measures, such as the initiative and referendum, by which voters could get issues onto the ballot without going through the legislature and the political parties. Outside of the political machines, major party financial backers including the liquor interests and the textile manufacturers opposed women's suffrage because of women's support for outlawing liquor and child labor. In turn, many women reformers felt that party politics was corrupt and their legitimacy with lawmakers was derived from their ability to remain nonpartisan. From 1868, suffragists testified before party committees seeking endorsement of the right for women to vote in the party platform to no avail (Kraditor 1981; Andersen 1996; Harvey 1998; Freeman 2000).

By the 1916 presidential election, the extension of suffrage to 4 million women voters in 12 states led both parties to endorse suffrage but neither party included support for a federal amendment in its platform. After women won the right to vote, the militant Congressional Union formed its own party, the National Woman's Party. Their leader Alice Paul authored the ERA and the party focused its efforts on gaining passage of the amendment through Congress. Meanwhile, NAWSA became the nonpartisan League of Women Voters, seeking to educate women for participation in politics and advocating for issues impacting women and children (Andersen 1996; Kraditor 1981; Flexner and Fitzpatrick 1996; Freeman 2000). With thousands of newly enfranchised women, the parties made aggressive efforts to mobilize women voters but remained reluctant to open the levers of power and influence within the party to women, namely elections, appointments, party policy, and money. The parties created women's divisions, bureaus, and committees and slowly began to expand women's representation on national and state party committees, in some cases adopting 50-50 rules for women's and men's representation (see Box 2.2 and Table 2.3). However, the criticism that the parties are more likely to utilize women in support roles than to give them positions of power persists today (Andersen 1996; Harvey 1998; Freeman 2000; Rymph 2006; Burrell 2009).

For most of the twentieth century the Republican Party was more open to the women's rights agenda than the Democratic Party. The Republicans endorsed suffrage before the Democrats and they were the first to support the ERA as labor unions, an important Democratic constituency, opposed the amendment throughout the 1960s. Early legislation for women, including the Equal Pay Act of 1963, the addition of sex to Title VII of the Civil Rights Act, and congressional passage of the Equal Rights Amendment in 1972, was passed with bipartisan support. However, neither party made women's rights a central part of its agenda.

Yet, by the 1970s, the second wave of the feminist movement and the antifeminist countermovement led to a realignment within the voting bases of the two parties with feminists aligning themselves with the Democratic Party and social conservatives moving to the Republican Party. By 1980 the

BOX 2.2

Women as Party Activists and Delegates to the Major Party Conventions

In 1900, Frances Warren of Wyoming became the first woman delegate to the Republican National Convention. In the same year, Elizabeth Cohen of Utah was chosen as an alternate to the Democratic National Convention. When another delegate became ill, Cohen became the first woman delegate to a Democratic National Convention and she gave a seconding speech for the party's presidential nominee, William Jennings Bryan (Andersen 1996; Center for American Women and Politics 2006).

After suffrage, women slowly increased their representation within the power structure of the political parties. By the late 1960s the parties were transformed as the proliferation of presidential primaries took the presidential nomination process out of the hands of party leaders and gave the voters the power to select the nominee. After the tumultuous 1968 Democratic National Convention that included riots in the streets of Chicago over civil rights and the Vietnam War, the Democrats appointed the McGovern-Fraser Commission to recommend reforms. The commission's recommendations included a directive that women, African Americans, and youth should be represented at Democratic Party conventions in proportion to their numbers in the electorate. These recommendations became a permanent part of the Democratic National Committee's charter in 1980. Similarly, in the early 1970s, the Republican Delegates and Organizations Committee recommended to the states, but did not require, equal representation for women at its conventions (Sanbonmatsu 2002; Freeman 2000; Baer and Bositis 1988; Baer 2003; Burrell 2009).

As a result of these changes, the number of women attending both conventions increased significantly in 1972. However, since 1972, there has been a greater percentage of women delegates at the Democratic than the Republican convention. Ironically, the expansion of women's representation at party conventions coincided with the decline of the party convention as a pivotal player in the nomination of presidential candidates as control over the nomination shifted from party elites to primary election voters (Sanbonmatsu 2002; Baer 2003; Burrell 2009). ■

Republican Party platform no longer supported the ERA and as conservatives in the mold of Ronald Reagan came to dominate over more moderate Republicans, the party embraced a strongly pro-life stance. Meanwhile, Democrats had adopted convention rules to require more diversity in party delegations by requiring equal representation of women and expanded representation of African Americans and youth. In the 1984 election, feminist groups were able to persuade Democratic presidential candidate Walter Mondale to choose Geraldine Ferraro as his vice presidential running mate in an effort to reach

TABLE 2.3

Women Delegates to the Major Party Conventions

Year	Democratic Delegates (% Women)	Republican Delegates (% Women)
1916	<1 (5 delegates)	<1 (6 delegates)
1924	11	14
1932	8	12
1940	8	11
1948	10	12
1956	16	12
1968	13	16
1972	40	29
1976	33	31
1980	49	29
1984	49	44
1988	48	33
1992	48	43
1996	53	36
2000	48	35
2004	50	44
2008	50	32

Source: 1916–1956 data, Andersen, Kristi. 1996. *After Suffrage: Women in Partisan and Electoral Politics before the New Deal.* Chicago: University of Chicago Press, p. 83; 1968–2000 data, Sanbonmatsu, Kira. 2002. *Democrats/ Republicans and the Politics of Women's Place.* Ann Arbor: University of Michigan Press, p. 43; 2004 data for Democrats from CNN (www.cnn.com/ELECTION/2004/special/president/convention/dnc/delegate) and Republican data from www.2004nycgop.org/; 2008 data for Democrats from Democratic National Convention Committee (www.demconvention.com/assets/downloads/Delegate-Diversity-1984-2008.pdf) and Republican data from CBS News (http://cbs2.com/politics/gop.poll.bush.2.807390.html).

out to women voters. Women's groups became a key player in the Democratic coalition. Still the alliance of both feminists and social conservatives with the parties remains uneasy and both groups have periodically threatened to abandon the party in favor of forming a third party committed to their cause or have threatened to demobilize or mobilize their followers behind other candidates (Freeman 2000; Wolbrecht 2000; Young 2000; Sanbonmatsu 2002; 2006; Baer 2003; Rymph 2006; Burrell 2009).

In addition to gaining leadership roles in the major parties, women have also sought the support of the parties in their bids for elective office. Both parties frequently ran women as sacrificial lambs (that is, had them oppose strong incumbents from the other party in a futile campaign rather than let the incumbent run unopposed in elections) or widows who were chosen to succeed their husbands in office in order to keep the seat in party hands and prevent an internal party struggle until a male frontrunner emerged (Burrell 1994;

BOX 2.3

Women as Party Leaders

In the early 1970s, two women, Jean Westwood and Mary Louise Smith, became the first (and to date the only) women to head the national Democratic and Republican parties. These women became leaders at the peak of the feminist movement when the advancement of women was a major issue in American politics. Congress had just passed the ERA in 1972 and the *Roe v. Wade* decision on abortion was handed down in 1973.

Yet the tenures of Westwood and Smith as party chairs also coincided with times of major crisis for their respective parties. Jean Westwood served as Democratic National Committee chair for only five months in 1972. A wealthy businesswoman from Utah who with her husband had built a fortune in several businesses including mink ranching, apartment construction, and swimming pool installation, Westwood was active in state politics and worked on presidential campaigns from Senator Robert F. Kennedy and Hubert Humphrey in 1968 to Bruce Babbitt in 1985. She was chosen to lead the Democratic Party after George McGovern earned the 1972 Democratic presidential nomination. She was known as a bold thinker who was willing to challenge allies. In the 1972 campaign, before Watergate and campaign finance reform, she advocated disclosing the names of campaign contributors even though the law did not require it. After McGovern lost the presidency to Richard Nixon in an election in which the Democratic candidate won only the Democratic strongholds of Massachusetts and Washington, D.C., Westwood resigned as chair (Molotsky 1997; Clymer 1998; Baer 2003).

Like Westwood, Mary Louise Smith led the Republican Party during an electoral loss and an internal battle for the ideological direction of the party. Appointed chair by Gerald Ford in 1974, Smith had the unenviable task of leading the party after the Watergate scandal and resignation of President Nixon. A devoted party loyalist, Smith worked her way up the party ranks from stuffing envelopes for the Iowa Republican Party to the national party chair. She served on the Republican National Committee for 20 years from 1964 to 1984. As a moderate who supported the ERA and affirmative action, Smith's views put her at odds with an increasingly conservative party. She stepped down as chair in 1977 and was replaced by Bill Brock, a conservative former senator from Tennessee. Ronald Reagan appointed her to the U.S. Civil Rights Commission in 1982, but her criticisms of administration policy on civil rights prevented her from being reappointed the next year (Pace 1997; Clymer 1998; Baer 2003).

Although Westwood and Smith remain the only women to achieve the pinnacle of power within the political parties, women have expanded their involvement in all aspects of party politics by serving as state party chairs and national party leaders during this time of heightened political competition (see *Profiles of party operatives Ann Wagner and Ann Lewis* on following pages). ■

PROFILES OF POLITICAL INFLUENCE

Ann Wagner, Republican National Committee Co-Chair and Chairwoman of the Missouri Republican Party (2001–2005)

Ann Wagner served as co-chair of the National Republican Party from 2001 to 2005. For a position traditionally reserved for a woman, President George W. Bush appointed her as co-chair because, according to Wagner, "he was looking for a suburban mother from the Heartland who knew how to win elections." As the first woman to chair the state Republican Party of Missouri, Wagner had a lot of experience in building the grassroots base of a party. Wagner got her start in politics in the late 1980s when her husband took a job as a legal adviser to then Governor John Ashcroft. Living in the Missouri capital of Jefferson City, Wagner says, "There are only a couple of things you can do if you live in a capital city—become involved in politics or work for the government." She did both, working for the Energy Division of the Missouri Department of Natural Resources and later, in 1991, becoming the director for the Republicans of the state House and Senate Redistricting Commission, a job that helps draw the district lines that govern elections to Congress and the state legislature for the ten years after a census. She then held a series of party posts in Missouri politics including state director of the Bush–Quayle presidential campaign in 1992 and adviser to John Ashcroft's 1994 Senate campaign.

After giving birth to her third child in 1995, Wagner took a year off from politics. However, when she returned to help organize state caucuses to choose the Republican nominee for president in 1996, Wagner was upset by the divisiveness and negativity of the supporters of Pat Buchanan, a candidate for the nomination and a conservative activist who had also run for the Republican nomination against President Bush in 1992. She told her husband that she needed to make a decision: either she would have a fourth child or she would plunge into Republican politics to change the direction of the party. She ran for a position on the Republican state party committee and in 1999 became the first woman to chair the state party. She continued to serve as state party chair through 2005. As state party chair, Wagner emphasized building up grassroots support for the party across the state. Under her leadership, Republicans saw a tremendous expansion of their electoral margins in Missouri, taking control of the majority of the seats in the Missouri delegation to the U.S. House of Representatives and winning majorities in the state legislature.

As national co-chair, Wagner devoted special attention to outreach to women as voters, party activists, and candidates. She designed the Republicans "Winning Women" program that, in addition to voter outreach, included recruitment of women as grassroots "Team Leaders" for the George W. Bush 2004 re-election campaign and leadership training programs designed to recruit Republican women

(Continued)

▶ PROFILES OF POLITICAL INFLUENCE (CONTINUED)

to run for office. Through their leadership training programs, Wagner says they get a commitment from the female participants to either run for office or take a key leadership role on a campaign. The networking opportunities and training the program provides has expanded the number of women serving at all levels of government from local boards and commissions to Congress.

Wagner believes it is important to expand the number of women participating in politics. Although she does not believe there are women's issues, she does say, "There are issues that women care deeply about. Being a daughter, mother, and wife builds who you are, it shapes how you approach issues" (McColl 2004). For Wagner, being a woman has never been a hindrance. Instead it has been an asset to advancement in politics—a fact that she attributes to often being the first woman in leadership roles and the novelty of that status. However, she thinks that we see fewer women in office because women have to be asked to run, which requires more aggressive recruiting efforts from the parties. She also sees the work–family balance as an issue for women. This is an issue she has personally faced in her roles as state party chair, national co-chair, and a mother of three school-aged children. "Sometimes it's like juggling an egg, a chainsaw and a bowling ball" (McColl 2004). When she first became national co-chair and began a heavy cross-country traveling schedule she often boarded the plane in tears, upset about missing one of her children's games. However, Wagner is in constant communication with them. Some evenings you would find her on the speakerphone in her Washington, D.C., office going over spelling homework with her nine–year old. Her work in politics also gives her an opportunity to instill values of public service in her children, expand their horizons beyond their home and school, and provide them with a front row seat to history by taking her children with her as she travels the nation on behalf of the Republican Party. After completing her tenure as national party co-chair in 2005, president Bush appointed Wagner to serve as the U.S. Ambassador to Luxemboug.

Sources: McColl 2004; biography provided by the Republican National Committee; personal interview by Michele Swers. ∎

Gertzog 1995; Sanbonmatsu 2002). Still, throughout most of the twentieth century, Republicans elected more women to office, particularly at the state legislative level. By the late 1980s and early 1990s the dynamic had shifted and Democratic women now comprise a larger percentage of their party's membership in Congress and the state legislatures in comparison to Republican women (Sanbonmatsu 2003; Wilcox and Norrander 2005; Burrell 2009) (see Chapter 7 for more information on this trend).

Responding to the feminist movement's demand for more women in elective office, the national Democratic and Republican parties began to create programs to recruit women candidates in the 1970s. For example, in 1974, the

◤ PROFILES OF POLITICAL INFLUENCE

Ann Lewis, Senior Advisor to the Hillary Clinton Presidential Campaign

Ann Lewis has been on the forefront of advancements for women in politics her entire life. Over the years, Lewis has worked for the Democratic Party, the nonprofit world, Congress, and the White House. Lewis attributes her interest in politics to her parents. Growing up in New Jersey just after World War II, her family took the values of democracy seriously. The experience of the war led her parents to stress the importance of choosing your leaders. "Once you accept the tenets of democracy and the important role people have to play in it, it becomes essential and necessary for you to do your part." Lewis began her political career as a volunteer handing out pamphlets for the presidential campaign of Adlai Stevenson in the 1950s. She later moved to Florida and went door-to-door for the Kennedy campaign in 1960. However, she found only two people who said they wanted to vote for him and they were going to be out of town and had not applied for absentee ballots. In the late 1960s she took a job with the mayor's office in Boston. While she was working there, a friend invited her to what turned out to be the convening meeting of the National Women's Political Caucus (NWPC), the first organization to actively promote the election of women to political office. At this and subsequent meetings Lewis began to feel the "irony of working hard to elect people who stood for equality yet had no intention to give women a share of the power—there were no women in power in politics."

The 1970s were a time of change for women in politics. It was the first time that feminists took an active role in electoral politics: "Most women in politics before this were not feminists; they were simply workers, volunteers." However, in the 1970s, "women decided they wanted to be more than just workers in politics and they began to work for equality for women in and through politics." Lewis headed the Massachusetts branch of the NWPC and began to develop two networks, traditional political friends and a growing group of women's rights friends. In 1974, she managed Barbara Mikulski's first campaign for the U.S. Senate, a race she lost with a surprisingly good showing of 43 percent of the vote. Mikulski later won a seat in the House of Representatives and Lewis served as her chief of staff.

Meanwhile women were pressuring the party to open its leadership ranks to women. The 50–50 rule requiring representation of women as half of all delegates to the national conventions originated with the McGovern Commission in 1972 but was not officially implemented until 1982. Lewis and other women's rights advocates viewed it "as a way to build women into the party structure, to ensure there was an entry level open to all." In the period leading up to the election of a new Democratic National Committee (DNC) chair in 1980, Lewis was part of a

(Continued)

▶ PROFILES OF POLITICAL INFLUENCE (CONTINUED)

group of women who pressured the party for more power for women. Because of this pressure, Lewis became the first female political director of the DNC serving from 1981 to 1985. By the 2004 electoral cycle the general election strategist, political director, and communications director were all women. This gave women a lot of power over the workings and message of the Democratic Party. Today, Lewis says, women have real power and influence in the Democratic Party.

During the 2004 electoral cycle, Lewis served as director of the DNC's Women's Vote Center (WVC). From this position, Lewis served as an advocate for women and kept information about women voters and their concerns flowing around the party. The center's Democratic Voice program they trained over 6,000 women to go into their communities and talk to other women about the Democrats. Lewis expanded the WVC's e-mail list from 3,000 to 65,000 people receiving weekly reviews from the party. The WVC kept track of women's voting and the issues that concerned them, breaking out every poll in terms of gender and the women's vote. According to Lewis, since women are the majority of the electorate and the majority of the swing voters that hold major power, women are very important to any political party.

In the 2008 elections, Lewis lent her knowledge of campaign strategy and women voters to the Hillary Clinton presidential campaign. During the primary election, Lewis served as a senior advisor to the Clinton campaign leading outreach to women voters and developing communications strategies. Lewis was proud to be a part of the first serious campaign for the presidency by a female candidate (Wildman 2008). She believes that women do have power now. She maintains, "There are no constraints for what women can do except for those we put upon ourselves. If we want to have equal power we have to demand it, fight for it, earn it. You have to keep pushing it just like they did with suffrage. Many women right now don't think they want power. Power is getting things to happen that might not have if you were not there. Women want the agency of power without the reputation."

Sources: Biography provided by the Democratic National Committee; Wildman, Sarah. 2008. "A Clinton Operative Plays Operator." *Guardian.co.uk* January 2.; personal interview by Research Assistant Kate Gentry Henningsen. ■

Democratic Party sponsored a Campaign Conference for Democratic women to help train women to run for office. In 1976, the National Federation of Republican Women began publishing a booklet, *Consider Yourself for Public Office: Guidelines for Women Candidates.* Since the 1992 "Year of the Woman" elections highlighted the underrepresentation of women in office and the potential benefit of women as outsider candidates, both parties have created various programs to recruit and train more women to run for elective office. The Republican Party's Excellence in Public Service Series is a political leadership development program led by groups of Republican women in several states. The typical program includes eight monthly sessions and three-day leadership seminars in Washington, D.C. The first program, the Richard Lugar Series, was founded in 1989 and the series continues to spread with more states adopting these programs every year (Burrell 2009).

The Congressional Campaign Committees, which recruit and fund candidates for the House and Senate, also have increased their outreach efforts to potential women candidates as party leaders and individual women members have set up their own PACs and programs to help women candidates. In 2002, Representative Nita Lowey (D-NY) and Senator Patty Murray (D-WA) became the first women to head their party's congressional campaign committees, the Democratic Congressional Campaign Committee (DCCC) and the Democratic Senate Campaign Committee (DSCC) respectively. Before becoming the chair of the DCCC, in 1999, Nita Lowey (D-NY) founded Women Lead, a fundraising subsidiary of the DCCC that targets women donors to contribute to women candidates. When Lowey became chair of the DCCC she appointed another congresswoman, Jan Schakowsky (D-IL) to head the program. Under Schakowsky's leadership Women Lead raised $25 million in the 2001-2002 campaign cycle for women candidates. Similarly, before rising to chair the DSCC, Patty Murray (D-WA) established the Women on the Road to the Senate program, which raised money for women Senate candidates and helped elect four new Democratic women to the Senate in the 2000 elections. In 2002, the program was renamed the Women's Senate Network. The elevation of Nancy Pelosi (D-CA) to Speaker of the House and her active involvement in candidate recruitment and funding decisions should also benefit future Democratic women candidates. Her close ally, Debbie Wasserman Schultz (D-FL) is currently vice-chair of the DCCC and is a leading contender for the DCCC chair when the current chair, Chris Van Hollen (D-MD), decides to step down (Burrell 2009; Rosenthal 2008).

On the Republican side, Elizabeth Dole (R-NC) is the only woman who has chaired a Republican congressional campaign committee. However, 2006 was not a good election year for Republicans and Dole's Republican Senate Campaign Committee faced a lot of criticism. Dole herself was defeated in her re-election bid in 2008. On the House side Anne Northup (R-KY) was in charge of recruitment for the National Republican Congressional Committee (NRCC) in the 2004 election cycle. As early as 1997, future Republican conference chair Deborah Pryce (R-OH) established VIEW (Value in Electing Women) PAC, a leadership PAC devoted to raising money for Republican women candidates. During the 2008 electoral cycle, NRCC chair Tom Cole appointed Candice Miller (R-MI) to lead an effort to recruit women candidates for the House but the initiative was not very successful (Burrell 2009; Kirchoff 2000). Contemporary Republican difficulties in recruiting women candidates stem from a combination of factors including the party's overall loss of standing in recent elections and a party culture and voter base that is less open to calls for diversity than is the Democratic Party (Evans 2005; Elder 2008). Still as campaigns continue to become more expensive and the parties enhance their recruitment activities, strong parties could benefit potential women candidates by providing them with the encouragement to run and strong financial backing (Wilcox and Norrander 2005; Burrell 1994, 2009).

Despite these more recent efforts, scholars disagree as to whether political parties have been a positive or negative force for the advancement of women in elective office. Some note that historically political parties have been an obstacle to the advancement of women in politics. Additionally, scholars have found that in their recruiting efforts, state party chairs have discriminated against women in these efforts either because they are more likely to recruit candidates like themselves—other men—or because they do not believe that voters will elect women (Niven 1998; Sanbonmatsu 2003, 2006). Alternatively, other scholars note that internationally there are more women in office in countries with strong parties that control the nomination process and those countries in which voters are loyal to a party rather than a particular candidate. Thus these scholars suggest that efforts to strengthen American parties and their control of the nomination and electoral process could only help women (Darcy, Welch, and Clark 1994; Norris 2003, Krook 2009). Similarly, other scholars note that women may benefit from the recruitment efforts of more active political parties because women are more likely than men to need to be asked to run for office whereas men naturally consider themselves potential officeholders (Lawless and Fox 2005, 2008; Niven 2006).

CONCLUSION

Our discussion of women's participation in social movements, interest groups, and political parties demonstrates a long, rich tradition of political activism among women. This activist tradition is marked by a great deal of diversity in the causes advocated by women, the ideological viewpoints of female activists, and the organizational tactics employed. Thus, during the fight for women's suffrage, women were active as both opponents and proponents of votes for women. Among the suffragettes, women supported the movement for different reasons and they varied in the extent to which they sought to challenge traditional gender roles. Some women advocated for women's rights based on principles of human rights and individual freedom whereas others viewed the ballot as a means to achieve other social reforms by allowing women to act as civic mothers, viewing politics as a natural extension of women's private sphere responsibilities. Still other women sought the vote for more nefarious reasons, seeking to counteract the influence of minorities and immigrants in an effort to preserve white supremacy. In contemporary politics, women's organizations represent a wide range of issues and ideological perspectives. Thus, feminist groups such as NOW promote equal rights for women and the elimination of barriers to women's full participation in society whereas conservative women's organizations like Concerned Women for America promote the values of the traditional family and the primacy of motherhood.

In addition to having varying goals, activist women have employed different tactics to achieve similar ends. Although they both sought the elimination of sex discrimination, the older branch of the feminist movement worked to achieve its goals through lobbying and legal reform while the younger branch sought to raise women's consciousness and to achieve women's liberation through profound change in societal gender relations.

Finally, women have employed varying political strategies to achieve their goals working outside of the political mainstream through social movements and seeking to achieve change by forming their own interest groups or working to gain influence within the political parties. Through their participation in movements, organizations, and parties, women have gained political skills that have allowed them to influence the direction of policy both by lobbying from the outside and by gaining election to the political offices that allow women to become the authors of policy change.

REFERENCES

Aldrich, John H. 1995. *Why Parties: The Origin and Transformation of Political Parties in America*. Chicago: University of Chicago Press.

Andersen, Kristi. 1996. *After Suffrage: Women in Partisan and Electoral Politics before the New Deal*. Chicago: University of Chicago Press.

Baer, Denise L. 2003. "Women, Women's Organizations, and Political Parties." In *Women and American Politics: New Questions, New Directions* ed. Susan J. Carroll New York: Oxford University Press. pp. 111–145.

Baer, Denise L. and David A. Bositis. 1988. *Elite Cadres and Party Coalitions*. Westport, Conn: Greenwood Press.

Baker, Paula. 1984 "The Domestication of Politics: Women and American Political Society, 1780–1920." *American Historical Review* 89, no. 3:620–647.

Barakso, Maryann. 2004. *Governing NOW: Grassroots Activism in the National Organization for Women*. Ithaca: Cornell University Press.

Barr, Cameron W., and Elizabeth Williamson. 2004. "Women's Rally Draws Vast Crowd: Marchers Champion Reproductive Rights, Opposition to Bush." *Washington Post* (26 April).

Berry, Jeffrey M. 1997. *The Interest Group Society*. New York: Longman.

Blair, Karen. 1980. *The Clubwoman as Feminist*. New York: Holmes and Meier Publishers.

Bordin, Ruth. 1981. *Woman and Temperance*. Philadelphia: Temple University Press.

Burrell, Barbara. 2009. "Political Parties and Women's Organizations: Bringing Women into the Electoral Arena." In *Gender and Elections: Shaping the Future of American Politics*, 2nd edition. Eds. Susan J. Carroll and Richard L. Fox New York: Cambridge University Press.

———. 1994. *A Woman's Place Is in the House: Campaigning for Congress in the Feminist Era*. Ann Arbor: University of Michigan Press.

Carabillo, Toni, Judith Meuli, and June Bundy Csida. 1993. *Feminist Chronicles 1953–1993*. Los Angeles: Women's Graphics.

Center for American Women and Politics. 2006. *Firsts for Women in U.S. Politics*. Accessed online at www.rci.rutgers.edu/~Cawp/Facts/Officeholders/firsts.html.

Clift, Eleanor, and Tom Brazaitis. 2003. *Madam President: Women Blazing the Leadership Trail*. New York: Routledge.

Clymer, Adam. 1998. "The Lives They Lived: Mary Louise Smith & Jean Westwood; First to the Party." *New York Times*. Section 6: (4 January):35.

Concerned Women for America. 2010. "About CWA." Accessed online at http://www.cwfa.org/about.asp

Conover, Pamela Johnston, and Virginia Gray. 1983. *Feminism and the New Right: Conflict Over the American Family.* New York: Praeger Publishers.

Conway, M. Margaret, David W. Ahern, and Gertrude Steuernagel. 1999. *Women and Public Policy: A Revolution in Progress.* 2nd ed. Washington, D.C.: Congressional Quarterly Press.

Costain, Anne N. 1992. *Inviting Women's Rebellion.* Baltimore: Johns Hopkins University Press.

Cushman, Clare, ed. 2001. *Supreme Court Decisions and Women's Rights: Milestones to Equality.* Washington, D.C.: Congressional Quarterly, Inc.

Darcy, R., Susan Welch, and Janet Clark. 1994. *Women, Elections, and Representation,* 2nd ed. Lincoln: University of Nebraska Press.

Davidson, Roger H., Walter J. Oleszek, and Frances E. Lee. 2009. *Congress and Its Members,* 12th ed. Washington, D.C.: Congressional Quarterly, Inc.

Day, Christine, Charles Hadley, and Megan Brown. 2001. "Gender, Feminism, and Partisanship Among Women's PAC Contributors." *Social Science Quarterly* 82: 687–700.

Dorr, Rheta Childe. 1910. *What Eight Million Women Want.* Boston: Small, Maynard & Company.

Elder, Laurel. 2008. "Whither Republican Women: The Growing Partisan Gap Among Women in Congress." *The Forum* 6: Issue 1, Article 13.

Evans, Jocelyn Jones. 2005. *Women, Partisanship, and the Congress.* New York: Palgrave MacMillan.

Ferree, Myra Marx, and Beth B. Hess. 1994. *Controversy and Coalition: The New Feminist Movement,* rev. ed. New York: Twayne Publishers.

Flexner, Eleanor, and Ellen Fitzpatrick. 1996. *Century of Struggle: The Women's Rights Movement in the United States.* Cambridge: Belknap Press of Harvard University.

Freeman, Jo. 1975. *The Politics of Women's Liberation.* New York: Longman Inc.

_____. 2000. *A Room at a Time: How Women Entered Party Politics.* New York: Rowman & Littlefield Publishers, Inc.

Gelb, Joyce, and Marian Lief Palley. 1996. *Women and Public Policies: Reassessing Gender Politics.* Charlottesville, VA: University Press of Virginia.

Gertzog, Irwin N. 1995. *Congressional Women: Their Recruitment, Integration, and Behavior.* 2nd ed. Westport, Conn: Praeger.

Hall, Richard, and Frank Wayman. 1990. "Buying Time Moneyed Interests and the Mobilization of Bias in Congressional Committees." *American Political Science Review* 84:797–820.

Harvey, Anna L. 1998. *Votes Without Leverage: Women in American Electoral Politics, 1920–1970.* New York: Cambridge University Press.

Hartmann, Susan M. 1989. *From Margin to Mainstream: American Women and Politics Since 1960.* Philadelphia: Temple University Press.

Independent Women's Forum 2004. *Agenda for Women 2004.* Washington, D.C.: Independent Women's Forum (26 January).

Institute for Women's Policy Research. n.d. *The Status of Women in the States Project Models for Action: Making Research Work for Women.* Washington, D.C.: Institute for Women's Policy Research.

Ireland, Patricia. 1996. *What Women Want.* New York: Dutton.

Kirchoff, Sue. 2000. "A Rising Republican's Quest for Balance." *CQ Weekly* (28 October): 2525–2527.

Klatch, Rebecca E. 1987. *Women of the New Right.* Philadelphia: Temple University Press.

Kraditor, Aileen S. 1981. *The Ideas of the Woman Suffrage Movement: 1890–1920*. New York: W.W. Norton & Company.

Krook, Mona Lena. 2009. *Quotas for Women in Politics: Gender and Candidate Selection Reform Worldwide* New York: Oxford University Press.

Klein, Ethel. 1984. *Gender Politics: From Consciousness to Mass Politics*. Cambridge: Harvard University Press.

LaHaye, Beverly. 1984. *Who But a Woman?: Concerned Women Can Make a Difference*. Nashville: Thomas Nelson Publishers.

Lawless, Jennifer L. and Richard L. Fox. 2005. *It Takes a Candidate: Why Women Don't Run For Office*. New York: Cambridge University Press.

———. 2008."Why are Women Still Not Running for Public Office?" *Issues in Governance Studies* 16: Washington, D.C.: Brookings Institution.

Mansbridge, Jane. 1986. *Why We Lost the ERA*. Chicago: University of Chicago Press.

Marshall, Susan. 1995. "Confrontation and Co-optation in Antifeminist Organizations." pp. 323–335 in *Feminist Organizations, Harvest of the New Women's Movement*, ed. Myra Marx Ferree and Patricia Yancey Martin. Philadelphia: Temple University Press.

McAdam, Doug. 1982. *Political Process and the Development of Black Insurgency, 1930–1970*. Chicago: University of Chicago Press.

McColl, Alicia. 2004. "Missouri's Dynamic Duo: Busy but Balanced." *St. Louis Women on the Move* 1, no.3, (April): 14–15, 20.

McGlen, Nancy E., Karen O' Connor, Laura van Assendelft, and Wendy Gunther Canada. 2002. *Women, Politics, and American Society*. 3rd ed. New York: Longman.

Molotzky, Irvin. 1997. "Jean Westwood Is Dead at 73; Led Democrats in Rout of '72." *New York Times* (23 August) Section 1: 10.

National Organization for Women. 2007. "NOW Political Action Committee Proudly Endorses Senator Hillary Rodham Clinton for President of the United States in 2008." Accessed online at http://www.now.org/press/03-07/03-28.html.

National Organization for Women. 2009. "NOW Joins Prop 8 Protests Nationwide and in the Nation's Capital." Accessed online at http://www.now.org/issues/lgbi/052809prop8.html.

National Organization for Women. 2010a. "About NOW." Accessed online at http://www.now.org/organization/info.html.

National Organization for Women. 2010b. "Frequently Asked Questions." Accessed online at http://www.now.org/organization/faq.html.

Comp: These references should be added in alphabetical order

Niven, David. 1998. *The Missing Majority: The Recruitment of Women as State Legislative Candidates*. Westport, CT: Praeger Publishers.

———. 2006. "Throwing Your Hat Out of the Ring: Negative Recruitment and the Gender Imbalance in State Legislative Candidacy." *Politics & Gender* 2:473–489.

Norris, Pippa. 2003. *Electoral Engineering: Voting Rules and Political Behavior*. New York: Cambridge University Press.

Norton, Mary Beth, David M. Katzman, Paul D. Escott, Howard P. Chudacoff, Thomas G. Paterson, and William M. Tuttle, Jr. 1986. *A People and a Nation: A History of the United States*. 2nd ed. Volume II: Since 1865. Boston: Houghton Mifflin Company.

Omolade, Barbara. 2004. "Ella's Daughters." In *Women's Lives: Multicultural Perspectives*, 3rd ed., Gwyn Kirk and Margo Okazawa-Rey. New York: McGraw-Hill.

Pace, Eric. 1997. "Mary L. Smith, Only Woman to Lead G.O.P., Dies at 82." *New York Times* (25 August): A21.

Raasch, Chuck. 2002. "Pro-Abortion Rights Group's Fundraising Power Could Be Wave of PAC Future." *Gannett News Service* (24 October).

Robnett, Belinda. 2000. *How Long? How Long?: African-America Women in the Struggle for Civil Rights*. Oxford: Oxford University Press.

Rosenthal, Cindy Simon. 2008. "Climbing Higher: Opportunities and Obstacles within the Party System." In *Legislative Women: Getting Elected, Getting Ahead*. Ed. Beth Reingold Boulder: Lynne Rienner Publishers.

Ryan, Barbara. 1992. *Feminism and the Women's Movement: Dynamics of Change in Social Movement Ideology and Activism*. New York: Routledge.

Rymph, Catherine E. 2006. *Republican Women: Feminism and Conservatism From Suffrage Through the Rise of the New Right*. Chapel Hill: University of North Carolina Press.

Sanbonmatsu, Kira. 2002. *Democrats/Republicans and the Politics of Women's Place*. Ann Arbor: University of Michigan Press.

_____. 2002. "Political Parties and the Recruitment of Women to State Legislatures." *Journal of Politics* 64:791–809.

_____. 2003. "Candidate Recruitment and Women's Election to the State Legislatures." Report prepared for the Center for the American Woman and Politics, Eagleton Institute of Politics, Rutgers, State University of New Jersey.

_____. 2006. *Where Women Run: Gender and Party in the American States*. Ann Arbor: University of Michigan Press.

Schreiber, Ronnee. 2002a. "Injecting a Woman's Voice: Conservative Women's Organizations, Gender Consciousness, and the Expression of Women's Policy Preferences." *Sex Roles* 47: 331–342.

_____. 2002b. "Playing 'Femball': Conservative Women's Organizations and Political Representation in the United States." In *Right-Wing Women: From Conservatives to Extremists Around the World*. ed. Paola Bacchetta and Margaret Power. New York: Routledge.

_____. 2008. *Righting Feminism: Conservative Women and American Politics*. New York: Oxford University Press.

Shanley, Mary Lyndon. 1988. *Women's Rights, Feminism, and Politics in the United States*. Washington, D.C.: American Political Science Association.

Skocpol, Theda. 1992. *Protecting Soldiers and Mothers*. Cambridge: The Belknap Press of Harvard University Press.

Slevin, Peter. 2009. "Slaying Raises Fears on Both Sides of the Abortion Debate." *Washington Post* (2 June).

Strolovitch, Dara. 2007. *Affirmative Advocacy: Race, Class, and Gender in Interest Group Politics*. Chicago: University of Chicago Press.

Tyler, Helen. 1949. *Where Prayer and Purpose Meet 1874–1949: The WCTU Story*. Evanston: The Signal Press National Woman's Christian Temperance Union Inc.

Wells, Mildred White. 1953. *The History of the General Federation of Women's Clubs*. Washington, D.C.: General Federation of Women's Clubs.

Wilcox, Clyde, and Barbara Norrander. 2005. "Change and Continuity in the Geography of Women Legislators." In *Women and Elective Office*, 2nd ed., Eds. Sue Thomas and Clyde Wilcox. New York: Oxford University Press.

Wildman, Sarah. 2008. "A Clinton Operative Plays Operator." *Guardian* (2 January).

Wolbrecht, Christina. 2000. *The Politics of Women's Rights: Parties, Positions, and Change*. Princeton: Princeton University Press.

Wood, Mary I. 1912. *The History of the General Federation of Women's Clubs for the First Twenty-Two Years of Its Organization*. New York: History Department, General Federation of Women's Clubs.

Young, Lisa. 2000. *Feminists and Party Politics*. Vancouver: UBC Press.

The Gender Gap in Elections and Public Opinion

A s Chapter 2 recounts, the struggle to achieve the right to vote for women spanned over 70 years of American history (1848–1920). As Table 3.1 demonstrates, though, the United States was neither the first nor last democratic nation to grant women's suffrage (see *Paths to Power: Women's Suffrage Around the World*). Underlying this struggle was the notion, among both the supporters and opponents of women's suffrage, that women held distinct political opinions and would vote differently than men. One argument that some proponents of female suffrage used in their arguments in favor of granting women the right to vote was that women voters would help "clean up" government and elect politicians committed to reforms that would help women and children, often involving enhanced regulation of industry. It was for that very reason that many business groups, fearful of such reform efforts, actively worked to stop ratification of the Nineteenth Amendment.

But after women won the right to vote, did a "women's" vote actually emerge as many had anticipated? Was it the case then, and is it the case now, that women and men actually have distinct views about politics and distinct patterns in their voting behavior? Is gender a powerful predictor of political behavior as many pundits and advocates claim that it is today?

In this chapter we examine differences in the voting behavior and political attitudes of men and women. The chapter traces the emergence of the gender gap in voting and explores the causes of this much talked about phenomena of American politics. We explore the efforts of the political parties to attract women's votes and examine whether women's position as a potential swing-voting group translates into political power and women-friendly policy. Finally, the chapter examines whether women voters constitute a key group of supporters for women candidates.

PATHS TO POWER

Women's Suffrage Around the World

In the United States, western territories were among the first to grant women's suffrage. Wyoming became the first territory to grant women the vote in 1869. Utah adopted suffrage the following year but the U.S. Congress repealed it because the Mormon Church had actively supported women's voting rights.[1] Colorado became the first state to allow women to vote in 1893. During the fight for the vote in the United States and abroad, some states and countries adopted limited suffrage for women allowing them to vote only in certain elections, such as for school board, municipal elections, or presidential elections (in the United States). These rights were later expanded to full suffrage. In 1971, Switzerland became the last democratic country to adopt women's suffrage. In contrast to the United States where the Nineteenth Amendment to the Constitution mandated full suffrage for women, the constitutional amendment adopted in Switzerland allowed local cantons (the equivalent of states in the United States) to adopt their own laws concerning suffrage in local elections and for one house of the Swiss Parliament. As a result, two Swiss cantons did not adopt full suffrage for women until 1989 and 1990 (Banaszak 1996). ∎

TABLE 3.1

Women's Suffrage in Select Democratic Countries

Year	Country
1893	New Zealand
1902	Australia*
1906	Finland
1913	Norway
1915	Denmark
1918	Germany, United Kingdom
1919	Netherlands, Sweden*
1920	United States
1944	France
1945	Italy
1952	Greece
1971	Switzerland

*Indicates that the right to vote was subject to conditions or restrictions.
Source: Interparliamentary Union: 2005. "A World Chronology of the Recognition of Women's Rights to Vote and to Stand for Election." www.ipu.org/wmn-e/suffrage.htm.

---

[1]Before becoming a state in 1896, Utah like other territories did not have the privileges of a sovereign state and was more stringently regulated by Congress. Therefore, Congress could repeal legislation concerning voting rights in national elections.

COURTING THE WOMEN'S VOTE: THE EARLY YEARS

Even before women won the right to vote, various political organizations and parties tried to anticipate what women would want in order to court or counter the potential women's vote. The passage of the Sheppard-Towner Act (1921), the first government-supported program for educating mothers about infant and prenatal care, was spurred by the desire of politicians to please a potential voting bloc that would soon make itself known at the polls. Many women's organizations lobbied heavily for the Act's passage, including the League of Women Voters, the General Federation of Women's Clubs, the National Consumers League, and the National Congress of Mothers (today known as the PTA) (Skocpol 1992; Klein 1984; Flexner and Fitzpatrick 1996). Similarly, in the early 1920s, at the behest of women's groups and in anticipation of a strong reform-minded women's vote, Congress passed the following legislation: the Cable Act (1922), equalizing citizenship requirements for men and women; the Packers and Stockyard bill (1921), requiring meat inspections to enhance consumer protection; and the Child Labor Act, (1924), giving Congress the authority to limit, regulate, or prohibit the employment of children under age 18 (Klein 1984).

Many ardent foes of women's suffrage had opposed giving women the right to vote because they feared that women would use their votes to impose reforms advocated by the numerous women's groups and female activists in the Progressive Era. Thus, business interests, including railroad, oil, meatpacking, and general manufacturing groups opposed women's suffrage because they feared that women would vote to outlaw child labor and demand improved conditions for working women. The political machines opposed suffrage because they doubted their ability to control women's votes and feared their reform proposals for clean government. The liquor manufacturers were among the most ardently opposed to suffrage because of the leadership of women in the temperance movement (Flexner and Fitzpatrick 1996). Speaking at the 1912 convention of the National Retail Dealer's Association, association president, Neil Bonner, declared: "We do not fear the churches, the men are voting the old tickets; . . . we need not fear the YMCA, for it does no aggressive work; but, gentlemen, we need to fear the Woman's Christian Temperance Union and the ballot in the hands of women; therefore, gentleman, fight woman suffrage" (quoted in Tyler 1949, 159).

Yet proponents and opponents of women's suffrage, who foresaw the potential of having women vote en masse, were wrong. In the years immediately following the adoption of the Nineteenth Amendment, women did not vote in large numbers and a women's bloc of votes loyal to a specific set of issues or a particular party did not emerge. A generation of women who were raised to believe that politics was a male domain did not cast a ballot. In the 1920 election, only one-third of eligible women voted and among those women, party affiliation, class, religion, and ethnicity rather than sex influenced their voting decisions. The greatest differences in turnout among women occurred among groups where sex role differences were most entrenched. Immigrant, rural, southern, and poor women voted in much smaller numbers than their male counterparts, whereas the turnout rates of native-born, middle-class women were closer to that of men (Klein 1984; Andersen 1996).

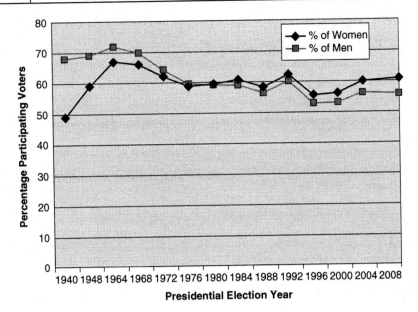

FIGURE 3.1

Percentage of Male and Female Eligible Voters Participating in Presidential Elections in Selected Years

Source: 1940 and 1948 data from Ethel Klein. *Gender Politics.* 1964–2008 data from Center for the American Woman and Politics. 2009. "Gender Differences in Voter Turnout."

During the Great Depression, New Deal Democrats courted women voters based on Roosevelt's social welfare policies. Thus, in 1936, First Lady Eleanor Roosevelt and Mary Dewson, the head of the Women's Division of the Democratic Party from 1932 to 1937, organized 60,000 women to canvass door-to-door for the Democrats. Women's voting participation first exceeded 50 percent of eligible women in the hotly contested presidential race of 1948 in which Harry Truman survived a split of his party that led Strom Thurmond to run on a Dixiecrat ticket and Henry Wallace to run under the Progressive banner (Klein 1984). The race was so close that the *Chicago Tribune* mistakenly declared Republican Thomas Dewey the winner in its early morning edition (Norton et al. 1986). By 1968 women's voting rates had largely caught up to the participation rates of men. Signaling the complete political integration of women in the realm of voting, since the 1984 election, women's participation rates in presidential elections have exceeded the rates of men across racial categories with the largest differences among African Americans (Center for the American Woman and Politics 2009) (see Figures 3.1 and 3.2).[2]

---

[2]According to the Center for the American Woman and Politics (CAWP) in 2000, the first year for which data are available, Asian Pacific Islander men voted at a slightly higher rate than Asian/Pacific Islander women at 24.9 percent for women and 26 percent for men.

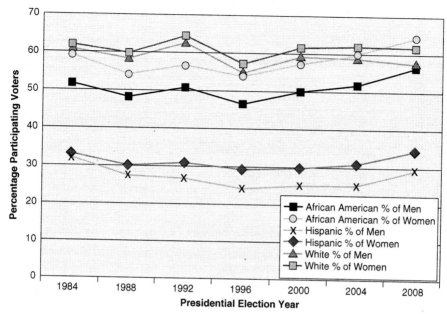

FIGURE 3.2

The Gender Gap by Race, 1984–2008 Presidential Elections

Source: Center for the American Woman and Politics. 2009. "Gender Differences in Voter Turnout."

THE EMERGENCE OF THE MODERN GENDER GAP

When most people think of the gender gap, they assume that it refers to the tendency of women to favor the Democratic Party. The media began paying attention to the gender gap in 1980 when Ronald Reagan's strong conservative politics, particularly his stances on the military and social welfare issues, gave him stronger support among men than women (Gilens 1988; Burrell 2005). However, this has not always been the case. Surveys of party identification and presidential voting since the 1950s demonstrate that women were aligned more closely with the Republican Party until 1964 (see Figure 3.3). This partially stems from the fact that in the 1950s and early 1960s the majority of women were homemakers whereas the majority of men were employed in blue-collar jobs. Homemakers and those in professional/managerial and clerical/sales jobs tend to vote Republican whereas employees in blue-collar/service jobs who are often unionized are more likely to vote Democratic. Thus, the fact that in 1956, 64.5 percent of women were homemakers and only 16.9 percent held blue-collar jobs, whereas less than 1 percent of men were homemakers and 64.8 percent were blue-collar workers helps explain the gender gap in partisanship and voting during this period (Seltzer et al. 1997; Norrander 2008).

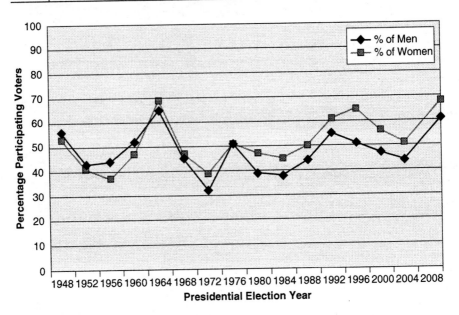

FIGURE 3.3

The Gender Gap in the Vote for the Democratic Presidential Candidate

Source: National Election Study Guide to Public Opinion and Behavior.

Other scholars point out that the gender gap resulted more from men leaving the Democratic Party than women realigning toward it (Kaufmann and Petrocick 1999; Norrander 1999, 2008; Kanthak and Norrander 2004). Beginning in the 1960s, men, particularly white southern men, increasingly became more Republican because of their opposition to the ascendancy of liberal views on civil rights and social welfare issues in the Democratic Party. At the same time, white southern women also became more Republican but at half the rate of white southern men. Outside the South, white men also affiliated more with the Republican Party but at a rate slightly lower than southern white women. However, white women's partisan preferences outside the South showed no change over time (Norrander 1999, 2008; Kanthak and Norrander 2004). In the 1990s, there is some evidence that white women began to turn toward the Democratic Party because of the Democrats more liberal positions on cultural issues (Kaufmann 2002).

In the contemporary period, the gender gap varies in size among demographic subgroups. The gap is more pronounced at higher education and professional levels and between single men and women in comparison to married men and women. Some scholars argue that we should expect a larger gender gap among highly educated professionals because labor force participation exposes women to gender inequalities they would not see as homemakers and gives these women a means of economic independence that shapes their political behavior. Thus, the expectation is that professional women will be attracted to

Democratic Party proposals related to equal pay and employment discrimination (Carroll 1988; Box-Steffensmeier, De Boef, and Lin 2004; Huddy, Cassese, and Lizotte 2008). Alternatively other scholars maintain that the professional advancement of highly educated women leads to more shared experiences with men and will lead to a convergence of the political views of educated, professional men and women (Box-Steffensmeier, De Boef, and Lin 2004).

Single women, with and without children, are a driving force behind the gender gap. According to exit polls from the 2008 elections, single women with children voted overwhelmingly for Democratic candidate Barack Obama. Seventy-four percent of single women with children supported Obama in comparison to 68 percent of single men with children. Similarly, 56 percent of unmarried men with no children voted for Obama in comparison to 69 percent of single women with no children (CNN 2008). The preference of single women for the Democratic Party is attributed to the fact that these women are the most economically vulnerable and thus the most likely to need the social welfare programs supported by the Democratic Party (Norrander 2008; Huddy, Cassese, and Lizotte 2008; Box-Steffensmeier, De Boef, and Lin 2004).

Figure 3.3 identifies the gender gap in voting for the Democratic presidential candidates since 1952, measured as the difference between the percentage of men and women who support the Democratic candidate. Thus, comparing the male and female vote for President Clinton in 1996 in his campaign against Bob Dole demonstrates that the gender gap reached a high point of 14 percent in 1996, as 65 percent of Democratic women voted for Clinton in comparison to 51 percent of men who did so.

As previously mentioned, women were slightly more likely to identify with the Republican Party until 1964. Thus, more women than men voted Republican in the 1948 through 1960 presidential elections. The contemporary gender gap in which women favor Democratic candidates emerged in Lyndon Johnson's 1964 election and continued until the 1976 election in which Jimmy Carter, a southern moderate governor of Georgia running in the aftermath of the Watergate scandal, was able to win enough votes from men to close the gap (Norrander 1999, 2008; Seltzer et al. 1997). The gap reemerged and began to gain media attention when strong conservative Ronald Reagan was elected in 1980. The gap continued to expand in the 1990s, peaking in the Clinton–Dole election of 1996 and remaining a strong 9 points in the hotly contested 2000 election, according to National Election Study figures. Other polls maintain that the magnitude of the gender gap remained at the same peak level in 1996 and 2000. Thus, Voter News Service reported that women favored Bill Clinton by 11 points (54 percent women to 43 percent men) whereas men favored Bob Dole by 6 points (44 percent men to 38 percent women). In 2000 women favored Al Gore by 12 points (54 percent women to 42 percent men) and men favored George W. Bush by 10 points (43 percent women to 53 percent men) (CAWP 1997, 2000). However, in the 2004 election the gender gap narrowed as women favored John Kerry over George Bush by only 7 points (CAWP 2004). In 2008 the gender gap remained at 7 points with women preferring Barack Obama (CNN 2008).

Although it is clear that the gender gap in presidential voting has expanded since the early 1990s, the reasons for this expansion remain unclear. Some scholars believe that the increasing polarization of the political parties at the elite level had a delayed impact on the mass level. Some argue that the election of Ronald Reagan in 1980 and his delineation of strong conservative policies in combination with a more strongly partisan Congress, particularly after the 1994 Republican Revolution, led to an ideological realignment in the partisan preferences of voters (Norrander 1999; Abramowitz and Saunders 1998; Box-Steffensmeier, De Boef, and Lin 2004). There is also evidence that over time, the gender gap expands when the country becomes more ideologically conservative, when the economy declines, and when there is an increase in the number of single women (a group that is more likely to need the social welfare services provided by the government) (Box-Steffensmeier, De Boef, and Lin 2004).

However, even at its peak, the gender gap remains smaller than other important voting gaps in American politics. In fact, race constitutes the largest gap in American politics. In the 2008 presidential election, exit polls indicate that 95 percent of African Americans voted for the Democratic and first African-American candidate Barack Obama in comparison to 43 percent of whites—a gap of 52 points. Similarly, the class gap is also much larger than the gender gap: 73 percent of voters in the lowest income bracket, voters who earned less than $15,000, voted for the Democrat, Barack Obama, in comparison to 52 percent of voters in the highest income bracket, voters earning $200,000 or more. This represents a 21-point voting gap (CNN 2008). The smaller size of the gender gap in comparison to other voting gaps in American politics may come as a surprise given the level of attention devoted to the gender gap by the media and political candidates. However, women constitute a larger potential pool of voters than the voters in other categories, women have higher turnout rates than men, and women are often perceived as swing voters by both the Republican and Democratic Parties (Norrander 2008, Burrell 2005). In an era when partisan competition is high and the margins to win control of Congress and the presidency are so small, the political parties more aggressively target potential swing voters. We will return to this point later in the discussion when we consider whether the gender gap brings women political power.

ISSUES THAT EXPLAIN THE GENDER GAP

To understand the nature of the gender gap and how likely it is that this gap will continue to manifest itself in electoral politics, one needs to examine the underlying causes of the gender gap in men and women's political attitudes and concerns. Beginning in the 1970s, survey research has demonstrated that women evince greater support for social welfare spending and a more activist government role in assisting the poor, in guaranteeing jobs, and in guaranteeing a standard of living (see Figure 3.4). In addition to differences in attitudes on social welfare issues, women are more likely to express feelings of insecurity and pessimism about the general economy and their own personal finances

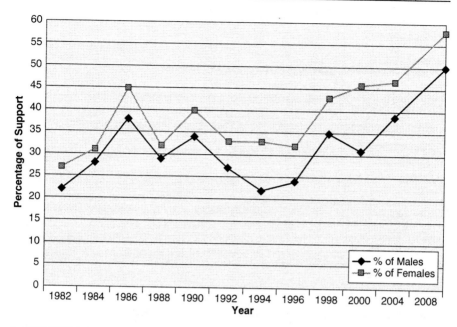

FIGURE 3.4

The Gender Gap in the Support for Increased Government Services and Spending

Source: National Election Study Guide to Public Opinion and Electoral Behavior.

(Shapiro and Mahajan 1986; Seltzer et al. 1997; Chaney, Alvarez, and Nagler 1998; Kaufman and Petrocik 1999; Box-Steffensmeier, De Boef, and Lin 2004; Norrander 1999, 2008). There are also some gender differences on environmental issues. Because women are more risk averse than men, a gender gap emerges on environmental regulations related to reducing risks such as health risks. However, there is no gender gap on issues where environmental protection is weighed against taxes or job growth (Norrander 2008).

Women's greater support for social welfare spending and government intervention in the economy may stem from the fact that, on average, women are more economically vulnerable than men. Women earn less than men, they are more likely to receive welfare benefits, and are more likely to be employed in social welfare occupations that rely on government funding (Norrander 1999, 2008). Additionally, there is some evidence that men are more likely to be pocketbook voters, basing their vote on their personal economic situation whereas women are more likely to be sociotropic voters who weigh societal conditions more heavily. Therefore, women's greater empathy for the poor may drive their support for increased social welfare spending (Huddy, Cassese, and Lizotte 2008). Since social welfare issues and government spending have constituted a major fault line between the Republican and Democratic parties since the New Deal, the gender gap will likely continue to be a feature of American politics for the foreseeable future.

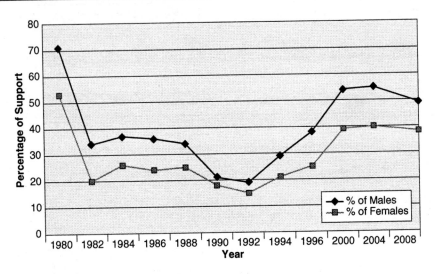

FIGURE 3.5

The Gender Gap in the Support for Increased Defense Spending

Source: National Election Study Guide to Public Opinion and Electoral Behavior.

Sex differences in support for the use of force constitute another important component of the gender gap (see *Profiles of Political Influence: Women and War*). Over time, women have been less supportive of military intervention than men and less supportive of increased defense spending (see Figure 3.5). These issues played a particularly important role in determining the gender gap in the 1980s when women were less supportive of Ronald Reagan's defense buildup and more in favor of a freeze on nuclear weapons development than were men (Shapiro and Mahajan 1986; Seltzer et al. 1997; Norrander 1999, 2008). A recent study on torture and the war on terrorism demonstrates that women are more likely than men to oppose the use of harsh interrogation techniques. Because women are more conscious of sexual violence than men, gender differences were largest regarding techniques that make the detainee feel the most personally vulnerable, such as sexually humiliating a detainee, forcing a detainee to go naked or holding a detainee's head under water (Haider-Markel and Vieux 2008). With regard to the use of force issues on the homefront, women are more likely to oppose capital punishment and to support gun control measures (Seltzer et al. 1997; Norrander 1999, 2008).

In contrast to conventional wisdom, feminist or women's issues are not an important component of the gender gap. Men and women express similar attitudes on gender roles, equality for women, and abortion. Although the media attributed the emergence of the gender gap in 1980 to Ronald Reagan's opposition to the ERA and his conservative position on abortion, research has shown that men and women were equally supportive of the ERA and equally likely to utilize it as a determinant of their vote (Mansbridge 1986).

PROFILES IN POLITICAL INFLUENCE

Women and War

Congresswoman Barbara Lee (D-CA) gained national attention and sacks of hate mail and death threats when she cast the lone vote against the resolution authorizing President Bush to use "all necessary and appropriate force" to retaliate against the terrorist attacks of September 11, 2001 (Hawkings and Nutting 2003). Lee is not the first congresswoman to take an unpopular stand against war. The first woman to serve in Congress, Jeannette Rankin (R-MT) (1917–1919 and 1941–1943), served for two terms each coinciding with the beginning of World War I and World War II. A pacifist, Rankin voted against war both times, casting the only no vote in the House or Senate against World War II (Kaptur 1996). Although these women took positions on war that ran counter to the majority view, are women as a group more peace oriented than men? Table 3.2 brings together polls from World War II to the contemporary Iraq War. From the table we can see that a majority of women have often supported the deployment of troops; however, women's support for war is consistently lower than support among men.

TABLE 3.2

Support for Use of Force, War

	Women	Men
World War II		
Suppose the German army gets rid of Hitler, gives up all the countries Germany has conquered, and offers to make peace. If that happens, should we make peace, or should we continue the war until the German army is completely defeated?		
% Should continue the war until German army is completely defeated	64%	76%

Source: Survey by Gallup, October 1943.

Korean War		
What do you think we should do now in Korea—keep trying to work out a way to stop the fighting in Korea, stop fooling around and do whatever is necessary to knock the Communists out of Korea once and for all even at the risk of starting WW III, or pull out of Korea right away and let them handle their own problems with the Communists?		
% Whatever is necessary to knock the Communists out	33%	45%

Source: Survey by the Roper Organization, October 1952.

(Continued)

▶ PROFILES IN POLITICAL INFLUENCE (CONTINUED)

		Women	Men
Vietnam War			

People are called "hawks" if they want to step up our
military effort in Vietnam. They are called "doves" if
they want to reduce our military effort in Vietnam.
Would you describe yourself as a "hawk" or a "dove"?

April 1968	Hawk	32%	50%
	Dove	49%	33%
	No Opinion	19%	17%
October 1969	Hawk	23%	39%
	Dove	63%	48%
	No Opinion	14%	13%

Source: Survey by Gallup, April 1968 and October 1969.

Persian Gulf War (1991)

Do you approve or disapprove of the United States
having gone to war with Iraq?

% Approve	68%	84%

Source: Survey by ABC News/*Washington Post*, January 1991.

Should American bombers attack all military targets in
Iraq including those in heavily populated areas where
civilians may be killed, or should American bombers
attack only those military targets that are not in heavily
populated areas?

% American bombers should attack all military targets	37%	61%

Source: CBS/*New York Times*, January 1991.

Iraq War (2003–current)

The Bush administration says it will move soon to disarm
Iraq and remove Saddam Hussein from power, by war
if necessary, working with countries that are willing to
assist, even without the support of the United Nations.
Overall, do you support or oppose this policy?

Support	51%	67%
Oppose	44%	31%
No Opinion	5%	2%

Source: Survey by ABC News/*Washington Post*, February 26–March 2, 2003.

▶ PROFILES IN POLITICAL INFLUENCE (CONTINUED)

	Women	Men
Do you think going to war with Iraq was the right thing for the United States to do or the wrong thing?		
Right	44%	56%
Wrong	48%	41%

Source: Survey by Quinnipiac University, May 18–24, 2004.

	Women	Men
Did the United States make a mistake in sending troops to Iraq?		
Mistake	61%	53%
Not a Mistake	37%	46%
Don't Know/Refused	2%	1%

Source: Survey by Gallup, May 2007.

	Women	Men
When it comes to the War in Iraq, should the United States withdraw all combat troops immediately, bring the combat troops home within a year, or stay until the mission is completed?		
Withdraw Immediately	19%	22%
Bring Troops Home within a Year	41%	35%
Stay Until Mission Complete	34%	41%

Source: Survey by Rasmussen Reports, August 2008.

Sources: Smith, Tom W. 1984. "The Polls Gender and Attitudes Toward Violence," Ladd, Everett Carll. 1997. "Media Framing of the Gender Gap" and 2003, 2004, 2007, and 2008 Iraq War Polls collected by the author from PollingReport.com, www.pollingreport.com and Rasmussen Reports. ■

However, there is some evidence that women do feel more intensely about their abortion position, particularly pro-life women. Moreover, women are more likely to hold positions at the extremes, either supporting abortion in all cases or prohibiting it in all circumstances (Seltzer et al. 1997; Norrander 1999, 2008; Kaufmann 2002; Jelen and Wilcox 2005). Perhaps related, there is also evidence that women are more religious and they express slightly more conservative attitudes on some additional social issues including school prayer, sexual mores (such as pornography and birth control), and civil liberties (Seltzer et al. 1997; Norrander 1999, 2008). However, women are generally more supportive of expanding rights for homosexuals than are men, including support for protections against discrimination in employment and support for gays in the military (Kaufmann 2002; Rhodebeck 2005; Norrander 2008).

DOES THE GENDER GAP BRING WOMEN POLITICAL POWER?

In the early 1980s, feminists and women's organizations, particularly the National Organization for Women (NOW), coined the term *gender gap* and worked to draw the attention of the media and party leadership to the potential importance of women as a voting bloc. Sending a monthly "Gender Gap Update" to several thousand reporters, Ellie Smeal (president of NOW) and other women leaders sought to parlay the gender gap into stronger support for the ERA and, in 1984, to pressure Walter Mondale, the Democratic nominee for president, to select a woman as his running mate. Although the campaign for the ERA ultimately fell three states short of ratification, women's groups and concerns about the gender gap did play a key role in Walter Mondale's decision to tap Congresswoman Geraldine Ferraro to be his vice presidential candidate (Bonk 1988; Frankovic 1988). Similarly, Ronald Reagan's concerns about his lack of support among women voters in 1980 led him to promise to appoint the first woman to the Supreme Court, a promise that he fulfilled with the appointment of Sandra Day O'Connor (Burrell 2005).

Throughout the 1990s, political competition between Republicans and Democrats intensified at all levels of government, aided in part by the realignment of many white southerners to the Republican Party. The 1994 Republican Revolution election gave Republicans control of both houses of Congress for the first time in more than 40 years. However, until Democrats regained control of Congress in 2006, the Republicans' majority control rested on only a handful of seats in both the House and Senate. Indeed, the decision of one Senator, Jim Jeffords (VT), to switch from the Republican Party to an independent gave the Democrats control of the Senate for part of the 107th Congress (2001–2002). Competition for votes has been equally tight at the presidential level. The presidential race in 2000 between Al Gore and George W. Bush was decided by such a small number of votes that the recounting of votes in Florida and the dispute over how to count those votes kept the outcome from being decided long after Election Day.

In such a highly competitive atmosphere, both parties seek to attract the elusive swing voter to expand their voting coalition to allow them to achieve a governing majority. Women are courted each election cycle, especially since they are less likely than men to be strong partisans and are more likely to decide on their vote later in the election cycle (Norrander 2008; Burrell 2005).

The Republican Party focuses particular attention on white, married, suburban women with children. Married voters lean Republican more than single voters, and married voters are more likely to turn out to vote than single voters. Married women are also more religious than singles, making them more open to the traditional family values message of the Republican Party (Norrander 2008; Brownstein 2008; Elder 2008). Thus, married suburban white women were the "soccer moms" that Bill Clinton and Bob Dole competed over in 1996. They were the voters that George W. Bush tried to appeal to in 2000 with his message of "compassionate conservatism." In 2004 these married, white suburban women became "security moms" who were concerned about the threat of terrorism and the security of their families (Martinez and Carey 2004; Kanthak and Norrander 2004; Norrander 2008; Brownstein 2008).

While Republicans work to increase turnout among subgroups of married white women, Democratic strategists target single women, especially single heads of households who are viewed as more economically insecure and, therefore, more inclined to support Democratic social policy initiatives. Single women under 40 and older women with grown children are particular targets of the get-out-the-vote efforts of the Democrats (Norrander 2008; Brownstein 2008). The group *Women's Voices, Women's Votes* was created to register and mobilize single women, as these women are less likely to vote than their married counterparts. To appeal to single women, Democrats emphasize issues such as abortion rights, access to emergency contraception for young single women, affordable health care, and for senior women, improvements to Medicare and Social Security (Martinez and Carey 2004).

At the presidential level, Burrell (2005) notes that in the period leading up to an election, presidents use the power of their office to create initiatives that will appeal to women voters. Thus, in an effort to mobilize women voters for the 1996 election, President Clinton increased the number of grants to combat violence against women, convened an Early Child Development and Learning Conference and a White House Conference on Child Care, held a roundtable on pay equity, and created a White House Office for Women's Initiatives and Outreach that held roundtables across the country on women's issues. He also proposed new legislation on pay equity and an expansion of family and medical leave (Burrell 2005).

Since the Iraq war and the threat of terrorism dominated the 2004 election, President Bush tried to appeal to security moms by demonstrating that he was a strong leader who was fighting the war on terror aboard in Iraq and Afghanistan to maintain security at home and make sure that we did not have to fight the war on American soil. The Bush campaign sponsored a "W stands for women" campaign complete with pink "W" baseball caps that could be purchased on the campaign website, to register and mobilize women voters. First Lady Laura Bush toured the country speaking to groups of women to highlight the president's achievements that would help women from the passage of the Medicare prescription drug bill to new freedoms enjoyed by Afghan women as a result of the war on terror (Gibbs 2004; Seelye 2004). During the Republican convention, three women who lost family members on 9/11 spoke during the prime–time television coverage on the first night of the convention. Appearing together on a dark stage under an illuminated sign reading "September 11, 2001," they spoke of the husbands and brothers they lost that day (Ozols 2004).

The Democratic candidate, John Kerry, a decorated Vietnam veteran, also tried to appeal to security moms by emphasizing his military background and his ability to keep the country safe. A separate group of 9/11 widows known as the "Jersey girls" who had been involved in the effort to establish the 9/11 commission appeared at campaign events across the country for John Kerry (Eccleston 2004; Harper 2004). The Kerry campaign also highlighted more traditional Democratic issues that appeal to women voters including health care and education.

In the end, President Bush was able to peel off enough female voters to push him to victory. In comparison to the 2000 Democratic candidate, Al Gore, John Kerry lost support among white women, working women, married women, and older women (Mock 2004; Morin and Balz 2004; Romano 2004; Scheiber 2004).

In 2008, working class women were intensely courted by both candidates. Obama turned to his former primary opponent, Hillary Clinton, to build support with working class women (Healy 2008a). The media described these voters as "hockey moms" and "Wal-Mart women" who "shop at Wal-Mart at least once a week, earn less than $60,000 a year, have less than a college education and hold a poor impression of Mr. Bush; they tend to call themselves independents and say their economic situation is fair or poor, listing the economy as their prime election issue" (Zerinke 2008). John McCain's selection of Alaska Governor and self-described "hockey mom" Sarah Palin as his running mate was an important part of his effort to reach working class women voters (Kaufman 2008; Healy 2008b).

It remains an open question whether the status of women as a swing-voting group empowers women in terms of the implementation of policy that benefits specific groups of women. For example, Susan Carroll (1999) argues that the courting of the "soccer mom" by Bill Clinton and Bob Dole in 1996

Republican vice presidential nominee Alaska Governor Sarah Palin signs an election poster during a rally.

actually disempowered women. Clinton appealed to these women by touting his support for policies including v-chips in televisions, school uniforms, and an expansion of the Family and Medical Leave Act to allow parents to attend parent–teacher meetings. Bob Dole campaigned with soccer moms at his side and promoted the ways in which his tax cuts would help soccer moms and their families. According to Carroll, the focus on the soccer mom and policy proposals related to children essentialized women as mothers, deflected attention away from the concerns of other subgroups of women (including older women, women on welfare, women of color, and professional women), and gave the campaigns the appearance of being responsive to the concerns of women while ignoring the majority of women. Therefore, despite the largest gender gap in presidential voting history—one that was not caused by the votes of soccer moms—activists representing various women's groups could point to no specific campaign promises that gave them a mandate to demand action on behalf of women on issues such as health care, abortion, welfare, employment, or child care (Carroll 1999).

By contrast, in her study of gender differences in the policy activities of members of the House of Representatives, Swers (2002) found that concern about the gender gap among the leadership of the Democratic and Republican parties raises the profile of women members of Congress, facilitates their efforts to gain positions of power in the party and committee structures, and enhances their ability to pursue policy initiatives related to women. For example, male and female members report that the desire of the Democratic Party to highlight issues and themes that reinforce its traditional advantage with women leads the party to seek out women members as speakers on the House floor and in the media on women's issues ranging from reproductive health to family and medical leave. Accepting these roles enables women members to raise their public profile and enhance their standing with the party leadership. These Democratic women can then use their enhanced standing to persuade party leadership to advance legislative proposals related to women's issues (Swers 2002).

To get their particular messages out to women, candidates from both parties also tailor their campaign activities to reach women voters. Thus, in 2008 Barack Obama frequently paid tribute to his mother who was a single mother and to his grandmother who helped raise him (Levey 2008). His wife Michelle Obama held numerous campaign events aimed at women voters (Healy 2008b). Oprah Winfrey endorsed Barack Obama during his primary fight against Hillary Clinton and actively campaigned for him. Through her television show and magazine Oprah reaches millions of potential women voters. Prior to endorsing Obama, Winfrey had never endorsed a political candidate, and her early support of Obama was viewed as a critical factor in his ability to gain traction in the Democratic primary against Hillary Clinton (Vedantam 2008; Zeleny 2007). Obama also made women's issues such as equal pay an important part of his campaign. He campaigned frequently with Lily Ledbetter, the woman who unsuccessfully sued the Goodyear Tire company for years of being paid less than her male colleagues and who was ultimately denied redress by the Supreme Court

(Zerinke 2008). Ledbetter made a campaign ad for Obama, and Obama invited her to ride with him on the inaugural train that brought him into Washington, D.C. The Lily Ledbetter Equal Pay Act was the first bill that Obama signed as President (Murray 2009).

These campaign events and Obama's outreach efforts to women took on added significance in 2008 as he aimed to heal the rifts left by the long primary contest for the Democratic nomination against Hillary Clinton. The difficult battle left many Hillary supporters angry about Obama's treatment of Hillary, and what they perceived as sexism in the campaign. Obama needed to heal that rift and unite Democratic women behind his candidacy. Hillary Clinton campaigned for Obama in the swing states of Florida, Pennsylvania, and Ohio to court the working class women who supported her in the primary. Seeing an opportunity to peel off some of Hillary Clinton's primary supporters, John McCain emphasized his great respect for Hillary Clinton throughout the general election campaign. Many media observers believed that McCain's surprise selection of Sarah Palin, the governor of Alaska who had served only two years in that office, as his running mate was partially motivated by his desire to capture women's votes. Throughout the campaign Palin referred to her respect for Hillary Clinton and the efforts both of them had made to crack the glass ceiling in politics. The McCain campaign also vocally denounced any perceived sexism leveled against Palin by the media and by Democratic activists (MacAskill and Goldenberg 2008; Healy 2008a, 2008b). McCain enlisted the support of high profile women to reach out to women voters, such

Oprah Winfrey with Michelle and Barack Obama as Oprah endorses and campaigns for Obama during the 2008 presidential election.

Hillary Clinton at the Democratic National Convention, moments after moving that Barack Obama be chosen as the Democratic nominee for president. She is joined by other members of the New York delegation, including fellow Senator Charles Schumer (left) and Governor David Paterson (right).

as the former CEO of Hewlett–Packard, Carly Fiorina and former E-bay CEO, Meg Whitman. He promised to increase the number of women in every part of his administration (Dinan 2008; Eilperin 2008).

Finally, both McCain and Obama appeared on television shows that target women voters including *The Oprah Winfrey Show*, *The View*, and *The Ellen DeGeneres Show* (Eilperin 2008; Zerinke 2008). Indeed, the number of campaign commercials aired during *The Oprah Winfrey Show* was second only to the number of commercials aired during the major news shows, a statistic that highlights the importance of women voters in the 2008 election (Zerinke 2008).

DO WOMEN VOTE FOR WOMEN?

It is often assumed that women provide a natural constituency of voters for women candidates. However, this is not necessarily the case, and current research provides conflicting evidence. The most important predictor of an individual's vote is party identification. Voters who identify as Democrats tend to vote for Democratic candidates. Similarly, voters who identify as Republicans are more likely to vote for Republican candidates.

Issues, the character and perceived competence of the candidates, and the nature of the campaign also influence voters (Campbell et al. 1960; Popkin 1991; Dolan 2004, 2008a). In congressional races the presence of an incumbent on the ticket has a strong impact on the outcome, as House incumbents have been reelected at rates above 90 percent since the late 1960s. House incumbents command numerous advantages over their challengers that reduce the competitiveness of House races, including the franking privilege that allows them to send mail to constituents, a large staff to assist them in doing casework for constituents, a record to campaign on and higher name recognition than the challenger. Additionally donors are more likely to give money to incumbents than challengers (Jacobson 2008; Herrnson 2007).

Given the overwhelming importance of party identification and incumbency, is there any room for a voter's sex to impact his or her candidate choice? Some research suggests an affinity affect does exist in which voters are more likely to support a candidate of the same sex. For example, Sanbonmatsu (2002) finds that voters have a standing baseline gender preference to vote for a male or a female candidate and women are more likely than men to express a gender preference and to prefer a female candidate. Others claim that women may be more likely to vote for women because of a shared gender consciousness that recognizes that women are underrepresented in government and that women's political futures are tied together (Rosenthal 1995; Rinehart 1992). Alternatively, women may vote for women because they trust them more on "group salient" issues that have a larger impact on women such as sexual harassment, child care, or abortion, especially when an election emphasizes these group salient issues (Paolino 1995; Dolan 2008b). Finally, some scholars indicate that certain subgroups of women are more likely to favor women candidates than others. These include feminists, liberals, African Americans, and well-educated women (Rosenthal 1995; Lewis 1999; Smith and Fox 2001; Palmer and Simon 2008).

In her comprehensive study of voting for women candidates from 1990 to 2000, Kathleen Dolan finds a limited impact for sex as women are more likely to vote for women in House races but not in Senate races. Additionally, when Dolan breaks down her data by election year, voter sex was only an important determinant of the House vote in 1992 (Dolan 2004, 2008a, 2008b). The finding that voter sex has an impact on House but not Senate races may be due to the fact that House races are often characterized as low-information elections in which the race is usually not covered extensively by the media and where voter knowledge of the candidates is often limited to party identification and incumbency. In this type of an election, the lack of information about the candidates may encourage voters to draw on other demographic characteristics such as sex and race to make inferences about the positions of the candidates (McDermott 1997). By contrast Senate elections are intensely covered by the media and voters focus more on issues when making evaluations of Senate candidates than House candidates (Kahn and Kenney 1999). Alternatively, it is possible that there is a glass ceiling for women candidates in which women voters and other voters are more willing to vote for women in House races but do not favor women candidates for higher, more prestigious offices such as the Senate (Dolan 1997).

Dolan (2004) also finds that women, particularly those with low to moderate levels of political knowledge, are more likely to vote for women if there is a gendered electoral context, meaning that gender and issues related to gender are highlighted in the media coverage about the electoral campaigns of a particular year and candidates are emphasizing issues and themes related to gender in their individual races. The 1992 election is the classic case of a highly gendered electoral environment in which issues such as sexual harassment and national health insurance were central to the presidential and congressional campaigns. The media dubbed the election "The Year of the Woman," focusing on the large numbers of women running for political office. Studies of the 1992 election indicate that those states or districts that featured a woman candidate attracted more media attention and enhanced the electoral involvement of women voters (Hansen 1997; Koch 1997; Sapiro and Conover 1997). Consequently, the importance that women voters and all voters give to candidate sex as a determinant of their voting decisions may increase or decrease depending on how relevant gender is to the electoral debate (Dolan 2004, 2008a, 2008b).

Finally, the ability to determine whether women vote for women is complicated by the fact that the gender gap in women's voting patterns favors Democrats, and more women candidates run as Democrats. For example, in the 2008 election among the 132 women running for the House of Representatives, 95 candidates were Democrats and 37 candidates were Republicans (CAWP 2008a). Therefore, it is possible that women are not voting for women but are simply more likely to vote for Democrats (Norrander 1999, 2008). Indeed, Dolan finds that voter stereotypes about the beliefs of women candidates have more of an impact on Democratic than Republican candidates. Male and female voters in the 1990–2000 elections, for example, were more likely to perceive female Democratic candidates as more liberal than their male counterparts whereas the sex of the candidate had no impact on the ideological evaluation of Republican candidates. Voters were also more likely to evaluate female Democratic candidates on stereotypically female issues such as health care and education but were not more likely to evaluate Republican women candidates on either stereotypically male or female issues (Dolan 2004).

However, other research shows that female Republicans are also able to shrink the gender gap by attracting more women's votes than male Republican candidates (Seltzer et al. 1997). Using data from a national survey sponsored by the Republican Network to Elect Women (RENEW), Matland and King (2002) found that Republican women are perceived as more moderate by voters than are male Republicans. This allows Republican women to attract more votes from independents and Democrats than do Republican men. However, this perceived moderation constitutes a handicap to women in gaining the nomination during the primary election because the Republican primary voter is more conservative than the general election voter and, therefore, is less likely to vote for a candidate who is perceived as more moderate than her male counterpart (Matland and King 2002).

Thus, the evidence on women voting for women demonstrates that women, like all voters, are most influenced by party identification and incumbency. However, women voters may be more likely to vote for female candidates in certain circumstances such as when the electoral context emphasizes issues related to gender or in races where voters have limited information about the candidates and, therefore, draw on the cue of candidate sex to help make inferences about ideological position and issue stands.

Hillary Clinton and the Women's Vote

While voters have long maintained that they are willing to vote for a woman for President, 2008 marked the first time that a woman was a serious contender for her party's nomination for the Presidency. Hillary Clinton's battle for the Democratic nomination against Barack Obama was groundbreaking for female and minority candidates and exceptional for the length and competitiveness of the fight. In recent years, the major party nominees are largely determined early in the campaign season after the Iowa Caucuses and New Hampshire primary. Party leaders do not expect the primary contest to last beyond Super Tuesday in March when multiple states hold their primaries and caucuses on the same day.

Yet the contest between Clinton and Obama remained competitive through the last primaries in June. For the first time, both candidates vigorously courted the superdelegates to try to shore up the nomination (Harwood 2008). Superdelegates include high ranking elected officials such as governors and members of Congress, party committee members, and some former elected officials. Unlike the delegates elected through the primaries and caucuses, the superdelegates are not bound to a particular candidate by their state's vote. The Democratic Party created superdelegates to give the party elite more influence over the nomination, believing that these officials would counterbalance liberal leaning primary and caucus voters by focusing on electability to help ensure that the party would nominate a candidate who could win the presidency and help down ballot candidates (Lazarus 2008; Maisel 2002). As the establishment candidate, Clinton held the early lead in superdelegate endorsements. However, as the primary season neared its end superdelegates began to break toward Obama in response to his lead in the pledged delegates won through primary and caucus victories (Harwood 2008).

While Obama campaigned on a message of change and Hillary portrayed herself as the candidate of experience, in state after state, the votes for each candidate followed a clear demographic pattern. As Table 3.3 shows, Hillary Clinton's base of supporters were women. With the exception of Connecticut and Wisconsin, when Clinton won the majority of women's votes, she won the primary and when she did not earn a majority of women's votes she lost (CNN 2008). Among women, Clinton's strongest supporters were women over age 50. Indeed, male and female older voters both preferred Clinton over Obama. Yet women supported her by the largest margins (Newport 2008; Seelye 2008; Huddy and Carey 2009). Many attributed Clinton's strong support among older women to the fact that these women most closely identified with her struggles as a woman competing in the male-dominated political world. Older women experienced the feminist movement and were more likely to have faced employment discrimination (Kantor 2008a, 2008b,

TABLE 3.3

The Gender Gap in the 2008 Democratic Primaries

States Clinton Won in the 2008 Primaries

	% Voting for Clinton		Gender Gap
	Women %	Men %	(% point difference)
Arizona	53	43	10
Arkansas	73	65	8
California	59	45	14
Florida*	54	42	12
Indiana	52	50	2
Kentucky	67	64	3
Massachusetts	62	48	14
Nevada	51	43	8
New Hampshire	46	29	17
New Jersey	58	48	10
New Mexico	52	43	9
New York	62	50	12
Ohio	57	50	7
Oklahoma	54	55	−1
Pennsylvania	59	49	10
Rhode Island	66	51	15
South Dakota	57	51	6
Tennessee	58	47	11
Texas	54	47	7
West Virginia	73	60	13

States Obama Won in the 2008 Primaries**

	% Voting for Obama		Gender Gap
	Women %	Men %	(% point difference)
Alabama	56	57	−1
Connecticut	45	59	−14
Delaware	51	58	−7
Georgia	65	70	−5
Illinois	64	67	−3
Louisiana	58	54	4
Maryland	55	62	−7
Mississippi	58	61	−3
Missouri	49	49	0

(Continued)

TABLE 3.3 (CONTINUED)

The Gender Gap in the 2008 Democratic Primaries

States Obama Won in the 2008 Primaries

| | % Voting for Obama | | Gender Gap |
	Women %	Men %	(% point difference)
Montana	50	64	−14
North Carolina	55	58	−3
Oregon	52	66	−14
South Carolina	54	54	0
Utah	50	65	−15
Vermont	56	64	−8
Virginia	60	68	−8
Wisconsin	50	67	−17

*Florida and Michigan disregarded Democratic Party rules when both states decided to hold primaries before Super Tuesday. Candidates pledged not to campaign in the states; Obama withdrew his name from the Michigan ballot, while Clinton let her name remain. Clinton and Obama both remained on the Florida ballot, since Florida law states that candidates cannot remove themselves from the ballot unless they withdraw completely from the general election. Delegates from Florida and Michigan each received half of a vote at the Democratic National Convention as a penalty for not abiding by party rules.

**Alaska, Colorado, Hawaii, Idaho, Iowa, Kansas, Maine, Minnesota, Nebraska, North Dakota, Washington, and Wyoming held caucuses rather than primaries, so no exit polls were conducted. Obama won these states.

Sources:
"Election Center 2008." CNN. www.cnn.com/ELECTION/2008/primaries/; "Proportions of Men and Women Who Voted for Hillary Clinton in the Super Tuesday Races of February 5, 2008." Center for American Women in Politics.2008c. www.cawp.rutgers.edu/fast_facts/voters/documents/SuperTuesday_Clinton.pdf
"Florida, Michigan Get all Delegates, but Each Gets Half Vote." CNN. 1 June 2008. www.cnn.com/2008/POLITICS/05/31/dems.delegates/index.html
The Hotline On-Call. The National Journal. 15 January 2008. http://hotlineblog.nationaljournal.com/archives/2008/01/team_obama_mich.html

Huddy and Carey 2009). Conversely, Obama dominated among younger voters. Eighteen to twenty-nine year olds were among Obama's strongest supporters and the only age demographic among women that did not trend toward Hillary Clinton (Newport 2008; Seelye 2008). These women were most excited about Obama's message of change; they did not experience the feminist movement and were less likely to have confronted employment discrimination (Kantor 2008a, 2008b).

Beyond gender and age, there were also clear divisions in the candidates' support based on race, education, and income. African Americans heavily favored Obama while Clinton won the support of white and Hispanic voters. Obama also faced some opposition from a minority of white voters, particularly in the South, who would not vote for him because of his race (Huddy and

Carey 2009). With regard to class and education, upper income and highly educated Democrats favored Obama, while lower income, blue-collar workers and those without a college education favored Clinton (Newport 2008). Clinton's ability to attract the support of whites, lower income, blue collar, and less educated voters is particularly striking when one considers the fact that these are the groups of voters that are assumed to be more difficult for a female candidate to win.

Ultimately, both Clinton and Obama earned about 18 million votes in the Democratic primaries, a record-breaking number for a primary campaign (Real Clear Politics 2008). The exact number of votes each candidate won, and who had more votes, was a subject of dispute between the two campaigns. Part of the feud stemmed from the fact that there was no agreement on whether and how to count the votes in the Florida and Michigan primaries, which Clinton won. Because these two states broke with party rules and held their primaries before Super Tuesday, the candidates agreed not to campaign in these states, and Obama even withdrew his name from the ballot in Michigan reducing the value of Clinton's victory in that state (Nasaw 2008; Romano 2008; Harwood 2008). However, when one looks at the states with the largest populations and thus the greatest number of votes in the Electoral College, Hillary Clinton won the popular vote in the three largest states, California, New York, and Texas. Clinton also won several large and important swing states such as Ohio and Pennsylvania. These states have swung between the Republican and Democratic presidential candidates in previous years and are perceived as the important battlegrounds in presidential contests. Other swing states won by Clinton included Arkansas, Nevada, New Hampshire, and New Mexico, while Obama won Colorado, Oregon, Minnesota, Iowa, Wisconsin, and Missouri (Saad 2008).

By the end of the hard fought primary campaign, the press was reporting that some of Clinton's supporters would not vote for Obama and might instead switch to McCain or sit out the election (Dickerson 2008). Many viewed McCain's choice of Sarah Palin as his vice presidential nominee as an effort to reach out to dissatisfied Clinton voters. However, in the general election, Clinton campaigned heavily for Obama, reaching out to the working-class white voters who were most skeptical of Obama (MacAskill and Goldenberg 2008; Healy 2008a, 2008b). On Election Day, most of the Clinton voters supported Obama. According to the CNN exit polls, 15 percent of voters who said they would have voted for Hillary Clinton if she were the general election candidate voted for McCain, while 84 percent voted for Obama (CNN 2008). Of those Clinton supporters who voted for McCain, 53 percent were women, while 47 percent were men (Ververs 2008). Furthermore, Obama's gender gap of seven points was exactly the same as the gender gap favoring Kerry in 2004. However, while Kerry earned only 51 percent of all of women's votes, Obama increased his majority earning 56 percent of women. Thus, Obama earned an even greater percentage of women's votes than Al Gore who benefited from a 10-point gender gap in the 2000 election against George W. Bush (IWPR 2008; CAWP 2008b).

What does Hillary Clinton's experience tell us about how voters will respond to future women candidates? As a Democratic candidate, Clinton benefited from women's stronger support for the Democratic Party. The fact that Democratic primary voters are more liberal than general election voters also helped Clinton as Palmer and Simon (2008) note that more liberal electorates are more supportive of women candidates. She gained the votes of lower income, less educated, white voters who are perceived as less supportive of women candidates. Still it remains an open question whether a female Republican presidential candidate will draw more support from women voters. Indeed, potential 2012 candidate and 2008 vice presidential nominee Sarah Palin's base of support is not women, but the Christian conservatives who are an important base within the Republican Party.

CONCLUSION

Since the 70-year-long struggle for the right to vote, candidates, political parties, and the media have tried to identify and attract the women's vote. Scholarly evidence indicates that the modern gender gap, in which women are prone to favor Democratic candidates, stems from men leaving the Democratic Party—not from women flocking to it. Social welfare issues and an increased support for government spending on these programs constitute a major source of the gender gap. Women's lower levels of support for defense spending and military action have also played a role in explaining the gender gap over time.

Although smaller than other voting gaps, particularly race and class, the gender gap expanded in the 1990s and became a major focus of presidential candidates during this period of close party competition as campaigns tried to identify and lure swing-voting groups of women from white middle class "soccer moms" to blue collar "hockey moms," and single mothers. It is an open question whether the aggressive courting of subgroups of women leads to policy changes to benefit women in society. Still, given that women are more likely than men to be undecided voters, it is likely that the gender gap will continue to play a role in future elections and political parties and consultants will work to identify and court new groups of undecided women.

REFERENCES

Abramowitz, Alan I., and Kyle L. Saunders. 1998. "Ideological Realignment in the U.S. Electorate." *Journal of Politics* 60:634–652.

Andersen, Kristi. 1996. *After Suffrage: Women in Partisan and Electoral Politics Before the New Deal.* Chicago: University of Chicago Press.

Banaszak, Lee Ann. 1996. *Why Movements Succeed or Fail: Opportunity, Culture, and the Struggle for Woman Suffrage.* Princeton: Princeton University Press.

Bonk, Kathy. 1988. "The Selling of the Gender Gap." In *Politics of the Gender Gap: The Social Construction of Political Influence*, ed. Carol Mueller. Newbury Park, CA: Sage.

Box-Steffensmeier, Janet, Suzanna De Boef, and Tse-Min Lin. 2004. "The Dynamics of the Partisan Gender Gap." *American Political Science Review* 98:515–528.

Brownstein, Ronald. 2008. "The Hidden History of the American Electorate." *National Journal* (18 October).

Burrell, Barbara C. 2005. "Gender, Presidential Elections and Public Policy: Making Women's Votes Matter." *Journal of Women, Politics, & Policy* 27:31–50.

Campbell, Angus, Phillip Converse, Warren Miller, and Donald Stokes. 1960. *The American Voter*. Ann Arbor: Survey Research Center, University of Michigan.

Carroll, Susan J. 1999. "The Disempowerment of the Gender Gap: Soccer Moms and the 1996 Elections." *PS: Political Science and Politics* 32:7–11.

———. 1988. "Women's Autonomy and the Gender Gap: 1980 and 1982." In *The Politics of the Gender Gap: The Social Construction of Political Influence*, ed. Carol Mueller. Newbury Park, CA: Sage.

Center for the American Woman and Politics (CAWP). 1997. *Fact Sheet: The Gender Gap: Voting Choices, Party Identification, and Presidential Performance Ratings*. New Brunswick: Center for the American Woman and Politics, Rutgers, State University of New Jersey.

———. 2000. *Fact Sheet: Gender Gap in the 2000 Elections*. New Brunswick: Center for the American Woman and Politics, Rutgers, State University of New Jersey.

———. 2004. "Gender Gap Persists in the 2004 Election." New Brunswick: Center for the American Woman and Politics, Rutgers, State University of New Jersey.

———. 2008a. *Fact Sheet: Summary of Women Candidates for Selected Offices 1970–2008 (Major Party Nominees)*. New Brunswick: Center for the American Woman and Politics, Rutgers, State University of New Jersey.

———. 2008b. "Gender Gap Evident in the 2008 Election-Women, Unlike Men, Show Clear Preference for Obama Over McCain." New Brunswick: Center for the American Woman and Politics, Rutgers, State University of New Jersey.

———. 2008c. "Proportions of Men and Women Who Voted for Hillary Clinton in the Super Tuesday Races of February 5, 2008." New Brunswick: Center for the American Woman and Politics, Rutgers, State University of New Jersey.

———. 2009. *Fact Sheet: Gender Differences in Voter Turnout*. New Brunswick: Center for the American Woman and Politics, Rutgers, State University of New Jersey.

Chaney, Carole K., R. Michael Alvarez, and Jonathan Nagler. 1998. "Explaining the Gender Gap in the U.S. Presidential Elections, 1980–1992." *Political Research Quarterly* 51:311–340.

CNN 2008. "Election Center 2008 Exit Polls." www.cnn.com/ELECTION/2008/results/polls/#USP00p1. Accessed March 25, 2009.

Dickerson, John. 2008. "The Great Snipe Hunt of 2008." *Slate* (June 13).

Dinan, Stephen. 2008. "McCain Vows to Appoint Women." *Washington Times* (15 June).

Dolan, Kathleen. 1997. "Gender Differences in Support for Women Candidates: Is There a Glass Ceiling in American Politics?" *Women & Politics* 17:27–41.

———. 2004. *Voting for Women: How the Public Evaluates Women Candidates*. Boulder: Westview Press.

———. 2008a. "Women Voters, Women Candidates: Is There a Gender Gap in Support for Women Candidates?" In *Voting the Gender Gap*. ed. Lois Duke Whitaker. Urbana and Chicago: University of Illinois Press.

———. 2008b. "Is there a 'Gender Affinity Effect' In American Politics?: Information, Affect, and Candidate Sex in U.S. House Elections." *Political Research Quarterly* 61:79–89.

Eccleston, Roy. 2004. "In Prime Time, the Focus Is on 9/11-Republican Convention." *The Australian* (1 September): 12.

Eilperin, Juliet. 2008. "McCain, Obama Reaching Out to Female Voters." *Washington Post* (12 June).

Elder, Laurel. 2008. "Whither Republican Women: The Growing Partisan Gap Among Women in Congress." *The Forum* 6: Issue 1, Article 13.

Flexner, Eleanor, and Ellen Fitzpatrick. 1996. *Century of Struggle: The Woman's Rights Movement in the United States.* Cambridge: The Belknap Press of Harvard University Press.

Frankovic, Kathleen. 1988. "The Ferraro Factor, the Women's Movement, the Polls, and the Press." In *Politics of the Gender Gap: The Social Construction of Political Influence,* ed. Carol Mueller. Newbury Park, CA: Sage.

Gibbs, Nancy. 2004. "What Do Women Want?" *Time Magazine* (3 October).

Gilens, Martin. 1988. "Gender and Support for Ronald Reagan: A Comprehensive Model of Presidential Approval." *American Journal of Political Science* 32:19–49.

Haider-Markel, Donald P. and Andrea Vieux. 2008. "Gender and Conditional Support for Torture in the War on Terror." *Politics & Gender* 4:5–33.

Hansen, Susan. 1997. "Talking About Politics: Gender and Contextual Effects on Political Proselytizing." *Journal of Politics* 59:73–103.

Harper, Tim. 2004. "Widows Back Kerry after Bush Rebuffs 9/11 Probe." *The Toronto Star.* (15 September): A10.

Harwood, John. 2008. "Democratic Primary Fight Is Like No Other, Ever." *The New York Times* (2 June).

Hawkings, David, and Brian Nutting. 2003. CQ *Politics in America 2004: The 108th Congress.* Washington, D.C.: Congressional Quarterly.

Healy, Patrick. 2008a. "Clinton Stumps for Obama, but with Little Fire at Palin." *The New York Times* (9 September).

_____. 2008b. "With Elbows in Check, Making a Pitch to Women." (21 September).

Herrnson, Paul. 2007. *Congressional Elections: Campaigning at Home and in Washington,* 5th ed. Washington, D.C.: CQ Press.

Huddy, Leonie, Erin Cassese, and Mary-Kate Lizotte. 2008. "Sources of Political Unity and Disunity Among Women: Placing the Gender Gap in Perspective?" In *Voting the Gender Gap.* ed. Lois Duke Whitaker. Urbana and Chicago: University of Illinois Press.

Huddy, Leonie and Tony E. Carey, Jr. 2009. "Group Politics Redux: Race and Gender in the 2008 Democratic Presidential Primaries?" *Politics & Gender* 5:81–95.

Interparliamentary Union. 2005. "Women's Suffrage: A World Chronology of the Recognition of Women's Rights to Vote and to Stand for Election." www.ipu.org/wmn-e/suffrage.htm. (Accessed May 28, 2009).

Institute for Women's Policy Research. 2008. "Women's Vote Clinches Election Victory: 8 Million More Women Than Men Voted for Obama." *Institute for Women's Policy Research* (November 6).

Jacobson, Gary. 2008. *The Politics of Congressional Elections,* 7th ed. New York: Longman.

Jelen, Ted G. and Clyde Wilcox. 2005. "Attitudes Toward Abortion in Poland and the U.S." *Politics & Gender* 1:297–317.

Kahn, Kim Fridkin, and Patrick J. Kenney. 1999. *The Spectacle of U.S. Senate Campaigns.* Princeton: Princeton University Press.

Kanthak, Kristin, and Barbara Norrander. 2004. "The Enduring Gender Gap?" In *Models of Voting in Presidential Elections: The 2000 Election,* ed. Herbert Weisberg and Clyde Wilcox. Stanford: Stanford University Press.

Kantor, Jodi. 2008a. "Clintons Bloc Becomes the Prize for Election Day." *The New York Times* (June 7).

———. 2008b. "Gender Issue Lives on as Clinton's Bid Wanes." *The New York Times* (May 19).

Kaptur, Marcy. 1996. *Women of Congress: A Twentieth Century Odyssey.* Washington, D.C.: Congressional Quarterly, Inc.

Kaufman, Jonathan. 2008. "Crossing Over: As the U.S. Economy Sputters, Working-Class Women Shift to Obama." *Wall Street Journal* (11 October).

Kaufmann, Karen M. 2002. "Culture Wars, Secular Realignment, and the Gender Gap in Party Identification." *Political Behavior* 24:283–307.

Kaufmann, Karen M., and John R. Petrocik. 1999. "The Changing Politics of American Men: Understanding the Sources of the Gender Gap." *American Journal of Political Science* 43:864–887.

Klein, Ethel. 1984. *Gender Politics.* Cambridge: Harvard University Press.

Koch, Jeffrey. 1997. "Candidate Gender and Women's Psychological Engagement in Politics." *American Politics Quarterly* 25:118–133.

Ladd, Everett Carll. 1997. "Media Framing of the Gender Gap." In *Women, Media, and Politics,* ed. Pippa Norris. New York: Oxford University Press.

Lazarus, Edward. 2008. "The Role of the Superdelegates: Could They Thwart the Choice of a Majority of Democratic Primary Voters?." *Findlaw.com* (February 14). http://writ.news.findlaw.com/lazarus/20080214.html (Accessed July 20, 2009).

Levey, Noam M. 2008. "Obama Courts Female Vote with His Family Stories." *Los Angeles* (4 September).

Lewis, Carolyn. 1999. "Are Women for Women? Feminist and Traditional Values in the Female Electorate." *Women and Politics* 20:1–28.

MacAskill, Ewen and Suzanne Goldenberg. 2008. "Barack Obama and John McCain Begin the Battle for Women Voters." *The Guardian* (6 September).

Maisel, L. Sandy. 2002. *Parties and Elections in America: The Electoral Process,* 3rd Edition. Lanham, MD: Rowman and Littlefield Publishers, Inc.

Mansbridge, Jane. 1986. *Why We Lost the ERA.* Chicago: University of Chicago Press.

Martinez, Gebe, and Mary Agnes Carey. 2004. "Erasing the Gender Gap Tops Republican Playbook." *CQ Weekly* (6 March): 564–570.

Matland, Richard E., and David C. King. 2002. "Women as Candidates in Congressional Elections." *In Women Transforming Congress,* ed. Cindy Simon Rosenthal. Norman: University of Oklahoma Press.

McDermott, Monika L. 1997. "Voting Cues in Low-Information Elections: Candidate Gender as a Social Information Variable in Contemporary U.S. Elections." *American Journal of Political Science* 41:270–283.

Morin, Richard, and Dan Balz. 2004. " 'Security Mom' Bloc Proves Hard to Find." *Washington Post* (1 October): A5.

Murray, Shailagh. 2009. "Fair-Wage Bill Clears the Senate." *Washington Post* (Jamuary 23).

Nasaw, Daniel. 2008. "Decision to Halve Disputed Democratic Primaries' Delegates Boosts Obama." *The Guardian* (June 1).

National Election Study. *Guide to Public Opinion and Behavior.* www.umich.edu/~nes/nesguide/nesguide.htm.

Newport, Frank. 2008. "Hillary Maintains Loyalty of Democratic Women Up to End." *Gallup* (June 3).

Norrander, Barbara. 1999. "Is the Gender Gap Growing?" In *Reelection 1996: How Americans Voted*, ed. Herbert F. Weisberg and Janet M. Box-Steffensmeier. New York: Chatham House Publishers.

_____. 2008. "The History of the Gender Gaps." In *Voting the Gender Gap*. ed. Lois Duke Whitaker. Urbana and Chicago: University of Illinois Press.

Norton, Mary Beth, David M. Katzman, Paul D. Escott, Howard P. Chudacoff, Thomas G. Paterson, and William M. Tuttle, Jr. 1986. *A People and a Nation: A History of the United States*. 2nd ed., Volume II: Since 1865. Boston: Houghton Mifflin Company.

Ozols, Jennifer Barrett. 2004. "He Can Make Us Safe: A Prominent 9/11 Widow—and Former Republican—Explains Why She Now Wants Kerry to Win the White House Race." Newsweek.com (17 September). Accessed online at http://www.newsweek.com/id/149875.

Paolino, Phillip. 1995. "Group-Salient Issues and Group Representation: Support for Women Candidates in the 1992 Senate Elections." *American Journal of Political Science* 39:294–313.

Popkin, Samuel. 1991. *The Reasoning Voter*. Chicago: University of Chicago Press.

Real Clear Politics. 2008. "2008 Democratic Popular Vote." www.realclearpolitics.com/epolls/2008/president/democratic_vote_count.html (Accessed July 19, 2009).

Rhodebeck, Laurie. 2005. "Partisanship, Religion, and Gay Rights: Another Perspective on the Gender Gap." Paper presented at the 2005 Annual Meeting of the Midwest Political Science Association, Chicago.

Rinehart, Sue Tolleson. 1992. *Gender Consciousness and Politics*. New York: Routledge.

Romano, Andrew. 2008. "Clinton's Popular Vote Claim? Close—But Not *Quite*" *Newsweek.com* (June 2) http://blog.newsweek.com/blogs/stumper/archive/2008/06/02/clinton's-popular-vote-claim-close-but-no-cigar.aspx (Accessed July 19, 2009).

Romano, Lois. 2004. "Female Support for Kerry Slips." *Washington Post* (23 September).

Rosenthal, Cindy Simon. 1995. "The Role of Gender in Descriptive Representation." *Political Research Quarterly* 48:599–611.

Saad, Lydia. 2008. "Hillary Clinton's Swing-State Advantage." *Gallup* (May 28).

Sanbonmatsu, Kira. 2002. "Gender Stereotypes and Vote Choice." *American Journal of Political Science* 46(1):20–34.

Sapiro, Virginia, and Pamela Johnston Conover. 1997. "The Variable Gender Basis of Electoral Politics: Gender and Context in the 1992 U.S. Election." *British Journal of Political Science* 27:523.

Scheiber, Noam. 2004. "Mothers of Invention." *The New Republic Online* (24 September).

Seelye, Katherine Q. 2008. "In Clinton vs. Obama, Age Is One of the Greatest Predictors." *New York Times* (22 April).

_____. 2004. "Kerry in a Struggle for Democratic Base: Women." *New York Times* (22 September).

Seltzer, Richard, Jody Newman, and Melissa Voorhees Leighton. 1997. *Sex as a Political Variable: Women as Candidates and Voters in American Elections*. Boulder: Lynne Rienner Publishers.

Shapiro, Robert, and Harpreet Mahajan. 1986. "Gender Differences in Policy Preferences: A Summary of Trends from the 1960s to the 1980s." *Public Opinion Quarterly* 50:42–61.

Skocpol, Theda. 1992. *Protecting Soldiers and Mothers*. Cambridge: The Belknap Press of Harvard University Press.

Smith, Eric R.A.N., and Richard Fox. 2001. "The Electoral Fortunes of Women Candidates for Congress." *Political Research Quarterly* 54:205–221.

Smith, Tom. 1984. "The Polls: Gender and Attitudes Toward Violence." *Public Opinion Quarterly* 48:384–396.

Swers, Michele L. 2002. *The Difference Women Make: The Policy Impact of Women in Congress.* Chicago: University of Chicago Press.

Tyler, Helen. 1949. *Where Prayer and Purpose Meet 1874–1949: The WCTU Story.* Evanston: The Signal Press National Woman's Christian Temperance Union Inc.

Vedantam, Shankar. 2008. "The Oprah Effect." *Washington Post* (1 September).

Ververs, Vaugh. 2008. "Who Were Those Clinton-McCain Crossover Voters?" *CBS News.com* (November 12). www.cbsnews.com/blogs/2008/11/12/politics/horserace/entry4596620.shtml?source=search_story (Accessed July 20, 2009).

Zeleny, Jeff. 2007. "Oprah Endorses Obama" *The New York Times* (May 3).

Zerinke, Kate. 2008. "Both Sides Seeking to Be What Women Want." *The New York Times* (15 September).

The Impact of the Media on Political Women

Shortly after President Bill Clinton's inauguration in 1993, First Lady Hillary Rodham Clinton was invited to address several groups in Congress, including the Congressional Black Caucus, the Congressional Hispanic Caucus, and the Congressional Caucus for Women's Issues. Clinton's joint meeting with the Congressional Black and Hispanic Caucus, where she discussed President Clinton's health care initiative, landed in the A section of the *Washington Post* ("Hillary Clinton Visits Minority Caucus" 1993). When Clinton met with members of the Caucus for Women's Issues, however, *Post* coverage of the event was relegated to the paper's style section. This placement infuriated members of the Caucus, prompting Congresswoman Pat Schroeder to decry the actions of the *Post* on the floor of the United States House of Representatives in a statement concerning the Violence Against Women Act. As listed in the *Congressional Record* of 24 February 1993, Schroeder remarked:

> We are also sending a letter to the *Washington Post*. As we met yesterday with Hillary Clinton, they put it in the style section. That is one of the problems with dealing with the very serious issues the caucus is dealing with. When we talk about women's health, women's economic status, and violence against women, it gets put on the style section by this city's major paper, and they talk about what we wear. It is time we move those issues to the front page. It is time that they are taken seriously. And it is time that women lawmakers are given the same play in the paper with their issues that the others are by that newspaper. (Quoted in Carroll and Schreiber 1997, 132)

More than 14 years later, when Hillary Clinton was serving as a U.S. Senator from New York and she was in the early stages of her bid for the 2008 presidency, she again made headlines in the *Washington Post* style section for a different reason: her cleavage! Robin Givhan, the longtime fashion writer for the

Washington Post, made her own headlines with her story about Clinton's neckline:

> There was cleavage on display Wednesday afternoon on C-SPAN2. It belonged to Sen. Hillary Clinton. She was talking on the Senate floor about the burdensome cost of higher education. She was wearing a rose-colored blazer over a black top. The neckline sat low on her chest and had a subtle V-shape. The cleavage registered after only a quick glance. No scrunch-faced scrutiny was necessary. There wasn't an unseemly amount of cleavage showing, but there it was. Undeniable   (Givhan 2007)

Givhan's article touched off a torrent of commentary and criticism, especially as the cable news outlets and talk radio had a field day with the story (Chris Matthews' show *Hardball* aired footage of Clinton in the outfit after the story broke with the caption that read "Senatorial Cleavage" [Media Report to Women 2007]). Ann Lewis, who was a senior advisor to the Clinton campaign, later wrote that "focusing on women's bodies instead of their ideas is insulting" (quoted in Media Report to Women 2008).

For decades, political women and feminist scholars have lamented the quality of media coverage surrounding the women's movement, women on the campaign trail, and female politicians once in office (Braden 1996; Niven and Zilber 2001; Witt, Paget, and Matthews 1994). This chapter examines this media coverage by starting with media treatment of suffrage and women's movements, continuing with more current assessments of how the media report on feminism. Do the media offer a balanced portrayal of feminism? What about women politicians? Are gendered frames employed in the media's treatment of women serving in Congress and in other elected offices? How do the media cover first ladies?

Many feminists argue that improvement in the coverage of female politicians, as well as the political and social issues that concern women most, will only improve with enhanced diversity among journalists and publishers. This chapter also examines the status of professional women in journalism and addresses the following questions: Do women journalists serve in equal numbers with men? Are they likely to cover the same sorts of stories as men or are they more likely to feature women's issues and use women as news sources? Are women well represented among the ranks of media management or ownership and does this matter?

THE NEWS MEDIA IN THE UNITED STATES

The importance of the news media to politics in the United States cannot be underestimated. The media provide publicity and coverage of political events, which is important as most individuals would not have access to such events otherwise. The media serve as agenda setters, helping to determine which political events are newsworthy and which problems "viewers regard as the nation's most serious" (Iyengar and Kinder 1987, 4). In this way, the news media help to determine the sorts of political issues Americans think about. Moreover, studies find that the media have a large "priming" effect on the public (ibid.). In other words, not only do the media help set the nation's political agenda, but they also help to determine the criteria by which the public rates politicians. For example, if the media consistently run stories about one or two political issues, such as the economy or jobs, and then link these issues to the decisions of politicians, the public is shown to rate the overall job performance of politicians based on these issues. In essence, the very livelihood and success of politicians can be affected enormously by media coverage (or the lack thereof). To that end, politicians and elected officials work very hard to influence the type of media coverage they receive through their press secretaries and communications offices—albeit with mixed success (see, for example, Cook 1998; Kedrowski 1996).

As renowned journalist Walter Lippman once pointed out many years ago, "The news is not a mirror of social conditions, but the report of an aspect that has obtruded itself" (Lippman 1922 [2000], 36). That is, it is impossible for the news media to accurately reflect a complete image of the political world. Instead, the media, by necessity, are selective in spotlighting some political events over others. And although journalists routinely claim that values such as objectivity, timeliness, and prominence are what guide their selection of news stories, the facts that reporters choose to emphasize often use a news narrative or "frame" to place them in context. As Pippa Norris (1997) points out, "Frames provide contextual cues, giving order and meaning to complex problems, actions, and events. Frames guide the selection, presentation, and evaluation of information, for journalists and reader, by slotting the novel into familiar categories" (2). For example, a frequent frame employed by journalists covering elections is the "horse race," in which journalists choose to peg their stories around which candidate is leading or lagging in the polls. Journalists could instead choose to cover different issues in campaigns, such as the candidates' backgrounds and experiences or their policy positions, but tend to focus on the competitive nature of the campaign because the news media favor conflict and novelty in their reporting. The "horse race" is a convenient and conventional way for journalists to report on elections, promoting a particular interpretation of campaigns.

The process of framing can have implications for women and politics, leading to gendered interpretations of political events. For instance, 1992 was routinely touted by the media as the "Year of the Woman" in American politics, as a record-breaking number of women were elected to the House and Senate, raising the number of women in Congress from 31 to 53. For example, the *Philadelphia Inquirer* noted in its front-page headlines that "Women's Gains Are Historic," while the *Washington Post* ran the following story: "Year of the Woman Becomes Reality as Record Number Win Seats" (Wostendiek 1992; Gugliotta 1992). Few of the stories about the "Year of the Woman," however, noted that women remained far from equal in their representation in Congress. Moreover, the stories about women's sudden "achievements" that year seldom considered that they came about as the result of years of struggle. Women politicians laid the groundwork for their success in Congress by moving up the political pipeline of state legislatures. In her syndicated column, Ellen Goodman wrote that the much-hyped "Year of the Woman" "reminds me of the 'overnight' singing sensation discovered after twenty years of training. The breakthrough came only after a generation of women moved in a slow and grueling pace through the system" (quoted in Braden 1996, 129).[1] Yet the frame of women's "breakthrough" in the "Year of the Woman" was too irresistible for most journalists to avoid. In a similar vein, journalists could not keep from framing the 1994 elections, in which Republicans gained the majority in both houses of Congress for the first time in decades, as the Year of the Angry White Male (Norris 1997). The media also brought us the "Year of the Soccer Moms" in 1996 during the presidential campaigns and touted the important role that they believed NASCAR Dads would play in the 2004 presidential elections.

Elections are not the only political events subject to "gendered" framing by the news media. As the previous example with the Congressional Caucus for Women's Issues highlights, a newspaper's decision to omit issues of concern to women from the front pages of the newspaper, and instead consign them to the paper's style section (if at all), can signify to readers that these issues are somehow less appropriate than other "real" political concerns. Leaders of the women's movement have criticized media coverage that too frequently employs sex stereotyping in its coverage of women's issues, women activists, and women politicians. When the media neglect to interview women leaders about political issues on talk shows or in news stories that are not overtly tied to so-called women's issues, such as national security or international affairs—and we will see later in the chapter that they often do not—they perpetuate the notion that most of politics remains a male bastion, undermining the credibility of women who serve in political office. These reasons are why it is vital to study the impact of the media on women and politics.

WHEN WOMEN UNITE: MEDIA COVERAGE OF THE WOMEN'S MOVEMENTS AND FEMINISM

Concerns about the media's impact on women and politics can be traced back to media coverage of women's movements in the United States, beginning with suffrage and extending through the "second wave" of women's activism in the 1960s and 1970s. (see Chapter 2 for a more extensive treatment of these political movements.) The cases of women's suffrage and the Equal Rights

---

[1]As Chapter 7 points out, another problem with the "Year of the Woman" frame is that it failed to demonstrate how the success for women happened predominantly among Democrats and not Republicans. Perhaps a more accurate frame would have been the "Year of the Democratic Woman."

Amendment (ERA) showcase two different outcomes when it comes to the relationship between the media and political movements. In the first case, media coverage did little to hurt the cause of women gaining the right to vote and, in fact, probably helped. However, the effect of the media on the later women's movement in the 1960s, which developed into the struggle for ratification of the ERA, was decidedly more mixed. Some critics believe the media, perhaps unknowingly, were instrumental in the defeat of the ERA.

Political and social movements depend on the media to enlarge the scope of their disputes by recruiting activists to their causes and raising awareness about the issues that concern them (Huddy 1997). For instance, the civil rights movement during the 1950s and 1960s in this country focused on improving conditions for African Americans. Under the leadership of Dr. Martin Luther King, Jr., civil rights activists drew media attention to their cause by planning carefully staged nonviolent protests, including marches, demonstrations, and "sit-ins" in restaurants and other venues that would not allow blacks to patronize their businesses. These sorts of practices are often employed by other social and political movements today, as organizations realize the importance of attracting positive media coverage to help advance their causes, build support among the public, and influence the work of elected officials.

However, the goals of social movements and the news media are rarely in sync, and it can be difficult for movements to gain media coverage, let alone sympathetic coverage. While movements need the media to help publicize their cause, the media expect such movements to provide "newsworthy" events that are dramatic and make for good "press." Moreover, the well-worn practices of the news business often lead the media to cover social movements in ways that can distort the goals and achievements of the movement. For instance, the media often portray a social movement as counterbalanced by some sort of opposition in order to keep their stories interesting but simple. This tendency, however, can imply that the two competing sides are of equal size and merit, which is not always the case (Huddy 1997). In his study of antiwar protestors in the 1960s, for example, Gitlin (1980) found that antiwar demonstrators dwarfed the number of pro-war protestors at rallies, yet the media often portrayed the two sides as fairly equal. In addition, the economics of journalism—the rush for deadline—often entails that journalists look to one or two favored leaders who routinely supply quotes or responses to their questions (Huddy 1997). This practice has the effect of portraying the political movements (and their opponents) as being less diverse than they actually are.

THE BATTLES FOR SUFFRAGE AND ERA

The first women's movement to receive widespread coverage by the news media in the twentieth century was the fight for women's suffrage, although women's organizations had been fighting for the right to vote since shortly after the Civil War. They undertook this struggle facing uniform hostility from the press, particularly after the Seneca Falls Convention in 1848. Scholar Eleanor Flexner (1959) quotes one editorial emblematic of the rest from the *New York Herald* in 1850:

> "What do the leaders of the women's rights convention want? They want to vote and hustle with the rowdies at the polls. They want to be members of Congress, and in the heat of debate subject themselves to coarse jests and indecent language . . . How funny would it sound in newspapers that Lucy Stone, pleading a cause [as an attorney], took suddenly ill in the pains of parturition and perhaps gave birth to a fine bouncing boy in court? . . . A similar event might happen on the floor of Congress, in a storm at sea or in the raging tempest of battle, and then what is to become of the woman legislator?". (Quoted in Flexner 1959, 820)

One result of such negative coverage was that early organizers for suffrage tried to generate support for the cause through their own publications. Perhaps best known of these efforts was the weekly newspaper *The Revolution*, which began publication by Elizabeth Cady Stanton and Susan B. Anthony in 1868 with the motto: "Men, their rights and nothing more; women, their rights and nothing less!" (Flexner 1959, 153). The impact of the newspaper, according to Eleanor Flexner, could not be underestimated: "It gave their movement a forum, focus and direction. It pointed, it led, and it fought, with vigor and vehemence" (ibid., 154).

Yet, by the turn of the century, the suffrage movement appeared moribund. American suffragists were buoyed, however, by the confrontational tactics employed by their counterparts in Great Britain in their fight for suffrage. Newly developed groups in the United States, such as Alice Paul's Congressional Union, adopted these strategies in their suffrage struggle, such as demonstrations, colorful parades, open-air meetings, and hunger strikes (while avoiding violent tactics, such as arson, that were sometimes employed by the British suffragists) (Lumsden 1997). Suffragists were also adept at marketing their cause through their own products and publications. For example, *Woman's Journal* was a popular, pro-suffrage monthly magazine published by the National American Women's Suffrage Association (NAWSA), which combined political and campaign information with inspirational stories as well as practical advice on dress and the domestic sciences (Finnegan 1999). Suffragists' successful self-promotion and public campaign tactics were ready-made for journalists at the time, resulting in a substantial increase in media coverage of the movement beginning around 1908 (Cancian and Ross 1981; Lumsden 1997). Increased coverage by the media, in turn, likely had a multiplier effect, with respect to recruiting more women (and men) to the cause of suffrage (Cancian and Ross 1981).

Media coverage of one event in particular helped build support for the movement. One day before the inauguration of Woodrow Wilson in March 1913, suffragists staged a national parade in Washington to bring attention to their cause. Thousands of women from across the county came, dressed in

Noted Suffragist leader Alice Stone Blackwell, seated, holds a copy of the *Woman's Journal and Suffrage News*, a popular pro-suffrage magazine published by the National American Women's Suffrage Association, which was instrumental in coordinating political action among suffragists nationwide.

colorful outfits carrying decorative banners. Yet a drunken riot broke up the peaceful assembly, one that was not stopped by the clearly undermanned District of Columbia police force, resulting in injuries to many female marchers (Lumsden 2000). Sympathetic media coverage of this event resulted in two important goals. First, future suffrage events were taken seriously by law enforcement, such as a parade in New York City held later that year. More important, however, media coverage of the Washington parade granted legitimacy to the movement (ibid.). Lumsden (2000) recounts one description of the parade by the *New York Tribune*, whose theme was oft repeated in other editorials of mainstream newspapers around the country: "There is no doubt that the sight thrilled many of the vast crowd that gazed, that it opened the eyes of the multitude and that the capital of the country is thinking, really thinking, about suffrage tonight as old Washingtonians never supposed it could think" (596).

Media coverage for the "second-wave" women's movement that emerged in the 1960s never reached as high a level as did the media's reporting of the suffrage movement (Cancian and Ross 1981). Moreover, media coverage of the movement was much slower to catch on. In fact, the *New York Times* placed news about the creation of the National Organization for Women (NOW) in November 1966 below a turkey recipe during Thanksgiving (Whitaker 1999). Compared with suffrage, the women's movement was difficult to cover. First, no single issue, such as the right to vote, was at stake.

Instead, the women's movement touched on a variety of issues of concern to women, leaving the media with a lack of focal point in its reporting (Cancian and Ross 1981). Furthermore, coverage of issues or public policy positions is typically downplayed by the media, which prefer instead to focus on "events" that are easier to cover—particularly those that provide good visuals and a sense of originality (Kahn and Goldenberg 1991a).

This emphasis on novelty explains why the media touted the "bra-burning" actions of feminist activists outside of the Miss America Pageant in 1968—the first demonstration of movement activists to generate national headlines. Susan Faludi (1991), however, points out that women's activists merely threw their brassieres—as well as stenographer's pads, hair rollers, high heels, and copies of *Playboy* magazine—into a trash can rather than set them ablaze. Nonetheless, the image of counter-culture, bra-burning feminists became a

The front page of the *Woman's Journal and Suffrage News* on March 3, 1913 features the headline "Parade Struggles to Victory Despite Disgraceful Scenes." That famous parade in Washington, which was covered by the major newspapers of the day, marked a turning point in the suffrage campaign, granting legitimacy to the movement for women's voting rights.

dominant theme in the news (and an image often invoked by opponents of the movement). As Susan Douglas (1994) notes, the media portrayed those protestors, and the movement activists who followed, as deviant and unstable:

> If these girls were out on the streets swinging bras around, why, they must be closet exhibitionists, narcissists, or simply hysterical . . . [t]he media also paid inordinate attention to the way feminists violated physical and social boundaries, and suggested that, by doing so, they were making spectacles of themselves . . . Feminists were cast as unfeminine, unappealing women who were denouncing the importance of the male gaze, yet who secretly coveted the gaze for themselves by protesting in public. These poor girls, it was suggested, sought to get through political flamboyance what they were unable to get through physical attractiveness. (156)

Not surprisingly, activists within the women's movement were often hostile to reporters, and press relationships were never routinized or given priority by feminist leaders, which further exacerbated the poor quality of media reporting about the movement (Freeman 1975; Kahn and Goldenberg 1991a). Combined with hostility from a male-dominated news industry—one in which few women journalists were able to cover hard news—early media coverage of the women's liberation movement was often either a "joke or a bore" (see, for example, Klemesrud 1971; Freeman 1975). For example, one female reporter from the *Atlantic Monthly* who reported on the movement lamented that newspaper editors often told reporters who covered the movement "to find an authority who'll say this is all a crock of shit" (North 1970, 105).

By the 1970s, however, the media began to take the women's movement more seriously. Part of the reason for the change may be due to small groups formed by feminist writers and researchers, which began to protest for better conditions for women reporters and for more serious treatment of the cause of women's liberation by the mainstream media (Freeman 1975). Although much coverage still denigrated women activists in their struggle for greater equality, other reporting was more positive, leading millions of people to embrace the goals of the movement. Stories concerning sex discrimination at work (including sex discrimination suits filed at major news organizations such as the *New York Times*), pay disparities between men and women, and the lack of decent child care had resonance with many Americans (Douglas 1994), often through the growing sophistication of women's interest groups, which began to realize the need for a coherent media strategy (Barker-Plummer 2000). One frame increasingly applied to the women's movement by the media at this time was that of the civil rights movement (Costain, Braunstein, and Berggren 1997). As Americans had watched African Americans struggle for equality and legal rights in the 1950s and 1960s, when the media began to frame the women's movement in a similar context, it resonated "strongly in a culture with a cherished Constitution and historic commitment to a policy setting system of courts" (ibid. 208). What further helped to galvanize supporters to the women's movement was the fight for ratification of the ERA, which was formally passed by Congress in 1972. By the mid to late 1970s, the majority of stories that the media wrote about women addressed women's rights, particularly as they related to the ERA (ibid.).

Although the battle for the ERA certainly provoked an increased amount of media coverage, critics claimed that treatment of the battle by the news media was often skewed or oversimplified. One common tactic used by the media in coverage of political movements is to zero in on one spokesperson or leader, even though political and social movements by their definition are collective ventures (Gamson and Wolfsfeld 1993). This was the case with the women's movement, when Gloria Steinem, a feminist journalist who was fairly new to organizational work in the movement, became the media's anointed leader. Unlike Betty Friedan, the founder of NOW and author of the path-breaking feminist work *The Feminine Mystique,* or outspoken Congress-woman Bella Abzug, Steinem was a young, glamorous woman who media moguls were sure would appeal to both men and women. Described by Douglas (1994) as "a feminist who looked like a fashion model" (230), Steinem appeared on the cover of *Newsweek* magazine in August 1971, in a feature that discussed the women's movement. *Newsweek*'s cover story had this description of Steinem, whom it recognized as the movement's "most sought-after spokesman," in its first paragraph:

> In hip-hugging raspberry Levis, 2-inch wedgies and a tight poor-boy T-Shirt, her long, blond-streaked hair falling just so above each breast and her cheerleader-pretty face made wiser by the addition of blue-tinted glasses, she is a chic apotheosis of cool. Her cheekbones are broad and high, her teeth white and even; the fingernails on her tapered hands are as long and carefully tended as a tong chief's and any old swatch of cloth rides like a midsummer's night dream on what one woman friend calls her "most incredibly perfect body". (*Newsweek* 1971, 51)

It is hard to imagine similar descriptions by the mainstream news media of any leaders of social movements who are male, at that time or now. Although certainly an effective spokesperson on behalf of the ERA, and one who was terrific at delivering memorable one-liners ("a pedestal is as much a prison as any small, confined space" and "if men could get pregnant, abortion would be a sacrament," http://womanshistory.about.com), Steinem was clearly not the only one fighting on behalf of its ratification. But media focus on the attractive and exceptional Steinem discounted the work of other feminists such as Abzug and Freidan, who were often portrayed as combative and shrill. It also implied that feminists themselves were divided in their fight for ERA ratification.

The emergence of grassroots conservative activist Phyllis Schlafly on the scene was in many ways a boon to the media. A Harvard-educated attorney, Schlafly was adept at using the media quite effectively, proving to be a perfect foil to Gloria Steinem. Schlafly routinely appeared on national and state news media programs to discount the ERA, which as of 1975 needed just three more states out of the 38 necessary to ratify it in order to meet the requirements of the Constitution, which requires three-quarters of the states to vote for ratification of constitutional amendments passed by Congress. With the battle being waged in her home state of Illinois, Schlafly took the lead in organizing the STOP-ERA campaign, claiming that ratification of the amendment would lead to women being drafted for combat duty and prompt other major changes in the roles of women and men. She was also effective at using media events to raise awareness of her cause, including the time she arranged for a man in a gorilla suit to interrupt a speech by the national president of the League of Women Voters, who was speaking in support of ratification of the ERA. In an attempt to embarrass the pro-ERA forces, Schlafly appeared after the arrival of the gorilla-suited individual to announce that many funds raised by the pro-ERA group came from *Playboy* magazine (Brown 2002). Schlafly also encouraged her followers to employ media-grabbing techniques. For example, in the state legislatures where the ERA was up for ratification, STOP-ERA forces brought home-cooked bread or cookies, complete with attached notes indicating how passage of the ERA would threaten the worth or even existence of homemakers (ibid.).

The national media attention that Phyllis Schlafly generated, juxtaposed with the attention received by Gloria Steinem, allowed the media to frame the debate about ratification for the ERA as a split among women. As Susan

Demonstrators opposed to the Federal Equal Rights Amendment gather outside the White House in February 1977.

Douglas (1994) argues, the media often portrayed the ERA as the "catfight par excellence" between Steinem and Schlafly:

> The stakes were higher than who got the boy, but we were back to the same old story we grew up with: Tinker Bell versus Wendy, Betty versus Veronica, the impossibility of female cooperation. And this is the primary reason we lost the ERA: if women themselves were so hopelessly divided over the amendment, why should it pass? While it's true that some women were deeply threatened by and anxious about the ERA and lobbied strenuously to defeat it, polls throughout the decade showed that they were the minority. The main struggle was between ERA proponents and male legislators, and behind-the-scenes corporate lobbyists, but this is not the struggle we saw on the nightly news. What we saw was the catfight.   (226)

The battle for ratification of the ERA was lost in 1982, when the amendment failed to be ratified by the necessary number of states. Opponents of the ERA campaign were successful in convincing legislators and citizens in the few remaining states needed to ratify the amendment that the ERA would lead to major changes in the role of men and women in society. In addition, there was growing legislative skepticism at that time about the consequences of giving the United States Supreme Court the authority to review state legislation that could potentially violate the amendment (Mansbridge 1986). Although these reasons help to explain the defeat of the ERA, some activists blame the loss, in part, on poor media coverage.

BACKLASH TO FEMINISM

By 1982, many feminists claimed that the failure to enact the ERA was endemic of a larger backlash by government, the American public, and the media toward feminism. The women's movement, which had touted the career, educational, and social gains made by women in the 1970s, began to be blamed for rising divorce rates and other social ills. A rash of stories appeared that portrayed formerly "liberated" women from the 1970s as unhappy women in the 1980s who were finding it increasingly difficult to balance their work and family life. Susan Faludi (1991) writes in *Backlash* that the press "acted as a force that swept the general public, powerfully shaping the way people would think and talk about the feminist legacy and the ailments it supposedly inflicted on women" (77). Trend journalism, which Faludi describes as a technique increasingly employed by the mass media that professes to offer "news of changing mores, yet prescribes more than it observes" (79), helped to coin terms that found themselves in the everyday lexicon of women including "man shortage," "biological clock," "mommy track," and "postfeminism" (77). Faludi contends that many of these "crises" among women were largely manufactured by the news media, yet had the effect of later influencing public opinion. For example, she recounts a sudden increase of news stories in the mid-1980s about how mothers were scared to leave their kids in dangerous day care centers. But this "trend" did not surface in national polls until 1988, when the confidence of parents in day care centers dropped from 76 percent in 1987 to 64 percent the following year (81). Similarly, another trend that made national headlines was the notion of the "mommy track," in which news reports insisted more and more women were opting for careers that paid less and offered fewer chances at professional advancement but that provided employees with a kinder work schedule, allowing for more time to be spent with family. Yet Faludi cites evidence that there was no such trend among women, including a 1990 Virginia Slims poll, which found that 70 percent of women called "mommy tracking" discriminatory and "just an excuse for paying women less than men" (91). Feminists believed that the media was too quick to cast these problems as repercussions of feminism, rather than blaming such trends on other reasons, such as (potentially) the conservative politics of the New Religious Right or the inability of business or social institutions to respond to increased numbers of women in the workforce (Faludi 1991).

As a result, the term *feminism* itself came into ill repute. Caryl Rivers (1996) argues that the media played a large role in creating what she calls "Fear of Feminism." She writes, "If you are constantly being told that the word equates with hairy, ugly man haters, that it dooms you to never getting married, never having children, being unloved and neurotic, getting depressed and anxious, and being a selfish hysteric to boot, you are probably not going to run headlong to the office of the National Organization for Women with your membership fee in hand" (111). Huddy's (1997) study on the use of the term *feminism* by the mainstream media over the past few decades finds that the term is typically limited to describing a small subgroup of organizations such as NOW—particularly those dedicated to reproductive rights—and leaders such as Gloria Steinem and Betty Freidan. The effect, says Huddy, is to paint feminism as a narrow movement with little appeal to ordinary women and men, leaving many individuals who otherwise support the goals of feminists to disavow the use of the term, a finding also supported by the research of political scientist Roberta Sigel (1996). Characteristic of many stories in the 1980s that questioned the success of feminism as a movement was a December 1989 *Time* cover story entitled "Women Face the '90s," which asked "Is there a future for feminism?" (Douglas 1994, 275). Douglas notes that the article discussed how women were "resentful" of the women's movement because things had not worked out as expected, yet failed to discuss other possible causes of the women's unhappiness (ibid.).

The arrival of a new century finds that many Americans remain ambivalent about the term *feminism* and women's relationship with power in the business, political, and academic worlds. A *Fortune* magazine article in October 2003 asked the question "Power: do women really want it?" The piece interviewed dozens of executive women and female politicians, most of whom were quoted as viewing power differently than their male counterparts. Many indicated that they would be less willing to take on the highest levels in their occupations because they lack the drive and ambition of men. Yet the article was short on compelling statistics. For instance, it noted that 26 percent of professional women who are not in the most senior posts say they don't want those jobs, and that of the 108 women who have appeared on the *Fortune 50* over the past five years, at least 20 have left these positions voluntarily (Sellers 2003, 3). In neither case, however, do these women make up the majority, nor are comparable statistics given for men. Although the article raises some interesting points, it smacks of the sort of "trend journalism" decried by Susan Faludi and other feminist critics.

In the late 2000s, feminists and feminist organizations are still a frequent target of the nationwide network of conservative radio and television hosts, including those with national prominence such as Rush Limbaugh, who is famous for coining the term "feminazi" in the 1990s to describe feminists. As recently as April 2009, he quipped on his nationally syndicated radio show, when discussing breast implants, that feminism was established "to allow unattractive women easier access to the mainstream of society" (quoted in Media Matters for America 2009). Syndicated radio show host Jim Quinn has referred to NOW as the "National Organization for Whores" and, like several prominent conservatives, was especially critical of NOW's opposition to Sarah Palin joining John McCain's presidential ticket in 2008. In September 2008, he had this to say about NOW and its supporters in wake of their criticism of Palin: "If you don't agree with the feminist scolds, then you're not a real woman—even if you are a very feminine working mom. But even if you're an actual man, never mind a childless feminist who looks like a Bulgarian weightlifter in drag, you're a real woman solely because you nod your head like a windup clapping monkey every time you read the latest editorial from *Ms. Magazine*" (quoted in Media Matters for America 2008).

While many Americans do not get their news or information from these conservative sources, a larger problem for groups like NOW has been that since the defeat of the ERA, the mainstream news media tend to link their coverage of feminist organizations almost solely to news concerning reproductive rights, which leaves the impression among many Americans that the sole concern of women's rights groups today is abortion. While these groups *are* defenders of abortion rights, they also promote and support a broader range of issues regarding gender equity, family and parental leave, child care, and family law—issues that more closely mirror the top priorities of women nationally than abortion (Barakso and Schaffner 2006).

Yet Americans, although reluctant to embrace the term *feminism*, still typically support efforts to "strengthen and change women's status in society" and generally support the goals of feminism (McGlen and O'Connor 1998; Sigel 1996). No doubt the support for such goals is grounded in women's experiences, especially of discrimination, either directly, secondhand, or even from the media. Although the media can be "our worst enemy" when it comes to ably representing the views and concerns of women in today's society, Susan Douglas also recognizes that it can be "our best ally in our ongoing struggle

BOX 4.1

The Gender Gap and Soccer Moms: Media Coverage of Women as Voters

Although the media often overlook political and social issues of importance to women, one issue that they have covered at length in the wake of the 1980 presidential elections is the gender gap, or the differences in voting behavior among men and women. It was in the 1980 election that women were 9 percent less likely to vote for Ronald Reagan than men, (Center for American Politics and Women 1997) a figure that caused scholars and pundits to begin to pay attention to gender differences in their analyses (Borquex, Goldenberg, and Kahn 1988). (see Chapter 3 for more information on the gender gap today in American politics.) As a result, the gender gap has not only held a prominent place on the political science research agenda, but also has become part of the continuing news stories of most elections.

By the 1984 election, one study reports that one in five campaign stories dealt with the gender gap, and that women as a "voting bloc" had become a prominent theme of stories featured in major newspapers such as the *New York Times* (Kahn and Goldenberg 1991). Coverage of the gender gap was no doubt made easier by NOW, which began releasing monthly "Gender Gap Updates" to reporters by 1982 to keep the issue alive. (*ibid.*) Many feminists attribute the nomination of Geraldine Ferraro as the first woman vice presidential candidate in 1984, in part, to their promotion of the gender gap. (*ibid.*) Others believe that media coverage of the gender gap in the 1980s "probably created a favorable atmosphere for female candidates and fostered more serious discussion of women's issues." (*ibid.* 107).

Yet some critics believe that the media's "discovery" of the gender gap in the 1980s was given more emphasis than it merited. For example, pollster Everett Carl Ladd argues that the media exaggerate the impact of gender on voting in comparison to other differences, such as the "race" gap or the "education" gap, two factors that have elicited much stronger electoral differences than gender (Ladd 1997). In reference to what he feels is an overstatement of gender gap accounts by the media, he writes that "the press displays an irresistible urge to make everything brighter and sharper than it actually is." (*ibid.* 115).

Nonetheless, the gender gap is a story that continues to influence political reporters. In 1996, for instance, the "swing voters" that candidates sought to influence most were the so-called "soccer moms," white, suburban mothers who were most concerned about issues relating to their children—or at least that was the major frame adopted by the media in covering the presidential elections that year. One study found that between July 1 and November 30, 1996, 211 articles were published concerning soccer moms in 55 different major newspapers (Carroll 1999). Political scientist Susan Carroll argues, however, that the soccer mom news frame actually hurt women more generally, as it led "to the disempowerment of most women through its narrow portrayal of women voters and their interests." (*ibid.* 10). In other words, missing from newspaper reports of the campaigns' attempts to appeal to these suburban, middle-class voters was discussion of issues that are more in tune with the feminist agenda, such as abortion, health care, sexual harassment, and job training.

In the 2004 election, reporters continued to cover gender gap concerns—although shifting from soccer moms to NASCAR dads. According to Democratic pollster Celinda Lake, a NASCAR dad is a "blue-collar family man who's been hurt by the economy and watched jobs shipped overseas and his brother shipped out to Iraq." (Quoted in Goodman 2003). While he used to be a Democrat and then became a Republican, some pundits believed his vote would be very much up for grabs in the 2004 election (although this theory never materialized, as such dads voted more often for Bush than Kerry). Regardless of the interpretation, it appears that gender differences in the electorate are still a major concern appealing to the news media today. ■

for equality, respect, power and love" (Douglas 1994, 294). Thanks to the media, boys and girls today are more likely than in times past to see strong female role models—both fictional and real—on television and in other media outlets. House Speaker Nancy Pelosi, former Senator and now Secretary of State Hillary Clinton, and Alaska Governor turned vice-presidential candidate Sarah Palin, for example, are now familiar faces on television.

In summary, the extent to which the media covers women's movements and organizations, as well as the tone and substance of that coverage, can have a large impact on the ability of such movements and organizations to be successful in the political arena. Suffragists were often quite adept at attracting sympathetic media attention, particularly in the latter years of their struggle. By contrast, activists in the women's movement were often hostile to mainstream coverage, although many within the movement began to see the importance of the media to building support for their cause. Even an increase in sympathetic media coverage was not enough for feminists to gain passage of the ERA. Yet the media in recent years have become better at more accurately depicting women's issues as well as offering positive female role models on television, although, as we will see in the next section, there is still room for improvement.

MEDIA COVERAGE OF FEMALE POLITICIANS AND FIRST LADIES

Part of the increase in coverage of women politicians and other female political actors is a result of more women engaged in the political process. Although it is no longer strange to see women politicians on television, how does media coverage of women politicians compare with their male counterparts? In Chapter 5, we more closely examine how the media cover women candidates who run for political office in comparison to men. Here we examine how the media react to women once they are elected. We also discuss media coverage of first ladies.

Media Coverage of Female Politicians

In Chapter 5, we show how female candidates often experience discriminatory, gendered treatment at the hands of the news media. The media discrimination that women sometimes face as candidates is often extended to them once they serve in office and is likely part of a larger bias of reporters when it comes to coverage of women more generally. For example, one study of the Freedom Forum found that approximately 15 percent of news stories appearing on the first page of both major and smaller-market newspapers feature women—who, more than half of the time, appear as crime victims (Hernandez 1996). In a 2002 study by Media Tenor of the three major evening news programs, the average percentage of female protagonists in news stories was 14 percent, and most often in stereotypical contexts, in stories concerning health, society, general interest, and the environment as opposed to stories concerning national defense or foreign affairs (Media Report to Women 2003b). National Security Advisor Condoleezza Rice was the most frequent female featured in network news in 2003, appearing 45 times (ibid.). In the case of women politicians, lack of coverage of their work in comparison to their male counterparts serves to reinforce the idea that politics is a male arena. Moreover, the stereotypical and conceptual frames that reporters sometimes use to describe women politicians and their concerns can be viewed as an artifact of this country's unresolved debate over a woman's "proper" role in society (Witt, Paget, and Matthews 1994).

Women politicians from the start have rarely had an easy time of it in the press. Take the case of Jeannette Rankin, the first woman to be elected to Congress in 1916 from Montana, a state that allowed women the right to vote before passage of the Nineteenth Amendment guaranteed women that right nationally. Although state and local press in Montana were generally encouraging of Ms. Rankin's election—noting that she had much political and organizational experience as a leading organizer of the national movement for suffrage—the national media viewed her as a curiosity and frequently commented on her appearance and her domestic habits. After her election was verified on November 11, 1916, the New York Times reported that she was "small, slight with light brown hair" and that she made "her own clothes and hats, and she [was] an excellent cook" (quoted in Braden 1996, 21). Another New York paper at that time noted that Rankin "has won genuine fame among her friends with the wonderful lemon meringue pie that she makes when she hasn't enough other things to do to keep her busy" (ibid.).

In addition to being the first woman elected to the House of Representatives, Jeannette Rankin is perhaps best known for her antiwar stances, fueled in part by media coverage. Although she was one of 16 members of Congress to vote against the entry of the United States into World War I, the national media chose to highlight her opposition separately. For instance, the New York Times reported in its headline on April 16, 1917, the following: "One Hundred Speeches were made—Miss Rankin, sobbing votes no." Although several eyewitnesses later recounted that Congresswoman Rankin did not weep when giving her speech against the war but did tear up, the papers neglected to mention the other cases in which several congress*men* became emotional in their own speeches (Witt, Paget, and Matthews 1994). The *Times* editorial page argued that her vote against the war came close to being "a final proof of feminine incapacity for straight reasoning"; other editors denounced her decision as well (Braden 1996). Rankin faced similar criticisms more than two decades later when she cast the lone vote in Congress against American entry into World War II.

For much of the twentieth century, political women who came to serve in Washington (and sometimes in the governor's office at the state level) followed the "widow's model," in that they were appointed to complete the terms of their departed spouses who had been elected first (see also Chapters 5 and 7). Press coverage always made mention of this fact upon their appointments and then typically ignored them while they carried out their husbands' terms (presumably until men could assume their "rightful" place). Those who were later reelected on their own merits were often cast by the media as atypical. Jeane Kirkpatrick (1974) pointed out that a double standard existed, affecting those women who replaced their spouses' seats but not those male politicians who were appointed to fulfill another man's seat: "The fact that Margaret Chase Smith[2] was initially appointed to serve out her husband's term seems more important to many than the fact that Walter Mondale was first appointed to the Senate to finish out the term of then Vice President Hubert Humphrey. Why? Because stereotypes persist. . . . Seeing political women as husbands' surrogates is a way of denying they are really political actors in their own right" (218–219).

But not all press coverage of these pioneering women politicians was negative. Women's magazines often urged their female readers to become more involved in politics. These magazines also profiled successful women politicians, including the *Women's Journal*, which in 1928 ran an article about three new women members of Congress (all named Ruth—Ruth Bryan Owen, Ruth Hanna McCormick, and Ruth Pratt), describing them as "notable for their personality and political leadership who won membership in Congress by campaigns rating with the best of men's" (quoted in Braden 1996, 37). These women's publications helped to challenge the perception that women were incapable of holding public office or of being politically active.

By the 1970s and beyond, most women elected to Congress were doing so in their own right. Yet the media are still more likely to define women members by their gender than male members. Relative to male members of Congress, press secretaries working for women members are considerably more likely to complain about unfair coverage (Niven and Zilber 2001). Press

---

[2]Smith (R-ME) went on to become the first woman elected in her own right to the United States Senate and even sought the Republican nomination for president in 1964. Serving much of her time in the Senate as the lone female, she was typically referred to as the "Lady from Maine" by the media (Braden 1996, 50). A former newspaper reporter, she understood the news business and was often successful at using it to her own advantage. She was also the first Republican to denounce the tactics of her fellow party member Joseph McCarthy in his fight against communism.

secretaries to female members of Congress more frequently report that media coverage of their bosses often mentions their family situation and is preoccupied with personality and appearance than do press secretaries to male members (ibid.). According to one press secretary, a reporter once asked about her female boss: "How does she have time for kids and Congress?" Her response was to ask this male reporter if he ever posed the same question to male members of Congress (ibid., 154).

In addition to an inordinate focus on family life in comparison to male members, female members of Congress often find that the press is most likely to interview them about so-called "women's issues," such as education, women's health care, or abortion rights (Carroll and Schreiber 1997)—despite attempts by members, through their websites or through their communications staff, to portray themselves as having diverse interests. Former Senator Nancy Kassebaum (R-KS), who served on the Foreign Relations Committee, notes that she was rarely asked to appear on the Sunday morning talk shows to discuss this area of expertise: "Maybe I'm just not as good at presenting the facts, but I think that most men tend to feel men present foreign policy a little more forcefully" (quoted in Witt, Paget, and Matthews 1994, 193).

Media coverage of Senator Kassebaum, from her election in 1978 through her retirement in 1997, was often gendered in tone, even as she gained more political seniority and clout, serving not just on the powerful Foreign Relations Committee but also as chair of the Labor and Human Resources Committee by 1995. Early stories that appeared after her first election often referred to her as "the soft-spoken" and "diminutive" Nancy Kassebaum—a theme that continued throughout her political career. For example, a front-page *Washington Post* profile of Kassebaum in May 1995 included this description: "In an age of shoot 'em dead politicians, she is from the school of grandmotherly love—more a gentle persuader than a political marksman" (quoted in Braden 1996, 162). It is hard to imagine many male senators being described as from the school of grandfatherly love.

On a more positive note, press portrayals of Nancy Pelosi, the first female Speaker of the House, have generally been more balanced in tone. In fact, Karen Kedrowski and Rachel Gower (2009) found that the news media covered Pelosi's ascent into the Speakership and her first two months "on the job" more so than any of the past six Speakers of the House save for the media-savvy Newt Gingrich, who assumed the Speakership after the historic 1994 elections in which Republicans gained control of both houses of Congress for the first time in forty years. Moreover, while about 10 percent of the news stories about Pelosi did focus on the historic nature of the "first woman" being elected as Speaker, the majority of news stories were not gendered in tone. In fact, most stories about Pelosi covered her ambitious plan to pass significant legislation in the first 100 days of Congress or they focused on her outspoken criticism of the war in Iraq (ibid.).

That is not to say that the news media completely avoided any discussion of Pelosi in gendered terms. For example, several stories noted that she was a mother and grandmother and often sought a more consensus-style of leadership. However, Kedrowski and Gower point out that this "motherly" image was one that Pelosi herself often used as a political strategy, such as in her acceptance speech on the floor of the House when she was handed the gavel for the first time as speaker, when she said, "For all of America's children, the house will be in order." Pelosi has won the respect of the media and others as a strongly disciplined and effective House Speaker.

Media Coverage of First Ladies

Elected Speaker of the House in 2006, Nancy Pelosi represents the highest-ranking elected female political leader in the United States. As we have yet to elect a female president, perhaps the closest women have come to influencing the Oval Office is through the position of first lady. As the role of first lady has changed, so has media coverage of the position. The earliest frame adopted by the media to cover the first "first ladies" was that of an escort or spouse, as when early newspapers referred to Martha Washington as "Lady Washington" or "the President of the United States and his lady" (Winfield 1997). Later, with Dolley Madison, the press began to acknowledge the social and ceremonial roles of the first lady. Even though many were aware that some presidential wives, such as Abigail Adams, had a large political influence on their husbands, such a relationship was never mentioned in the early press. By the start of the twentieth century, national magazines began to pay more attention to the wives of the president and presidential candidates. A frequent frame employed by reporters at this time was the "noblesse oblige" role—reporting on the first lady's charitable works (ibid.).

Then came Eleanor Roosevelt, a first lady who defied classification. Before FDR's election as president in 1932, *Good Housekeeping* referred to Eleanor Roosevelt in 1930 as "the ideal modern wife" (quoted in Winfield 1997). A journalist who was also politically powerful in the Democratic Party upon her husband's election, Eleanor offered to serve as a national sounding board on the Great Depression, inviting citizens to write her letters about their conditions and concerns. Although many Americans embraced her, particularly minorities and other dispossessed groups that she visited and spoke on behalf of, the press criticized her independence and self-appointed political role. For example, the *New York Times* wrote in an editorial on January 28, 1933, that "it is not indelicate or impolite to express the hope that she will refrain from such utterances in the future. The very best helpers of a President are those who do all they can for him, but keep still about it" (ibid., 173). Yet Eleanor Roosevelt was often very savvy in her use of the press. While she continued to write a syndicated column for local newspapers, she also made sure that the press covered the more traditional duties of the first lady (Winfield 1997).

After Eleanor Roosevelt, press coverage of the first lady reverted back to the more traditional, stereotypical coverage, embodied especially by coverage of Jacqueline Kennedy, the young and beautiful wife of President John F. Kennedy. Although Jackie Kennedy had had a previous career in journalism, media coverage focused on her escort and social roles, particularly her looks and keen fashion sense. Winfield (1994) notes that stereotypical stories about the first lady's appearance or decorating tastes in the White House are "easy, comfortable stories to do" by the media (71).

Beginning with Jackie Kennedy, first ladies developed a more formal, managed relationship with the press. While Kennedy was the first to hire a staff member specifically to handle press relations, Lady Bird Johnson was the first to have a Press Secretary (Burns 2008). In more recent decades, the advent of television and celebrity journalism has prompted more media attention toward first ladies (as well as the wives of prominent presidential candidates). Scholar Lisa Burns (2008) notes that one result of media fascination with the position is a "cult of celebrity" around the first lady, one in which "journalists often expect first ladies to embody traditional gender roles and [yet] reflect the changing times, simultaneously modern and traditional (6)"—a position that is often impossible for first ladies to completely embody. In her historical analysis, Burns argues that press coverage of first ladies is often reflective of larger trends in women's roles. She argues that during the Great Depression, World War II and the Cold War, the press framed the first lady as portraying a domestic ideal, while the feminist movement of the 1960s and 1970s led to press coverage that often praised more "activist" first ladies who managed to balance both the more traditional aspects of the position with the promotion of outside (though typically non-political) causes. However, Burns says that in the period between 1980 and 2001, a backlash to feminism led reporters to question more critically any political role sought by first ladies. She writes: "Concerned with the 'hidden power' of first ladies, journalists framed political wives who overstepped the boundaries of first lady and gender performance as political interlopers whose influence allegedly trespassed too far into the male political sphere (15)."

In fact, in one study comparing the tone of media coverage of three recent first ladies—Nancy Reagan, Barbara Bush, and Hillary Rodham Clinton—researchers found that the more politically involved first ladies become, the more negative the news coverage (Scharrer and Bissell 2000). Part of the reason for this finding is that the "watchdog function" of the press becomes more pronounced as the political role of the first lady expands. However, part of this change in tone is also the likely result that the public might not feel comfortable having a first lady make political decisions (ibid.).

Political pundits and journalists alike reflected this unease in their coverage of Hillary Rodham Clinton as candidate Bill Clinton's wife during the 1992 presidential campaign. Late-night comedians joked about the "co-presidency" that Bill and Hillary Clinton would develop if elected (a co-presidency that they had earlier touted in the campaign themselves), while many reporters made note of Hillary Clinton's own political ambitions. One *New York Times* report in September 1992 found that the press had made no fewer than 50 references to Hillary Clinton as Lady MacBeth, causing scholar Caryl Rivers (1996) to ask if male advisers to the president were ever presented as accessories to murder! The first few years of media coverage of Hillary Clinton's role as first lady were decidedly mixed. After being selected to head President Clinton's Health Care Task Force, she received praise from the media and elsewhere for early, effective testimony that she provided in hearings about health care reform on Capitol Hill. As it became clear that the Task Force was unable to put together a winning plan for a universal health care system, however, Hillary Clinton was blamed for the failure, resulting in negative media coverage. The press also went after her involvement with a failed land deal in Arkansas, called Whitewater, with abandon, often trying to equate the scandal with Watergate (Winfield 1994). Inevitably, the press resorted to the more traditional coverage of Hillary Rodham Clinton as first lady by focusing on her fashion and changing hairstyles, and even sympathetically portrayed her as the "wronged wife" during the Monica Lewinsky scandal, which helped to boost her popularity among the American public.

Hillary Clinton's upsurge in popularity toward the end of her time as first lady helped to convince Democrats in New York that she should consider running for the Senate seat that was being vacated by Daniel Patrick Moynihan—a seat that she easily won. Hillary Clinton's election as U.S. Senator marked the first time that a first lady has been elected to public office—and some pundits speculated that a new era of heightened political involvement for first ladies could be imminent.

Yet Clinton's successor, Laura Bush, largely embodied the more stereotypical role of presidential spouse. While eschewing any political or policy-making role, Laura Bush received high marks after the events of September 11, 2001, when she went around the nation recounting her experiences and serving as "Therapist in Chief" for the nation (Ma 2002). Becoming a fixture in women's magazines, *Media Industry Newsletter* notes that Laura Bush was honored by *Woman's Day Magazine*, interviewed by *Family Circle*, and appeared on the cover of *Good Housekeeping* and *Ladies' Home Journal* in the three months after the 9/11 terrorist attacks (*Media Industry Newsletter* 2002). Although she actively campaigned for her husband's re-election in 2004, Bush largely eschewed political and policy matters and was seldom featured in television news or print media alone from her husband after 9/11. This did not stop her, however, from being one of the most admired women in America, even when her husband faced dismal popularity rankings late in his time in office.

In contrast to Laura Bush, the news media (and many Americans more generally) are fascinated with the nation's first African-American first lady, Michelle Obama, who has taken a higher public profile than her immediate predecessor. Obama was an effective campaigner for her husband during his election campaign, although some conservative commentators portrayed her as an "angry" black woman, particularly after she said in one February campaign event that "For the first time in my adult life, I am proud of my country because it feels like hope is finally making a comeback" (Merida 2008). First Lady Laura Bush defended Obama against detractors who claimed she was unpatriotic by saying that her words were largely misconstrued. The most egregious statement about Michele Obama was likely when a Fox news commentator likened her celebratory "fist bump" with

The infamous *New Yorker* cover that satirizes the fist bumb betweem Michelle and Barack Obama during a campaign event, dubbed a "terrorist fist jab" by conservative commentators.

Barack Obama, after clinching the Democratic Party nomination in June 2008, as a "terrorist fist jab," which was parodied by a now-infamous *New Yorker* political cover.

By and large, however, later coverage of Michelle Obama during the remainder of the campaign and as a first lady has been largely positive, with the media emphasizing several causes that she has championed, such as the plight of military families and her commitment to promoting healthy lifestyles for young people, as demonstrated by her decision to plant an organic vegetable garden on the White House lawn. The media is also enamored of her own personal style and fashion sense, as well as her lovely young family, which includes daughters Malia and Sasha and the much-heralded "First Dog," Bo, who arrived at the White House in spring of 2009. In March 2009, she became the second first lady to be featured on the cover of *Vogue* magazine, and the media's apparent obsession with her toned arms and her propensity to wear sleeveless dresses led the President to quip at the White

In March 2009, First Lady Michelle Obama—
known for her keen fashion sense—appeared
on the cover of the popular women's fashion
magazine *Vogue*.

House Correspondents' Association's annual dinner in May 2009 about his wife: "She's even begun to bridge the differences that have divided us for so long, because no matter which party you belong to we can all agree that Michelle has the right to bare arms." (White House Transcript 2009). Whether Michelle Obama will seek out a public path that emphasizes a more overtly political agenda remains to be seen.

In this section, we have considered media coverage of women politicians and first ladies. The media have certainly become more balanced in their coverage of women politicians from the early days of Jeannette Rankin, the first woman elected to the House of Representatives. For instance, coverage of the first female Speaker of the House, Democrat Nancy Pelosi, has been overwhelmingly neutral. Yet it is not uncommon for the media today to lapse into stereotypical coverage of women candidates and leaders, often by emphasizing their "feminine" traits and appearance. Moreover, some women politicians report difficulty in getting the media to accept them as spokespeople for *all* political issues, not just those that are often associated with women and children. As our next section discusses, perhaps these barriers that women politicians face from the media will be further broken down by the growing number of women in journalism.

WOMEN IN MEDIA TODAY: A FAIR BALANCE?

One reason that media coverage of the women's movement and early female politicians often relied on gendered norms that often belittled their subjects was no doubt due in part to the small number of news writers who were women. Many argue that coverage of female politicians, as well as the political and social issues that concern women most, has improved as more women have joined the journalism profession. Yet some stereotypical coverage of women remains, which begs the question: What exactly is the status of professional women in journalism? In this section, we ask whether or not women journalists serve in equal numbers as men. Does it matter to have more women serving as reporters when it comes to the status of women in politics? We also take a look at the role of women in higher media management. How do women fare when it comes to media management and ownership?

Historically, women first began to enter the ranks of journalism as a result of various social movements, including abolitionism, temperance, and suffrage. For these women, becoming reporters allowed them the opportunity to publicize and write about their causes. But when larger numbers of female reporters began to cover "hard news," they were often stopped in their tracks. For example, when women correspondents in Washington numbered more than 10 percent in 1879, they were banned from the Capitol Hill press galleries, which had the effect of banning women reporters from covering political news for much of the next century (Witt, Paget, and Matthews 1994). Instead, women reporters were often relegated to covering society news.

There were two other outlets, however, that female reporters had in the late nineteenth and early twentieth centuries aside from the gossip pages. Some young women reporters became "stunt girls," including the most famous of all, Nellie Bly, who reported for Joseph Pulitzer's paper *The World* (Ross 1936). These stunt girls were young women reporters who would often put their own safety or lives at risk to create sensational stories, often posing as beggars, balloonists, or street women who would then write about such experiences. Nellie Bly, for instance, faked insanity to be placed in an asylum. The enthralling tales she wrote of her mistreatment in the pages of *The World* led to reforms in the treatment of the mentally ill (Witt, Paget, and Matthews 1994). Perhaps her most famous escapade, however, involved her well-publicized trip around the world, which was designed to beat the time of the fictional Phileas Fogg, the hero of Jules Verne's *Around the World in Eighty Days*. Bly reported from exotic locales, riveting readers with her escapades in foreign lands. When she returned in 72 days to much acclaim, *The World* proclaimed in its headline on the front page, "Father Time Outdone!" (Ross 1936). The other type of reporting available to women was the role of the "sob sister." These female reporters, such as Winifred Black (who wrote under the pen name Annie Laurie in her columns for the *San Francisco Examiner*), wrote tear-jerking human interest stories that were geared at reform. Black is redited, for example, with exposing San Francisco's poor treatment of underprivileged women in city hospitals, causing reforms in the method by which ambulances were allocated. Although female reporters were largely only permitted to assume these two reporting roles, these pioneering "stunt girls" and "sob sisters" often had a political and social impact above their entertainment value. Not only did these women push the norms and expectations of women in society at the time, but also they often affected public policy at the local level, "describing the human costs and validating the unique authority women were thought to be able to bring to the political system" (Witt, Paget, and Matthews 1994, 190).

The cause of women's journalism was helped by Eleanor Roosevelt, who insisted that her press conferences be covered by women reporters only. Given her large political role, Roosevelt's request caused many news outlets to hire women reporters for the first time (Braden 1996). Several of the women assigned to cover Mrs. Roosevelt noted that these appointments also allowed them greater access to covering hard political news, including Beth Campbell Short of the Associated Press:

> I would not have admitted Mrs. Roosevelt's importance at the time. I had never felt discrimination at my early jobs and never felt it at the Associated Press. It didn't matter if there was a story on the Hill, or if Mrs. Roosevelt was doing something. If I was the one who was free, they sent me. But I've thought about it lately. If the woman hadn't insisted on press conferences and if she hadn't had the policy of only women covering then . . . well, that's what really gave people like me . . . our break. (Quoted in Mills 1988, 44–45)

Yet the women reporters who covered Mrs. Roosevelt were the exception to the rule when it came to the presence of female journalists in Washington, D.C. Although a few women journalists and columnists did have a national following, such as Anne O'Hare McCormick, the first woman to join the editorial board of the *New York Times* and the first woman to win a Pulitzer Prize in journalism in 1937, women were largely relegated to the society pages, as they had been in the nineteenth century (Braden 1996). Many women reporters briefly were promoted to the news desk during World War II but then were forced to return to the women's sections of the papers after the return of the men from the war. Braden (1996) notes, however, that it was not just that men wanted their old jobs back upon the end of the war that forced women away from news coverage. It was also the mind-set among male news editors that it was safer for men to be assigned stories concerning crime and corruption, and that women were not as capable as men of being objective or analytical in their reporting. Braden cites a survey of news editors by *Mademoiselle* magazine in 1949, in which male editors hired men as reporters because "women lack evenness of temperament, dependability, stability, quickness, range, understanding, knowledge, and insight" (quoted in Braden 1996, 173).

By the late twentieth century, the opportunities for women in journalism increased dramatically, aided in part by the path-breaking work of journalists such as Helen Thomas, the longtime White House correspondent for United Press International (and later Hearst Newspapers) who began her beat with the Kennedy administration (see *Profiles of Political Influence*). Whereas women made up 20 percent of working journalists in 1971, they increased their ranks to 34 percent in 1982—a figure that remained relatively steady for the next two decades (Weaver 1997; Becker 2003). According to the Bureau of Labor Statistics, women made up 45 percent of people in the news analysts, reporters, and correspondents category in 2008—although their numbers differ with respect to the type of media in which they work (Catalyst 2009). For example, the American Society of Newspaper Editors (2009) reported in 2009 that the percentage of women reporters who work on daily newspapers is about 37 percent—a figure that has remained virtually unchanged in the past decade. Catalyst, a research organization that tracks women's representation in numerous industries, reports that 40 percent of television news staffs and 23 percent of radio news staffs, respectively, are women (Catalyst 2009). Women fare worse, however, when it comes to national network news. Turning to the national television news programs, 28 percent of news stories on the "big three" news outlets (ABC, CBS, NBC) were reported by women in 2006 (Center for Media and Public Affairs 2007). However, television history was made that same year when Katie Couric became the sole anchor of *The CBS Evening News*, a post held for 24 years by Dan Rather (see *Profiles of Political Influence*). In December 2009, Diane Sawyer, the longtime popular host of ABC's morning television show *Good Morning America* became the second woman to assume the anchor position of a major network news program when she replaced Charlie Gibson as host of ABC's *World News Tonight*.

Despite the gains that women have made in the news business, particularly in print, there are still areas in which women are greatly underrepresented, especially those that are known for their "agenda-setting" functions. There are far fewer women than men who are syndicated political columnists and women are less likely to appear as authors of op-ed pieces in newspapers. In one example, Geneva Overholser writes that in the week after the September 11 attacks in 2001, the *New York Times* and *Washington Post* together had 65 signed op-ed pieces—just four of which were written by women (Overholser 2001). A more recent study by media watchdog and journalist Howard Kurtz of the *Washington Post* found that in March 2005, women wrote just 20 percent of op-eds in the *LA Times* and 10 percent of op-eds in the *Washington Post*, respectively (Kurtz 2005).

Few women journalists regularly appear on the Sunday morning talk shows, nor are women likely to be invited as guests. One study of five major Sunday talk shows, such as *Meet the Press*, found that women represented just 11 percent of guest appearances (The White House Project 2002). And in one of the fastest-rising forms of political communication—the political weblogs or blogs—women also appear to be underrepresented (see Box 4.2).

PROFILES OF POLITICAL INFLUENCE

Helen Thomas

Often referred to as "The First Lady of the Press," Helen Thomas served for 57 years as a reporter with United Press International (UPI), beginning her stint as White House correspondent in 1960 with president-elect John F. Kennedy (AEI Speakers Bureau n.d.) Thomas has covered every president since Kennedy, including, most recently, Barack Obama.

Thomas was born in Kentucky in 1920 and raised in Detroit, Michigan, the daughter of Lebanese immigrants. Her first job was as a copy girl in the early 1940s with the *Washington Daily News*, a now defunct Washington paper, making $17.50 a week ("I thought I had arrived") (Danini 2003, 3B). She was hired by UPI in 1943, first covering the news of the federal government before becoming White House correspondent in 1960. In 1971 she married fellow White House correspondent (and Associated Press competitor) Douglas Cornell, who died in 1982 of Alzheimer's disease (Helen Thomas: *Doyenne of the Washington Press Corp*, 2001).

Thomas is notable for several "firsts" for women journalists. She was the only print journalist to cover President Nixon's path-breaking trip to China in 1972, which normalized relations between the United States and that country. She says of that event: "Going to China with President Nixon was one of the greatest stories I ever covered. It really was like landing on the moon. But this was a great opening, and we were able to write stories with 'new eyes'" (ibid.). She was the first woman officer of the National Press Club, the first female officer of the White House Correspondents Association, and the first female member of the Gridiron Club. She was also named one of the 25 Most Influential Women in America by the *World Almanac* (ibid.).

A syndicated columnist with Hearst Newspapers until her retirement in 2010, Thomas made headlines recently when she denounced the Iraq war as immoral. At a speech at the University of North Carolina in November 2003, she asked, "Who is demanding to know why we invaded Iraq—a country that did absolutely nothing to us?" ("Helen Thomas Blasts Iraq War . . ." 2003). Her long career abruptly ended in 2010 when she was forced to resign after making offensive comments about Jews and Israel.

Thomas acknowledges that women journalists have made great strides in the past but that young women in this profession "still have mountains to climb." (Quoted in Danini 2003, 3B). Yet she also notes that journalism is an extremely rewarding profession, telling young women, "Go for it! You'll never feel unhappy when you go into journalism. When your job gives you an education, every day is worth it." (Quoted in Falk 1999). ∎

PROFILES OF POLITICAL INFLUENCE

CBS Evening News Anchor, Katie Couric (right) interviews former Alaska governor and Republican vice-presidential nominee Sarah Palin in what was heralded as one of the most important television moments of the 2008 Presidential Elections.

Katie Couric

In September 2006, Katie Couric made history by becoming the anchor of the CBS Evening News, the first woman to solo-anchor one of the "big three" broadcast evening news programs,[3] to much fanfare and media hype (Brewer and Macafee 2007). She came to the position with solid credentials as a reporter and popular longtime television host of NBC's Today show, where she co-anchored the morning broadcast for 15 years. CBS signed Couric for a five-year stint for a reported $75 million, with a goal of bringing in new viewers to the long-running program, which had long been mired in third place in the ratings behind NBC Nightly News and ABC's World News Tonight (Guthrie 2008).

After an initial jump in ratings for the first few weeks of Couric's tenure as anchor, CBS fell back to third place. Many were critical of Couric's performance and some of the show's attempts to revamp the format of the news program to play to her strengths as a conversationalist. However, her so-called "chatty" style did not come across well in a format that relies on brief overviews of the day's events. Efforts to retool the program back into a more traditional hard-news broadcast have had mixed results. In fact, prominent insiders predicted that Couric would leave the broadcast after the 2008 presidential elections.

However, Couric appears to have hit her stride, especially with her coverage of the 2008 presidential elections, aided in no small part by her much-hyped interview with Alaska Governor Sarah Palin, shortly after she was selected by John McCain to be his running mate. Couric's interview with Palin was, for many, a turning point in the election as it highlighted Palin's lack of knowledge about many important political issues, especially foreign affairs. (No doubt, Saturday Night Live's famous send-up of the interview, featuring comedians Tina Fey as Palin and Amy Poehler as Couric, also helped raise Couric's

---

[3]In 1976, Barbara Walters briefly co-anchored ABC's World News Tonight with Harry Reasoner and in 1993 to 1995, Connie Chung co-anchored the CBS Evening News with Dan Rather. More recently, Elizabeth Vargas co-anchored ABC News Tonight for about 5 months from December 2006 to May 2006 (Ryan, Lake, and Mapaye 2008).

PROFILES OF POLITICAL INFLUENCE (CONTINUED)

profile). In 2009, Katie Couric won a Walter Cronkite Award (given annually for excellence in television political journalism by the University of Southern California's Annenberg Norman Lear Center) for Special Achievement for National Impact on the 2008 Campaign for her interview with Palin, as judges called the interview "a defining moment in the 2008 presidential campaign" (www.reliableresources.org/winners09.html). Couric went on to land big interviews with Joe Biden and John McCain, which were generally well-received. Talks about her dismissal from CBS have largely dissipated; however, the ratings for CBS Evening News have still not greatly improved.

But blaming Couric for failing ratings at CBS may not be entirely fair. In general, viewership for the big three networks is in a state of decline, as more and more Americans are turning to newer forms of media, such as the Internet, to get news and information at their convenience. One study by the Project for Excellence in Journalism estimates that evening news viewership over the last 25 years has decreased by at least one million viewers per year (Ryan, Lake, and Mapaye 2008). Moreover, cable news programs have drawn many viewers away from the networks with their 24-hour news coverage and have filled an important niche for those viewers who look for news and commentary that is more ideological in tone, as FOX news tends to draw more conservative viewers and MSNBC is increasingly becoming its liberal foil. Nonetheless, national broadcast news remains the "Gold Standard" in terms of news for many Americans as more people continue to get their news from this source than from any other. Having Katie Couric as a sole anchor and managing editor of a nightly network broadcast, then, is an important milestone for women journalists. ∎

BOX 4.2

Women, Politics and the Internet

The traditional mainstream news media—particularly print journalism—often discriminates against women in terms of their representation as journalists, story sources, and commentary experts. Moreover, many of the issues about which women care deeply are often ignored or seldom reported on, in part because of gatekeeping, a journalism practice that recognizes that there is a limited amount of space in newspapers and on broadcast television for certain topics to be covered.

(Continued)

BOX 4.2 (CONTINUED)

Many women's rights advocates believed that the Internet, especially the practice of blogging, would bring more attention to such issues and provide political news and commentary less dependent on gender stereotypes. Also, political theorists believed that the Internet would have the potential to provide more open spaces for a variety of new voices; that it would, in essence, become an "electronic marketplace" of ideas, providing a "form of citizen journalism that offers a wider spectrum of perspectives" (Harp and Tremayne 2006, 248). Moreover, the Pew Internet and American Life Project found in 2004 (Rainie 2005) that 57 percent of blogs are written by men and 43 percent are written by women, which shows that women are active in the blogosphere. But do women blog about politics? And, if so, are their voices carrying resonance in politics?

In terms of politics, initial research suggests that the Internet may not be proving to be the great democratizing force that political theorists envisioned—at least when it comes to women and gender issues. For example, researchers Dustin Harp and Mark Tremayne (2006) analyzed the 30 top political blogs for a one-year period (June 2004–May 2005) and found that only three were women-authored. Turning to the more established news sources and their on-line coverage, several studies have found that women are again less likely to be the subjects of news articles and that the coverage of news stories is often gendered and stereotyped. For example, one study examined the coverage of women in popular on-line newsmagazines from four different nations, including the United States, which featured analysis of *Time* magazine for a one-month period (Yun et al. 2007). They found that women made up only 3 to 5 percent of the news subjects of articles, and that while almost all of the news stories portrayed men as leaders (92 percent), roughly just two-thirds of the women depicted in the news stories had leadership positions. Moreover, the stories about women were more likely to focus on their personal qualities in addition to their professional ones compared with men.

Another study that examined the lead stories of such American news sources as CNN.com, FoxNews.com, and NYT.com (the *New York Times'* online version) found that almost six times as many men were quoted in news stories than women (Burke and Mazzarella 2008).

However, not all the news for women concerning the Internet and politics is bad. For example, while the comparative study undertaken by Hyun Jung Yun and her research colleagues found very few stories in which women were the news subjects of the articles, they did find that those pieces focused on women tended to avoid gender stereotypes and that women as news subjects were actually less open to criticism than men in their sample. Also, during the past several years, several notable political websites have been developed and edited by women, including the Huffington Post, founded in 2005 by Greek heiress-turned-liberal political activist Arianna Huffington and the Daily Beast, founded in 2009 by Tina Brown, the former editor of *Vanity Fair* and the *New Yorker*. ■

PROFILES OF POLITICAL INFLUENCE

Signe Wilkinson, Cartoonist

One of the few women today who serves as a political cartoonist for a major metropolitan newspaper, Signe Wilkinson was the first woman to win the Pulitzer Prize for cartooning in 1992 (Signe Wilkinson 2004).

Wilkinson began her career as a reporter for the *Daily Local News* in West Chester, Pennsylvania, but soon found that she was "drawing the people she was supposed to be reporting on." ("Background about Signe Wilkinson" n.d.). Soon after, she attended the Pennsylvania Academy of Fine Arts and landed her first full-time job cartooning with the *San Jose Mercury News* in 1982 (ibid.). Three years later, she became the political cartoonist for the *Philadelphia Daily News*, where she has drawn five political cartoons a week for close to 20 years.

Wilkinson herself notes the challenges that face women in this industry. She jokingly insists that the reason that 9.85 out of 10 political cartoonists are men is because of khaki:

> At the office, the cartoonists wear khaki slacks. At summer cartoonist conventions, it's khaki shorts. And for evening dinners, where they pick up their awards for the year's most insightful cartoon on problems of the misunderstood insurance industry, the cartoonist adds a tie and navy blue blazer to his khaki outfit. You can see why it's a tough arena for women to enter. We girls just don't do as much with khaki." (Wilkinson 1998, 1).

(Continued)

▶ PROFILES OF POLITICAL INFLUENCE (CONTINUED)

In a more serious vein, however, she says part of the problem is "group-draw." In other words, (often) male news editors seem most comfortable with humor that ranges from "Jay Leno all the way to David Letterman monologue material," which is often "puerile and pointless." (ibid.) Wilkinson believes that women often have a different sense of humor than men—one not favored by editorial staffers—resulting in fewer women being drawn to the profession. (In fact, she reports that most children who show her their work are boys, not girls.)

Yet Wilkinson notes that this was not always the case. Historically speaking, there were almost two dozen women suffragists active as political cartoonists, who viewed their cartooning as a tool of social change. Wilkinson finds inspiration from these women, noting today that "cartoons can fight for ideas, defend the downtrodden and, most important, use humor to subvert the status quo." (Wilkinson 1998, 2). Her hope is that an increasing number of women will become political cartoonists as more women enter politics.

For more examples of Signe Wilkinson's work, go to www.signetoons.com. ∎

Although the general public does not always watch the Sunday morning talk shows, read the op-ed sections, or go online to read political web-logs, each of these sources has influence with political elites and often provides a crucial source of political discussion. As the White House Project concludes, by leaving women out of these outlets, the "public perception that men have greater ability to address political topics persists" (ibid.). This perception is likely only enhanced by the fact that official sources used in the news stories from more traditional outlets, such as newspapers and television news, are overwhelmingly male (Armstrong 2004; Zoch and VanSlyke Turk; Project for Excellence in Journalism 2005).

Does the growth in the number of women journalists translate into different types of coverage, and coverage that potentially helps women's causes or women in politics? There is little consensus about such an effect. Many female reporters and politicians insist that the news has little gender bias. For example, there are few noticeable differences between men and women journalists when it comes to ranking news priorities (Weaver 1997). These findings reflect the strong socialization norms inherent in the journalism profession, taught at journalism schools and reinforced in newsrooms across the country. Most journalists, regardless of gender, work within the constraints of their news organizations and must meet the expectations of their employers, peers, and audiences (ibid.). Senator Nancy Kassebaum does not believe that having more women reporters makes a difference in the coverage of women because reporters still oversimplify issues, regardless of their gender: "They still pigeonhole and lump women together" (quoted in Braden 1996, 168). Moreover, some female politicians believe that because women reporters fight against stereotypes of weaknesses, they often are tougher on female politicians. Interviewed by scholar Maria Braden (1996), Geraldine Ferraro believed that female reporters often came down harder on her than male reporters: "They were trying to find themselves. A lot were torn because they were happy about my nomination but they had to prove themselves by being objective" (Braden 1996, 117).

Yet others insist that women journalists bring a different perspective to the news business and affect both the substance and style of political coverage, in part because women bring with them different life experiences than men. Many female reporters argue that their elevation to the newsrooms has resulted in coverage of issues of concern to women that heretofore were ignored by men, such as domestic violence, hormone replacement, and toxic shock syndrome. According to Rena Pederson, a reporter for the *Dallas Morning News*: "Women absolutely bring a different perspective to issues addressed on the editorial page. Without women's input, editorial pages would have been much slower to discuss battered women, child abuse, and rape. It isn't that men didn't care, but it wasn't their primary interest" (quoted in Mills 1997, 52). Moreover, this new emphasis by women on women's issues has allowed men, especially male editors, to be more open to stories that affect women than they used to be.

Others suggest that increasing numbers of female reporters have positively shaped the political climate for women, by bringing women as candidates into the mainstream of coverage (Mills 1997). Kahn and Goldenberg (1991b) found in one study that female reporters placed greater emphasis on the "female" issues, especially in their coverage of female candidates for U.S. Senate, which they argue could lead to more positive evaluations of female candidates. They conclude that an increase of women reporters "may be an important resource for female candidates running for electoral office" (196). Former Texas Governor Ann Richards believes that women reporters are more "in tune" with female politicians: "Women reporters pick up on body language and nuance, not just what you say but how you say it. They're much more sensitive to that" (Braden 1996, 166).

Studies also suggest that female reporters are more likely to use women as news sources in their stories, as the work of journalism professor Cory Armstrong demonstrates. Her content analysis of 18 American newspapers found that the overall frequency of male mentions in newspaper articles was nearly three times that of females (Armstrong 2004). She also found that the presence of a female writer in a story had a positive impact on the number of female sources mentioned in a story. Moreover, the presence of a female writer meant that female sources had a more prominent mention or emphasis in the story, such that women were featured more prominently near the beginning of the piece. However, she cautions that her research is preliminary and does not get at *why* women reporters have a bearing on the gender of news sources. It could be that the results may be driven by story types, as women reporters are often assigned more "soft news" stories as opposed to hard news. Nonetheless, Armstrong points out that source selection and placement are important and can affect perceptions of public status. She writes that "if males are continually used as knowledgeable sources and women are repeatedly underrepresented or misrepresented in news coverage, an inaccurate reflection of society will be presented" (*ibid.*, 140).

Although there is no consensus about the impact of more women journalists on political reporting, it is clear that women remain far behind when it comes to media management and ownership, where some say the root of power really lies. A recent study by the Annenberg Public Policy Center at the University of Pennsylvania of the 57 largest companies and conglomerates in entertainment, telecommunications, cable, and publishing found that fewer than one in five of their board members were women (Koss-Feder 2002). Moreover, women were even less likely to be directors and executives of these firms, making up just 12 percent of directors and 16 percent of executives of the 23 largest telecommunications and cable providers (ibid.). The lack of women at the top of these industries is a major inequity for an industry that markets half of its products to women. It is also an inequity that has led many feminists to begin their own "counterculture" publications (see *Paths to Power* box). And for those women who do break through the glass ceiling in the communications industry, they are still likely to earn less than men. A General Accounting Office report shows that in 2000, women managers in the communications field earned just 73 cents for each dollar earned by a male manager (Media Report to Women 2002a). In the newspaper industry, women hold only about 35 percent of newspaper management jobs, which is low considering that women in general hold 44 percent of managerial positions in the United States (Media Report to Women 2002b.) And fewer women are promoted to the top editorial positions of major newspapers. Journalist Kay Mills believes this is because of the tendency of men to hire and promote people just like themselves— "other white males from the same economic and cultural background" (Mills 1988, 334).

Long gone are the days of women reporters assigned strictly to society pages and to novelty news. Women now make up a significant portion of the news media business, from producers, reporters, bloggers, and on-air personalities, including political commentators who represent a wide variety of views. Having more women in these important positions will likely have some ramifications for women and politics, as female reporters are able to bring to view the sorts of issues that have often been overlooked by the male news establishment in the past, such as sex discrimination, sexual or physical abuse, and women's health concerns. Moreover, an increase in the number of women journalists likely means that female politicians are taken more seriously as well.

PATHS TO POWER

Feminist Media

Many feminists have routinely called for greater numbers of women to be involved in the mainstream media, from reporting to media ownership. However, other feminists have instead eschewed the mainstream media in favor of their own alternatives. Beginning with the women's movement in the 1960s, when reporters routinely ignored or demeaned the concerns of feminism, women's activists relied on their own alternative media to help spread the word about their causes (Douglas 1994). Feminist publications at this time ran the gambit, from the more professional works such as *Ms. Magazine* to the handcrafted newsletters of local activists.

One resource that has tracked feminist media both small and large has been the Women's Institute for Freedom of the Press, founded by the late Donna Allen in 1972. Allen believed that because women lack economic equality with men, they have had fewer opportunities to voice their experiences through the mass media, which is why Allen started an annual Index to Women's Media, to make alternative feminist publications better known (Beasley 1992). (This index is available online at www.wifp.org/DWM/DirectoryWomensMedia.html). Allen also believed that the mass media is run as a business, depriving individuals of their means to communicate on an equal basis—particularly women and other marginalized groups. The development of an alternative feminist media in Allen's mind would lead to a greater protection of the First Amendment and a healthier democracy (Beasley 1992).

In addition to providing an index of women's media, the Women's Institute for Freedom of the Press continues to promote a list of principles that it feels is consistent with feminist journalism. For example, it believes that men tend to define "news" as conflict and violence whereas women-owned media define news differently, seeking "to generate harmony and interconnection by taking care that there are works and images that nurture and affirm our wholeness" (Allen 1991, 36). In addition, it insists that the journalistic goal of women's media is "the effective use of media as an instrument of change," whereas male-owned media claim the goal of objectivity (ibid.). Focusing on the continuing struggle of the women's movement, the Women's Institute believes that unlike male-owned media, women-owned media are nonhierarchical and do not stress competition in the news business but rather cooperation (Allen 1991).

In the 1990s, the Internet allowed for the development of various publications by "third-wave" feminists. According to Baumgardner and Richards (2000), third-wave feminism shares with the generation of second-wave feminists the goals of legal, political, and social equality for women, although trying to appeal to young women who feel disenfranchised from older movement activists. Unlike second-wave feminists, third-wave feminism is much more comfortable being embedded in popular culture, citing MTV, the fashion industry, and television shows as being influential in their lives (Shugart, Waggoner,

(*Continued*)

and Hallstein 2001). While referencing popular culture, third-wave feminists use alternative forms of media, such as the Internet, art, radio programs, and their own in-house publications or zines (their term for "magazines") to "raise consciousness about, provide political commentary on, and resist and educate against racism, child abuse, rape, domestic violence, homophobia and heterosexism, ablism, fatism, environmental degradation, classism, the protection of healthcare rights, reproductive rights, and equity" (Garrison 2000, 141). One popular third-wave feminist group using alternative media to this purpose is Riot Grrrl, a young feminist subcultural movement that "combines feminist consciousness and punk aesthetics, politics, and style" (ibid.). Many activists in the movement believe that these third-wave publications will help raise feminist consciousness among younger women in the United States, who are often turned against feminism but not the goals or policies that it promotes. ■

CONCLUSION

In many cases, media coverage of women's involvement in politics has been skewed or incomplete, replete with stereotypes. Early mainstream media coverage of the women's movement in the 1960s, for example, often belittled the concerns of women activists. More recent coverage of feminism, in which feminists are often portrayed as "man-hating," bitter women, has led many Americans to reject the term outright (although not necessarily the goals of the movement).

As more women have entered the political arena, however, there have been improvements in both the substance and amount of media coverage of women politicians. By and large, most female politicians are taken seriously by the media. Nancy Pelosi, the first woman Speaker in the House, has received largely balanced media attention. However, subtle (and not-so-subtle) biases sometimes remain. Media coverage of former First Lady, Senator, and now Secretary of State Hillary Rodham Clinton has often captured both the not-so-subtle biases references to her cleavage, for example and subtle biases (her visit to the Congressional Caucus for Women's Issues featured in the style section of the *Washington Post*) that the media continue to exhibit in their treatment of women in politics. When mainstream journalists continue to talk about the appearance or family life of female politicians at greater rates than they do about male politicians, this holds women elected officials to a different standard than men. When the Sunday morning talk shows continue to invite more male politicians to appear on their programs, the public once again believes that men are better suited to a career in elective office.

Part of the problem may lie in the fact that women make up a minority of working journalists. Women journalists may be more sympathetic to the potential stereotypes that face women politicians and could help to avoid perpetuating them in their own coverage. In addition, women journalists have been credited with raising awareness of important social and political issues that face women, putting these concerns on the political agenda. The good news is that we are likely to find more women in this field in the future. Women now make up the majority of both undergraduate and graduate students in journalism programs.

REFERENCES

"A pedestal is as much . . . " 2004. http://womanshistory.about.com/cs/quotes/a/qu_g_steinem.htm. Accessed January 5, 2004.

AEI Speakers Bureau. n.d. "Helen Thomas." www.aeispeakers.com/speakerbio.php?SpeakerID=1002. Accessed June 2, 2010.

Allen, Donna. 1991. "Women News." *The Quill.* (May): 36–37. www.wifp.org/reportwomensmedia.html.

American Society of Newspaper Editors. 2009, "Diversity in Newspapers' Newsrooms: Newsroom Employment Census." www.asne.org/index.cfm?id=5660. (6 April). Accessed May 24, 2009.

Armstrong, Cory L. 2004. "The Influence of Reporter Gender on Source Selection in Newspaper Stories," *Journalism & Mass Communication Quarterly.* 81, no.1: 139–154.

Barakso, Maryann and Brian F. Schaffner. 2006. "Winning Coverage: News Media Portrayals of the Women's Movement, 1969–2004." *Harvard International Journal of Press/Politics.* 11, no. 4:22–44.

Barker-Plummer, Bernadette. 2000. "News as a Feminist Resource? A Case Study of the Media Strategies and Media Representation of the National Organization for Women, 1966–1980." pp. 121–159 in *Gender, Politics, and Communication,* ed. Annabelle Sreberny and Liesbet van Zoonen. Cresskill, NJ: Hampton Press, Inc.

Baumgardner, Jennifer, and Amy Richards. 2000. *Manifesta: Young Women, Feminism, and the Future.* New York: Farrar, Straus, and Giroux.

"Background About Signe Wilkinson." www.cartoonistgroup.com/properties/signe/about.php. Accessed March 3, 2004, 1.

Beasley, Maurine. 1992. "Donna Allen and the Woman's Institute: A Feminist Perspective on the First Amendment." *American Journalism 9*, nos. 3 and 4:154–166.

Becker, Lee B. 2003. "Gender Equality Elusive, Surveys Show." (15 December). www.freedomforum.org/templates/document.asp?documentID=17784.

Borquez, Julio, Edie N. Goldenberg, and Kim Fridkin Kahn. 1988. "Press Portrayals of the Gender Gap." pp. 124–148 in *The Politics of the Gender Gap: The Social Construction of Political Influence,* ed. Carol Mueller. Newbury Park, CA: Sage.

Braden, Maria. 1996. *Women Politicians and the Media.* Lexington: University Press of Kentucky.

Brewer, Paul R. and Timothy Macafee. 2007. "Anchors Away: Media Framing of Broadcast Television Network Evening News Anchors." *The Harvard International Journal of Press/Politics.* 12, no. 3: 3–19.

Brown, Ruth Murray. 2002. *For a "Christian America": A History of the Religious Right.* Amherst, NY: Prometheus Books.

Burke, Cindy, and Sharon R. Mazzarella. 2008. "A Slightly New Shade of Lipstick": Gendered Mediation in Internet News Stories." *Women's Studies in Communication.* 31, no. 3:395–418.

Burns, Lisa M. 2008. *First Ladies and the Fourth Estate: Press Framing of Presidential Wives.* DeKalb, IL: Northern Illinois University Press.

Cancian Francesca M., and Bonnie L. Ross. 1981. "Mass Media and the Woman's Movement: 1900–1977." *Journal of Applied Behavioral Science* 17, no. 1:9–26.

Carroll, Susan J., and Ronnee Schreiber. 1997. "Media Coverage of Women in the 103rd Congress." pp. 131–148 in *Women, Media, and Politics*, ed. Pippa Norris. New York: Oxford University Press.

Carroll, Susan J. 1999. "The Disempowerment of the Gender Gap: Soccer Moms and the 1996 Elections." *PS: Political Science & Politics.* 32(1): 7–11.

Catalyst. 2009. "Women in Media: Quick Takes." www.catalyst.org/publication/248/women-in-media. March.

CBS News. 2006. "Katie Couric Moves to CBS." April 5, 2006. Accessed online at www.cbsnews.com/stories/2006/04/05/national/main1472375.shtml.

Center for American Politics and Women. 1997. "The Gender Gap Voting Choices, Party Identification, and Presidential Performance Ratings." www.cawp.rutgers.edu.

Center for Media and Public Affairs. 2007. "Media Monitor: 2006 Year in Review." 21, no. 1: Winter 2007. Accessed online at www.cmpa.com/files/media_monitor/07winter.pdf.

Cook, Timothy. 1998. *Governing with the News: The News Media as a Political Institution.* Chicago: University of Chicago Press.

Costain, Anne, Richard Braunstein, and Heidi Berrgren. 1997. "Framing the Women's Movement." pp. 205–220 in *Women, Media, and Politics*, ed. Pippa Norris. New York: Oxford University Press.

Danini, Carmina. 2003. "Museum Honors Noted Columnist; Thomas Receives Woman of Achivement Award." *San Antonio Express-News* (17 September): 3B.

Douglas, Susan J. 1994. *Where the Girls Are: Growing Up Female with the Mass Media.* New York: Times Books.

Falk, Ariana. 1999. "Helen Thomas Describes Life at the White House." *Yale Daily News.* (18 November). www.yaledailynews.com.

Faludi, Susan. 1991. *Backlash: The Undeclared War Against American Women.* New York: Crown Publishers.

Finnegan, Margaret. 1999. *Selling Suffrage: Consumer Culture and Votes for Women.* New York: Columbia University Press.

Flexner, Eleanor. 1959. *Century of Struggle: The Woman's Rights Movement in the United States.* Cambridge: The Belknap Press of Harvard University Press.

Freeman, Jo. 1975. *The Politics of Women's Liberation.* New York: David McKay Company, Inc.

Gamson, William, and Gadi Wolsfeld. 1993. "Movements and Media as Interacting Systems." *Annals, AAPSS* 528 (July): 114–125.

Garrison, Ednie Kaeh. 2000. "U.S. Feminism-Grrrl Style! Youth (Sub) Cultures and the Technologies of the Third Wave." *Feminist Studies* 26, no. 1:141–170.

Gitlin, Todd. 1980. *The Whole World is Watching: Mass Media and the Making and Unmaking of the New Left.* Berkeley: University of California Press.

Givhan, Robin. 2007. "Hillary Clinton's Tentative Dip Into New Neckline Territory." *Washington Post.* (20 July): C1.

Goodman, Ellen. 2003. "It's About Gender, Not Race." *Boston Globe* (9 November). www/boston.com/news/politics/primaries/new_hampshire/articles/2003/11/09/its_about_gender_not_race.

Gugliotta, Guy. 1992. "'Year of the Woman' Becomes Reality as Record Number Win Seats." *Washington Post* (4 November): A30.

Guthrie, Melissa. 2008. "Couric to Leave Anchor Desk Soon." *Broadcasting & Cable.* (14 April). 3, 53.

Harp, Dustin, and Mark Tremayne. 2006. "The Gendered Blogosphere: Examining Inequality Using Network and Feminist Theory." *Journalism & Mass Communication Quarterly*. 83, no. 2:247–264.

"Helen Thomas Blasts Iraq War as 'Immoral'." 2003. *WorldNetDaily* (25 November). www.worldnetdaily.com/news.

"Helen Thomas: Doyenne of the Washington Press Corp." Fall 2001. www.agingresearch. org/living_longer/fall01/print_legend.html.

Hernandez, Debra Gersh. 1996. "Women and Front-Page News." *Editor & Publisher* 12:37.

"Hillary Clinton Visits Minority Caucus." 1993. *Washington Post* (3 March): A5.

Huddy, Leonie. 1997. "Feminists and Feminism in the News." pp. 183–204 in *Women, Media, and Politics*, ed. Pippa Norris. New York: Oxford University Press.

Iyengar, Shanto and Donald R. Kinder. 1987. *News that Matters: Television and American Opinion*. Chicago: University of Chicago Press.

Kahn, Kim Fridkin, and Edie Goldenberg. 1991a. "The Media: Obstacle or Ally of Feminists?" *Annals, AAPSS* 515 (May): 104–113.

———. 1991b. "Women Candidates in the News: An Examination of Gender Differences in U.S. Senate Campaign Coverage." *Public Opinion Quarterly* 55:180–199.

Kedrowski, Karen. 1996. *Media Entrepreneurs and the Media Enterprise in the U.S. Congress*. Hampton, NJ: Hampton Press.

Kedrowski, Karen and Rachel Gower. 2009. "Gender and the Public Speakership: News Media Coverage of Speaker Nancy Pelosi." Paper presented at the Southern Political Science Association's Annual Meeting, New Orleans (January).

Kirkpatrick, Jeane J. 1974. *Political Woman*. New York: Basic Books.

Klemesrud, Judy. 1971. "In Small Town USA, Women's Liberation Is Either a Joke or a Bore." *New York Times* (22 March): 54.

Koss-Feder, Laura. 2002. "Study: Few Women at the Top of Media Companies." Women's E-News. 1–3. www.womensenews.org/article.cfm/dyn/aid/1048/context/archive.

Kurtz, Howard. 2005. "For One Ed, Strong Op: Susan Estrich Addresses the Male." *Washington Post* (7 March): C1.

Ladd, Everett Carll. 1997. "Media Framing of the Gender Gap." pp. 113–128 in *Women, Media, and Politics*, ed. Pippa Norris. New York: Oxford University Press.

Lippman, Walter. 1922. *Public Opinion*. New York: Simon & Schuster. pp. 36–43 reprinted in Doris Graber, ed. 2000. *Media Power in Politics*. Washington, D.C.: CQ Press.

Lumsden, Linda J. 1997. *Rampant Women: Suffragists and the Right of Assembly*. Knoxville: University of Tennessee Press.

———. 2000. "Beauty and the Beasts: Significance of Press Coverage of the 1913 National Suffrage Parade." *Journalism and Mass Communications Quarterly* 77, no. 3:593–612.

Ma, Lybi. 2002. "Therapist in Chief Laura Bush." *Psychology Today* 35, no. 6:34–38.

Mansbridge, Jane. 1986. *Why We Lost the ERA*. Chicago: University of Chicago Press.

McGlen, Nancy, and Karen O'Connor. 1998. *Women, Politics, and American Society*, 2nd ed. Upper Saddle River, NJ: Prentice Hall.

Media Matters for America. 2008. "Women, minorities, autistic children: Conservative radio's vitriol not reserved for Obama." www.mediamatters.org/print/research/200811130002. 13 November.

———. 2009. "Discussing Breast Implants, Limbaugh again claims 'feminism was established so as to allow unattractive women easier access to the mainstream of society.'" www.mediamatters.org/print/clips/200904100020. 10 April.

Media Report to Women. 2002a. "Another Glass Ceiling: Women in Communications Losing Ground" 30, no. 1:1.

_____. 2002b. "Progress Stalled for Newspaper Women; Greater Numbers But Not Greater Advancement" 30, no. 1:1.

_____. 2003a. "Keep an Eye on Coverage of Democratic Leader Pelosi, Other Women in Politics" 31, no. 1:2.

_____. 2003b. "Media Tenor Study: U.S. Television News Ignores Women; Only 14 Percent Depicted Are Female" 31, no. 2:1.

_____. 2007. "Women and Media: Still Like Gazing Into Funhouse Mirrors." 35, no. 3:23.

_____. 2008. "Gender Bias in Clinton Coverage: Journalists, Bloggers React." 36, no. 1: 1–2.

Merida, Kevin. 2008. "A Defining Moment; In Denver, Michele Obama Takes a Deep Breath and Steps Up to the Podium and Her Supporting Role." *Washington Post* (26 August): A19.

Mills, Kay. 1988. *A Place in the News: From the Women's Pages to the Front Page.* New York: Dodd, Mead, and Company.

_____. 1997. "What Difference Do Women Journalists Make?" pp. 41–55 in *Women, Media, and Politics,* ed. Pippa Norris. New York: Oxford University Press.

Newsweek. 1971. "Gloria Steinem: The New Woman." 78, no. 7:51–55 (16 August).

Niven, David, and Jeremy Zilber. 2001. "'How Does She Have Time for Kids and Congress?' Views on Gender and Media Coverage from House Offices." *Women & Politics* 23, no. 1/2:147–165.

Norris, Pippa ed. 1997. *Women, Media, and Politics.* New York: Oxford University Press.

North, Sandie. 1970. "Reporting on the Movement." *Atlantic Monthly,* Volume 225 (March) pp. 105t.

Overholser, Geneva. 2001. "Where Are the Women's Voices?" www.maynardije.irg/columns/guests/020514_blethen/011102_overholser. Accessed September 27, 2001.

Project for Excellence in Journalism. 2005. "The Gender Gap: Women are Still Missing as Sources for Journalists." 23 May. www.journalism.org/node/141. Accessed May 29, 2009.

Rainie, Lee. 2005. "The State of Blogging." *Pew Internet & American Life Project.* http://pewInternet.org/pdfs/PIP_blogging_data.pdf.

Rivers, Caryl. 1996. *Slick Spins and Fractured Facts: How Cultural Myths Distort the News.* New York: Columbia University Press.

Ross, Ishbel. 1936. *Ladies of the Press: The Story of Women in Journalism by an Insider.* New York: Harper & Brothers.

Ryan, Kathleen, Hillary Lake and Joy Chavez Mapaye. 2008. "Newsqueens? A Comparative Analysis of Women's Roles in Network News." Paper Presented at the annual meeting of the International Communication Association, Montreal, Canada. May 21. www.allacademic.com/meta/p232203_index.html.

Scharrer, Erica, and Kim Bissell. 2000. "Overcoming Traditional Boundaries: The Role of Political Activity in Media Coverage of First Ladies." *Women & Politics* 21, no. 1:55–83.

Sellers, Patricia. 2003. "Power: Do Women Really Want It?" *Fortune Magazine* 148(8): 80–100 (13 October).

Shugart, Helene A., Catherine Egley Waggoner, and D. Lynn O'Brien Hallstein. 2001. "Mediating Third-Wave Feminism: Appropriation as Postmodern Media Practice." *Critical Studies in Media Communication* 18, no. 2:194–210.

Sigel, Roberta. 1996. *Ambition and Accommodation: How Women View Gender Relations*. Chicago: University of Chicago Press.

"Signe Wilkinson." http://thegalleriesatmoore.org/publications/cartoons/signe.shtml. Accessed March 3, 2004.

Weaver, David. 1997. "Women as Journalists." pp. 21–40 in *Women, Media, and Politics*, ed. Pippa Norris. New York: Oxford University Press.

"While Laura Bush Suddenly Became a Woman's Magazine Superstar." 2002. *Media Industry Newsletter* 55, no. 2:1.

Whitaker, Lois Duke. 1999. *Women in Politics: Outsiders or Insiders?* 3rd edition. Upper Saddle River, NJ: Prentice Hall.

The White House Project. 2002. "Who's Talking? An Analysis of Sunday Morning Talk Shows." www.thewhitehouseproject.org/research/who_talking_overview.html.

White House Transcript 2009 Dinner Speech. 2009. http://www.whca.net/2009dinnerspeech.htm. Accessed May 21, 2009.

Wilkinson, Signe. 1998. "The Rare Female Cartoonist: If Only She Wore Khaki." The American Editor, (December) www.asne.org, 1.

Winfield, Betty Houchin. 1994. "'Madame President': Understanding a New Kind of First Lady." *Media Studies Journal* 8, no. 2:59–71.

———. 1997. "The First Lady, Political Power, and the Media: Who Elected Her Anyway?" pp. 166–179 in *Women, Media, and Politics*, ed. Pippa Norris. New York: Oxford University Press.

Witt, Linda, Karen M. Paget, and Glenna Matthews. 1994. *Running as a Woman: Gender and Power in American Politics*. New York: The Free Press.

Wostendiek, John. 1992. "Women's Gains Are Historic." *Philadelphia Inquirer* (5 November): A1.

Yun, Hyun Jung, Monica Postelnicu, Nadia Ramotour, and Lynda Lee Kaid. 2007. "Where is she? Coverage of women in online news magazines/*Journalism Studies* 8(6):930–947.

Zoch, Lynn and Judy VanSlyke Turk. 1998. "Women Making News: Gender as a Variable in Source Selection and Use." *Journalism & Mass Communication Quarterly* 75, no.1:762–75.

Women as Candidates for Elective Office

INTRODUCTION: NORTH CAROLINA'S 2008 SENATE RACE

In one of the most closely watched elections of the 2008 election cycle, Democrat Kay Hagan unseated first term incumbent and former presidential candidate Elizabeth Dole for one of North Carolina's U.S. Senate seats. It was the only Senate race in 2008 that featured two women running against one another and was only the eighth such race in the history of the United States. It was also the first time in the history of U.S. Senate elections that a female challenger unseated a female incumbent (CAWP 2008b). What was also remarkable about the race was that both of the women running had accumulated sufficient political experience to justify labeling them career politicians, and, unlike many previous races featuring women candidates, the race was extraordinarily expensive and negative, with both sides launching personal attacks on the other.[1]

Kay Hagan and Elizabeth Dole diverge in many ways from "typical" female candidates but they also share many things in common with the women who preceded them in pursuit of political office. They certainly have come a long way since Elizabeth Cady Stanton made history in 1866 as the very first woman to run for United States Congress (Griffith 1984, 125). For one, both Hagan and Dole could cast ballots for themselves. Stanton could not do so since women were barred from voting and would not gain the right for another 53 years.

This chapter examines female candidates' experiences, challenges, and opportunities as they contest political office in the United States. More specifically, it addresses the following questions: Who runs for office? Why are women less likely to run than men? How do women deal with voter stereotypes and media coverage that sometimes turns sexist when they are on the campaign trail?

---

[1]Much scholarship finds that female candidates tend to shy away from personal attacks and instead challenge the issue positions of their opponents (Benze and DeClerq 1985; Bystrom and Kaid 2002; Fox 1997; Procter et al. 1994).

PROFILES OF POLITICAL INFLUENCE

Elizabeth Cady Stanton: A Political Pioneer

Elizabeth Cady Stanton is probably most well known for hosting the 1848 Women's Rights Convention in Seneca Falls, New York, and for drafting the Declaration of Sentiments and Resolutions, a document closely modeled after the U.S. Declaration of Independence in its insistence that women, as well as men, are created equal. Today, she is honored for her tireless work on behalf of American women at the Women's Rights National Historical Park in Seneca Falls, New York, where visitors can tour her historic home and the church where the 1848 women's rights meetings were held.

She is far less well known as the very first woman to run for the U.S. Congress (Griffith 1984, 125). In 1866, Elizabeth Cady Stanton made her historic bid for a seat to represent what was then the Eighth Congressional District of New York in the U.S. House of Representatives, some six years before Victoria Woodhull made history as the very first woman to run for the U.S. presidency. Although states prohibited anyone except white, propertied men from voting, they imposed no such gender-based criteria on those seeking public office. Thus, Stanton could legally run for public office, as she did, but could not legally vote for her own candidacy! Stanton surely would have been disappointed to learn that it took another 50 years for Jeannette Rankin to become the first woman elected to the U.S. Congress and an additional 12 years more before the first woman was ever elected to represent her home state of New York. ■

To answer these questions, the chapter is divided into two sections: the various factors that influence political women's decisions to run for office and the types of challenges they face while on the campaign trail. In addition, special attention is devoted to the historic presidential and vice presidential candidacies of both Hillary Clinton and Sarah Palin, and the ways in which each woman attempted to convince the American public that she was the right woman for the job.

RUNNING FOR OFFICE IN THE UNITED STATES: WHO DECIDES TO RUN?

There are hundreds of thousands of elected offices up for grabs in the United States. At minimum, each state elects a governor and various other statewide officials,[2] numerous state legislators, hundreds of city council members and

---

[2]The most common elective statewide positions include lieutenant governor, attorney general, treasurer, and secretary of state.

county commissioners, and countless more school board members. In addition, each state sends two representatives to the U.S. Senate, anywhere from 1 to 53 members to the U.S. House of Representatives, and selects officials for a variety of additional offices, ranging from state judges to sheriffs to dogcatchers. Although less than 1 percent of the U.S. population ever runs for elective office (Fox and Lawless 2004), remarkably fewer women than men decide to throw their hat into the ring.

In general, the higher the level of political office sought, the larger the difference between the proportion of women and men who decide to run. At the highest level, in her race for the U.S. Presidency in 2008, Hillary Clinton broke the political glass ceiling with her extraordinary bid for the Democratic nomination. Running alongside Clinton in the primaries were seven Democratic men and seven Republican men, outnumbering her by a margin of 14:1. In primaries for U.S. Senate races in 2008, female candidates were outnumbered by male candidates by about 10 to 1. Also in 2008, women made up nearly 20 percent of House primary candidates, their highest percentage to date. But even so, men outnumbered them by nearly a 5:1 margin.[3]

Men greatly outnumber women as candidates for state legislative and municipal offices, too (Seltzer, Newman, and Leighton 1997). It is only at the very lowest levels, for school board seats, that the numbers of female candidates come close to the number of male candidates. In the late 1990s, about 40 percent of candidates for school board seats in the United States were women (Deckman 2003). Why do women lag so far behind? Some 80 years after women won the right to vote, why is it that they are more reluctant than men to try their hand at politics? Various theories have been advanced over the years to explain why women continue to lag behind men:

1. Women are simply less interested and less politically ambitious than their male colleagues.
2. Women's career choices and professional backgrounds are less likely than men's to facilitate making a run for political office.
3. Women's roles as wives and mothers delay their candidacies, narrowing the pool of potential female candidates.
4. Discrimination from the political parties effectively discourages those who have an interest in participating.

Let us look at each of these theories in more detail.

WHY WOMEN ARE LESS LIKELY TO RUN: 4 THEORIES

1. Political Engagement, Interest, and Ambition

Are women actually less interested in politics than men? Less politically ambitious? National surveys of American voters suggest as much, even if the differences are slight. Indeed, when asked how interested they are in politics,

---

[3]Many thanks to Barbara Palmer and Dennis Simon for sharing these data with us.

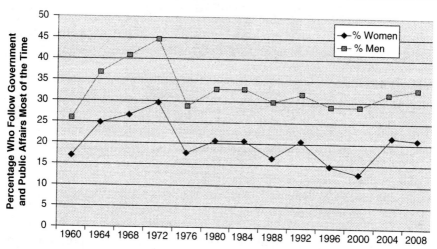

FIGURE 5.1

Political Interest Among Women and Men

Source: The American National Election Studies. Data accessed online at www.umich.edu/~nes/nesguide/
2ndtable/tbd_5_4.htm. Updated with data from the 2008 NES.

more men consistently claim to follow public affairs most of the time (see Figure 5.1). Since 1960 an average of 12 percent more men than women indicate that they pay attention to public affairs most of the time. Perhaps because they are less interested in politics, women are also less politically knowledgeable than men with similar educational backgrounds (Delli Carpini and Keeter, 1996; Verba, Burns and Schlozman, 1997). Because citizens are not likely to run if they are not interested in public affairs, we may see women continue to lag behind men until their interest levels are commensurate.

Why are women less interested in politics than men? Scholars theorize that sex-role socialization is partly to blame (Verba, Burns and Schlozman 1997; Conway, Steuernagel and Ahern 2005). If politics is perceived as a man's game, then girls and women may simply write it off as uninteresting, pay little attention, and show little interest. Or, even if girls and women are somewhat interested, the dearth of women in politics may signal that politics is simply not for them. Until 2008, very few women had been highly visible in U.S. politics at any one given time. But in 2008, Hillary Clinton made her historic bid for the Democratic nomination for the U.S. Presidency, Sarah Palin ran as the first female vice presidential candidate on the Republican ticket, Congresswoman Nancy Pelosi served as Speaker of the House of Representatives, and Condoleezza Rice served as Secretary of State. All of these women appeared regularly on television and in the print media and were highly visible to even the most casual observer of U.S. politics. Recent research suggests that women's engagement in politics and likely future participation increase when they see highly qualified women running for office (Campbell and Wolbrecht

2006; Atkeson 2003; Verba, Burns and Scholzman 1997). With four such high profile women in the public eye, perhaps we will see increased political interest among women in the near future.

Political Ambition What about political ambition? Even among politically astute individuals, interest alone does not necessarily translate into the desire to hold public office. How do politically interested women compare to similar men? Early research suggested that women were less politically ambitious than men. Time and again, these studies demonstrated that politically active women simply evinced less desire to run for higher office or picked much more modest, lower-level offices when they did indicate a desire to move ahead in politics (Bledsoe and Herring 1990; Burt-Way and Kelly 1992; Carroll 1985; Costantini 1990; Costantini and Bell 1984; Costantini and Craik 1972; Farah 1976; Jennings and Farah 1981; Jennings and Thomas 1968; Kirkpatrick 1976; Sapiro and Farah 1980). Whereas men aspire to the presidency and United States Congress, women set their sights much lower, such as city council or state legislative seats.

Why might this be the case? As told by many politically active women, part of their reluctance stems from the fear of being summarily dismissed by voters. Even when well qualified to run, women often question their own skills and abilities, convincing themselves that they are not worthy candidates (Fox and Lawless 2004; Keyserling 1998; Witt, Paget, and Matthews 1994). When former South Carolina state legislator Harriet Keyserling was considering her first run for office, for a seat on the local county council, she doubted her own qualifications, explaining "I conjured up so many reasons not to run—I was shy, I was afraid of speaking in public, I didn't know enough about government or the men who ran it. These are pretty typical reasons most women give for not running for office. They would rather work for candidates, stuffing envelopes and making phone calls, than be candidates" (Keyserling 1998, 47).

Congresswoman Louise Slaughter's apprehensions were slightly different. After winning her first term to the New York State Assembly in 1982, the incumbent serving in her U.S. House district decided to retire, leaving an open seat up for grabs. With incumbency reelection rates nearing 90 percent in most years for House seats, an open seat presents a golden opportunity for those with political aspirations. Slaughter recognized as much but decided not to pursue the seat. As she explained, it was a mixture of her own fears about losing her newly acquired seat and concerns about whether or not voters would consider her qualified for the position (Fowler and McClure 1989). Having just been elected to her first term in the New York State Assembly, Slaughter felt uncomfortable running for Congress so soon thereafter, worried that she might jeopardize her young legislative career. A few years later, she did run for and win the congressional seat and has served ever since.

Slaughter's apprehension is fairly typical for political women, who generally spend more time in lower-level offices or gaining other relevant political experience before pursuing higher offices (Burt-Way and Kelly 1992; Carroll and

Strimling 1983). As political consultant Cathy Allen tells it, "Men decide to run in two hours after someone in the law firm says, 'You've got to run,'. . . The average woman takes two years to decide. She'll wait until she has the perfect campaign manager, the right 17 endorsements, until she's gotten down to a perfect size 10 and the kids are out of school" (Collins 1998).

Scholars theorize that female candidates put off running for longer periods of time in order to build up their confidence, to develop new skills, and to master their current environment before pursuing new challenges. This was certainly the case for Slaughter. Although she very much desired the U.S. House seat, she also explained that she simply lacked the confidence to contest the seat for the higher office. For whatever reason, this lack of confidence or skepticism about their own qualifications is also more common for women seeking office than for men (Fox and Lawless 2004; Keyserling 1998). A recent study indicates that junior high girls are more confident in their political abilities than boys, but the pattern is reversed for senior high school students, college students, and adults (Elder 2004).

Further, many politically active women never throw their hat into the ring because of their own perceived lack of qualifications. While most previous research examined the ambitions of women and men already holding public office, new scholarship more closely examines individuals within the "eligibility pool," those occupations that most frequently serve as stepping-stones to political office (law, business, education, and the government and non-profit sectors). In their path-breaking study of more than 2,000 men and women in the eligibility pool, Lawless and Fox (2008) find women are significantly less likely than men to plan to run for political office sometime in the future. Even when these women are highly qualified by all objective standards, they are still more likely than men to cite their own qualifications as a reason not to run. For men, the perception of their own qualifications weighs less heavily on their decision to run.

Sometimes positive encouragement from supporters, such as party officials, advocacy groups, friends, and family is just the boost women need to jump-start their candidacies (Fox and Lawless 2004; Fowler and McClure 1989; Margolies-Mezvinsky 1994; Witt, Paget, and Matthews 1994). Pat Schroeder, first elected to the U.S. House in 1972 from the state of Colorado, got her start in politics after her husband came home from a political meeting and told her she had been identified as a potential candidate to challenge Denver's first-term incumbent in the U.S. House (Schroeder 1998). Schroeder admits that neither she nor her husband thought she had a prayer of winning. After winning her primary, she went on to defeat the incumbent to become the first woman to serve in Congress while raising young children. Ann Wynia, a six-term state legislator who made history as the first woman Democratic majority leader for the Minnesota House of Representatives, first seriously considered running for the state legislature when her representative announced he was not seeking reelection. Although Wynia had always been interested in running, she credits a phone call from a friend as the support she needed to commit to running. She won the race and served for 12 years before running unsuccessfully for a U.S. Senate seat in 1994 (Watkins and Rothchild 1996). For both Schroeder and Wynia, essential encouragement came from their family and friends. In the United States, we also expect political parties to play this role. But as many scholars have found, women are less likely to be recruited by the parties than are men (Lawless and Fox 2008; Niven 1998, 2006; Sanbonmatsu 2006).

Stepping into this void, a variety of organizations host training seminars and schools to provide training opportunities for women interested in running for office. One of the largest is the White House Project, an organization originally founded with the goal of electing a woman to the White House by 2008 ("A Woman's Place is in the White House" 1998). Today they focus more broadly on giving women the tools they need to mount competitive candidacies. Since 2007, they have hosted nearly 20 trainings in seven different states through their *Go Run!* program and have set a goal of training 36,800 women by 2013 (see Table 5.1 for more information about campaign training schools geared toward women).

As this section makes clear, the confidence barrier can definitely be overcome, but women seemingly need more support and encouragement from others and take a longer time to realize their own potential before they commit to running. Until this changes, we will likely see fewer women than men running for office.

Political Motivation and Reasons for Running Candidates typically cite a variety of reasons for becoming involved in politics: a sense of civic duty and commitment to public service, a desire to advance a particular cause or issue, and personal ambition or the desire to advance one's own career. Both male and female candidates usually mention a combination of these goals. Many studies indicate that women are much more likely to run out of concern for a particular issue and less likely to cite personal ambition as something that motivates them (Carroll and Strimling 1983; Darcy, Welch, and Clark 1994; Fox 1997; Van Hightower 1977; van Assendelft and O'Connor 1994). The 1992 congressional elections are a case in point. Professor Anita Hill came forth in the fall of 1991 with charges that Clarence Thomas, her former boss and pending nominee for a seat on the United States Supreme Court, had sexually harassed her while they worked together at the Equal Employment Opportunity Commission. In the Senate hearings that followed, many women were appalled by the way in which the all-male Senate Judiciary committee grilled Professor Anita Hill. For many women, the committee hearings demonstrated just how out of touch sitting members of Congress were and just how few women held office. Many of the women who ran for office in 1992 credit the Thomas–Hill hearings as the impetus that convinced them to run (Palley 1993; Witt, Paget, and Matthews 1994; Margolies-Mezvinsky 1994).

On the other hand, a recent study of school board candidates found that greater numbers of men than women identified policy-related goals as something that motivated them to run (Deckman 2003). To be sure, majorities of

TABLE 5.1

Campaign Training Schools and Seminars for Women

Organization	Campaign Training Details	website
White House Project	*Go Lead!* Program trains women in the nuts and bolts of running a political campaign. Offers one and two-day programs on a regular basis.	www.whitehouseproject.org
EMILY's List	Runs Political Opportunity Program (POP) for pro-choice Democratic women.	www.emilyslist.org/programs/pop
WISH List	Runs the Tillie Fowler Campaign Training Program for pro-choice Republican women.	www.thewishlist.org/
The Women's Campaign School at Yale University	Nonpartisan, issue-neutral campaign training program for women. Five-day comprehensive training offered in the summer.	www.wcsyale.org
Jo Ann Davidson Leadership Institute	Hosts an eight-month long program to "encourage and train women in business and civic leadership to assume more prominent roles, elected or appointed, in government and in the Republican Party."	www.jadleadershipinstitute.com

men and women expressed the desire to influence government policy as a key motivator. These findings run counter to the preceding findings and suggest that the level of office may affect a candidate's reasons for running. The studies highlighted previously all examine women running for higher offices, such as state legislatures and the United States Congress. As such, it may be that women's and men's reasons for running diverge to a greater degree when running for higher office.

Some female candidates get political experience by working on a particular cause and decide that the next logical step is to run for elected office (Mandel 1981; Tolchin and Tolchin 1973; Margolies-Mezvinsky 1994; Witt, Paget, and Matthews 1994). Since the fight for suffrage, women have devoted their time and energy to a variety of social causes, often selecting roles that complement their traditional roles in the family. As Harriet Woods, former candidate and president of the National Women's Political Caucus, puts it, "Most women begin with community concerns, not ambition" (Collins 1998). Women often become involved in politics through a desire to do something for their family or to work on a policy issue of particular concern and interest to women or the family (Burkett 1998; Flammang 1997; Fox 1997; Stanwick 1983). Women's historical links to such causes may also explain why they are more likely to run for office at the local level than at other levels. Indeed, if they are prompted to become active by issues that concern their family or home, local office likely affords greater opportunity to do so.

As this section demonstrates, the political ambitions of women and men do appear to be slightly different. Compared to men, female citizens repeatedly indicate less political interest and political knowledge, women officeholders and party faithful aspire to lower offices and have less desire to run for higher office, and different factors prompt them to run in the first place. This does not mean that women will never have the same political desires as men but that we should view their political behavior through slightly different lenses.

2. The Eligibility Pool: Women's Professional Qualifications for Office

A second explanation for women's reluctance to pursue political office is that they are less likely than men to possess professional and occupational qualifications that facilitate running for office, thus making up a smaller portion of the pool of most eligible candidates for office. Once women start amassing the career backgrounds and professional qualifications common among officeholders, the theory suggests, they will begin running for and winning offices in greater numbers (Palmer and Simon 2008). They will start with lower-level offices, such as school board, city council, and the state legislature, and then gradually work their way up the hierarchy.

But the American workforce remains remarkably segregated by sex, with the majority of men and women employed in different occupations (Lewis 1996). Further, fewer women than men work full-time. Because more women have either been absent from the workforce or have traditionally worked in low-status occupations offering fewer opportunities to transition to elected office, the theory suggests that we will only see an increase in the number of female candidates once their occupational choices afford them greater opportunity to do so (Carroll 1994; Darcy, Welch and Clark 1994).

What positions typically serve as springboards to elective office? The professions of law and business are disproportionately represented in the United States Congress and in state legislatures (Stanley and Neimi 2001; Hawkings and Nutting 2003; Davidson and Oleszek 2000; Niven 1998). But men have always outnumbered women in high-ranking legal positions. Men today make up 67 percent of all lawyers in the United States while women dominate the ranks of legal assistants (88 percent are women) (U.S. Bureau of the Census 2007, table 596). Women are steadily increasing their share of the legal profession and now receive nearly half of all law degrees awarded in the United States (U.S. Bureau of the Census 2002; U.S. Department of Education 2001).

Although women are making steady inroads into "feeder" occupations, they are still far more likely to be employed in traditionally feminine areas, such as nursing and teaching (U.S. Department of Labor 2001). And so it is not particularly surprising that female candidates more often come from these backgrounds than do their male counterparts. More than 20 years ago, Susan J. Carroll (1994) found teaching elementary and secondary education the most frequent occupation among female political candidates, with the professions of nursing and social work more common professions than law. Although changing somewhat, a fair number of female candidates continue to come from traditionally female occupations. Even when running for school board seats, where we would expect high numbers of both women and men from education backgrounds, more female educators than male educators run (Deckman 2003). Of course, women are more likely to be teachers in the first place; the U.S. Census Bureau (2004) reports that 71 percent of teachers in 2000 were women. The very first African-American woman ever elected to the United States Congress, Shirley Chisholm, was a nursery school teacher and director of a child-care center before she ran for the New York state legislature (Gill 1997). Both Congresswomen Lois Capps and Eddie Bernice Johnson spent some 20 years in the field of nursing before they were elected to the U.S. House of Representatives (Gill 1997), and U.S. Senator Barbara Mikulski was a social worker before she first ran for city council in Baltimore.

Besides different occupational training and experience, fewer women than men work full-time. However, much research reports that women often acquire political skills and know-how through volunteer work or through an association with a women's organization or other nonprofit organization (Darcy, Welch, and Clark 1994; Kirkpatrick 1974; Merritt 1977; Van Hightower 1977). In her study of women's political life in Santa Clara County, California, Janet Flammang (1997) notes that many elected women were previously active on educational issues (PTA, school boards, protesting the lack of traffic signals near public schools) and neighborhood issues (conservation, safe bike paths near the schools, neighborhood development issues, etc.). Thus, even if they do not have continuous experience in the paid workforce, women can and often do develop political skills through other channels.

3. Family Constraints

The third explanation posits that situational constraints effectively diminish women's likelihood of putting themselves forward as candidates. As Ruth Mandel (1981) explains,

> The political world does not work on the steady, weekly routine of an office, factory, or retail business schedule. Mothering requires predictable scheduling, whereas politicking requires availability for erratic scheduling. (p. 86)

Holding public office is notoriously time-consuming, can demand long and irregular hours, and can require trips away from the home district to conduct legislative business in the state or national capitol. Because American women continue to bear a disproportionate share of childrearing and housekeeping responsibilities for their families, many women simply postpone their political careers until their children are grown and have left the household. Although men certainly face family constraints in their pursuit of public office, they do not appear to weigh as heavily on men's decisions to run as women's (Carroll and Strimling 1983; Elder 2004). For men considering a run for public office, having small children at home is not all that atypical. For women, however, it is fairly atypical. Political women are far less likely than political men to have small children at home (Carroll and Strimling 1983).

Former Congresswoman Patricia Schroeder campaigned for her U.S. House seat and subsequently served in office while raising small children. Besides voters' persistent questions about her motives and ability to serve while simultaneously fulfilling her role as mother, other political women were not always so enthusiastic about her choice. When she first met Bella Abzug, an outspoken feminist and sitting congresswoman from New York City, Abzug said to her, "I hear you have little kids . . . You won't be able to do this job" (Schroeder 1998, 24). More recently, Representative Mary Bono's mother-in-law publicly lamented that her grandchildren "would essentially become orphans open to abuse by strangers" if Ms. Bono was successful in her bid to fill the seat vacated by her late husband Sonny Bono (Henneberger 1998). Not surprisingly, then, women are usually older than men when they first become candidates for office (Bernstein 1986; Burrell 1998).

The family constraints theory may help explain why women run far more often for seats on school boards and city councils than for state legislative or congressional seats. Local offices are closer to home and are often part-time positions with more flexible hours. For example, many city councils meet once a week or less, and school boards typically meet even less frequently. As such, women considering a run for public office may decide to begin locally so as to more easily balance their work and family responsibilities.

4. Discrimination by Parties

The fourth explanation for women's underrepresentation in the ranks of political candidates in the United States is that the political parties discriminate against female candidates, effectively discouraging them from running. In fact, early research suggested that female candidates faced notable discrimination from the parties, which dismissed their political ambitions, recruited them to serve disproportionately as "sacrificial lambs," and failed to provide meaningful support once their campaigns got underway.

When asked, female officeholders generally report positive experiences with their party, indicating similar recruitment experiences, and comparable encouragement and financial assistance when compared to men (Carroll and Strimling 1983). But these women were successful in their bids for elected office, so generalizing from their experiences is somewhat problematic. Other political women report that party leaders actively discouraged them from running (Fox 1997; Mandel 1981; Niven 1998; Tolchin and Tolchin 1973). Many women tell stories about approaching their party to seek support, only to be told that the timing was not right or that the party had someone else in mind for the position. As Tammy Baldwin, elected in 1998 as the first female congresswoman from the state of Wisconsin, tells it,

> I was projected to lose every competitive race I entered. People told me that I wouldn't be able to win, that I should get out of the race to ensure a clean primary, or that I should step aside to ensure that a candidate who "could win in the general election" would win our primary. Well, I proved them all wrong, having won every race I was supposed to lose.   ("No Limits for Women," 2002, 12)

Why would the parties be reluctant to recruit and support female candidates? David Niven (1998) suggests that unconscious discrimination on the part of party elites is to blame. As he argues, party leaders have a tendency to select candidates who look and behave like themselves. Because women traditionally enter politics through community service or activism in local organizations, their qualities and credentials are often discounted by male party elites, who more often rise through the ranks of the party leadership or enter politics through business connections.

Furthermore, women have traditionally played supporting rather than leadership roles within the party ranks (Fowlkes, Perkins, and Rinehart 1979; Porter and Matasar 1974; Carroll 1994; Watkins and Rothchild 1996; Tolchin and Tolchin 1973), making them relatively invisible to party elites when it comes to seeking out prospective candidates. If women are largely seen but not heard in party organization ranks, their chances of coming to the forefront as viable candidates certainly diminish. And as mentioned earlier, men and women generally come from different occupational backgrounds. If male party elites tend to choose candidates who look like themselves, they may discount perfectly viable female candidates because they do not appear to fit the mold. Female party elites appear more supportive of and open to the possibility of women as candidates, however, so greater gender balance in party leadership ranks may increase women's chances in the future (Niven 1998; Wells and Smeal 1974).

Political parties sometimes do actively recruit female candidates. In fact, women were historically recruited and supported disproportionately as sacrificial lambs (Carroll and Strimling 1983; Carroll 1994; Diamond 1977; Gertzog and Simard 1981; Mandel 1981; Tolchin and Tolchin 1973; Van Hightower 1977). That is, the parties would seek out female candidates more frequently for seats in which the party had no realistic chance of winning, such as where a strong incumbent was already serving, or where party registration numbers were heavily tilted toward the opposing party. Before she ran for the United States Congress, Republican Susan Molinari got her start in city politics in New York City. With a city council entirely controlled by Democrats, Molinari was approached and encouraged to run by Staten Island political leaders. For all practical purposes, she had no realistic chance of winning—she was challenging a Democratic incumbent in a district that was more heavily Democratic than Republican, she was only 26 years old and had never held political office before, and she was running as a conservative Republican in a liberal Democratic city. On the plus side, her father was a long-serving and well-respected member of Congress, giving her excellent name recognition in her district. She ended up winning the seat and served for four years before eventually running for and winning her father's old congressional seat (Molinari 1998).

More recent scholarship stresses that the parties actively recruit female candidates, recognizing their potential and attempting to cash in when the political climate seems favorable to electing more women (Biersack and Herrnson 1994; Burrell 1993, 1994; Fox 1997). The 1992 elections, widely referred to as the "Year of the Woman," are a case in point. Perceiving that voters were fed up with politics as usual and looking for change, female candidates fit the bill. Indeed both parties courted female candidates, a record number 117 women won their party nominations, and 48 emerged victorious in November (CAWP 2002a).

Yet clearly not every election year will be a "Year of the Woman." If women candidates are actively recruited only in particular election cycles, when the climate seems particularly favorable, it will be a long time before we see women running in numbers anywhere close to men. Further, recent scholarship suggests that the electoral context is not the only factor that influences women's recruitment. In her study of state legislative party leaders, Sanbonmatsu (2006) finds that party leaders do not think all districts are equally winnable by female candidates. That is, they readily acknowledge that women cannot win in all legislative districts. If this is the case, we can assume that women are not recruited to run across the board, but only for a limited number of legislative seats. This finding echoes the work of Palmer and Simon (2008) who have studied women's candidacies for the U.S. House going back to 1956. In their research, they uncover what they term "women friendly districts." According to Palmer and Simon, certain types of congressional districts elect a disproportionate share of women. These districts are typically urban, wealthier than average, and racially diverse. Thus, if only a fraction of the total legislative seats are open to women's candidacies, it will be a long time indeed before women reach anything approaching parity in elected offices.

Nevertheless, it appears that women candidates today find themselves in a much warmer and more supportive environment than did their sisters some 20 or 30 years ago. The days of fielding women disproportionately as sacrificial lambs are waning or over, and both the Democrats and Republicans now take active steps to identify potential female candidates, help them secure the tools necessary to run, and support them with financial and other sorts of campaign assistance. This does not guarantee that the parties will be equally successful in fielding female candidates, however. In fact, recent research suggests that since 1988, the Democratic Party has fielded a greater proportion of female candidates than has the Republican Party (Palmer and Simon 2001). We explore some of the potential reasons for this divergence later in the chapter.

Summary: Why So Few Women Run

As this section makes clear, there is no single explanation why women continue to lag significantly behind men as candidates. Rather, it is likely a mix of factors that inhibits women from becoming candidates: their own apprehensions about their qualifications and competency shaped, in part, by professional and occupational experiences that differ from those of political men, a desire to put family first and forgo political careers until their children have grown, and unexpected resistance from party leaders.

CHALLENGES ON THE CAMPAIGN TRAIL AND STRATEGIES FOR SUCCESS

Even though women appear more reluctant than men to contest office, women's success rates at the polls are encouraging. Scholars argue that voter discrimination worked against women in the 1960s and 1970s, but most public polls today demonstrate that very few voters flat-out refuse to vote for female candidates. The result is that most scholars today conclude that "when women run, women win" (Darcy, Welch, and Clark 1994; Burrell 1988, 1992; Welch, Ambrosius, Clark, and Darcy 1985; Seltzer, Newman, and Leighton 1997). Whether in primary or general election contests, female candidates now compare very favorably to their male counterparts.

If women tend to win about as often as men, why are so few women sitting in elected office? First, incumbency is a major factor. The majority of incumbents are still men, and it is very difficult to unseat incumbents in the United States (Fiorina 1977). Combined with the fact that the vast majority of incumbents seek reelection year after year, quality electoral opportunities present themselves relatively rarely to women and other newcomers to politics. Second, as mentioned previously, a limited number of congressional districts have sent a disproportionate share of women to Congress (Palmer and Simon 2008). If women are electable in some, but not all, districts, we may reach a plateau where women continue to replace other women in office, but fail to increase their numbers overall as they cannot make inroads into other less friendly districts. At the state legislative level, this may be occurring already. In the last decade, women's representation at the state legislative level has remained fairly stagnant (going from 21.8 percent in 1998 to 23.7 percent in 2008) (CAWP 2008a). Women have continued to make incremental progress in the United States Congress, increasing from 12.1 percent to 16.8 percent over the past 10 years (CAWP 2009). Thus, even if women begin running and winning in similar numbers, the power of incumbency, combined with a limited number of "women friendly districts" virtually ensures that it will take many years to significantly alter the existing gender imbalance in elected positions.

Relatively similar success rates at the polls do not necessarily mean that women and men face the same challenges and constraints on the campaign trail. Rather, much evidence indicates that voters perceive female and male candidates through different lenses, that the press treats their candidacies differently, and that women and men themselves behave somewhat differently when they run. The next section examines each of these areas in more detail.

Voter Stereotypes about Female Candidates: A Double Bind

All political candidates must figure out a way to appeal to a general public that pays relatively little attention to politics and election campaigns. Most citizens devote very little time to informing themselves about candidates, instead relying on cues like party identification and incumbency when it is time to cast their ballots. Especially true in local, low-stimulus elections (such as city council or school board elections), voters tend to take shortcuts when deciding for whom to vote. That is, most people simply do not have the time or interest to painstakingly research all of the candidates running, compare and contrast their policy positions and experiences, and select the candidate who most closely approximates their own ideals. It is far easier to rely on a few shortcuts, such as party identification and/or incumbency. If the incumbent has performed relatively well in office, or has at least avoided scandal or controversy during his or her tenure, voters more often than not decide to return him or her to office (Jacobson 1997). Voters also rely on partisan identification to simplify their voting decisions. Thus, if all else is equal, voters tend to pick the candidate who shares their own partisan identification.

Gender likewise serves as a voting cue, but in a more complicated way than party identification and incumbency. For voters, the generic male and female candidates simply stand for different things. In assessing candidates, voters tend to use gender stereotypes and apply them to the particular candidates running for office, regardless of whether or not the individual candidates fit the stereotypes. As Kim Fridkin Kahn (1996) explains the process,

> When developing impressions of others, people routinely give priority to judgments based on stereotypes rather than judgments based on new

information. People prefer to limit their cognitive efforts by drawing stereotypical impressions rather than processing new information that may alter their initial assumptions. (4)

As such, voters presume that female candidates possess certain feminine personality traits whereas men possess certain masculine traits. Female candidates are seen as more compassionate, moral, honest, and ethical than are men. Voters perceive men as tougher, better able to handle crises, more qualified, and more decisive than women (Alexander and Andersen 1993; Kaid, Myers, Pipps, and Hunter 1984; Koch 1999; Sapiro 1981–82). If both sets of personality characteristics were valued equally, female candidates would be on relatively equal footing with male candidates. But voters value masculine traits over feminine traits (Huddy and Terkildsen 1993; Rosenwasser and Dean 1989; Rosenwasser and Seale 1988). As such, we can expect that voter stereotypes will hurt women more often than they will help them. In the widely acclaimed "Year of the Woman" in 1992, voters were said to be in the mood for change and eager to throw out incumbents who were guilty of overdrawing their official checking accounts in the House of Representatives. Believing that women were more honest, moral, and ethical, the political climate was favorable for women in that year and 24 new women were elected to the U.S. House. Ten years later, in the aftermath of September 11, 2001, and with war against Iraq on the horizon, voters were presumably looking for tough, masculine candidates. Only seven new women were elected to the House of Representatives.

Second, voters presume that women are more competent in dealing with issues such as health care, Social Security, and education whereas men are better at dealing with the economy and taxes, the military, and crime (Alexander and Andersen 1993; Brown, Heighberger, and Shocket 1993; Mueller 1986; Rosenwasser and Dean 1989; Rosenwasser and Seale 1988; Sanbonmatsu 2002; Sapiro 1981–82). Accordingly, women's electoral fortunes can be expected to rise and fall depending on the issues deemed most salient immediately preceding an election. If voters are particularly concerned about the economy, terrorism, or military crises, they tend to assume that male candidates are more capable for the job. On the other hand, women can be expected to do better in election years in which education, health care, or other social issues are on the forefront of citizens' minds.

Third, voters tend to assume that female candidates are more liberal than they really are (Koch 1999, 2000; McDermott 1997, 1998). For certain women, such as Republican women running in moderate to liberal districts or Democratic women running in liberal or very liberal districts, such perceptions may work to their advantage. For women running in more conservative districts, however, the public's overestimation of female candidates' liberalism may work against them at the polls. This may explain why fewer Republican women than Democratic women have been running for Congress over the last decade. Palmer and Simon (2001) show that although the percentage of Republican and Democratic female congressional candidates was relatively equal until 1988, Democratic women now lead the way. More Democratic women seek their party's nomination in the primary, and more Democratic women win their party's nomination to go on to the general election. If the public assumes that Republican women are more liberal than they are, contesting a Republican Party primary may prove quite difficult for these women because primary voters are typically more ideologically extreme than are those who vote in the general election (Baer and Bositis 1988). Even if these Republican women candidates are quite conservative, primary elections are often low-information races and these are the type of races in which voters are most likely to rely on voter stereotypes. Also problematic for Republican female candidates running for Congress, according to Simon and Palmer (2005), is that "the districts where Republican women have the best opportunity to win a nomination are districts where their prospects in the general election are lowest." Their research examines the political geography of congressional districts to determine whether or not certain districts are friendlier to female candidates than are others. They find that such districts do exist, but that Republican women tend to do less well in these seats than do their Democratic sisters.

One encouraging note for Republican women is that they have done fairly well at the school board level. Across the United States, school board candidates are more likely to identify themselves as Republicans than as Democrats, and female school board candidates fit this pattern. That is, there are more Republican than Democratic women running for school board seats, regardless of the type of community (Deckman 2003). These Republican women may potentially benefit from voter stereotypes about their ideological leanings. In a low-information race like a school board election, voters may assume that a Democratic male and a Republican female are fairly similar in ideological terms but give the woman the edge because of her presumed expertise in the area of education. But data from a nationwide survey of male and female school board candidates suggest that voter assumptions are off the mark. In fact, there are many more conservative women running for school board seats than there are liberal women, so voters would be safer to assume that female school board candidates, especially Republican ones, are fairly conservative (Deckman 2003).

What can female candidates do, if anything, to counteract such damaging voter stereotypes about their capabilities and ideological leanings? As communications scholar Kathleen Hall Jamieson (1995) contends, female political candidates run up against what she terms a "double bind," a Catch-22 situation that expects women, but not men, to simultaneously exhibit stereotypical feminine and masculine traits. A woman that comes across as very masculine invariably invokes criticism for being too harsh, aggressive, and unladylike (read "bitchy"), whereas a woman who is too feminine will be dismissed for lacking the skills necessary to compete and survive in the rough-and-tumble world of politics. Thus, the challenge for political women is to convince the public that they are sufficiently aggressive and tough without being tagged as an "Iron Lady," a woman who has lost touch with her feminine side (Fenn 2008). As former Congresswoman Pat Schroeder put it, "The electorate seems to be looking for representatives that are half-Marine, half-legislator.

That's tough for a woman to pull off" (Mashek and Healy 1986). Former Congresswoman Susan Molinari (1998), when running for the City Council in New York, echoed Schroeder's comments:

> As a woman candidate you are forced into a constant battle to convince voters that even though you weigh less than one hundred pounds you're still tough enough to do the job.   (x)

Female candidates deal with the double bind in a variety of ways. Mary Beth Rogers, a campaign manager for the late Texas Governor Ann Richards, explained that the campaign made a concerted attempt to present Richards as both a tough, savvy politician and as a caring, compassionate family woman. They emphasized her experience in a traditionally masculine domain, as state treasurer responsible for the fiscal health of the state. After a particularly nasty primary battle involving plenty of negative advertising, Richards softened her image for the general election by airing commercials that showed her in maternal roles, both with her grandchildren and ailing father (Morris 1992; Tolleson-Rinehart and Stanley 1994). Other female candidates have done the same—while leveling negative attacks against their opponents, they remind voters of their feminine side by airing positive ads showing themselves in loving relations with family members, in stereotypically feminine situations (homemaker, mother), or speaking to stereotypically feminine issues (Sheckels 1994; Sullivan 1998).

A close examination of the 2008 presidential elections suggests that both Hillary Clinton and Sarah Palin also confronted the double bind in their campaigns, but in different ways. The next section looks more closely at Clinton and Palin's campaigns, paying particular attention to their strategies for overcoming the double bind.

The Double Bind in the 2008 Elections: Hillary Clinton and Sarah Palin

Existing research tells us a great deal about how the media and voters evaluate women, but we know far less about how female candidates attempt to deal with the double bind. "How do they position themselves and sell their candidacies to a public that will likely see them as women first and as political candidates second?". By focusing on their own communications, we examine Hillary Clinton and Sarah Palin's strategies for dealing with the double bind.

Hillary Clinton and the Double Bind   When Hillary Clinton began her presidential campaign in January of 2007, both she and her campaign advisers painted a picture of her as tough, strong, and experienced. As told by campaign aides, chief campaign strategist Mark Penn's overall strategy was to make Clinton look presidential, to portray her as "one tough woman" (Baker and Kornblut 2008). They reiterated this message in their campaign communications, their spin, and with her own words.

In the first campaign brochure Clinton distributed to Iowa voters in July of 2007, she featured "Ready to Lead" as a prominent campaign slogan and repeatedly emphasized her experience throughout the entire brochure (Kornblut 2007a). Further, in numerous television advertisements, Clinton's tag line was a variation on her strength ("the strength to fight"), her experience ("the experience to lead"; "time for a president who is ready") or both. Perhaps the most widely covered ad was her "3:00 a.m." spot, which touted her preparedness and resolve. Throughout the ad, a phone rings unanswered in the background while children sleep soundly in their beds. The male narrator asks:

> "It's 3 A.M. and your children are safe and asleep. But there's a phone in the White House and it's ringing. Something is happening in the world. Your vote will decide who will answer that call, whether it's someone who already knows the world's leaders, knows the military, someone tested who is ready to lead in a dangerous world . . . who do you want answering the phone?"

Clinton's campaign advisers rarely missed an opportunity to tout her toughness and experience. After an October 2007 debate in Philadelphia, in which her Democratic rivals repeatedly attacked Clinton in their responses, one Clinton adviser said "Ultimately, it was six guys against her, and she came off as one strong woman" (Kornblut and Balz 2007b). Clinton also made remarks on the campaign trail to shore up any voter doubts about her ability to compete in the masculine world of politics. When asked what lessons she learned from John F. Kerry's failed 2004 presidential bid, Clinton responded "When you're attacked, you have to deck your opponents. . . . [Y]ou can count on me to stand my ground and fight back" (Kornblut and Balz 2007b).

Throughout the campaign, Clinton reminded voters that she was tough, experienced, and ready to lead. And voters appeared to embrace this message. In poll after poll, voters gave Clinton the edge when asked who would be the toughest commander-in-chief, toughest on terrorism, and best able to deal with the situation in Iraq (Saad 2007; *Washington Post*-ABC News 2008). From early in 2007 throughout the nomination campaign, Democrats in the majority of states thought Clinton would be a more effective commander-in-chief than would Obama or John Edwards (CNN 2008; NBC/WSJ 2008). Similarly, at the height of the Democratic primary battle between Clinton and Obama, voters indicated Clinton would be better than Obama at dealing with leaders of foreign countries and dealing with the war in Iraq (NBC/WSJ 2008).

Voters also thought Clinton brought stereotypically masculine character traits to the table. When asked who was the strongest leader and who was the candidate with the best experience to be president, Clinton consistently outpaced both Obama and Edwards. This was true from early 2007 all the way through at least February of 2008. Just a month before the Democratic primaries and caucuses got underway, 61 percent of Democratic-leaning voters identified Clinton as the strongest leader in the Democratic field, more than three times the number that thought either Obama or Edwards were the strongest leader. This gap narrowed over time, but Clinton enjoyed a 24-point lead over Obama on this measure going into Super Tuesday, February 5, 2008 (*Washington Post*-ABC News 2008).

Yet while the polling numbers always demonstrated that the public found her strong, intelligent, and qualified for the job, she often lagged behind Barack Obama on measures of trustworthiness, honesty, and compassion, traits for which female candidates are usually given the edge. In numerous polls, Obama bested Clinton by nearly 20 points when asked who was more honest and trustworthy. Clinton and Obama were closer in voters' minds when it came to their compassion and concern for others, but Obama again typically outpaced her by 10 or more points (NBC/WSJ 2008).

Political scientists Susan B. Hansen and Laura Wills Otero (2006) argue that voters typically prefer presidential candidates who are both strong *and* compassionate leaders. Combined with the aforementioned double bind, female candidates who are perceived to be strong leaders must also take steps to remind voters that they are not Iron Ladies, that they have not lost touch with their feminine side. Veteran political communications consultant Peter Fenn puts it this way: "the most personal vote a voter will cast is for the Presidency of the United States. Voters want to like the person they are voting for, to feel like this person is like them and understands what makes them tick" (Fenn 2008). For Clinton, the challenge was to convince voters that she could be tough but still compassionate, the most experienced candidate who also happened to understand their problems and concerns.

There is ample evidence that the Clinton campaign understood the challenges of presenting her as a warm and caring woman and took many steps to humanize her throughout the campaign. Her campaign often quipped that "she is the most well known person that nobody knows." Their challenge was to reintroduce her to the public, hoping to get beyond the image of a cold and calculating political operator created during her years in the White House and get voters to appreciate her on her own terms. Clinton herself acknowledged this problem when she appeared on *The Ellen DeGeneres Show* in September of 2007, noting that the biggest misperception of her is that she is "some kind of creature from an alien world" (Kornblut 2007b).

To dispel these perceptions, Clinton and her campaign team tried a variety of tactics to show just how warm, compassionate, and likable she was throughout the campaign. They tried to soften her image by showing her as a loving mother, daughter, and friend. For example, when Clinton kicked-off her campaign in January of 2007, she did so from the comfort of her home in Washington, D.C., taking on what one journalist called "the demeanor of a kaffe-klatching neighbor" (Hornaday 2007). While she did not mention the fact that her aging mother lived with her in Washington, D.C., the fact eventually came to light in the campaign (Koncius 2007).

Many of her television ads likewise attempted to soften her image, presenting her as a caring, warm, and compassionate woman. The visual imagery of the ads was often vibrant and pleasing, with soothing or triumphant background music in the background. Clinton was routinely shown in close contact with individuals from all walks of life, including the elderly, children, families, women, African Americans, and blue-collar workers, and they all looked genuinely delighted to be with her. Clinton was often shown listening intently to voters, nodding in agreement with them, and sometimes gently touching them. While she definitely communicated her policy priorities in the ads, the unspoken message was that Clinton cared deeply about people, she listened to them, and she would always do what she could to help them.

The campaign also launched "The Hillary I Know" campaign on its website, which consisted of numerous testimonials from "constituents, friends, and leaders whose lives Hillary has touched." One testimonial is from Hillary's mother, Dorothy Rodham, explaining that she wants to let people know "what a good person [Hillary] is" and how she has spent her life helping people. One particular advertisement features Dorothy Rodham and Chelsea Clinton prominently, reminding viewers that Hillary has loving relationships with both of them. At the end of this spot, we see Chelsea in close contact with a group of voters while Clinton looks on as a proud mother in the background.

In the early stages of the campaign, the strategy to remind voters that Clinton had a softer side appeared to be working. In fact, many voters in both Iowa and New Hampshire expressed how the Hillary they met in person differed substantially from the person they had seen portrayed in the media. One woman in Grinnell, Iowa, after seeing Clinton at the local high school said "People say she's cold, but I thought she was quite warm" (Kornblut and Balz 2007b). After a town hall meeting with Clinton in Davenport, Iowa, another woman took the media to task for portraying political candidates too often as caricatures rather than real people. As she explained "With Hillary, [the media] have her painted as a cold fish. That's absolutely what you do not get in person. She's very warm and intelligent" (Balz 2007). A woman in Concord, New Hampshire, concurred, noting that Hillary Clinton in person is "much more inspirational and much more genuine" (Marcus 2007).

Hillary Clinton also used humor to soften her image, showing that she had a fun side and did not take herself too seriously. For example, during one debate in New Hampshire, the debate moderator asked her how she would respond to New Hampshire voters who liked her resume, but thought Barack Obama scored higher on the likeability factor. Without missing a beat, Clinton tilted her head to the side and playfully said, "Well, that hurts my feelings." She paused for a few moments while the audience laughed and then continued, feigning dejection, "but I'll try to go on." She continued by saying that she agreed that Obama is a likeable guy, but that she didn't think that she was all that bad. When the cameras panned to Obama, he was busy taking notes. Without looking up at the cameras, he muttered "You're likable enough, Hillary" and she graciously responded "I appreciate that" (Democratic Presidential Debate 2007). She maintained her sense of humor throughout the entire exchange, smiling, remaining playful yet confident. In fact, many commentators contrasted her grace under fire with Obama's cool response to her, suggesting that he came across as snarky and dismissive.

During another one of the New Hampshire debates, a group of communications consultants gave Clinton high marks for her nonverbal cues, noting that

Leading up to the Iowa Caucuses, daughter Chelsea Clinton and mother Dorothy Rodham joined Hillary Clinton on the campaign trail, reminding voters of Hillary's softer side.

she came across as both strong and calm, commanding and warm. In one particular exchange, Tim Russert pointed out that Bill Clinton's stated position on torture differed from Senator Clinton's. She confidently responded, "Well, he's not standing here right now." While the audience cheered and laughed heartily, Clinton nodded her head in agreement. Russert followed up, stating "So there is a disagreement . . .". Clinton then smiled sheepishly and said sweetly, "Well, I'll talk to him later," prompting more audience laughter and cheering. According to the consultants, her tone of voice clearly communicated that she was in charge, but the smile and use of humor conveyed warmth on her part (Argetsinger 2007).

But the one incident that went the furthest toward softening her image was not likely planned by the campaign. After finishing third in the Iowa caucus, Clinton was behind Obama by about 10 points going into the New Hampshire primary, a short five days after the Iowa caucuses. In a coffee shop in Portsmouth, New Hampshire, a female supporter asks her "How do you do it? How do you keep upbeat and so wonderful?" After taking a moment, Clinton responded that it wasn't easy, and went on to talk about the reasons she was running. But rather than a standard stump speech, her response was heartfelt and human, showing a vulnerable side of her rarely seen in public. As she said,

> You know, this is very personal for me. It's not just political, it's not just public. I *see* what's happening [in this country] and we have to reverse it. And some people think elections are a game, they think it's like who's up

or who's down. It's about our country, it's about our kids' futures, and it's really about all of us, together.

Her voice begins to break about halfway through, her eyes go moist, and she almost demurely rests her chin in her left hand for a few seconds while she speaks ("Clinton Wells Up" 2008). As one journalist noted, Clinton, "had a jarring moment of vulnerability" (Givhan 2008). Her moment of vulnerability received much media attention, and seemed to be just the thing many female voters needed—they were already convinced of her intelligence, experience, and toughness, but also wanted to know that she was a real woman, sometimes vulnerable and breakable. Clinton went on to eke out a victory in the New Hampshire primary, coming from well behind Obama to beating him by 2 percent of the vote, and many identified her rare display of emotion as partially responsible for her victory. In fact, among those who said that they made their vote choice on the basis of which candidate "cares about people like me," a standard measure of compassion, Clinton was the top vote getter. Edwards did best among this group in Iowa, but Clinton edged him out in New Hampshire and also beat Obama by a 2-1 margin among this group (Dionne 2008).

So why did Clinton ultimately lose the Democratic nomination to Barack Obama? Political campaign consultant Peter Fenn, who began advising female candidates over 20 years when he worked for vice presidential candidate Geraldine Ferraro, argues that she was unable to convince enough voters that she was likeable and compassionate. When asked what advice he would have given Clinton, he said a good strategy would have been to focus on overcoming her negatives. One way to do so, he suggested, would be to return to what had worked so well for her in New York. When she ran for the U.S. Senate seat in New York in 2000, she embarked on a "Listening Tour," traveling throughout the state to meet with people in every county, focused on hearing what they had to say instead of telling them what she thought. In doing so, she was able to convince the people of New York that she was a good listener and empathetic. As Fenn continued, "People know that she's smart and that she knows the issues. But she needed to let the entire country know that she was empathetic." Part of the problem with her campaign strategy in Iowa, according to Fenn, was that she spent too much time giving speeches in crowded auditoriums and not enough time engaging people at the grassroots, in small diners and other intimate settings. Her frontrunner and celebrity status no doubt made this more difficult, but Fenn argues that the campaign should have figured out how to make it work (Fenn 2008).

Although voters who met her in person often commented on how warm and funny she was, the grueling and compressed schedule of primaries and caucuses made it nearly impossible to sustain personal interactions with so many voters after the first contests wrapped up in Iowa and New Hampshire. With 22 states holding their primaries and caucuses on Super Tuesday, a mere four weeks after the New Hampshire primary, all of the candidates were forced to rely more heavily on the mass media for communicating their message. And for Hillary Clinton, this may have been particularly challenging.

Unfortunately for Clinton, voters seemed to have more misgivings about her as an individual than they did about the other candidates. No doubt voters' impressions of her were influenced by her eight years in the White House and the intense media scrutiny she received as a politically involved and active first lady. She was widely blamed for the failure of her husband's health care plan in 1994 (Bernstein 2007), and was tarnished by her involvement in many other missteps of the Clinton administration. Few other candidates faced such a challenge in redefining themselves for the electorate.

What can we learn from Senator Clinton's campaign? Did she dismiss once and for all that presumption that political women cannot compete on masculine policy issues or that voters will automatically give male candidates the edge on such issues? That they will never be perceived as tough or strong leaders? It is tempting to conclude that voters now pay less attention to candidate gender and more attention to their record when assessing their capabilities, but it would be premature to do so. For one, Senator Clinton is unlike any other female politician who has gone before her. Never before has a sitting first lady run for and won a U.S. Senate seat, and never before has a former first lady run for the U.S. presidency. Because of her unique status, Senator Clinton enjoyed far greater name recognition and media attention than the rest of her colleagues while in the U.S. Senate. For better or for worse, the public felt like they knew her and could judge for themselves her character traits and capabilities across a variety of policy issues. As such, voters hardly needed to rely on gender cues in evaluating her candidacy. For female candidates with less name recognition, such as Republican vice presidential nominee Sarah Palin, we might expect gender cues and stereotypes to carry more weight. We turn now to discussing the challenges faced by Sarah Palin in the 2008 campaign.

Sarah Palin and the Double Bind   The challenges to overcome voter stereotypes were quite different for vice presidential candidate Sarah Palin. In contrast with Clinton's struggles to convince voters she was likable, Palin's toughest challenge was convincing voters that she was qualified for the job. When John McCain announced her as his running mate on August 29, 2008, 7 out of 10 Americans had never heard of her or did not know enough to have an opinion about her. When asked if she was qualified to assume the presidency if needed, a mere 39 percent of registered voters agreed that she was up to the task while almost an equal number (33 percent) said that she was not qualified. According to Gallup, only former Vice President Dan Quayle scored lower on perceived qualifications following his nomination (Gallup Poll 2008).

Recognizing that most voters knew very little about Palin at this juncture, perhaps these numbers are not particularly surprising. In the absence of much information about her, we can expect voters to rely on gender as a cue. And because the office of the vice presidency has never been held by a woman, voters may simply have been resorting to gender stereotypes about what female candidates can and cannot do. But as the campaign progressed, voters did not change their minds about her qualifications for the job. She never did convince a majority of voters that she was qualified as a vice presidential candidate or potential president (Survey by *Newsweek* 2008).

Where Palin did well with voters was on stereotypical feminine traits like compassion, trustworthiness, and likeability. Seventy percent of registered voters rated her as likable a few weeks before the election, and approximately 60 percent of voters agreed that she was honest, trustworthy, and cared about the problems of people like themselves throughout the campaign (Polling Report 2008; Survey by *Newsweek* 2008; ABC News 2008).

So how did the McCain campaign address the double-bind problem for Sarah Palin? Their presentation of her suggests that the campaign was trying to present her as both masculine and feminine, showing her as both tough and compassionate, as a political executive with real experience who was also an outsider committed to reform. She talked tough, leveled negative attacks against Obama, and reminded voters that she was hockey mom and a hunter. But she also stressed her feminine traits: a small town regular "gal" rather than a polished politician, a mother and wife, and someone who could finally shatter "the highest, hardest glass ceiling in America."

From the start, the campaign sought to portray her as a "caring mom who can be tough"(Shear and Murray 2008). When he announced her as his running mate, McCain touted her experience fighting against "oil companies and party bosses and do-nothing bureaucrats," and assured voters that she was tough enough to stand up for what's right, not letting "anyone tell her to sit down." After she concluded her acceptance speech at the Republican National Convention, the 1970s song "Barracuda" blasted over the airwaves, a clever nod to the nickname "Sarah Barracuda" she had earned for her exploits on the basketball court during high school.

Like many vice presidential candidates before her, she adopted the role of an attack dog on the campaign. Her convention acceptance speech criticized Democratic nominee Barack Obama not only for his policy stances but also called into question his character. She mocked his previous experience as a community organizer, suggesting her own experience as a small town mayor was better preparation for the presidency. As she quipped, "a small town mayor is sort of like a community organizer, except you have actual responsibilities." She also took a number of personal digs at Obama, suggesting he was more interested in self-promotion than serving his country and that his campaign was a self-indulgent "journey of personal discovery" that the country could hardly afford (Palin's Speech 2008). While on the campaign trail, she continued to attack Obama, accusing him of "palling around with terrorists" on numerous occasions.

The campaign was careful to showcase her feminine side, too. When she was first introduced by McCain, her seven-year-old daughter Piper stood close by her side while her husband and three of her other four children appeared in the background. As we soon learned, her eldest son was a soldier in the Army getting ready to ship off to Iraq. Palin described herself as "just your average 'hockey mom'", and "a mother of one of our troops" (CBS 2008). And the campaign made no secret of the fact that they thought she would be very appealing to many female voters who were disappointed that Clinton did not win the Democratic nomination (Baird 2008).

The campaign also highlighted her status as an outsider who would help McCain bring change to Washington. This strategy often works well for female candidates, as voters perceive women as more trustworthy and ethical than men. Indeed, part of the campaign's strategy appeared to be to present her as the campaign's antidote to Barack Obama. If he could bring change to Washington, so could she. McCain touted his own maverick status throughout the campaign in an attempt to distance himself from an unpopular president of his own party, and concluded many of his campaign ads with the slogan "Change is coming." But as a U.S. Senator with more than 25 years of experience in Washington, his message of change was hard for many to swallow. Governor Palin, a relative unknown before she was selected as McCain's running mate, could more persuasively sell the message of change. Elected as Governor of Alaska just two years before, she was not a career politician and had never lived in Washington, D.C. In her own acceptance speech at the Republican convention, Palin reminded voters that she is not part of the "permanent political establishment." Further, as a 44 year-old woman, she looked a lot more like the face of change than did the 72 year-old McCain.

Reminding voters that she is a mother of five, Governor Palin campaigns in Nevada with daughters Piper and Willow and son Trig (daughter Willow is holding Trig).

While the campaign was successful in presenting her as a tough but caring mother and an outsider, they were less successful in convincing voters that she was qualified to be president. After pundits and Democrats questioned her thin resume, the campaign tried to portray her as a proven leader by crediting her as being the only candidate in the race with executive experience: first as a mayor and then as a Governor. Time and again, they repeated the mantra that she had more executive experience than did Barack Obama.

Even more troubling for the campaign was her lack of experience in the most stereotypically masculine domain: foreign policy. When the issue turned to her lack of foreign policy experience, the campaign tried to deflect attention away from her inexperience by emphasizing that McCain was at the top of the ticket, not her, or they emphasized that she was part of a team, a quick study who would learn much as vice president. When CNN anchor Campbell Brown asked campaign spokesman Tucker Bounds why he thought Sarah Palin was ready to be commander-in-chief, he responded, "Governor Palin has the good fortune of being on the ticket with John McCain, who . . . is the most experienced and has shown proven judgment on the international stage" (Brown 2008). After another campaign adviser acknowledged that Palin could be criticized for her lack of foreign policy experience, he offered the assurance that "[s]he's going to learn national security at the foot of the master for the next four years" (Cooper and Bumiller 2008). Another adviser explained that "she doesn't pretend to be a foreign policy expert," but offered that she was remarkably up to speed on Middle East issues (Abramowitz and Eilperin 2008).

The campaign also argued that her experience as an executive provided opportunities to engage in foreign policy, as did Alaska's geographical proximity to Russia. When CNN anchor Campbell Brown pressed Tucker Bounds to explain Palin's (rather than McCain's) foreign policy experience, Bounds changed the subject and argued that Palin had as much executive experience as Barack Obama. When Brown continued to press for a response about foreign policy experience, Bounds offered that her role as commander of the Alaska National Guard qualified as foreign policy experience, but he struggled to explain any decisions she had made as commander of the National Guard. In her interview with ABC anchor Charlie Gibson, Palin herself suggested that Alaska's geographical proximity to Russia gave her special insights into foreign relations with the country. When Gibson asked her "What insight into Russian actions . . . does the proximity of the state give you," Palin responded "They're our next door neighbors. And you can actually see Russia from land here in Alaska" ("Sarah Palin Holds Forth." 2008). She reiterated the same line during her interview with CBS anchor Katie Couric, also adding that Alaskan trade missions with Russia gave her opportunities to engage in diplomacy.

At the end of it all, voters were not convinced that Palin had a sufficient grasp of foreign or domestic policy issues. Some began to question her command of the issues following high-profile televised interviews with Charlie Gibson (ABC News) and Katie Couric (CBS News) and following her debate performance with Democratic vice presidential candidate Joe Biden. While Palin did not commit any major guffaws in these appearances, she also did not come across as very well-versed in the issues. Her poll numbers reflect as much. Following her convention speech in August, a high of 47 percent of voters thought Palin was prepared to be vice president. By late October, only 35 percent of likely voters thought she was prepared (CBS/NYT 2008; CBS 2008b). When asked about whether or not she was well informed about the issues, Palin's numbers took a similar turn for the worse, going from 45 percent in late September to 35 percent in late October (Survey by *Newsweek* 2008; Survey by Pew Research Center 2008).

What can we learn about Palin's candidacy? It is tempting to conclude that Palin is a personification of the female candidate too feminine to be taken seriously. As an attractive and stylish mother of five, described by some as the "Hottest VP from the Coolest State" or the "Hottest Governor," Palin had to demonstrate that she was more than a pretty face, that she was knowledgeable and aggressive enough to play the part. In portraying her as a "caring mom who can be tough," the campaign was successful in convincing voters that she was tough enough and likable enough for the job. But by relying so heavily on selling her as an outsider and an agent of change, the campaign had a difficult time dispelling voter concerns about her qualifications and preparedness for office. That is, it proved difficult to sell her inexperience and outsider status as a plus on the one hand and then turn around and argue that it should not be held against her when she lacked the knowledge and experience that voters sought.

Further, the McCain campaign shot itself in the foot in some ways. Before McCain had selected Palin as his running mate, he argued that the most important issue for him in selecting a running mate would be that person's ability to be commander-in-chief. When Governor Palin was unveiled as his running mate, members of the media were quick to investigate her foreign policy credentials. If McCain had not placed such emphasis on the commander-in-chief issue, perhaps the campaign could have done a better job of selling Palin as experienced and qualified enough to be one heartbeat away from the presidency.

But in the end, the public was not convinced that she was qualified for the job. Despite the fact that majorities of voters thought Palin was likable and compassionate, the campaign could not convince them that she had what it takes to be president of the United States.

Media Coverage of Female Candidates

Depending on the level of office sought, most candidates will have to interact with the media in some way, shape, or form. Local races for mayor, city council, or school board often receive coverage in local newspapers and radio programs. As one moves up the hierarchy of elected offices, candidates generally rely more heavily on media coverage to communicate with voters. Some state legislative candidates and virtually all congressional and gubernatorial candidates attempt to secure some sort of television coverage—either for free (free media) or by purchasing airtime themselves (paid media). For presidential and vice presidential candidates, media coverage is essential.

Free media consists of all coverage that a news organization decides to bestow upon a candidate. For newspapers and other print media sources, this might include publishing a profile or interview with the candidate or a question-and-answer session designed to elicit various policy positions held by the candidate. Typical formats for free broadcast media consist of coverage of press conferences held by the candidate, televised debates between candidates, or video footage of candidates in action, perhaps giving a speech, meeting with citizens, or staging media events. Free media cost nothing financially, but the candidate cannot be certain that a positive image will be conveyed. For this reason, candidates also rely on paid media, or newspaper, radio, and television spots for which they foot the bill.

What types of media coverage do male and female candidates report? Do they receive similar amounts of coverage by media outlets? Are more stories devoted to men's or women's candidacies? Does the press take seriously women's policy positions? Do they focus disproportionately on their personal and physical characteristics? After reviewing the existing scholarship, we then turn to more closely examine the media coverage received by women running for the presidency and vice presidency: Elizabeth Dole, Hillary Clinton, Geraldine Ferraro, and Sarah Palin.

Many female candidates complain that the media do not take their candidacies seriously. An extreme example is told by former Reagan appointee Margaret Heckler, who years before she served as Reagan's Secretary of Health and Human Services won a primary election bid for a state legislative seat by challenging the sitting Speaker of the Massachusetts House in 1966. As she explains, her candidacy received absolutely no media coverage except for a story that said "Margaret Heckler is a candidate, but is not going to win" (Tolchin and Tolchin 1973, 22). More recently, there is continued evidence that female candidates for high-ranking offices continue to receive less media coverage than similarly situated men, and the coverage that they receive is often more negative (Aday and Devitt 2000; Heldman, Carroll, and Olson 2000; Kahn 1994, 1996; Kahn and Goldenberg 1991; Rausch, Rozell, and Wilson 1999).

For lower level offices, there is some evidence that media coverage appears to be more balanced. For example, male and female state legislative candidates receive relatively similar amounts of press coverage in their races; further, there appears to be no gender disparity in terms of "horse race" coverage, or the emphasis of who is ahead in the polls, at this level (Miller 2001). However, press articles are more likely to mention the incumbency status of male state legislative candidates than female state legislative candidates (ibid.).

At the school board level—the level at which more female candidates run than any other—gender differences with respect to the media are not apparent.[4] When asked to describe if the media are liberally or conservatively biased in covering their school board elections, very few candidates—either male or female—make such claims. Women and men candidates are just as likely to find that the media coverage of their campaigns is accurate, although most agree that media coverage is not, in their opinions, sufficient. Over half of all female and male candidates rate the media as being not very important in their elections.

In dealing with the media, many women lament that the press sexualizes them, doubts their competence and credibility, does not pay sufficient attention to their policy positions and the issues they discuss, but rather pays untold attention to their family arrangements, hairstyle, clothing, and physical appearance. As told by Joan Growe, former secretary of state for the state of Minnesota and a candidate for the U.S. Senate in 1984,

> When you're running for an office few women have run for before, you might as well be a green-headed toad. The press was almost worse than the public. It was subtle discrimination by then, which I think is more difficult to ideal with than overt discrimination. (Watkins and Rothchild 1996, 229)

What types of discrimination did she face? Reporters would steer conversation toward questions about her children when she was in the midst of discussing arms control policy, and she felt the press held her to a different standard in demonstrating her knowledge about policy issues, a concern echoed by other political women. In reflecting on her experiences in dealing with the media, and strategizing about how she'd do things differently if she ran again, she said the following:

> If I were to do it again, I'd gather every reporter in my office and I'd say, "This is off the record. You now get to ask all your insane, asinine, stupid questions—about my health, my body, my bra size, who I'm sleeping with, anything else you want to ask me. And after this, no more sexist questions." (Watkins and Rothchild 1996, 230)

The media likewise scrutinizes marital status, family arrangements, and physical appearance much more closely for female than male candidates (Aday and Devitt 2000; Bystrom, Robertson, and Banwart 2001; Devitt 1999; Heldman, Carroll, and Olson 2000). When running for governor of Virginia

---

[4]Approximately 40 percent of school board candidates are women and women are just as likely to win as their male counterparts (Deckman 2003).

in 1993, Democratic candidate Mary Sue Terry indicated that the media were preoccupied with her marital status (she is single) while they paid no attention to the marital status of two single congressmen from Virginia. "Nobody writes about Rich Boucher, who is my age and has never been married, or about Bobby Scott, who was married only briefly," said Terry, leading her to conclude that male politicians are not subject to the same scrutiny as are female candidates (Baker 1993).

One need not look far to find examples of the press paying greater attention to women's than men's physical appearance. When Linda Smith challenged incumbent U.S. Senator Patty Murray for her Senate seat in 1998, *Time* magazine devoted an entire paragraph to comparing their appearances:

> [T]hey are definitely not using the same hairdresser. Murray, known as the mom in tennis shoes in 1992 when she won office in the year of the woman, could be in a Wheat Thins commercial or an Eddie Bauer catalog; Smith looks like she's just come from Talbots and is on her way to accept the Dry Cleaning Woman of the Year award. (Lopez 1998 p. 56)

It is hard to imagine that the same type of coverage would have appeared if two men were running against one another. Jan Jones, a former Las Vegas mayor who ran for governor of Nevada in 1998, is described in one article as having "a generous nimbus of frosted hair" and "a penchant for extremely high heels" (Bruni 1998). As Jones herself explains, "I'm often described as flamboyant and flashy with big hair. I'll take flamboyant and flashy, but I don't have big hair." She goes on to add, "I think the press covers women more harshly, and I think it's a different approach. A man is considered to be of substance unless he shows he's not, and a woman must first prove she has substance" (Morrison 2000). And according to Jane Danowitz, former director of the Women's Campaign Fund, such coverage "knock[s] women down a peg or two on the credibility ladder . . . News stories focusing on appearance detract from and dilute a candidate's message" (Jahnke 1992).

Not only do female candidates endure greater attention and stories about their physical appearance, but they also suffer from being tagged as less viable candidates than similar men (Heldman, Carroll, and Olson 2005; Kahn and Goldenberg 1991; Kahn 1994). And as if to add insult to injury, the press pays less attention to female candidates' policy positions than they do for men, even when female candidates devote greater attention to policy issues in their own political communications (Devitt 1999; Aday and Devitt 2000; Kahn 1994, 1996; Kahn and Goldenberg 1991; Kahn and Gordon 1997; Gilmartin 2001). An unfortunate implication of such slanted coverage is that voters may come away with the impression that female candidates are unworthy contenders. By emphasizing females' physical appearance over their policy expertise, their poll numbers over their policy stances, media coverage does little to dispel the stereotype that women are more style than substance.

This type of treatment by the media serves to illustrate the difficulties women encounter in portraying themselves as candidates first and women second. Because women are still more of an anomaly than a standard fixture in politics, their appearance sets them apart from men in obvious ways, but usually in ways that have nothing to do with their ability to be effective public servants.

Media Coverage of Female Presidential and Vice Presidential Candidates In 1984, Geraldine Ferraro made history when Democratic presidential candidate Walter Mondale selected her to be his running mate in his bid for the U.S. presidency. Before Ferraro, no woman had ever been selected to be on a major party ticket for the U.S. vice presidency. Twenty-four years later, in 2008, Sarah Palin made history as the first Republican woman to be nominated for the office of the vice presidency. Also in 2008, Hillary Clinton proved herself the most viable female presidential candidate in the history of the United States. Although she lost the Democratic nomination to Barack Obama, the first African American to win a major party nomination for the presidency and to win the presidency, she was long considered the favorite to win the Democratic nomination. Previous to Clinton, Elizabeth Dole made a bid to become the Republican Party's presidential nominee in the 2000 elections, becoming the most viable Republican woman to run for the presidency.

Now that four viable women have made the run for the White House, we have an opportunity to examine the types of media coverage they received. Did the press pay undue attention to their appearance and family arrangements? Cover their candidacies more negatively than their male counterparts? Question their credibility? This section looks more closely at each of these questions.

Ferraro, Dole, and the Media In 1984, three-term Congresswoman Geraldine Ferraro was selected by Walter Mondale to be his running mate in his unsuccessful bid to unseat incumbents Ronald Reagan and George H.W. Bush. Initial media coverage of Ferraro was largely positive, although the media soon began to focus on her husband, real estate businessman John Zaccaro, and his alleged (but never proven) financial improprieties and supposed family ties to the mafia in generations past, which were little more than rumors—albeit run in respectable news outlets such as the *Wall Street Journal*. Ferraro recounts in her memoirs: "There wasn't even sufficient documentation for the paper [the *WSJ*] to run the piece in the news section of the paper. It was run on the editorial page. And other journalists cried foul" (Ferraro and Francke 1985, 235).

The media also focused inordinately on Ferraro's appearance and personal characteristics. One study found that almost 30 percent of her media coverage contained references to clothing, hair, make-up, and other feminine characterizations (Heith 2003). As Ferraro cynically remarked, "When you're the only one wearing a bright-colored dress and wearing lipstick, it's pretty obvious who the woman candidate is" (*ibid.*, 126). The media also engaged in a long-running debate as to whether Mondale should kiss or touch Ferraro in public and who should walk first on stage at political events, signaling that they were not sure what to make of Ferraro's candidacy (Braden 1996).

More disturbing, however, were questions that Ferraro received from journalists concerning her "toughness" for the office and her ability to serve as commander in chief, particularly as the United States found itself in the middle of a Cold War with the former Soviet Union. Ferraro recalls one heated exchange between herself and reporter Marvin Kalb on *Meet the Press*, who pointedly asked her "Are you strong enough to push the button?" She responded, "I could do whatever is necessary to protect this country" (Ferraro and Francke 1985, 273). Ferraro expressed distaste at a similar interview she had with Ted Koppel, who grilled her on a misstatement she had made during a debate with Vice President George Bush, whom she believed had "bought into the stereotype that women can only deal with children's and women's issues" (Braden 1996, 110).

Fifteen years after Ferraro's candidacy, Elizabeth Dole announced that she was seeking the Republican Party's 2000 presidential nomination. Dole, a Harvard-trained lawyer, was a well-known Republican who had served as a cabinet secretary in both the Reagan and Bush administrations before eventually becoming president of the American Red Cross. She was also the wife of Senator Robert J. Dole, who had unsuccessfully run for President against Bill Clinton in 1996. Americans were quite familiar with Elizabeth Dole and many pundits gave her high praise for the poise and political skills she displayed while campaigning for her husband's presidential campaign, especially after her performance at the 1996 Republican National Convention. Many Republican insiders encouraged her to run for president and she was largely discussed as the first viable woman to seek the office (Hall 2000).

After launching her bid for the presidency to much fanfare, Dole bowed out of the race within less than a year, months before the Iowa Caucuses. She cited fund-raising difficulties, as popular Texas Governor George W. Bush quickly became the consensus candidate among the party faithful. But some speculated that her decision to withdraw was also linked to the poor media coverage she received. In a detailed content analysis of more than 70 daily newspapers, Heldman, Carroll, and Olson (2005) found significant differences in the type of media coverage that Dole received compared with the men running for the GOP nomination in 2000. Despite high name recognition, high favorability ratings, and a consistent second-place showing among likely Republican voters in early public opinion polls, Dole received far less coverage than not only George W. Bush, which was expected given his early front-runner status, but also Senator John McCain, who was less well-known than Dole and who consistently finished in third place among likely GOP voters in similar early polls. Instead, her coverage "more closely resembled the coverage received by lesser-known, far less popular candidates" for the GOP nomination, such as Steve Forbes, Gary Bauer, and Alan Keyes (*ibid.* 321).

Heldman, Carroll, and Olson (2005) also found that, compared with the male candidates for the nomination, the press paid much more attention to Dole's personality traits, appearance, and her familial ties (as the spouse of Bob Dole). For example, they found that about 17 percent of newspaper stories focused on Dole's appearance while more than 60 percent focused on her personality traits or mentioned Bob Dole as her husband (323). Scholar Diane Heith (2003) recounts one complaint made by Ari Fleischer, Dole's spokesperson at the time, who noted that reporters often asked Dole about walking an entire parade route in high heels: "Men don't get questions about their footwear!" (127).

Reporters frequently featured Dole's status as the first serious female contender for the U.S. presidency in their stories (Anderson 2002; Heith 2003; and Heldman, Carroll, Olson 2005). Heldman and her colleagues (2005) found that almost two-thirds of all the newspaper stories they analyzed made explicit reference to the fact that she was a woman (325). Karrin Vasby Anderson's (2002) work on Dole's media coverage, which included newsmagazines and television news in addition to print journalism, verified the findings by Heldman and her colleagues, leading Anderson to conclude that such media portrayals made it hard "for a voter to imagine her as president" (Anderson 2002, 107).

The Dole and Ferraro candidacies demonstrate that media coverage of presidential campaigns involving women differs in important respects from those involving only male candidates. In both cases, the mainstream news media were more likely to focus on the physical characteristics and familial ties of Dole and Ferraro than their male counterparts. In the case of Ferraro, reporters also concentrated on whether she had the "toughness" to be Commander in Chief; in the case of Dole, she systematically received less coverage from the news media than male candidates who did not match her in terms of name recognition or high favorability ratings. In both cases, Dole and Ferraro were unsuccessful, and it is important to realize that their defeats were the result of many more factors than their media coverage, including the enormous popularity of their rivals at the time. However, the tone of the media coverage, with its gendered frames, likely did little to help their campaigns.

Were things different in 2008 for the candidacies of Hillary Rodham Clinton and Sarah Palin? Were gendered frames employed or was the reporting largely free of such frames? Did these women candidates receive markedly less coverage than their male counterparts, or was the tone different?

Hillary Clinton and the 2008 Primary Elections Hillary Rodham Clinton, as the early front-runner for the 2008 Democratic nomination, received more media coverage than any other candidate running for president—Democratic or Republican—in the earliest stages of the primary election season, according to the Pew Research Center's Project for Excellence in Journalism (2007). Pew examined more than 40 sources including major newspapers, network and cable news shows, notable Internet sources, and radio programs and found that fully 17 percent of stories were about Clinton, followed by 14 percent about Barack Obama (ibid.). However, Obama's coverage was almost twice as likely to be positive in tone (47 percent) than Clinton's coverage (27 percent). Deckman's (2009) study of Democratic primary campaign coverage in the *New York Times* also found that a larger percentage of Obama's stories were positive than were stories about Hillary Clinton.

As the primary season rode on, however, and the Democratic field narrowed to Clinton and Obama, the Pew Research Center found that media coverage of the personal character qualities of Obama and Clinton was comparable and overwhelmingly positive, despite insistence from many of Clinton's supporters that the media was biased in favor of Barack Obama (Pew Research Center's Project for Excellence in Journalism 2008a). The top positive character narrative in media stories about Clinton concerned her preparedness to lead the country, which corresponds quite well with the Clinton campaign's efforts to paint her as the most experienced and qualified candidate. Conversely, questions regarding Clinton's likeability and whether she represented the "status quo" were also frequent narratives in the news media, although positive stories heavily outweighed negative ones, especially earlier in the race (ibid).

Previous research finds that the media more often focus on the physical appearance of female candidates than their male counterparts on the campaign trail; moreover, media coverage of female candidates for executive positions often employ a "first woman" frame. However, preliminary evidence from a content analysis of election coverage in two papers, the *New York Times* and the *New York Post*, finds that neither paper typically referred to either Clinton's appearance or used the "first woman" frame, which is an improvement from the media treatment faced by both Elizabeth Dole and Geraldine Ferraro in previous presidential elections (and perhaps showcases the viability of Clinton's candidacy) (Deckman 2009).

Sarah Palin and the 2008 General Election   Media studies that compare coverage of male and female candidates often find that male candidates receive more coverage than their female counterparts, as Elizabeth Dole found out in 2000 in her bid for the presidency (Heldman, Carroll and Olson 2005). This was not the case for Alaska Governor Sarah Palin, the Republican vice-presidential nominee, whose media coverage far outweighed her Democratic rival for vice president, Senator Joe Biden. In fact, Palin-related stories were the third most frequent storyline for the entire campaign during the six crucial weeks between the end of the Republican Convention on September 8, 2008, to the final debate between Barack Obama and John McCain on October 16, 2008. Only campaign stories about the economy and financial crisis and stories about the presidential debates received more attention (Pew Research Center's Project for Excellent in Journalism 2008b). Overall, the Pew Research Center found that three times as many stories focused on Palin than Biden (Pew Research Center's Project for Excellence in Journalism 2008b). Some of this coverage was related to Tina Fey's spot-on parodies of

Palin, aired on *Saturday Night Live* (SNL) for many weeks during the height of the campaign.

Contrary to some expectations, Palin received a slight bump in news coverage following her much-maligned interview with CBS Evening News Anchor Katie Couric, most of which was negative (Pew 2008b). Overall, negative coverage of Palin far outweighed positive coverage, but most of the negative coverage stemmed from reporters examining her record as governor in Alaska (*ibid*).

In several ways, Palin's news coverage was more gendered in tone than was the coverage of Hillary Clinton. Unlike Clinton, for example, many early stories about Palin featured a "first woman" frame, which is likely explained by Palin's status as the first woman to appear on the Republican Party's presidential ticket. And, unlike coverage of Hillary Clinton, the media paid far more attention to Palin's appearance. Early profile stories of her almost always mentioned her background as a beauty pageant contestant (she was runner-up in the Miss Alaska pageant). And while stories about Palin's family and personal life made up a relatively small percentage of her total media coverage, most media outlets did run stories discussing Palin's role as a mother of five children, including an infant, Trig, with Down Syndrome who was born to Palin while she was governor. The pregnancy of her unwed 17-year-old daughter Bristol also generated headlines, sparking debate among many Americans as to the governor's decision to run for the vice presidency. Typical was this front-page story in the *New York Times*, which ran during the Republican National Convention entitled "A New Twist on the Debate on Mothers," in which two female reporters interviewed dozens of women as to their opinions about Sarah Palin's candidacy: "With five children, including an infant with Down syndrome and, as the country learned Monday, a pregnant 17-year-old, Ms. Palin has set off a fierce argument among women about whether there are enough hours in the day for her to take on the vice presidency, and whether she is right to try" (Kantor and Swarns 2008). Critics of Palin said reporting about her children and role as a mother was legitimate given that (1) Palin routinely referred to herself as a "hockey mom" while on the campaign trail and that (2) McCain likely chose Palin as his running mate to boost his credentials with his party's socially conservative base, in part because of her strong pro-life views. However, the McCain camp was quick to denounce as sexist the media's pursuit of stories involving Sarah Palin's family.

Was the media's attention to Palin's family life and appearance sexist? And was the media unduly harsh on Palin in terms of attacking her credentials and fitness for office and did they do so because of her gender? It is hard to say. In comparison to stories about Joe Biden, the media did spend an inordinate amount of time writing about her family situation and appearance. Had Palin been a man, it is hard to believe that the media would have spent as much time writing about her family life or engendering debates as to her fitness for office given that she was the parent of small children. (Indeed, young, photogenic children are often viewed as a political asset for male candidates for president or vice-president; for example, Barack Obama was likely helped by having an attractive young family.)

In comparing 2008 presidential election media coverage, one gendered theme that was largely missing from the coverage of both Clinton and Palin, and that plagued Geraldine Ferraro, was whether either Clinton or Palin were "tough enough" to handle the job of president or vice president. In fact, Hillary Clinton was more likely to be critiqued for being too tough and not feminine enough. When she did have a tearful moment in New Hampshire, several critics even insisted that the moment was contrived for political purposes. Questions did arise in media coverage as to Palin's fitness for office, but it is doubtful that many of these questions derived because of Palin's gender, but instead were likely the result of her relatively thin political resume, her performance as Alaska's governor, and her mediocre interview performances with Katie Couric and other journalists.

In terms of the 2008 presidential campaign and media coverage, Clinton and Palin's historic candidacies offered exciting politics and the mainstream media's coverage of both women was an improvement over the coverage received by either Geraldine Ferraro or Elizabeth Dole before them. The mainstream press largely avoided gender stereotypes when it covered Clinton, although the media did generate some stories about whether Palin's motherhood factored into her fitness for office and also discussed her attractiveness in some cases. Some blatant sexist coverage persisted for both candidates, however, in certain outlets. Nonetheless, the media generally took the candidacies of both women seriously and it is likely that strong, viable women who run for president or vice president in the future will face media treatment that is even less steeped in gendered frames.

Clinton and Palin: Sexism on Talk Radio and Cable News   Overtly sexist treatment of either Hillary Rodham Clinton or Sarah Palin was hard to come by in mainstream media outlets in 2008 (Deckman 2009). However, the same cannot be said of alternative forms of media, including talk radio and cable television, in which discussions about Sarah Palin and especially Hillary Clinton were often dripping with sexist rhetoric. We highlight several notable examples below.

Talk Radio   Sexist treatment of Hillary Clinton and Sarah Palin appeared all too commonplace on right-wing talk radio. The influence of right-wing talk radio cannot be underestimated. For example, the Rush Limbaugh Show is routinely cited as the most popular talk radio show in the country and his influence in Republican Party politics is quite extensive (Jamieson and Cappella 2008). An ardent conservative, Limbaugh has never been a big fan of either Bill or Hillary Clinton, but his critiques of Hillary Clinton during her race for president were quite misogynistic. For example, in describing Clinton's power within the Democratic Party, he referred to her so-called "testicle lockbox," saying that "her testicle lockbox can handle everybody in the Democratic hierarchy." He later claimed that "Clinton reminds men of the worse characteristics of women they've ever encountered over their life: totally controlling, not soft and cuddly. Not sympathetic. Not understanding" (Media Matters 2008a).

But such sexist vitriol was not limited to Rush Limbaugh. Milwaukee radio host Mark Beilling said on his program "when you think of Hillary Clinton," the word "bitches" come to mind (Media Matters 2008c). Nationally syndicated columnist Jim Quinn also referenced the "bitch" term in his discussions of Hillary Clinton, by playing the Elton John song "The Bitch is Back" in introducing segments about Clinton on air (*ibid.*), while San Francisco talk radio host Lee Rodgers described Clinton's voice as that "screechy, fingernails-on-the-blackboard voice of hers" (*ibid.*)

Ironically, conservative radio hosts, who supported Sarah Palin's candidacy, frequently used sexist terms to describe her physical appearance. For example, Limbaugh referred to her as a "babe" (Farmer 2009) while talk radio host Chris Baker referred to her as "a smoking-hot chick from Alaska" (Media Matters 2008c). In discussing Palin"s debate performance against Joe Biden, Baker later said Palin "shoulda had a little cleavage going" and that he "noticed a panty line on her" (*ibid.*).

Cable News   Conservative talk radio is not exactly known as a bastion of women's rights, so such sexist banter is not entirely unexpected in that format. Perhaps somewhat more surprising was the sexist and mean-spirited treatment that the two candidates, especially Hillary Clinton, received on cable news. For example, on FOX News, analyst Neil Cavuto suggested of her campaign strategy that she was "trying to run away from this tough, kind of bitchy image"("Cavuto: Hillary Running Away . . ." 2008). On CNN, news commentator Jack Caverty described Clinton as a "scolding mother, talking down to a child" (Media Matters 2008b). Tucker Carlson, former host of a talk show on MSNBC, frequently described Clinton in emasculating terms, such as in the following examples: "[T]here's just something about her that feels castrating, overbearing, and scary" adding "when she comes on television, I involuntarily cross my legs" (quoted in Farmer 2009). Hillary Clinton's laughter was derided as a "cackle"by several cable talk show hosts and in and of itself became a political topic. And more than one pundit claimed that the only reason Hillary Clinton won in New Hampshire was because she acted in a stereotypically female way by crying. For example, Bill Kristol, formerly of the *National Journal*, said on FOX News about her victory: "It's the tears. She pretended to cry, the women felt sorry for her, and she won" (Wakeman 2008).

Probably one of the worst offenders in terms of sexist treatment of Clinton was MSNBC's Chris Matthews. Media Matters for America, a liberal media watchdog group, documented numerous sexist affronts toward Clinton that Chris Matthews made on his MSNBC program, in which he (among other things) "featured a Photo-shopped image of Clinton sporting 'She Devil Horns' while discussing Republican efforts to demonize her; repeatedly likened Clinton to 'Nurse Ratched,' the scheming, heartless character from the psych ward movie *One Flew Over the Cuckoo's Nest*; described her laugh as a 'cackle,' suggesting she was 'anti-male,' 'witchy,' and was on a 'short leash;' and . . . claimed that 'some men' say Clinton's voice sounds like 'fingernails on a blackboard'"(Media Matters 2008b). Clinton's sexist treatment by cable news' outlets, particularly MSNBC, led some of her supporters and feminist organizations to sponsor cable news boycotts and letter writing campaigns to raise awareness about the use of sexist terms by the news media. In response to Clinton's treatment by the press, NOW also started a campaign to highlight its "Media Hall of Shame," which documents examples of sexist language used by the mainstream news media on its website (Seelye and Bosman 2008).

Sarah Palin's candidacy was also viewed through a gendered lens, as mainstream news outlets such as CNN raised concerns about her ability to be vice president as a mother to an infant with special needs. Witness the following exchange from CNN anchor John Roberts and CNN congressional correspondent Dana Bash. John Roberts said "The baby [Trig] is slightly more than 4 months old now. Children with Down syndrome require an awful lot of attention. The role of vice president, it seems to me, would take up an awful lot of her time, and it raises the issue of how much time will she have to dedicate to her newborn child?" Dana Bash's response, "That's a very good question, and I guess . . . that perhaps the line inside the McCain campaign would be, if it were a man being picked who also had a baby . . . born with Down syndrome, would you ask the same question?"

Even on cable news and on talk radio—the above examples not withstanding—most of the press treatment of Hillary Clinton and Sarah Palin did not rely on gender stereotypes nor was it misogynistic in nature. These examples do demonstrate, however, that sexism in presidential news coverage was alive and well in 2008, and are problematic despite cable's relatively small viewership or talk radio's relatively small listenership by the American public, given that topics first discussed on such outlets that might not be initially considered newsworthy often find their way onto the pages of mainstream newspapers or onto network news broadcasts.

Fund-Raising

Money is referred to as the "mother's milk" of politics for good reason. Without money, candidates will have a tough time communicating their message to voters. Television and radio ads, leaflets, brochures, yard signs, and campaign consultants all cost money. Without spending money, it is unlikely that candidates will be able to deliver their message to voters or that the average citizen will know anything about their candidacies. Thus, candidates must fashion a fund-raising strategy: How much money will they need to mount an effective campaign? From whom will they seek funds? What organizations and individuals will likely support them and contribute to their campaign coffers? In general, the higher the level of office, the more money a candidate can expect to raise in order to compete.

How successful have women been at fund-raising? Looking solely at their campaign receipts, it appears that female candidates do as well as male candidates running in similar situations (Uhlaner and Schlozman 1986; Fox 1997; Werner 1997). That is, female incumbents raise about as much money as do male incumbents, female challengers about as much as male challengers, and the same holds true for open-seat candidates, male or female.

Yet political women have historically reported greater difficulties in raising funds, receiving smaller average campaign contributions that require more time and energy to amass than do large contributions. Some evidence suggests that women raise larger amounts of money from individual contributors whereas men get larger proportions from PACs (Political Action Committees) (Stanwick 1983; Tolleson-Rinehart and Stanley 1994; Witt, Paget, and Matthews 1994). But this difference is likely a function of women's status as challengers, who typically have a more difficult time raising funds and receive smaller proportions of their contributions from PACs. For example, incumbent Senator Elizabeth Dole raised more than twice as much money as did her challenger Kay Hagan ($19,508,712 versus $8,555,412) and received almost three times more PAC dollars than did Hagan ($2,637,840 versus $920,069). As a challenger, Hagan relied more heavily on individual donations than did Dole (85 percent of Hagan's funds raised were from individuals while 69 percent of Dole's were from individuals) (Open Secrets 2008).

Women historically reported difficulties in getting the party to back them with financial support, but more recent evidence suggests that the parties are gender neutral when it comes to allocating campaign dollars (Biersack and Herrnson 1994; Burrell 1993, 1994, 1998; Fox 1997). That is, once women have received their party nomination, the parties are as likely to back their candidacies as they would similarly situated male candidates. This does not mean that the parties willingly provide financial assistance to all women's campaigns. As organizations with limited resources, the parties behave strategically in deciding how to allocate campaign dollars, hoping to secure the greatest potential return on their investments. This fact often escapes many newcomers to politics, women and men alike, who are dismayed when their party fails to get behind their candidacies.

Women and men tend to raise campaign funds from slightly different sources, too. First of all, there are a number of PACs that give money primarily or solely to female candidates (see Table 5.2.) The largest of these is EMILY's List, founded by Ellen Malcolm in Washington, D.C., in 1985. EMILY's List (Early Money Is Like Yeast—it makes the "dough" rise) is the largest and most successful of the women's PACs. Donating money and providing campaign services to pro-choice, Democratic women, the PAC was the brainchild of Ellen Malcolm, the daughter of a Republican committeewoman who came of age in the antiwar movement and changed her party affiliation to Democrat. The beneficiary of a trust based on the fortune of her grandfather, a founder of IBM, Malcolm began anonymously donating money to liberal causes and

TABLE 5.2

PACs Focused on Electing Women

Name of PAC and Year Founded	Gives To	Types of Races Supported
National Organization for Women PAC (1966)	Feminist women and men	Federal, state, and local
Women's Campaign Forum (1974)	Pro-choice women	Federal, state, and local
National Women's Political Caucus PAC (1975)	Women	Federal and state
Minnesota Women's Campaign Fund (1982)	Pro-choice women	Federal, state, and local
EMILY's List (1985)	Pro-choice Democratic women	Federal, gubernatorial
Susan B. Anthony List (1992)	Pro-life women and men	Federal and state
WISH List (1992)	Pro-choice Republican women	Federal, state, and local
Women in Leadership (1993)	Pro-choice women	Federal, state, and local
Value in Electing Women PAC (View PAC) (1997)	Republican Women	Federal, House of Representatives
Women Under Forty PAC (WUF-PAC) (1999)	Women 40 years old and younger	Federal and state
National Association of Women Business Owners (various)	Women and men	Federal

organizations such as the National Women's Political Caucus and the Women's Legal Defense Fund.

After years of anonymous donations, Malcolm decided to reveal her identity and utilize her political skills and connections to work for the advancement of women in office (Clift and Brazaitis 2003). In 1985 Malcolm gathered 25 women in her basement to create the network that would become EMILY's List. The women brought their Rolodexes to write letters to friends to seek donations for viable pro-choice Democratic women candidates. Each member of EMILY's List had to pay a $100 membership fee and contribute at least $100 to two women candidates. From there Malcolm went across the country holding "Rolodex parties" in people's living rooms.

Ellen Malcolm, left, President of Emily's List, and Michigan Governor Jennifer Granholm enjoy cheers from guests at the EMILY's List 20th Anniversary Luncheon on Monday, October 17, 2005, in Washington, D.C.

By the close of the 1986 election cycle, EMILY's List raised over $350,000 and helped elect Barbara Mikulski, the first Democratic woman to be elected to the Senate in her own right (Clift and Brazaitis 2003). Today EMILY's List raises millions of dollars for women candidates and regularly tops the list of leading fund-raisers keeping pace with and often surpassing leading national fund-raisers including the National Rifle Association and major business associations (Raasch 2002; Schatz 2002). In the 2008 election cycle, EMILY's List spent approximately $43 million in helping to elect female candidates (EMILY's List 2009).

The Republican counterpart to EMILY's List is the WISH List (Women in the Senate and House), an organization that bills itself as "the nation's largest political fund-raising network for mainstream Republican women." Like EMILY's List, WISH List gives funds only to pro-choice women and asks its members to contribute to at least two candidates per election cycle. Unlike EMILY's List, however, WISH List also supports women for lower-level offices (WISH List 2003).

Also located in Washington, D.C., the Women's Campaign Forum (WCF) is the oldest PAC that gives solely to female candidates. Founded in 1974, the WCF bills itself as a "non-partisan national network dedicated to achieving parity for women in public office" (WCF 2010). To these ends, the organization contributes to both Democratic and Republican pro-choice women and supports women running for national as well as state and local offices.

On the whole, conservative women's organizations have not been as active in forming PACs and distributing campaign dollars. For example, Concerned Women for America's (CWA) tax status does not allow it to endorse political candidates, it has not formed a PAC to raise money for candidates, and it does not see putting more women into office as a priority. Instead the organization limits itself to publishing voter guides on priority issues and encouraging its members to register to vote and recruit others to vote. It is possible that CWA and other conservative women's groups have not embraced the goal of electing conservative women to office because such a path conflicts with their views of women's traditional roles and advocacy of a return to family values and biblical principles.

However, one organization, Susan B. Anthony List, has taken up the cause of electing socially conservative women. Founded in 1992 in reaction to the increased number of pro-choice, Democratic women elected during the "Year of the Woman" elections, the group raises money and provides campaign training and services for pro-life women. In addition to supporting pro-life women, the group also endorses pro-life men who are running against pro-choice female candidates in an effort to reduce the ratio of pro-choice women in Congress (Susan B. Anthony List 2003). As more conservative women continue to run for office, it is possible that conservative women's organizations will become more involved in electoral politics.

CONCLUSION

Female candidates have surely come a long way since Elizabeth Cady Stanton ran for Congress over 140 years ago. By many measures, female candidates today seem to be equally as competitive and likely to win their elections as their male counterparts. They no longer run disproportionately in hopeless districts, they raise as much if not more money than male candidates, and they continue to wage competitive campaigns in their pursuit of public office.

Yet some challenges clearly remain. As the discussions of both Hillary Clinton and Sarah Palin reveal, the double bind continues to be problematic for female candidates. Even more revealing, this is true for women running at the highest levels where we might expect plentiful information about the candidates to drive out gendered stereotypes about their capabilities and character traits. In addition, while Clinton and Palin received more media coverage than did their male counterparts, more of this coverage was negative and in Palin's case, focused on her family and appearance. Not only does such coverage give voters reason to call into question women's fitness for office, but it may also discourage other women from running in the future.

On a more positive note, emerging research suggests that regardless of whether they win or lose, simply seeing high-profile women campaign for office increases girls' and women's overall interest in politics. While women continue to lag behind men in terms of political interest and political knowledge, perhaps seeing both Hillary Clinton and Sarah Palin on the national stage in 2008 will convince more women young women that politics is for women, too, and will prompt additional women to try their hand at politics. Only time will tell.

REFERENCES

"A Woman's Place is in the White House." 1998. *The Globe and Mail* (12 June): A15.

ABC News. 2008. *ABC News / Washington Post Poll.* October 2nd. Accessed through Polling the Nations.

Abramowitz, Michael, and Juliet Eilperin. 2008. "Experts Helping Palin Brush Up on Foreign Policy." *Washington Post* (5 September): A25.

Anderson, Karrin Vasby. 2002. "From Spouses to Candidates: Hillary Rodham Clinton, Elizabeth Dole, and the Gendered Office of the US President." *Rhetoric and Public Affairs* 5, no. 1:105–132.

Argetsinger, Amy. 2007. "Read Her Lips, and Hands, Oh, and Eyes, Too: Nonverbal Cues May Speak Louder than Words." *Washington Post* (28 September): C1.

Aday, Sean, and James Devitt. 2000. *Newspaper Coverage of Female Candidates: Spotlight on Elizabeth Dole.* Women's Leadership Fund.

Alexander, Deborah, and Kristi Andersen. 1993. "Gender as a Factor in the Attribution of Leadership Traits." *Political Research Quarterly* 46, no. 3:527–545.

Atkeson, Lonna Rae. 2003. "Not All Cues Are Created Equal: The Conditional Impact of Female Candidates on Political Impact." Journal of Politics 65, no.4: 1040–1061.

Baer, Denise L., and David A. Bositis. 1988. *Elite Cadres and Party Coalitions.* New York: Greenwood Press.

Baird, Julia. 2008. "From Seneca Falls to . . . Sarah Palin?" *Newsweek* (22 September). Accessed online at www.newsweek.com/id/158893.

Baker, Donald P. 1993. "From Early Years, Powerful Lessons." *Washington Post* (17 October): A1.

Baker, Peter, and Anne E. Kornblut. 2008. "Turning it Around; Down in the Polls After an Iowa loss, Hillary Clinton had no victory speech for New Hampshire." *Washington Post* (10 January): A1.

Balz, Dan. 2007. "Mixed Reviews for Clinton in Iowa." *Washington Post* (29 January): A1.

Benze, James G., and Eugene R. Declerq. 1985. "Content of Television Political Spot Ads for Female Candidates." *The Journalism Quarterly* 62:278–283, 288.

Bernstein, Robert A. 1986. "Why Are There So Few Women in the House?" *Western Political Quarterly* 39, no. 1:155–164.

Bernstein, Carl. 2007. *A Woman in Charge: The Life of Hillary Rodham Clinton.* New York: Vintage Books.

Biersack, Robert, and Paul S. Herrnson. 1994. "Political Parties and the Year of the Woman." pp. 161–180 in *The Year of the Woman: Myths and Realities*, ed. Elizabeth Adell Cook, Sue Thomas, and Clyde Wilcox. Boulder, CO: Westview Press.

Bledsoe, Timothy, and Mary Herring. 1990. "Victims of Circumstances: Women in Pursuit of Political Office." *American Political Science Review* 84, no. 1:213–223.

Braden, Maria. 1996. *Women Politicians and the Media.* Lexington, KY: University Press of Kentucky.

Brown, Campbell. 2008. Television interview with McCain spokesperson Tucker Bounds. (2 September). Accessed through YouTube at www.youtube.com/watch?v=UYYiw_y2qDI

Brown, Clyde, Neil R. Heighberger, and Peter A. Shocket. 1993. "Gender-Based Differences in Perceptions of Male and Female City Council Candidates." *Women & Politics* 13, no. 1:1–17.

Bruni, Frank. 1998. "Las Vegas Mayor Runs for Governor, Undaunted by Cancer." *New York Times* (4 August): A9.

Burkett, Elinor. 1998. *The Right Women.* New York: Touchstone.

Burrell, Barbara C. 1988. "The Political Opportunity of Women Candidates for the U.S. House of Representatives in 1984." *Women & Politics* 8, no. 1:51–68.

_____. 1992. "Women Candidates in Open-Seat Primaries for the U.S. House: 1968–1990." *Legislative Studies Quarterly* 17, no. 4:493–508.

_____. 1993. "John Bailey's Legacy: Political Parties and Women's Candidacies for Public Office." pp. 123–134 in *Women in Politics: Outsiders or Insiders?* ed. Lois Lovelace Duke. Englewood Cliffs, NJ: Prentice Hall.

_____. 1994. *A Woman's Place Is in the House.* Ann Arbor: University of Michigan Press.

_____. 1998. "Campaign Finance: Women's Experience in the Modern Era." pp. 26–37 in *Women and Elective Office,* ed. Sue Thomas and Clyde Wilcox. New York: Oxford University Press.

Burt-Way, Barbara J., and Rita Mae Kelly. 1992. "Gender and Sustaining Political Ambition: A Study of Arizona Elected Officials." *Western Political Quarterly* 45, no. 1:11–25.

Bystrom, Dianne, and Lynda Lee Kaid. 2002. "Are Women Candidates Transforming Campaign Communication? A Comparison of Advertising Videostyles in the 1990s." pp. 146–169 in *Women Transforming Congress,* ed. Cindy Simon Rosenthal. Norman, OK: University of Oklahoma Press.

Bystrom, Dianne G., Terry A. Robertson, and Mary Christine Banwart. 2001. "Framing the Fight: An Analysis of Media Coverage of Female and Male Candidates in Primary Races for Governor and U.S. Senate in 2000." *American Behavioral Scientist* 44, no. 12:1999–2013.

Campbell, David E., and Christina Wolbrecht. 2006. "See Jane Run: Women Politicians as Role Models for Adolescents." *Journal of Politics* 68, no. 2:233–247.

Carroll, Susan J. 1985. "Political Elites and Sex Differences in Political Ambition: A Reconsideration." *Journal of Politics* 47, no. 4:1231–1243.

_____. 1994. *Women as Candidates in American Politics,* 2nd ed. Bloomington: Indiana University Press.

Carroll, Susan J., and Wendy S. Strimling. 1983. *Women's Routes to Elective Office: A Comparison with Men's.* New Brunswick, NJ: Center for the American Woman and Politics.

"Cavuto: Hillary Running Away from Her 'Tough, Bitchy Image." (19 February). www.hufffingtonpost.com/2008/02/19/cavuto-hilary-running-a_n_87441.html.

CBS. 2008a. "America: Meet Sarah Palin." (29 August). Accessed through YouTube at www.youtube.com/watch?v=Gg0darQB7r4.

CBS News. 2008b. *Public Opinion Poll.* (8 September). Accessed through Polling the Nations.

CBS/NYT. 2008. *CBS News/New York Times Poll.* (30 October). Accessed through Polling the Nations.

Center for the American Woman and Politics (CAWP). 2002a. *Women Candidates for Congress 1974–2002: Major Party Nominees.* Center for the American Woman and Politics, Eagleton Institute of Politics, Rutgers University.

———. 2008a. *Women in State Legislative Office 2008.* Center for the American Woman and Politics, Eagleton Institute of Politics, Rutgers University.

———. 2008b. *Woman versus Woman: Congressional and Gubernatorial Races 1944–2008.* Center for the American Woman and Politics, Eagleton Institute of Politics, Rutgers University.

———. 2009. *Women in the U.S. Congress 2009.* Center for the American Woman and Politics, Eagleton Institute of Politics, Rutgers University.

Clift, Eleanor, and Tom Brazaitis. 2003. *Madam President: Women Blazing the Leadership Trail.* New York: Routledge.

"Clinton Wells Up: 'This is Very Personal.'" 2008. WMUR-TV, New Hampshire. (7 January). Accessed online at www.youtube.com/watch?v=pl-W3IXRTHU.

CNN. 2008. CNN Exit Polls. Accessed online at www.cnn.com/ELECTION/2008/results/polls/#val=USP00p3.

Collins, Gail. 1998. "Why the Women Are Fading Away." *New York Times* (25 October).

Conway, M. Margaret, Gertrude A. Steuernagel, and David W. Ahern. 2005. *Women and Political Participation.* 2nd edition. Washington, D.C.: CQ Press.

Cooper, Michael, and Elizabeth Bumiller. 2008. "Alaskan in McCain's Choice; First Woman on GOP Ticket." *New York Times* (30 August): A1.

Costantini, Edmond. 1990. "Political Women and Political Ambition: Closing the Gender Gap." *American Journal of Political Science* 34, no. 3:741–770.

Costantini, Edmond, and Julie Davis Bell. 1984. "Women in Political Parties: Gender Differences in Motives Among California Party Activists." pp. 114–138 in *Political Women: Current Roles in State and Local Government,* ed. Janet A. Flammang. Beverly Hills: Sage.

Costantini, Edmond, and Kenneth H. Craik. 1972. "Women as Politicians: The Social Background, Personality, and Political Careers of Female Party Leaders." *Journal of Social Issues* 28, no. 2:217–236.

Darcy, R., Susan Welch, and Janet Clark. 1994. *Women, Elections and Representation.* Lincoln, NE: University of Nebraska Press.

Davidson, Roger H., and Walter J. Oleszek. 2000. *Congress and Its Members.* Washington, D.C.: CQ Press.

Deckman, Melissa M. 2003. "Women Running Locally: How Gender Affects School Board Elections." Paper presented at the Japanese and American Women Political Scientsts' Symposium, University of Delaware (August).

———. 2009. "Style or Substance? An Examination of Media Coverage of Hillary Clinton and Sarah Palin in the 2008 Presidential Elections." Paper presented at the Japanese and American Women Political Scientists' Symposium, Tokyo (July).

Delli Karpini, Michael X, and Scott Keeter. 1996. *What Americans Know About Politics and Why it Matters.* New Haven: Yale University Press.

Democratic Presidential Candidates Debate. 2007. Hosted at Dartmouth College, New Hampshire. (27 September). Accessed online at www.youtube.com/watch?v=t1c10kwZWL4.

Devitt, James. 1999. *Framing Gender on the Campaign Trail: Women's Executive Leadership and the Press*. Women's Leadership Fund.

Diamond, Irene. 1977. *Sex Roles in the State House*. New Haven: Yale University Press.

Dionne, E.J., Jr. 2008. "A Shocker, in Hindsight." *Washington Post* (10 January): A21.

Elder, Laurel. 2004. "Why Women Don't Run: Explaining Women's Under-representation in America's Political Institutions." *Women & Politics* 26 no. 2:27–56.

EMILY's List. 2009. "About Emily's List: Where We Come From." www.emilyslist.org/about/where_we_come_from/. Accessed July 14, 2009.

Farah, Barbara G. 1976. "Climbing the Political Ladder: The Aspirations and Expectations of Partisan Elites." pp. 238–250 in *New Research on Women and Sex Roles*, ed. Dorothy G. McGuigan. Ann Arbor, MI: University of Michigan Press.

Farmer, Ann. 2009. "The Media's Gender Bias." *Perspectives: A Newsletter for & about Women Lawyers*. Winter. 17(30): 4-7.

Fenn, Peter. 2008. Personal interview conducted with author. (May 16): St. Paul, Minnesota.

Ferraro, Geraldine, with Linda Bird Francke. 1985. *Ferraro: My Story*. Toronto: Bantam Books.

Fiorina, Morris P. 1977. *Congress: Keystone of the Washington Establishment*. New Haven: Yale University Press.

Flammang, Janet A. 1997. *Women's Political Voice: How Women Are Transforming the Practice and Study of Politics*. Philadelphia: Temple University Press.

Fowler, Linda L., and Robert D. McClure. 1989. *Political Ambition: Who Decides to Run for Congress*. New Haven: Yale University Press.

Fowlkes, Diane L., Jerry Perkins, and Sue Tolleson Rinehart. 1979. "Gender Roles and Party Roles." *American Political Science Review* 73, no. 3:772–780.

Fox, Richard Logan. 1997. *Gender Dynamics in Congressional Elections*. Thousand Oaks, CA: Sage Publications.

Fox, Richard L., and Jennifer L. Lawless. 2004. "Entering the Arena: Gender and the Decision to Run for Office." *American Journal of Political Science* 48, no. 2: 264–280.

Gallup Poll. 2008. "Palin Unknown to Most Americans." (August 30th). Accessed online at www.gallup.com/poll/109951/Palin-Unknown-Most-Americans.aspx.

Gertzog, Irwin N., and M. Michele Simard. 1981. "Women and 'Hopeless' Congressional Candidacies: Nomination Frequencies 1916–1978." *American Politics Quarterly* 9, no. 4:449–466.

Gill, LaVerne McCain. 1997. *African American Women in Congress: Forming and Transforming History*. New Brunswick, NJ: Rutgers University Press.

Gilmartin, Patricia. 2001. "Still the Angel in the Household: Political Cartoons of Elizabeth Dole's Presidential Campaign." *Women & Politics* 22, no. 4:51–67.

Givhan, Robin. 2008. "A Chink in the Steely Façade of Hillary Clinton." *Washington Post* (8 January): C1.

Griffith, Elisabeth. 1984. *The Life of Elizabeth Cady Stanton*. New York: Oxford University Press.

Hall, Jane. 2000. "Hillary and Liddy: Old and New Stories in Reporting on Women Candidates." *Media Studies Journal* 14, no. 1:68–75.

Hansen, Susan, and Laura Wills Otero. 2006. "A Woman for U.S. President? Gender and Leadership Traits Before and After 9/11." *Journal of Women, Politics and Policy* 28, no. 1:35–60.

Hawkings, David, and Brian Nutting, eds. 2003. *Politics in America 2004: The 108th Congress*. Washington, D.C.: CQ Press.

Heith, Diane J. 2003. "The Lipstick Watch: Media Coverage, Gender and Presidential Campaigns." pp. 123–130 in *Anticipating Madam President*, ed. Robert P. Watson and Ann Gordon. Boulder: Lynne Rienner Publishers.

Heldman, Caroline, Susan J. Carroll, and Stephanie Olson. 2000. "Gender Differences in Print Media Coverage of Presidential Candidates: Elizabeth Dole's Bid for the Republican Nomination." Paper presented at the Annual Meeting of the American Political Science Association, Washington, D.C., August 31–September 3.

Heldman, Caroline, Susan J. Carroll, and Stephanie Olson. 2005. "She Brought Only a Skirt: Media Coverage of Elizabeth Dole's Bid for the Republican Presidential Nomination. Political Communication 22, no. 2:315–335.

Henneberger, Melinda. 1998. "No Escaping Motherhood on Campaign Trail." *New York Times* (13 June): A1.

Hornaday, Ann. 2007. "Throwing Her Hat on the Web: Clinton's Announcement Combines Internet Savvy and Polished Production." *Washington Post* (21 January): D1.

Huddy, Leonie, and Nayda Terkildsen. 1993. "The Consequences of Gender Stereotypes for Women Candidates at Different Levels and Types of Office." *Political Research Quarterly* 46, no. 3:503–525.

Jacobson, Gary C. 1997. *The Politics of Congressional Elections.* 4th ed. New York: Longman.

Jahnke, Christine K. 1992. "Beauty Pageant: How to Avoid Gender Issues in Your Campaign." *Campaigns & Elections* (January).

Jamieson, Kathleen Hall. 1995. *Beyond the Double Bind: Women and Leadership.* New York: Oxford University Press.

Jamieson, Kathleen Hall and Joseph N. Cappella. 2008. *Echo Chamber: Rush Limbaugh and the Conservative Media Establishment.* New York: Oxford University Press.

Jennings, M. Kent, and Barbara G. Farah. 1981. "Social Roles and Political Resources: An Over-Time Study of Men and Women in Party Elites." *American Journal of Political Science* 25, no. 3:462–482.

Jennings, M. Kent, and Norman Thomas. 1968. "Men and Women in Party Elites: Social Roles and Political Resources." *Midwest Journal of Political Science* 12, no. 4:469–492.

Kahn, Kim Fridkin. 1994. "The Distorted Mirror: Press Coverage of Women Candidates for Statewide Office." *Journal of Politics* 56, no. 1:154–173.

———. 1996. *The Political Consequences of Being a Woman: How Stereotypes Influence the Conduct and Consequences of Political Campaigns.* New York: Columbia University Press.

Kahn, Kim Fridkin, and Edie N. Goldenberg. 1991. "Women Candidates in the News: An Examination of Gender Differences in U.S. Senate Campaign Coverage." *Public Opinion Quarterly* 55, no. 2:180–199.

Kahn, Kim Fridkin, and Ann Gordon. 1997. "How Women Campaign for the U.S. Senate: Substance and Strategy." pp. 59–76 in *Women, Media and Politics*, ed. Pippa Norris. New York: Oxford University Press.

Kaid, Lynda Lee, Sandra L. Myers, Val Pipps, and Jan Hunter. 1984. "Sex Role Perceptions and Televised Political Advertising: Comparing Male and Female Candidates." *Women & Politics* 4, no. 4:41–53.

Kantor, Jodi, and Rachel L. Swarns. 2008. "A New Twist in the Debate on Mothers." *New York Times* (2 September): A1.

Keyserling, Harriet. 1998. *Against the Tide: One Woman's Political Struggle.* Columbia, SC: University of South Carolina.

Kirkpatrick, Jeane J. 1974. *Political Woman.* New York: Basic Books.

_____. 1976. *The New Presidential Elite: Men and Women in National Politics.* New York: Russell Sage Foundation.

Koch, Jeffrey W. 1999. "Candidate Gender and Assessments of Senate Candidates." *Social Science Quarterly* 80, no. 1:84–96.

_____. 2000. "Do Citizens Apply Gender Stereotypes to Infer Candidates' Ideological Orientations?" *Journal of Politics* 62, no. 2:414–429.

Koncius, Jura. 2007. "The Woman Behind the Room Behind Hillary Clinton." *Washington Post* (1 February): H1.

Kornblut, Anne E. 2007a. "In Iowa, Clinton Camp Scripts Bill's Role to Keep Focus on Hillary." *Washington Post* (1 July): A4.

Kornblut, Anne E. 2007b. "The Trail." *Washington Post* (5 September): A6.

Kornblut, Anne E., and Dan Balz. 2007a. "Clinton Begins Her Run in Earnest: Iowa 'Town Hall' Draws a Crowd." *Washington Post* (28 January): A1.

Kornblut, Anne E., and Dan Balz. 2007b. "Clinton Regroups as Rivals Pounce." *Washington Post* (1 November): A1.

Lawless, Jennifer L., and Richard L. Fox. 2008. *Why Are Women Still Not Running for Public Office?* Washington, D.C.: Brookings Institution.

Lewis, Gregory B. 1996. "Gender Integration of Occupations in the Federal Civil Service: Extent and Effects on Male–Female Earnings." *Industrial and Labor Relations Review* 49, no. 3:472–483.

Lopez, Steve. 1998. "An Unconventional Fight." *Time* (2 November): 55+.

Mandel, Ruth B. 1981. *In the Running: The New Woman Candidate.* New Haven: Ticknor & Fields.

Marcus, Ruth. 2007. "The War She Hasn't Won." *Washington Post* (14 February): A19.

Margolies-Mezvinsky, Marjorie. 1994. *A Woman's Place: The Freshmen Women Who Changed the Face of Congress.* New York: Crown Publishers.

Mashek John W., and Melissa Healy. 1986. "A Woman's place Is on the Ballot in '86." *U.S. News & World Report* (3 November): 21.

McDermott, Monika L. 1997. "Voting Cues in Low-Information Elections: Candidate Gender as a Social Information Variable in Contemporary United States Elections." *American Journal of Political Science* 41, no. 1:270–283.

_____. 1998. "Race and Gender Cues in Low-Information Elections." *Political Research Quarterly* 51, no.4:895–918.

Media Matters for America. 2008a. "Limbaugh returned to 'testicle lockbox;"claimed Clinton 'reminds men of the worst characteristics of women.'" (15 February). http://mediamatters.org/research/200802150004.

_____. 2008b. "For Chris Matthews, Misogyny Pays." (16 April). http://mediamatters.org/print/columns/200804160002.

_____. 2008c. "Women, minorities, autistic children: Conservative radio's vitriol not reserved for Obama." (13 November). http://mediamatters.org/print/research/200811130002.

Merritt, Sharyne. 1977. "Winners and Losers: Sex Differences in Municipal Elections." *American Journal of Political Science* 21, no. 4:731–743.

Miller, Geralyn. 2001. "Newspaper Coverage and Gender: An Analysis of the 1996 Illinois State Legislative House District Races." *Women & Politics* 22, no. 3: 83–100.

Molinari, Susan. 1998. *Representative Mom: Balancing Budgets, Bill and Baby in the U.S. Congress*. New York: Doubleday Books.

Morris, Celia. 1992. *Storming the Statehouse: Running for Governor with Ann Richards and Dianne Feinstein*. New York: Charles Scribner's Sons.

Morrison, Jane Ann. 2000. "Study Finds Uneven Political Reporting." *Las Vegas Review-Journal* (24 January).

Mueller, Carol. 1986. "Nurturance and Mastery: Competing Qualifications for Women's Access to High Public Office?" *Research in Politics and Society* 2:211–232.

NBC News/*Wall Street Journal*. 2008. "NBC News/*Wall Street Journal* Poll, Study #6080." March 2008. Accessed online at http://online.wsj.com/public/resources/documents/WSJ-20080312-poll.pdf

Newsweek. 2008. *Newsweek* Poll. October 10th. Accessed through Polling the Nations.

Niven, David. 1998. "Party Elites and Candidates: The Shape of Bias." *Women & Politics* 19, no. 2:57–80.

———. 1998. *The Missing Majority: The Recruitment of Women as State Legislative Candidates*. Westport, CT: Praeger Publishers.

———. 2006. "Throwing Your Hat Out of the Ring: Negative Recruitment and the Gender Imbalance in State Legislative Candidacy." *Politics & Gender* 2, no. 4:473–489.

"No Limits for Women: The Official Word." 2002. *In These Times* (22 July): 12.

Open Secrets. 2008. "2008 Race: North Carolina Senate." Accessed online at www.opensecrets.org/races/summary.php?cycle=2008&id=NCS1

Palin's Speech at the Republican National Convention. 2008. Transcript available at http://elections.nytimes.com/2008/president/conventions/videos/transcripts/20080903_PALIN_SPEECH.html.

Palley, Marian Lief. 1993. "Elections 1992 and the Thomas Appointment." *PS: Political Science and Politics* 26, no. 1:28–31.

Palmer, Barbara, and Dennis Simon. 2001. "The Political Glass Ceiling: Gender, Strategy, and Incumbency in U.S. House Elections, 1976–1998. *Women & Politics* 23, no. 1–2:59–78.

———. 2008. *Breaking the Political Glass Ceiling: Women and Congressional Elections*. 2nd ed. New York: Routledge Press.

Pew Research Center's Project for Excellence in Journalism. 2007 (29 October). "The Invisible Primary—Invisible No Longer: A First Look at Coverage of the 2008 Presidential Campaign." 29 October. www.journalism.org/node/8187.

———.2008a. "Character and the Primaries of 2008 (29 May). www.journalism.org/node/11266.

———. 2008b. "Winning the Media Campaign." (22 October). www.journalism.org/node/13310.

Polling Report. 2008. "Campaign 2008." Accessed online at www.pollingreport.com/wh08.htm.

Porter, Mary Cornelia, and Ann B. Matasar. 1974. "The Role and Status of Women in the Daley Organization." In *Women in Politics*, ed. Jane S. Jaquette. New York: John Wiley and Sons.

Procter, David E., William J. Schenck-Hamlin, and Karen A. Haase. 1994. "Exploring the Role of Gender in the Development of Negative Political Advertisements." *Women & Politics* 14, no. 2:1–22.

Raasch, Chuck. 2002. "Pro-Abortion Rights Group's Fundraising Power Could Be Wave of PAC Future." *Gannett News Service* (24 October).

Rausch, John David, Jr., Mark J. Rozell, and Harry L. Wilson. 1999. "When Women Lose: A Study of Media Coverage of Two Gubernatorial Campaigns." *Women & Politics* 20, no. 4:1–22.

Rosenwasser, Shirley Miller, and Norma G. Dean. 1989. "Gender Role and Political Office: Effects of Perceived Masculinity/Femininity of Candidate and Political Office." *Psychology of Women Quarterly* 13:77–85.

Rosenwasser, Shirley M., and Jana Seale. 1988. "Attitudes Toward a Hypothetical Male or Female Presidential Candidate—A Research Note." *Political Psychology* 9, no. 4:591–598.

Saad, Lydia. 2007. "Democrats Prefer Clinton Over Rivals on Most Policy Issues." October 4th. Accessed online at www.gallup.com/poll/101710/Democrats-Prefer-Clinton-Her-Rivals-Handle-Most-Policy-Issues.aspx

Sanbonmatsu, Kira. 2002. "Gender Stereotypes and Vote Choice." *American Journal of Political Science* 46, no. 1:20–34.

_____. 2002. "Political Parties and the Recruitment of Women to State Legislatures." *Journal of Politics* 64, no. 3:791–809.

_____. 2006. "Do Parties Know that 'Women Win'? Party Leader Beliefs About Women's Electoral Chances." *Politics & Gender* 2, no. 4:231–250.

Sapiro, Virginia. 1981–82. "If U.S. Senator Baker Were a Woman: An Experimental Study of Candidate Images." *Political Psychology* (Spring/Summer): 61–83.

Sapiro, Virginia, and Barbara G. Farah. 1980. "New Pride and Old Prejudice: Political Ambition and Role Orientations Among Female Partisan Elites." *Women & Politics* 1, no. 1:13–36.

"Sarah Palin Holds Forth on Bush Doctrine, Pakistan." 2008. ABC Interview with Charles Gibson. Aired September 11th. Accessible online at www.youtube.com/watch?v=Z75QSExE0jU

Schatz, Amy. 2002. "EMILY's List Supports Abortion-Rights Candidates, Sees Slow Start This Year." *The Austin American Statesman* (28 September).

Schroeder, Pat. 1998. *24 Years of House Work . . . and the Place Is Still a Mess.* Kansas City, MO: Andrews McMeel Publishing.

Seelye, Katharine Q., and Julie Bosman. 2008. "Critics and News Executives Split Over Sexism in Clinton Coverage." *New York Times* (13 June): A1.

Seltzer, Richard A., Jody Newman, and Melissa Voorhees Leighton. 1997. *Sex as a Political Variable.* Boulder, CO: Lynne Rienner.

Shear, Michael D., and Shailagh Murray. 2008. "Back on the Stump, Candidates Attack Each Other on Economy: McCain, Obama Shift Messages Back to Political Center." *Washington Post* (6 September): A1.

Sheckels, Theodore F., Jr. 1994. "Mikulski vs. Chavez for the Senate from Maryland in 1986 and the 'Rules' for Attack Politics." *Communication Quarterly* 42, no. 3:311–326.

Simon, Dennis, and Barbara Palmer. 2005. "The Political Geography of Women Friendly Districts, 1972–2000." Paper presented at the 2005 Annual Meeting of the Southern Political Science Association. New Orleans, LA, January 6–8.

Stanley, Harold W., and Richard G. Neimi. 2001. *Vital Statistics on American Politics.* Washington, D.C.: CQ Press.

Stanwick, Kathy A. 1983. *Political Women Tell What It Takes.* New Brunswick, NJ: Rutgers: CAWP.

Sullivan, David B. 1998. "Images of a Breakthrough Woman Candidate: Dianne Feinstein's 1990, 1992, and 1994 Campaign Television Advertisements." *Women's Studies in Communication* 21, no. 1:7–26.

Survey by Newsweek and Princeton Survey Research Associates International. 2008. (October 22-October 23). Retrieved July 30, 2009 from the iPOLL Databank, The Roper Center for Public Opinion Research, University of Connecticut. www.ropercenter.uconn.edu.ezproxy.macalester.edu/ipoll.html.

Survey by Pew Research Center for the People & the Press and Princeton Survey Research Associates International. 2008. (September 27-September 29). Retrieved (July 30), 2009 from the iPOLL Databank, The Roper Center for Public Opinion Research, University of Connecticut. www.ropercenter.uconn.edu.ezproxy.macalester.edu/ipoll.html.

Susan B. Anthony List. 2003. "About SBA List: History." www.sba-list.org/index.cfm/section/about/page/history.html. Accessed July 8, 2003.

Tolchin, Susan, and Martin Tolchin. 1973. *Clout: Womanpower and Politics.* New York: Coward, McCann, & Geoghegan, Inc.

Tolleson-Rinehart, Sue, and Jeanie R. Stanley. 1994. *Claytie and the Lady: Ann Richards, Gender, and Politics in Texas.* Austin: University of Texas Press.

Uhlaner, Carole Jean, and Kay Lehman Schlozman. 1986. "Candidate Gender and Congressional Campaign Receipts." *Journal of Politics* 48, no. 1:30–50.

U.S. Bureau of the Census. 2002. *Statistical Abstract of the United States.* Washington, D.C.: Government Printing Office.

——. 2004. "Special Edition Press Release: Teacher Appreciation Week." (May) www.census.gov/Press-release/www/releases/archives/facts_for_features_special_editions.

——. 2007. *Employed Civilians by Occupation, Sex, Race, and Hispanic Origin: 2007.* Table 596. www.census.gov/compendia/statab/tables/09s0596.pdf

U.S. Department of Education. National Center for Education Statistics. 2001. *Digest of Education Statistics.* Washington, D.C.: Government Printing Office.

U.S. Department of Labor, Women's Bureau. 2001. 20 Leading Occupations of Employed Women 2001. www.dol.gov/wb/wb_pubs/20lead2001.htm. Accessed July 7, 2003.

van Assendelft, Laura, and Karen O'Connor. 1994. "Backgrounds, Motivations and Interests: A Comparison of Male and Female Party Activists." *Women & Politics* 14, no. 3:77–92.

Van Hightower, Nikki R. 1977. "The Recruitment of Women for Public Office." *American Politics Quarterly* 5, no. 3:301–314.

Verba, Sidney, Nancy Burns, and Kay Lehman Schlozman. 1997. "Knowing and Caring About Politics: Gender and Political Engagement." *Journal of Politics* 59, no. 4: 1051–1072.

Wakeman, Jessica. 2008. "Misogyny's Greatest Hits: Sexism in Hillary Clinton Coverage." FAIR: Fairness & Accuracy in Reporting. May/June. www.fair.org/index.php?page=3407 www.fair.org/index.php?page=3407

Washington Post / ABC News. 2008. Washington Post-ABC News Poll. (4 February). Accessed online at www.washingtonpost.com/wp-srv/politics/polls/postpoll_020308.html

Watkins, Bonnie, and Nina Rothchild. 1996. *In the Company of Women: Voices from the Women's Movement.* St. Paul: Minnesota Historical Society Press.

Welch, Susan, Margery M. Ambrosius, Janet Clark, and Robert Darcy. 1985. "The Effect of Candidate Gender on Electoral Outcomes in State Legislative Races." *Western Political Quarterly* 38, no. 3:464–475.

Wells, Audrey Siess, and Eleanor Cutri Smeal. 1974. "Women's Attitudes Toward Women in Politics: A Survey of Urban Registered Voters and Party Committeewomen." In *Women in Politics*, ed. Jane S. Jaquette. New York: John Wiley and Sons.

Werner, Brian L. 1997. "Financing the Campaigns of Women Candidates and Their Opponents: Evidence from Three States, 1982–1990." *Women & Politics* 18, no. 1:81–97.

WISH List. 2003. "FAQs About the WISH List." www.thewishlist.org/FAQs.htm. Accessed (July 8), 2003.

Witt, Linda, Karen M. Paget, and Glenna Matthews. 1994. *Running as a Woman: Gender and Power in American Politics.* New York: The Free Press.

Women's Campaign Forum. 2010. "Our Mission." Accessed online at http://www. wcfonline.org/sites/wcf/index.php/sn/mission/.

Women in Local Politics and Government

In the early twentieth century, several communities experienced what would become known as "petticoat politics," in which women would become so frustrated with the corruption and inability of local male officeholders to operate government that they would run an all-female slate of candidates with the goal of reform in mind. This occurred in Jackson, Wyoming, in 1920, when five women defeated an all-male ticket (including two husbands of female candidates), as well as in smaller towns in Oregon, New York, Ohio, Colorado, and Michigan during the next decade (Gruberg 1968). The typical pattern was for the women to balance the budget, root out fraud, and retire shortly thereafter upon completion of these tasks, typically after one term in office.[1] However, these pioneering women seldom sparked a desire among large numbers of women to become involved more routinely in local politics as elected officials.

Today, women are more likely to serve at the local level of government than at the state or national level. One reason is obvious—there are many more opportunities to participate. As of 2007, there were more than 85,000 government units in the United States, ranging from school boards, townships, counties, municipalities, and "special districts," which are independent government units designed for a specific special purpose, such as handling public transportation (U.S. Census Bureau 2007). Table 6.1 lists the numbers and types of local governments according to the U.S. Census Bureau. Combined, these local governments allow for the election of almost 500,000 public

---

[1] Although in one instance, *The Literary Digest* reports in 1937 in its article "Henpecked Kansans: Males Endanger Beer, Vote Complaining Women into Office" that the election of several women to local political office in Craighead County, Kansas, was engineered (unbeknownst to them) by the town's male inhabitants, who "were tired of the female criticism of the way they had the village" (7). However, upon election, the women officials promised to limit men's ability to buy alcohol. As the newly elected Mayor Katherine Ermie claimed, "We're in for two years at least and there won't be any places licensed to sell beer" (ibid.).

> **TABLE 6.1**
>
> **Type of Local Governments in 2007**
>
> | Type of Government | Number |
> |---|---|
> | Federal Government | 1 |
> | State Governments | 50 |
> | Local Governments | |
> | General Purpose: | |
> | County | 3,033 |
> | Municipal | 19,492 |
> | Township | 16,519 |
> | Special Purpose: | |
> | School Districts | 13,051 |
> | Special Districts | 37,381 |
>
> *Source:* U.S. Census Bureau. 2007. "Government Units in 2007." *U.S. Census of Governments.*

officials nationwide. In 1992—the most recent year for which such data are available by gender—more than 20 percent of those elected officials were women (ibid.).

Not only are women more likely to be elected at the local level of government, but enhanced opportunities to affect public policy also exist for women in local bureaucracies and in grassroots, nongovernmental organizations (Palley 2001). In many ways, the daily lives of women (and men) are deeply touched by local governments. Though less glamorous than national or state politics, local politicians grapple with issues that impact women and children disproportionately, such as education, social services, and domestic violence. In addition, local government is where public access to elected officials is greatest. Given that decentralization is a hallmark of American government and politics, examining the impact and activism of women in local politics is important.

This chapter takes a look at women in local politics in three broad areas. First, we examine women in local elected office, both at the executive level and legislative level. How often are women elected to these sorts of positions? Does having women in these elected offices actually improve the status of women in their communities? Do women pursue different policies than men at the local level, or is gender even a factor?

In addition to examining women in local elective office, we also study women in local bureaucracies and public administration. As Marian Lief Palley (2001) notes, many women bureaucrats may be "hidden players" in terms of affecting and developing public policy, from the agenda-setting stage to policy implementation. Bureaucrats often hold appointed positions, from small town police officers and school principals to city managers in large metropolitan areas. How well are women represented among local bureaucrats? And do they behave any differently than their male counterparts?

We then turn to examining women in grassroots activism and nongovernmental organizations (NGOs), recognizing that participation in these areas often results in demands for government to address a variety of concerns like environmental issues, labor disputes, and economic development. How or why do women activists at this level differentiate themselves from men? We profile several cases of local activism in which women made a unique contribution. Lastly, we take a look at women in the private sector. Given the importance of economic development to local communities, both urban and rural, business leaders often have a large hand in politics as well. How are women faring as leaders in the private sector, and does this have any spillover effects in terms of local politics?

WOMEN IN LOCAL ELECTIVE OFFICE

Women as Locally Elected Executives

Many localities have elected female mayors and county supervisors. The first woman to be elected mayor in the United States was Susan Madora Salter, elected in 1886 as mayor of Argonia, Kansas (Bystrom n.d.). Serving as mayor or as an elected county supervisor can be an important stepping-stone for political office. U.S. Senator Dianne Feinstein, for example, gained national attention as the mayor of San Francisco. Feinstein, then president of the San Francisco Board of Supervisors (the city council), was made mayor after the assassination of George Moscone in 1978; she went on to be elected to two terms as one of the most popular mayors in San Francisco history before successfully running for the U.S. Senate in 1992. Feinstein also founded the Women Mayors' Caucus in 1983, an offshoot of the U.S. Mayors' Conference that brings together female mayors from across the country so that they can meet informally and exchange information (Maharaj 2004).

Women are not as well represented as locally elected executives as they are in legislative bodies, with their numbers having held steady since the early 1990s. In 1971, just 1 percent of cities with a population of 30,000 or more had female mayors; that number increased to 17 percent by 2009 (CAWP 2009). As of January 2009, 11 women served as mayors of the 100 largest cities in the United States; of the 1,142 U.S. cities with populations over 30,000, 193 or 16.9 percent were female (CAWP 2009) (see Table 6.2). Unfortunately, no data show the proportion of females serving as mayor in smaller cities and towns. Our profile of Mayor Margo Bailey of Chestertown, Maryland, sheds some light on what it is like to be the mayor of a small town (see *Profiles of Political Influence*). Bailey's experience is compared to that of Shirley Franklin, the former mayor of Atlanta and the first African-American woman to serve as mayor for such a large city.

There is relatively little research to document whether or not female mayors behave differently than do male mayors. One early study found that the presence of a female mayor boosted the number of women in the municipal workforce, particularly in nonclerical and professional or administrative positions (Saltzstein 1986). Barbara Crow's (1997) case study of female

TABLE 6.2

Percentage of Female Mayors in Cities with More Than 30,000

Year	Percentage
1971	1%
1975	5
1979	7
1983	9
1987	11
1991	17
1995	18
1999	21
2001	21
2003	17
2009	17

Source: Compiled by the Arizona Women's Political Caucus, with information from the Center for the American Woman and Politics (CAWP), the National League of Cities, and the U.S. Conference of Mayors.

PROFILES OF POLITICAL INFLUENCE

Margo Bailey, Mayor of Chestertown, Maryland

Margo Bailey is the first woman to serve as mayor in Chestertown, a small historic town of 4,500 on Maryland's Eastern Shore. She was first elected in 1990, after two years of serving on the city council. Before trying her hand in politics, Bailey operated a newsstand for ten years—a business that in a local community meant she frequently interacted with a large, diverse group of people. She found that her business also allowed her the chance to help people, particularly members of the minority African-American community, who often came to her for assistance with problems such as tenant issues. These very same people eventually persuaded her to run for local office, indicating that they "didn't feel comfortable" with the current male officeholders and wanted instead someone "they could talk to" in the government (Bailey 2004). After losing her first race by one vote and learning more about how campaigns work at the local level, she was handily elected on her second try. She decided to run for mayor when the incumbent decided not to seek reelection and because she was angry at attempts by Wal-Mart to open a store in the small community. She believed that such a move would only offer low-end jobs in the town and would pose a threat to other local businesses (Bailey has successfully led the effort to stop Wal-Mart in a bitter protracted legal battle with the company.)

▶ PROFILES OF POLITICAL INFLUENCE (CONTINUED)

Although Bailey did not raise gender as an issue herself when she was first running for office, she did face some initial resistance from voters because she was a woman. For example, she reports that at one candidate gathering, she was told "my skirts were too short." Other voters, typically older people of her parents' generation, wanted to know if elected, who would be home to "cook the food or run the household?" A mother of four, Bailey waited to enter politics until after her children were older, being first elected at age 50. This decision is similar to other women who run for local offices (see also Chapter 5).

As mayor of Chestertown, Bailey believes that her gender has had both advantages and disadvantages. Although she reports that her interactions with other government and elected officials are generally positive, relations with local business leaders, often men, are sometimes more contentious. She says that many male chief financial officers are not used to having to deal with a female mayor. She says that some male business leaders "just didn't think I could figure out" how to do work effectively with local industry—a vital task of any elected mayor. She found initially that in meetings with such male leaders, they would often ask questions or direct comments to the male town manager, upon which she would have to remind them that she was the one in charge. Ultimately, Bailey feels that dealing with members of the business community is not a "gender thing" and has worked hard to establish ground rules, refusing to be intimidated because she is a woman.

Bailey does note, however, that there may be some advantages to being a female executive. First, she believes that women leaders are better at asking questions than men, having the "ability to walk in and not be embarrassed" to ask for help. She believes that people love to be asked for their assistance and are generally open to her inquiries. She also believes that she, like other women, has a different approach to governance. "You can be firm and strong," she says, "but you can always be kind." She also points to the fact that, as a woman, she knows lots of other women in the community and works hard to bring them into local government as volunteers by asking them to serve on local commissions. Finally, a benefit of being one of the few women mayors in Maryland has been a heightened profile in the state. Bailey's success has attracted attention, and she has been asked to serve on various state commissions and as an activist in the Maryland Municipal League, where she makes it a point to mentor newly elected female officials.

Bailey believes that it is difficult as a mayor in a small town to guide public policy in a way that specifically benefits women and children—most social policies and programs are instead developed at the state level of government in Maryland. Indirectly, however, as a member of various state committees, Bailey tries to influence policy in that direction for the entire state. Another way that she helps

(Continued)

PROFILES OF POLITICAL INFLUENCE (CONTINUED)

women and girls is as a role model. For instance, she is asked regularly to speak to "at-risk" groups of teen girls, discussing self-esteem issues. Although she has been approached by many people to run for higher office, Bailey is more than content to keep her current position, finding the job of local mayor both fun and rewarding. ■

PROFILES OF POLITICAL INFLUENCE

Shirley Franklin, Atlanta's First African-American Female Mayor

In 2001, Atlanta citizens elected Democrat Shirley Franklin as mayor—the first African-American woman chief executive of any major Southern city (Schoenberger 2003). A former city administrator in her first elected position (she was cultural affairs commissioner under Maynard Jackson in the 1970s and city manager for Andrew Young during the next decade), the 65-year-old Franklin has won wide praise among community and business leaders and members of both political parties. *Governing* magazine described her as having "engineered a remarkable turnaround of the city's credibility and public demeanor" (Gurwitt 2004, 2). She was easily re-elected in 2005. Among other accolades, she was named the 2004 Public Official of the Year by *Governing* Magazine and *Time* Magazine named her one of the top five mayors in the country in 2005, the same year in which she won the John F. Kennedy Profile in Courage Award.

Prior to Franklin, Atlanta had suffered under the former mayor, Bill Campbell (1994–2002), who alienated the business community during his term and left Franklin's administration to deal with a large budget deficit and a sewage crisis (Shipp 2004). After being inaugurated in January 2002, her first year in office was spent trying to make up a deficit estimated to be more than $80 million. She went about cutting jobs, reducing government spending, and raising property taxes. She also voluntarily took a pay cut of more than $40,000 to demonstrate her belief that such changes, although painful, were necessary for the city (Schoenberger 2003). Such moves demonstrated to many that she was willing to have the city take responsibility for its management as opposed to looking for federal and state government to bail it out. The sewer mess—which had been ignored by city leaders for years—was a much more expensive problem to fix. The century-old sewage system needed upgrading desperately, as it often dumped raw sewage into the South and Chattahoochee rivers after heavy rainstorms. Worse, the federal government had issued consent decrees after Atlanta was sued for violating the Clean Water Act and

▶ PROFILES OF POLITICAL INFLUENCE (CONTINUED)

threatened fines, contempt of court citations, and a ban on new sewer hookups, which would effectively put a halt to local development (Gurwitt 2004). Initially, Franklin made little headway when appealing to the state legislature for help in funding the renovations for the sewer, which were estimated to cost the city more than $3 billion (National Public Radio 2004). But eventually, after a series of direct talks between Franklin and state political leaders (which followed her creation of a task force of community and business leaders to address the problem), Franklin was able to persuade the Republican governor and state legislature to use the state's credit to borrow money and got permission to allow the Atlanta City Council to vote for a property tax increase, which passed in spring 2004.

Franklin does have her critics, which could be linked in part to her gender. Despite having a generally warm relationship with most business leaders, others in the "old boy's network" have labeled her "disrespectful," claiming she "acts like a queen" (Campbell 2004, 3E). Franklin claims this is because many people have an expectation that women leaders should be just like men leaders, although men often learned their leadership styles "from their own experiences, like teams sports, and I think we're seeing in Atlanta [which also has a female city council president] the emergence of different women's styles" (Quoted in Campbell 2004, 3e). Moreover, Franklin says that Atlanta has learned that she is not just "some man's pawn," and that "women can be equally strong in a different way," which has rubbed some people the wrong way (ibid.).

Her initiatives to raise various taxes and city budget cuts have not been popular in the poor, black community either. Now that the sewer and budget crises have been averted, however, Franklin is turning her attention to poverty issues in a city where close to a quarter of the population lives below the poverty line. "The city of Atlanta's interactions with people of low income around issues of poverty are [limited to] law enforcement," she says. "That's how we interact with them. Well, we've got to shift that model" (Quoted in Gurwitt 2004, 8). She spearheaded an initiative to address homelessness, opening the 24/7 Gateway Center in 2005 that serves 500 homeless people daily in collaboration with community partners and instituted a $150 million Quality of Life Bond Program through the Public Works Department to beautify the city and fix and repair roadways and sidewalks (City of Atlanta n.d.). She raised her national profile, as well, by becoming a co-chair of the 2008 National Democratic Convention held in Denver, Colorado, and was a former president for the Conference of National Democratic Mayors.

Overall most Atlantans have been impressed with the 5-foot, 2-inch dynamo. According to Shirley Franklin's friend Michael Lomax, who heads the United Negro College Fund and is a longtime Atlanta political figure, "I always thought she was little and cute, but I'd say 'Beware!' that first impression. She's a powerful intellect, a tough personality and a person of extraordinary integrity. She's become formidable in her mature years (Gurwitt 2004, 5)."

Because Atlanta imposes term limits on its mayors, Franklin did not run for re-election in 2009. She was succeeded by Kasim Reed, her former campaign manager. ■

mayors in Ontario, Canada, found that most were attracted to this local level because it offered a chance to directly affect the lives of individuals and their families. As one mayor stated, "The issues that were paramount to me were those day to day issues, the community infrastructure, the way that we talk to people, respect for the individual. These were things that I could make a difference at, I felt, and they were at the municipal level" (Crow 441). Crow argues that female mayors in Canada, at least, view the more traditional policies pursued at this level of government, such as economic development and land use, as being interrelated to the "private" spheres that are assumed to best serve the interests of women and families, leading her to conclude that women mayors perhaps do not seek substantively different policies upon election than their male counterparts.

Two more recent studies suggest that women mayors in the United States may be more likely to advance policy goals through the budgetary process, at least in larger cities. In her study of budget data from close to 200 cities, Holman (2008) finds that cities that have a female mayor are more likely to spend more on welfare programs than cities that have a male mayor. Further, another study of 120 U.S. mayors composed of 65 female and 55 male mayors, found that women mayors were more likely than their male counterparts to change budgeting procedures to address policy goals and were more likely to view the budgetary process as a way to encourage more community participation in government (Weikart et al 2006). This same study, however, found few gender differences in terms of governing styles or political goals for mayors. More striking in the study was the difference of perceptions concerning gender discrimination. Women mayors were far more likely to agree that women in elected office faced particular obstacles because of their gender than were men mayors, citing personal experience they faced with respect to gaining credibility among many community and business leaders and being taken seriously, particularly when it came to business-related decisions.

Local Councils: Women in Country and City Government

Counties trace their heritage back to English shires, which served as administrative arms of the national government (National Association of Counties 2003). Counties and cities are still viewed as arms of the states, which confer all formal powers to local governments through state constitutions or by acts of the state legislature (Ross and Levine 2001). Currently, all states except Rhode Island and Connecticut have functioning county governments, although in Alaska they are known as "boroughs" and in Louisiana they are known as "parishes" (NAC 2000). There are a total of 3,033 counties in the United States, including 34 city-county governments, which are cities that share government functions with their surrounding counties (NAC 2003). However, almost 10 percent of the total U.S. population is not served by county government, as many of the most populous cities have separate municipal government structures not affiliated with counties (U.S. Census of Governments 1992). In other words, some people live in cities that have their own separate governments apart from counties in the states. Local legislatures at the county level are typically known as county councils, boards of supervisors, or boards of commissioners. As of 1992, there were 17,274 elected officials serving on county legislatures (ibid.).

There are three basic forms of county government. The most popular is the commission form, in which legislative and executive powers are shared. Currently, about three-quarters of county governments use the commission structure, with one of the commissioners acting as the presiding officer (Bowman and Kearney 1999). Other counties have a commission with an appointed administrator, who often has responsibility for a broad range of powers, such as hiring and firing county employees. Approximately 800 counties have this arrangement. The last form of county government is the council-executive, which is predicated in the separation of powers and used by close to 400 counties. Here county executives are elected separately from the council and typically have veto power over the legislative abilities of council members in addition to hiring authority and other administrative responsibilities. The ability to oversee county employees is an important one, as county governments currently employee more than 2 million individuals nationwide (NAC 2003).

Traditionally, counties performed state-mandated duties such as record keeping, assessing property, maintaining and building local roads, administering local elections, law enforcement, and judicial functions—tasks that still make up the bulk of what county governments do. But counties have increasingly taken on more responsibilities in the wake of the "devolution revolution" that has been occurring in American politics since the late 1980s. Devolution involves shifting policy responsibilities from the federal government to the state and local levels. Local government power was probably most curtailed in the 1960s, with the federal government taking a more proactive role in trying to coordinate and fund public programs geared at tackling poverty, health care, economic development, and education in urban, suburban, and rural areas. However, as it became clear that a nationally mandated focus was making little headway in actually solving these intractable problems, and as both state and local governments began to chafe under the regulations that accompanied the grant money given to address these issues, calls came for greater freedom for such governments to handle social services and design policies that better suited their own localities. Of course, critics of devolution point out that this greater "freedom" has meant reduced spending on the part of the federal government, meaning that states and localities have either had to raise more money independently or cut back on social services. Although counties vary nationwide regarding the extent to which they provide such services, local shares of domestic expenditures on such programs grew dramatically from the 1970s to the 1990s, indicating that subnational governments such as counties have risen in importance as devolution has taken place (Weber and Brace 1999).

Unlike county government, most municipal governments operate under a council-manager system. The council-manager system operates in approximately half of municipal governments, followed by the mayor-council system; the commission form of government is the least common organized structure of urban government (Ross and Levine 1999).

The most recent data available examining the number of women serving in locally elected legislatures such as county and city councils are dated (Table 6.3). For example, in 1992, the U.S. Census of Governments reported that almost 13 percent of elected county council members were women, which was and remains smaller than the percentage of women serving in state legislatures (18.7 percent in 1992; 24.2 percent in 2009, [U.S. Census of Governments 1992; CAWP 1992, 2009]). There is little reason to suspect that this number has not increased, however, as women posted tremendous gains at this elected position from the 1970s into the early 1990s. In 1987, 8.6 percent of county council members were women, more than triple the number of women serving at this position in 1975 (Manning 1988). Region appears to be a factor when it comes to female representation on elected county councils. As Table 6.3 demonstrates, women are much more likely to be elected to county councils in the West than in the South. This finding corresponds with the heritage of the "frontier" woman in the West, where women were often permitted to vote and run for political office well before suffrage. In the South, more traditional views of the role of women likely predominate in many rural areas in which county councils exist, explaining the paucity of such women serving on these elected boards.

Women are better represented in city councils than on county councils. Additionally, on city councils, there is a positive relationship between city size and the proportion of female council representation, as data from the International City/Council Management Association (ICMA) show in Table 6.3. In 2001, the ICMA found that 22 percent of city council members were women. Although still the minority on boards, women lack presence on only 23 percent of city councils according to the 2001 ICMA data; having a larger council improves the chances that at least one woman will serve on a city council (Alozie and Manganaro 1993).[2] Commission forms of governments, even in urban areas, tend to have the smallest number of members (MacManus and Bullock 1993).

The proportion of the nonwhite population has also been linked to higher levels of representation of minorities at different levels of political office,

---

[2]Women serving on city councils are overwhelmingly white. One study found that in 1988, black women make up about 5 percent and Latinas make up 3 percent of city councils in areas that have at least 10 percent of blacks and Latinos, respectively (Darcy, Welch, and Clark 1994). Yet women of color make up more than one-third of minority elected officials at the local level, whereas fewer than one-fourth of white elected officials are women ("GenderGap in Government" 2004).

TABLE 6.3

Women Serving in Local Councils

County Council	1992	
Percent of Women Serving on County Councils	12.6%	
By Region		
Northeast	14.4	
Midwest	12.1	
South	8.1	
West	18.0	

Source: U.S. Census of Governments, 1992.

City Council	1991	2001
Percent of Women Serving on City Councils		
Total, All Cities	18.7%	22.1%
Percent Women by Population Group		
Over 1,000,000	24.4	33.8
500,000–999,999	24.1	34.9
250,000–499,999	25.9	32.6
100,000–249,000	27.4	28.6
50,000–99,999	22.2	25.9
25,000–49,999	22.4	23.7
10,000–24,999	19.0	22.0
5,000–9,999	17.7	20.4
2,500–4,999	17.0	20.6
Under 2,500	16.3	23.0
Percent Women by Size of City Council		
Fewer than 4 council members	14.9	17.0
4–6	18.3	21.9
7–9	19.6	22.8
More than 9	20.8	23.9
Percent Women by Form of Government		
Mayor-Council	17.4	21.7
Council Manager	20.2	22.8
Commission	10.3	15.3
Town Meeting	18.4	19.8
Representative Town Meeting	24.2	23.6
Percent Women by Method of Election		
Nominated and elected at large	19.7	NA
Nominated by district, elected at large	17.4	NA
Nominated and elected by district	16.3	NA
Other	17.4	NA

Source: MacManus Susan A., and Charles S. Bullock. 1993. "Women and Racial/Ethnic Minorities in Mayoral and Council Positions." *The Municipal Yearbook.* Washington: ICMA, 70–84; International City/County Management Association. 2001. *Municipal Form of Government Survey.*

including county, municipal, and school board offices. In one path-breaking study known as the Gender and Multicultural Leadership Project (see *Paths to Power* box) researchers found that African Americans, Asian Americans, and Hispanic Americans enjoyed more electoral success in districts that were racially diverse—although large percentages of minority groups in districts (or states) does not always result in equitable parity when it comes to office-holding for men or women of color (Hardy-Fanta et al. 2006). For female elected officials of color, the authors define equitable parity as "the extent to which women of color elected officials have reached a share of a given level of office proportionate to their share in the population" (ibid. 16). Indeed, they find that parity ratios differ with respect to race, level of office, and state. For example, women of color, especially Latina and Asian-American women, often enjoy higher parity values in terms of elected representation than do (non-Hispanic) white women (the findings are more mixed for African-American women), depending on the level of government.

One of the most examined questions with respect to the election of women to city councils concerns the relationship between electoral structure and the representation of women. Racial minorities have long argued that single-member districts are more beneficial to their groups because the costs of waging a campaign in a single district are less expensive than running at large. Furthermore, minorities argue that it is easier to be elected in single-member districts because neighborhoods tend to be segregated racially; hence, the odds of electing a minority from a minority-majority district are likely higher than facing several opponents at large as most blacks vote for black candidates and most whites vote for white candidates (see, for example, Browning, Marshall, and Tabb 1984).[3]

By contrast, many feminists have long argued that at-large elections would provide more opportunities for women to serve on city councils. Unlike minorities, women are not geographically isolated in city neighborhoods. The thinking is that women would do better in citywide races because voters would not be faced with a zero-sum choice as they would in a single-district race that elected just one member, in which voting for a woman would mean not choosing a man. When voters can make several choices (as opposed to one choice in a single-member district), they are more likely to want to balance and diversify the ticket (Thomas 1998).

The data, however, do not support these suppositions. Most scholars conclude that women are not advantaged in at-large elections, at best finding only a weak relationship as women are slightly more likely to serve in at-large seats (Karnig and Walter 1976; Welch and Karnig 1979; Bullock

---

[3]There does not appear much evidence to suggest that Hispanics do better in single-member districts than at-large ones, though this has not stopped activists in the Latino community from supporting district-based elections (Darcy, Welch, and Clark 1994).

PATHS TO POWER

The Gender and Multi-Cultural Leadership Project

Women of color have enjoyed large gains in elected office holding at the national, state, and local levels of government in recent years, which is not particularly surprising given that the United States is undergoing dramatic demographic changes. The election of such women of color has greatly increased minority representation in government more generally. In fact, "the election of Black female officeholders accounts for all the gains in the number of African American elected officials over the past ten years (Hardy-Fanta et al 2006, 11)."

To better understand how gender and race/ethnicity are shaping leadership at all levels of government in the twenty-first century, several notable political scientists have undertaken a massive research study to explore the intersectionality of race and gender in American politics, known as the Gender and Multi-Cultural Leadership Project (www. gmcl.org). According to Dr. Christine Sierra, one of the study's principal investigators, the project's origins stem from a 1994 Center for Women and American Politics conference at Rutgers University, in which scholars who specialized in the politics of women of color networked and recognized the need for more systematic research and data on elected officials that examined women of color across all levels of government and was multi-cultural in its approach (Sierra 2009).

More than a decade later, with funding from the Ford Foundation, the GMCL Project has amassed an impressive database of more than 10,000 elected officials of color (both men and women) who serve in Congress, state legislatures, county commissions and boards of supervisors, city councils and school boards across the country. The creation of such a database serves as "a reference point, a baseline for understanding new political leadership at the beginning of the 21st century," according to Dr. Sierra. Researchers and the public alike can find out where elected officials of color govern nationally through the website's interactive map, which shows the distribution of elected officials of color by race and state (www.gmcl.org/database.htm).

In addition, the GMCL researchers surveyed a large sample (N=1,354) of these officials, from summer 2006 to spring 2007, in what is the first comprehensive study of elected officials of color at various levels of government. The survey reveals some interesting gender and cultural differences. For example, men of color are more likely to be represented in state legislatures and in county and municipal offices than women, while men and women of color make up approximately equal shares of school board members. Elected women of color were older than men when they first ran for office; such women are far less likely to be married than men, too. The interaction of race and gender also reveals some interesting findings. While women of color were far more likely than men to have been raised in political families, the gap is especially large between Latinas and Latinos (see "Elected Officials of Color in the US: A Portrait of Today's Leaders" at www.gmcl.org).

The researchers are currently analyzing attitudinal data by race and gender, which is revealing some surprising findings, according to Dr. Sierra. For example, the team finds

(Continued)

that black officials are very supportive of public schools offering courses in language other than English, which runs counter to much of the tension that is often reported between African Americans and immigrant communities in the news. Dr. Sierra says that perhaps one of the most surprising findings came with respect to the issue of voting by legal non-citizens. Female African-American elected officials were the group that was most supportive of allowing legal non-citizens the right to vote in school boards. Dr. Sierra believes that this may be "an indication of where intersectionality might be at work—that perhaps African American women are the most conscious of differences and differential treatment given their own experience and they are inclined to believe if you have kids in schools, you should have a voice in how those schools are run."

While the GMCL project research team continues to analyze and explore their data, they believe that in the short term, at least, the electoral future looks bright for women of color at the state and local levels of politics. Dr. Sierra encourages young women and men who are interested in politics to seize on the numerous opportunities that can provide them with skills that are vital to politics: "how to talk with people, how to organize, and how to work for and with others." Dr. Sierra and her fellow researchers hope that the GMCL Project can contribute in some way to larger public policy debates on issues of importance to people of color in the United States and to provide opportunities for civic education on America's changing leadership. ■

and MacManus 1991; Alozie and Manganaro 1993; MacManus and Bullock 1993; Darcy, Welch, and Clark 1994).[4] This finding is confirmed by the data in Table 6.3, at least for 1991. This is not to say that some electoral structures necessarily elect more women to office, though. One study has found that the few cities that have multimember districts, in which voters can choose to elect more than one person per district, for example, have the most equitable representation in terms of women (Herrick and Welch 1992). Internationally, proportional representation systems, which predominate in Europe, appear to do a better job of ensuring that more women are elected to office (Darcy, Welch, and Clark 1994). Ultimately, however, single-member, at-large districts, or a combination thereof, predominate in municipal elections in the United States (MacManus 1999).

Gender, Leadership Style, and Policy Outcomes in Local Government

"Women are forced to deal with down-home realities of husbands and kids, getting the dinner and the sitter; while men leave home behind when they go to work. So women have a greater ability to understand. They are

---

[4]This finding carries over for African American women, whose success is not affected by electoral structure (Herrick and Welch 1992). African American men, however, are advantaged in single-member districts.

not as slick. They are more personal and better at one-on-one. This is good because these qualities have been missing from politics." (Quoted in Flammang 1985, 111)

The above quote comes from a county council woman who served on the County Commission in Santa Clara County, California, and highlights potential differences that women, as opposed to men, may bring to their service in locally elected government positions. Having more women serving in local politics could be important if women bring with them different experiences, leadership styles, and policy concerns than men. Indeed, political theorists and modern-day interest groups have often argued that only when women achieve greater numbers of elected seats in government will women, as a group, have their concerns and preferences reflected in policy outcomes (see Chapter 7 for an extended discussion of concepts of representation). So, what difference does having women serve in local government actually make?

Once elected to city councils, both female and male municipal councilors face the same administrative tasks and policy responsibilities as elected county councilors. However, cities bring with them challenges that rural and suburban areas are less likely to face (or less willing to address), such as gang violence, drug abuse, homelessness, and poverty. According to MacManus (1999), 42 percent of the nation's poor live in cities with more than 25,000 residents. As a result of the greater duties that city councils often confront, city councils have become more institutionalized in American cities over the past few decades, hiring more paid staff and increasingly relying on subcommittees to carry out their workload (National League of Cities 2003b). City councilors report that the personal cost of their service is high in terms of the time away from their family and other work and campaign expenses (ibid.).

The many everyday responsibilities that are charged to city councilors, such as making sure the garbage is picked up, potholes are filled, taxes are collected, and public parks are open and safe, are largely done in a gender-neutral fashion. Yet the implementation of many public policies, and in turn the way that local politics are conducted, can be gendered at this level of government. Paul Schumaker and Nancy Burns (1988) conducted an analysis of 30 policy decisions in one city—Lawrence, Kansas (home of the University of Kansas)—and found what they called "gender cleavages" on 20 policies.[5] They found that male councilors and policy elites were more supportive of economic growth policies, such as proposals to build shopping and retail centers, and less supportive of restrictive construction regulations (which could

---

[5]Moreover, Schumaker and Burns found that gender cleavages were more frequent than other types of cleavages based on factors such as socioeconomic status, race, and partisan identification. Cleavages predicated on neighborhoods and ideology, however, were more frequent than those based on gender.

potentially limit development), whereas female officials and elites were more supportive of neighborhood preservation policies and increasing financial contributions to social services. However, when strong gender cleavages emerged around issues, male activists were more successful in implementing their preferred policies than were females, leading them to conclude that men's participation in local government has a greater impact than women's participation. Even though they caution that their findings are limited to one city, they note that even stronger gender differences could emerge in cities that have less support for women in public life than Lawrence, which is a fairly progressive city in a college setting in which women are well represented as local elected officials.

An earlier case study comparing male and female representatives in municipalities in Connecticut also found a disconnect between support for policy issues and the ability to implement such policies by women elected officials. Although Mezey (1978) found that while female city councilors in Connecticut were more supportive of feminist policies than their male counterparts, such as establishing rape crisis centers and increasing the number of quality day care facilities for working parents, they were just as likely as men to rank other concerns, such as roads and transportation, public recreation, and pollution ahead of feminist concerns when it came to prioritizing them. When controlling for other factors, moreover, Mezey found that ideology was a more important predictor in determining support for feminist policies than gender. Her conclusion? Electing more women to local legislatures may not necessarily result in more feminist policies, at least not in Connecticut.

Although the findings with respect to women's ability to implement different types of policies than men might be discouraging in terms of substantive representation—at least for feminists—it should come as no surprise that women elected officials are more supportive of increased spending on social welfare programs and policies geared at preserving neighborhoods. Another case study examined female officials in Santa Clara County, California, dubbed the "feminist" capital of the nation in the 1980s due to the large numbers of women elected there. For instance, by the mid-1980s, four cities in the county had female mayors, while 14 of the 15 city councils had female members, including female majorities on the San Jose City Council and on the Santa Clara County Board of Supervisors (Flammang 1985). Flammang found that newly elected women in Santa Clara County— both feminists and nonfeminists alike—linked their policy concerns, and their ability to handle their new positions effectively, to their homemaking and childrearing experiences, as the quote earlier demonstrates (Flammang 1985). Female elected officials in Santa Clara County believed that their backgrounds provided them with unique but bona fide management skills that were conducive to politics. Many of these women argued that they were better at constituency service, more honest, more empathetic, more courteous, and better listeners than men. Some argued that they sensed a distinctive female understanding of power as elected officials, including this council member: "We are softer, more compassionate, yet still firm . . . There are advantages to being a woman in business and politics: we can get our way, not by batting eyelashes or anything like that, but by using methods men cannot use. Men always feel they have to compete with each other" (108).

This notion that women perhaps approach local governance differently is supported by the experiences of the first county council to have a completely female majority, which was Missoula County, Montana, when in 1985 all three seats of the county board of commissioners were held by women (Manning 1988).[6] According to Ann Mary Dussault, one of the elected commissioners, "I think that women, regardless of whether they are in council positions or commission positions or legislative positions, do bring that nurturing and, in a lot of cases, a far less aggressive or combative style to the position. I think those things play into a kind of management style that is done on an instinctive level rather than an intellectual level" (Manning 1988, 5). The council was generally given high marks by local community leaders, described by one member of the chamber of commerce as the "most well-reasoned, stable, trustworthy body" that he had dealt with in many years (ibid.). Their success came somewhat unexpectedly to the commissioners themselves, as the women believed that expectations for an all-female board were low. As Commissioner Janet Stevens remarked, "People said we probably don't know much about roads and things like that, and we would probably bicker and argue. There are people who would like to see us go at each other with our fingernails" (2).

Not everyone was happy with their stewardship, however, including the male county sheriff, who had unsuccessfully sought a court order seeking an injunction against the commission, which had ordered tighter controls over the use of sedatives in the local jail upon an audit of the police department. The sheriff described the three women as "overzealous" and complained that the three women "tend to stick together more than three men would" (4). All in all, though, the women believed that the community had largely been accepting of them and appreciative of their willingness to listen to the concerns of voters. This experience on behalf of the three commissioners is not surprising given that other studies have found that locally elected women spend more time on their jobs than men and believe that their constituents place greater trust in them than they would in men (Merritt 1980; Antolini 1984). Moreover, many voters see women candidates for local office as superior to men candidates in dealing with the community (Brown, Heighberger, and Shocket 1993).

---

[6]This distinction, which was recognized by the *Congressional Record*, perhaps is not surprising considering that Missoula was the county in which Jeannette Rankin, the first woman ever to be elected to Congress, was raised (Manning 1988).

Although there are documented differences in terms of how women serving in local legislatures not only view their jobs as elected officials compared with men but also in how they relate with their constituents, the ability of women to make gains in terms of substantive representation is questionable. The irony is that some women may be drawn to service on local governments such as city councils and county boards of commissioners, as compared with state or national government, because they believe that this level of government has the greatest impact on the day-to-day lives of families, yet might find themselves limited in their abilities to make systematic policy changes that result in more supportive social policies. Given the paucity of research at the local level of government, however, such a generalization is preliminary. More systematic and updated research at this level of government is needed, such as a recent study that examined the relationship between descriptive representation and levels of political trust among constituents in 70 different municipalities. Stacy Ulbig (2007) found that levels of political trust among men and women differed as the number of women serving in city councils rose. Among citizens with a moderate awareness of politics and government, women exhibited higher levels of political trust as their city councils gained more women members, while the opposite happened for men. While the study does not examine specific policies enacted by such councils, it does demonstrate that legitimacy in ones' government can be related to the gender of who is serving in office and perhaps illustrates why having diversity in government is important. (For a look at women serving in another form of local government—tribal government among Native Americans—see *Profiles of Political Influence*: *Women as Tribal Leaders*).

PROFILES OF POLITICAL INFLUENCE

Women as Tribal Leaders

Out of the more than 500 Native American tribes recognized by the Bureau of Indian Affairs, 61 had women leaders in 1990 (McCoy 1992). Local tribes, often located on Indian reservations, have their own responsibilities for local governance and face many of the same challenges as other local governments. Yet native tribes are not monolithic and bring with them different cultural heritages and practices toward governance, including the inclusion of women in tribal decisions. For example, Prindeville and Gomez's study of female Native America political activists in Pueblo tribes in New Mexico found that women faced much hostility from the men who dominated tribal government (Prindeville and Gomez 1999). In most Pueblo communities there, women are prohibited from attending tribal council meetings, from voting, and from holding tribal office. The Pueblo and several other communities often link their exclusion of women in formal politics to their traditional religious practices.

▶ PROFILES OF POLITICAL INFLUENCE (CONTINUED)

Other tribes, however, have been more accepting of women's participation in tribal governance, often citing a matrilineal tribal culture that was in place before such Native cultures were upended by white colonization. In one fascinating study of the Upper Skagit Tribe in Washington State, Bruce Miller found that, unlike state legislatures or Congress, women have actually held a majority of elected tribal council seats since the establishment of the first modern elected tribal council in 1975 (Miller 1994). Miller argues that women candidates in this tribe have several electoral advantages over men, as most have higher levels of education and most benefit from the close familial ties that characterize community-voting preferences in the small Indian community. That women constitute a majority of voters and activists in local government has also helped women candidates to reach their majority status.

In another study of women leaders drawn from numerous Native American tribes, Melanie McCoy found that the average female tribal leader is age 52, college educated, married with two children, and came to her position after serving on a local tribal council or in a paid position in the tribal government (McCoy 1992). Of the 19 women she interviewed, 17 indicated that their gender played a role in how they governed. One theme that emerged was that it was harder for women to participate in tribal politics because women leaders must be "superwomen," balancing their roles as elected officials with their roles as wives and mothers. Moreover, women leaders indicated that they felt pressure to fit into the male world of tribal politics by adopting the same leadership style as men. Because of this pressure, they believe that women have a harder time participating in tribal politics at the state and national levels. Finally, several women acknowledged that they believe women tribal leaders deal with people differently and try harder to communicate and bring in more viewpoints about concerns than do men. But whereas the women tribal leaders in McCoy's study acknowledge that gender might be one factor on how they approach their jobs, they are often limited more by the scarce resources many tribes face and the realities of tribal life, which include communities beset with high rates of poverty, unemployment, and alcohol and drug abuse. Tribal leaders, regardless of gender, seem to give priority to issues that concern survival of their people, such as economic development and fostering independence from the federal Bureau of Indian Affairs (Prindeville 2002).

One notable trendsetter among female Native Americans was Wilma Mankiller (1945-2010), who was elected in 1987 as the first woman chief of the Cherokee Nation, the second largest tribe in the United States. As of the early 1990s, the Cherokee Nation had an enrolled tribal population of more than 140,000, an annual budget of more than $75 million, and more than 1,200 employees (Mankiller and Wallis 1993). The Cherokee Nation has its roots in the southeastern United States but lost most of its people during the forced relocation known as the Trail of Tears in the nineteenth century to the

(Continued)

PROFILES OF POLITICAL INFLUENCE (CONTINUED)

area that would later become Oklahoma. Mankiller first gained notice among tribal leaders for spearheading the Bell Community Revitalization Project to rebuild and develop homes and water projects for this downtrodden community in the Cherokee Nation in 1981. It soon became a model for other nations to follow. Her success and national attention propelled her into the elected position of deputy chief in 1985, and she assumed the role of acting chief later that year when the elected chief retired from office.

Mankiller wrote that she faced a lot of hostility in her initial campaign for deputy chief and later chief of the tribe: "I heard all sorts of things—some people claimed that my running for office was an affront to God. Others said having a female run our tribe would make the Cherokees a laughingstock of the tribal world. I heard it all. Every time I was given yet another silly reason why I should not help run our government, I was certain that I had made the correct decision" (Mankiller and Wallis, 241). Mankiller, a proud feminist, proved her critics wrong and won high praise for her leadership ability from both men and women. In 1992, she was reelected with more than 80 percent of the vote.

Mankiller believed that her time in office until she retired in 1995 has inspired more women, especially girls, to become active in local and national tribal politics—a role that is more in tune with the history of Cherokee women. She wrote: "We are returning the balance to the role of women in our tribe. Prior to my becoming chief, young Cherokee girls never thought they might be able to grow up and become chief themselves. . . . From the start of my administration, the impact on the younger women of the Cherokee Nation was noticeable. I feel certain that more women will assume leadership roles in tribal communities" (ibid., 246).

In more recent years, women continue to make gains in tribal governments. In 2005, Cecilia Fire Thunder became the first woman ever to head the Oglala Sioux in South Dakota, a large tribe of 46,000 whose most famous leader historically was Sitting Bull. Her tenure was marred with controversy, however, when she announced in 2006 her intent to start a Planned Parenthood Clinic on the reservation, which would not be subject to state regulation. (She did this in response to the state's passage of a near universal ban on abortion in 2006, which was eventually overturned in federal court.) The tribal council later announced its own ban on abortion procedures on its tribal land and removed Fire Thunder from office, replacing her with the president pro tempore, Alex White Plume. However, the Oglala Sioux elected another women to the position in 2008, and Theresa Two Bulls serves as its elected chief until 2010.

Native American women also have raised their profile as national leaders in other respects. The current executive director of the National Congress of American Indians is Jacqueline Johnson Pata (www.ncai.org). This trend should largely continue given that women currently make up two-thirds of students at tribal colleges nationwide, according to the American Indian College fund. ■

School Boards

In the late 1860s, several women were elected to school boards in Massachusetts (where they are known as school committees), marking the first elected political position held by women in the nation (Darcy, Welch, and Clark 1994). Moreover, many states granted women the limited right to vote in school board elections long before women gained universal suffrage in 1920. Historically, education has been viewed as a special prerogative of women, given many women's status as mothers. Even today, women devote more of their civic activism to education than to other political issues (Schlozman, Brady, Verba, and Donahue 1995).

It should come as no surprise, then, that school boards represent the local political office to which women are most likely to be elected. In 2002, 39 percent of school board members were women (Hess 2002). The ranks of women at the school board level have increased from the early 1970s, when the National School Boards Association estimated that 12 percent of board members were women (Blanchard 1977).

Although some view school board elections as akin to community service, many important political decisions are decided by school boards. School board elections have become a hotly contested venue in the "culture wars" of American politics. As pitched battles over sex education, censorship, and school prayer demonstrate, the school district is one arena in which moral values often intersect with education (Deckman 2004; Gaddy, Hall, and Marzano 1996). School boards help to establish the direction of local education policy by selecting and monitoring school administrators and they also establish district priorities through budgeting. School boards are also springboards to higher office as many national and state political leaders, such as former President Jimmy Carter and U.S. Senator Patty Murray, got their start as elected school board members. In terms of the political pipeline theory, many argue that women will not go on to pursue higher political office until they have more experience at local offices such as school boards.

How do men and women compare as school board candidates? Data from a national 1998 survey of school board candidates show that 38 percent were women, corresponding closely to their ranks as elected school board members (Deckman 2004, 2006).[7] These same data show that women and men win school board seats at roughly the same rates, as 65 percent of women candidates and 62 percent of men candidates succeeded in their elections. Gender remains an insignificant factor in terms of predicting school board success when controlling for other variables such as incumbency, campaign resources, and type of district (ibid.). Although male and female school

---

[7]Data come from a survey conducted by Deckman in 1998, in which 300 school districts were randomly selected nationwide, stratified by size, and asked to provide lists of candidates who ran in the most recent school board elections. A total of 1,220 school board candidates were identified, and after two waves of mailing, 671 usable responses were received, for a response rate of 55 percent.

board candidates share similar socioeconomic backgrounds, female candidates are more liberal than their male counterparts. Yet more Republican women run at this level than at other levels.

What happens after the elections are over? Do male and female school board members behave differently once in office? Why might we expect gender to emerge as an important factor in terms of guiding the behavior of candidates once elected? Several possibilities emerge. First, women and men could have different policy prerogatives once elected to school boards that have important gender implications. For example, research finds that women legislators at the national and state levels are more likely to champion policies to help the disadvantaged and women. If this were similar at the school board level, we might find that female school board members would be more proactive in supporting special education, racial equality, and vocational education. With respect to education policy that directly impacts girls, some research suggests that girls are more likely to face discrimination in the classroom by teachers in terms of time and attention, and girls are less likely to take science and math classes than boys (AAUW 1992, 1998). Moreover, the number of lawsuits filed concerning Title IX enforcement has grown tremendously at the secondary school level as parents seek to address the imbalance of funds and resources devoted to boys' sports at the expense of girls (Pennington 2004).

If so, one plausible hypothesis is that women school board members will be more likely to advocate for policies that help girls and disadvantaged youths. However, this is not necessarily true. Although Jesse Donahue's research of school board or committee members in Massachusetts finds that 79 percent of women board members agree that "public education needs to do more to foster equality for girls," compared with just 50 percent of male board members, very few women (8 percent) have ever worked on gender equity measures designed to help girls in their school districts, which is comparable to men (Donahue 1999). Donahue believes this discrepancy is due to a lack of women's interest groups to lobby on behalf of these issues at the school board level, the lack of formal powers that many school boards have to address such changes, and to the substantial minority of board members who strongly disagree that girls need extra help in public schools. As Donahue notes, "At best, women [school board members] demonstrate an informed interest in the topic [of gender equality] but frequently fail to pursue measures that would help girls in their system. At worst a substantial minority of women committee members are openly hostile to the very idea that they should be representing girls in their school systems . . ." (Donahue 1999, 77). Instead, men and women board members spend more time discussing more "mainstream" agenda items such as budgeting, curriculum, staff, facilities, and class size (Donahue 1997).

Aside from policy advocacy, a second way that gender could impact school board service is related to *how* members approach their positions. In other words, do male and female board members perceive their roles as board members differently? For example, how do they interact with school superin-tendents? One study from the early 1970s found that male superintendents viewed female board members as more difficult to interact with compared with male members, including this Boston superintendent: "By and large, women on school committees (boards) are nitpicking, emotional, use wiles to get what they want, demand to be treated as equals but have no hesitancy at all to put on the pearls and insist on 'respect' when the going gets rough—and they talk too much" (quoted in Mullins 1972, 27). This superintendent was speaking from limited experience with female board members in a different era and his perspective diverged from the findings of other scholars in the 1970s, who concluded that female and male board members were remarkably similar in how they approached their jobs. More recently, Donahue (1997) has found that women school board members actually talk on average *less* than men during board meetings, a finding based on the condition that men are more likely than women to chair school boards, and board chairs have a larger speaking role as facilitators of the meetings.

These findings beg the question—does it matter that women are under-represented in school board politics? On the one hand, the most recent research suggests that gender does not matter when it comes to school board governance, both in terms of substantive representation in the form of helping advance gender equality in schools and in terms of doing the actual day-to-day work of school boards. Instead, school board members of both genders likely conform to the role of school board member once elected. On the other hand, gender might still impact school board governance in ways that have not been quantified or documented. For instance, some speculate that because school boards are still predominantly male in most districts, it is harder for women to be appointed as school superintendents (Czubaj 2002). Thus, this important administrative position remains male dominated nationally. Also, research from almost three decades ago found that female board members were more likely than male board members to say serving as a community liaison was a vital aspect of their jobs. This finding corresponds with findings about women serving in other legislative bodies and demonstrates that women might bring their own unique understanding to what the role of legis-lators should be even at this local level of government. More updated research is needed at the school board level to determine if women school board members still view this aspect of the position differently than their male counterparts.

In summary, the number of women serving in local legislatures, such as school boards, county boards of commissioners, or city councils has increased dramatically in the past three decades. Although women have made gains in these areas, the most recent data suggest that their numbers might be leveling off. The good news is that for women who run for local office, electoral struc-ture or discrimination on the part of voters does not appear to hinder their success. Women candidates win at the same rates as male candidates. The bad news is that women still show a reluctance to take the initial step to become candidates in the first place, for a variety of reasons that Chapter 5 explores more fully. It is perhaps not until women serve in larger numbers on local legislatures that women will make gains in promoting public policies at the local level that benefit women and families.

WOMEN IN THE BUREAUCRACY

Elected officials are not the only individuals who can affect public policy at the local level of government. Although often overlooked, bureaucrats or public administrators not only have a hand in determining how the policies established by elected officials are overseen but also in shaping their political dimensions. Michael Lipsky calls public-service workers who interact directly with citizens, particularly at the local level, "street-level bureaucrats" and argues that they are important policy actors (Lipsky 1992 [1980]). He writes: "Whether government policy is to deliver 'goods'—such as welfare or public housing—or to confer status—such as 'criminal' or 'mentally ill'—the discretionary actions of public employees are the benefits and sanctions of government programs and determine access to government rights and benefits" (476). In this section, we examine how gender affects the administration of public policy in local bureaucracies. Our definition of bureaucrats includes the "usual suspects" one considers when thinking about public administration, such as city managers and school superintendents. We also consider a broader definition of bureaucrats, however, by examining women as college presidents and women in policing. How well are women represented in these important positions, and does gender have an impact on the way they do their jobs and in the sorts of policies that they pursue?

According to the Equal Employment Opportunity Commission, 42.7 percent of full-time local government employees—of which there are more than 3.6 million—are women (EEOC 2005). More than half of county (53.1 percent) and special district employees are women (50.3 percent), whereas women make up a minority of employees in cities (30.8 percent) and townships (27.4 percent) (ibid.). Women have made great strides in terms of their overall representation in both state and local governments since the mid-1970s, yet this improvement for women was more significant for minority women excluding African Americans (who reported no major increases in the last decade). One study showed that between 1990 and 1997, for instance, 3 percent of white women actually lost jobs due to the downsizing of state and local governments nationally; men lost jobs, too (Burheide 2000). Although the percentage of women working in local and state governments has increased in the past few decades compared with men, men and women are often "segregated" into particular jobs. Men, for example, are still likely to be overrepresented as administrators, whereas women make up the bulk of clerical workers, administrative support, and "paraprofessional" jobs such as home health care and child-support workers (EEOC 2005).

Even among the professional administrative ranks, however, there appears to be gender segregation at work in state government agencies depending on the type of functions they perform. For example, women are underrepresented among administrative and professional ranks in state governmental units dealing with distributive functions, such as construction, repair, parks, and recreations, and regulatory functions, such as police protection, prison operation, and business and labor regulation—although there has been some improvement in terms of female representation in recent years (Kerr, Miller, and Reid 2002). Women fare much better in administrative and professional positions for agencies that primarily serve a redistributive function, such as those that manage welfare and employment programs or provide public-health services (ibid.). Women earn less than men working in state and local government, in no small part due to occupational segregation. The median annual salary for full-time state and local government employees in 2005 was $44,090 for men and $36,417 for women (EEOC 2005). In the EEOC's study of eight different job categories, including administrative and professional positions, men made a higher median salary than women (ibid.).[8]

One important local administrator in terms of power and responsibility is the city manager, found in the council-manager form of government. The city manager is an appointed position first developed around the turn of the century as part of a larger movement to reform government, particularly in urban areas. Popular at this time was the idea that administration could be separate from politics, known among public administration scholars as the "politics–administration" dichotomy. Yet it became clear as time passed that administrators, particularly those appointed to leadership positions such as city manager, had much discretion in their jobs and the ability to influence both the priorities and actions of elected officials and to influence policy more directly. In some cases, elected officials find it hard to challenge long-serving city managers, in part because of their reliance on them for the day-to-day tasks of governing the city and their expertise or because of their long-standing ties to the community (Svara 1990; Hassett and Watson 2004). More frequently, though, there is little evidence that long-standing city managers tend to "abuse" this power. There is a recognition that although managers often have a large hand in guiding policy implementation while working with the council, they typically try and stay above partisan politics, relying on the professional standards developed by groups such as the International City/County Management Association (Montjoy and Watson 1995).

---

[8]The eight categories include officials/administrators, professionals, technicians, protective service workers (including police), paraprofessionals, administrative support (including clerical workers), skilled craft workers, and service-maintenance. See EEOC 2001, page xxxi, for a full description of job categories.

Women currently make up about 12 percent of city managers—a number that has remained relatively stagnant in the last decade despite rapid growth in the profession by women in the 1970s and 1980s (Symborksi 1996; Renner 2001; Watson and Hassett 2004). Some suggest that women actually eschew the top position in favor of serving as assistant city managers because this level is more amenable to a stable family life (Hassett 2004). In 1994, 35 percent of assistant city managers were women (Symborksi 1996).

Rising to the top of this profession often requires hard personal choices. Individuals on the career path to the position of city manager frequently move and the job can be extremely demanding in terms of time and responsibility. One city manager, Jan Dolan of Menlo Park, California, acknowledges that having a family and doing this job would be difficult: "I always assumed I would not have children. I thought it would be too hard to do both well" (Wood 1994, 29). Judy Kelsey, city manager of Eureka, California, also put off marriage because "I thought a council wouldn't hire me because I wouldn't be able to convince my husband to move (ibid.)." After 17 years on the job, she finally decided to get married. Yet other women do not see a necessary conflict between their roles as mothers and as city managers, such as Susan George, the city manager of Woodside, California: "I think if you decide to have a child, you really have to learn how to juggle (ibid.)." Some women acknowledge that they still face discrimination and unrealistic expectations from city council members, who are typically male. One thing that could help women break through to this level of management is mentoring, which can boost the confidence of women and allow them the ability to build management skills and make contacts in the profession (Symborski 1996).

Once women become city managers, does gender play a factor in their job performance? On the one hand, gender might not make much difference. For example, when ranking the priorities of city managers, no gender differences emerge with respect to many of the most important responsibilities of city managers such as managing fiscal issues (such as balancing the budget), maintaining city infrastructure, and managing personnel (Fox and Schuhmann 1999, 2000). Further, city managers, regardless of gender, are often limited in their abilities to prioritize policies by their budgets and other factors, such as the importance placed on the norms of their profession that seek to limit city managers from instituting their own personal or political values (Fox and Schuhmann 1999).

On the other hand, there are several documented differences between men and women city managers, some of which could impact job performance. Female city managers are more politically liberal, and characterized the mayors with whom they work as more liberal than the male managers characterized the mayors with whom they work (Fox and Schuhmann 2000). However, it could be that women city managers are more likely to be hired in liberal settings than their male counterparts. Women managers do differ from men managers in the area of community relations, with women being more likely than men to place a high priority on using citizen input in their decision making (Fox and Schuhmann 1999, 2000). Women city managers are more likely to place higher priority on effective communication as well. For example, when given hypothetical scenarios such as creating a new recreation facility and dealing with a personnel problem, female managers were more likely than males to include citizen input in their decision making (in the first case) and to view themselves as mediators between the council and employee (in the second) (Fox and Schuhmann 1999). As Menlo Park city manager Jan Dolan says, "I think women generally have better people skills" (Wood 1994, 26). These findings appear to support the earlier work of social psychologist Carol Gilligan, who argues that men and women perceive social reality differently, speaking in "different voices." In other words, women tend to be more caring and nurturing, whereas men are more individualistic, embracing an adherence to rules (see Chapter 9 for more on Gilligan's work). Fox and Schuhmann's research on gender differences in public management corresponds with work on women managers in the private sector (Rosener 1995).

One area in public administration that many would expect women to be more influential than others is education. As Palley (2001) notes, school district employees and administrators have the discretion to make many important decisions regarding educational policy and development, even while complying with state and federal regulations. This is especially true for school superintendents, who are relied on by school boards for advice in numerous areas. Meier and Wilkins (2002) describe school districts as "classic glass ceiling organizations" in the sense that while women predominate at the lower levels, they have trouble reaching higher administrative posts. Teaching is dominated by women: men make up less than one in four teachers, with the vast majority of those teaching at the high school level (Snyder 2008). Yet women make up a minority of school principals by a factor of almost two to one, despite the fact that the vast majority of principals begin their careers as teachers (Holloway 2000). However, women are less likely to want to leave teaching than men, citing the long hours working in administration as well as the thankless nature of the job as barriers to their interest in pursuing careers in education administration (Adams 2004).

It is not surprising, then, to find that only about 13 percent of school superintendents are female (McCabe 2001). One national study of school superintendents also found that women are not typically well-positioned to become high-level education administrators, as few administrators come from the ranks of elementary school teachers (where women predominate) nor do they have as much experience in fiscal management as men—a criterion that boards of education increasingly consider when hiring superintendents (Glass 2000). Women superintendents also face discrimination in their fields, as research indicates they are more likely to be assigned to work in less desirable locations and for lower pay than male superintendents (Wolverton 1999). One result of having so few women superintendents is that some often feel the need to distance themselves from their gender, as they must overcome perceptions from those they work with that they are somehow different or more emotional than male superintendents (Gardiner, Enomoto, and Grogran 2000).

Women also face barriers in seeking college presidencies—an administrative position that can have important political ramifications. The American Council of Education reports that the percentage of female college presidents has more than doubled since 1986 from 9.5 to 23 percent in 2006 (American Council on Education 2007), but the rate of growth has slowed. Women are best represented as presidents of two-year institutions (29 percent) and make up 13.8 percent of college presidents at doctorate-granting institutions (ibid.). Female college presidents face salary and other types of discrimination (Manzo 2001), as do women administrators in other fields. One study of women college presidents found that some had difficulties with "old-time" board members who were skeptical of a woman's ability to lead; others indicated that they were more scrutinized for their appearance than men presidents and worried more about handling the conflicting demands of work and family. According to Dr. Martha T. Nesbit, president of Gainesville College, "Women still have to worry about juggling more than men do" (Manzo 2001, 14). One notable achievement for women in the field of higher education came with the appointment of Muriel A. Howard, president of Buffalo State College, as president of the American Association of State Colleges and Universities in 2009 (AASCU); she is the first African American to lead one of the six presidentially based higher education associations in the nation (American Association of State Colleges and Universities 2009).

Although the field of education is in many ways dominated by women, at least below the administrative level, the same cannot be said for policing, where in 2002, women made up just 11 percent of all sworn law enforcement personnel in the United States (National Center for Women and Policing 2002). According to the 2002 study by the National Center for Women and Policing, women fared better in large police departments with more than 100 sworn personnel, of which 13 percent were female. By contrast, women comprised just 8 percent of personnel in small and rural police departments (fewer than 100 personnel) (ibid.). The current numbers of women as police chiefs are downright bleak. Of the 18,000 police departments across the United States, the National Center for Women and Policing (NCWP)'s Director Margaret Moore estimates that in 2009, only about 224 police departments have women chiefs (Moore 2009). The current numbers of women as police chiefs are downright bleak. Of the 18,000 police departments across the United States, the National Center for Women and Policing (NCWP)'s Director Margaret Moore estimates that in 2009, only about 224 police departments have women chiefs (ibid.).

The NCWP argues that the lack of female representation among police officers is due to a widespread bias in police hiring, which keeps the number of women officers artificially low. They believe that too much emphasis is placed on physical prowess, which might keep otherwise qualified women from serving (NCWP 2002). Police departments have had good success, however, when they have actively sought to recruit women to their ranks; organizations such as the Institute for Women in Trades, Technology, and Science offer police departments tools and resources to help them in this endeavor (Polisar and Milgram 1998; Milgram 2002). One recent national survey of police women found that a strong majority believe that they were "made to feel as welcome as their male counterparts upon entering the field of law enforcement" (Seklecki and Paynich 2007, 28), which suggests that the bigger hurdle may be actually getting women to pursue jobs in policing, not in getting them to stay.

Current policing practices offer a more welcoming environment for women recruits than in years past. According to many, the policing field has begun to shift its emphasis away from a paramilitary structure in wake of police brutality scandals to one that emphasizes communication and community relations more prominently—a structure in which women officers can potentially excel ("Women . . ." 2004). Studies show that women officers rely on a less physical style of policing and are better at deescalating violent confrontations with citizens; they are particularly effective in

Cathy Lanier is the first woman to serve as Police Chief of the District of Columbia and won praise for her handling of Barack Obama's Inauguration Ceremony in January 2009.

BOX 6.1

Women Firefighters

Firefighters often serve as the first line of defense for local communities, not only handling local fires but also medical emergencies, terrorist threats, natural disasters, water rescues, and hazardous materials spills—not to mention the occasional cat that gets stuck up in a tree. There are more than 1 million firefighters in the United States, 73 percent of whom are volunteers (National Volunteer Fire Council 2003). Yet women hold very few of these important local positions. For instance, there are only around 6,200 women who serve as career firefighters or hold fire officer positions in the United States (International Association of Women in Fire and Emergency Services 2008). In addition, between 35,000 and 40,000 women are estimated to serve as volunteer firefighters in local communities (ibid.). Nationally, this means that women's service in the paid sector of firefighting is around 2 percent and around 5 percent as volunteers. However, Cornell's Institute for Women and Work found in 2008 that more than half (51.2 percent) of the nation's largest metropolitan regions have no paid female firefighters (Lang 2008).

Historically, the first known woman firefighter was Molly Williams, an African-American slave who volunteered with Oceanus Engine Company #11 in New York City in the early 1800s. Her work with the company was notable, as she was said to be "as good a fire laddie as many of the boys" (Women in the Fire Service 2004a). Another famous female volunteer firefighter was San Francisco heiress Lillie Hitchcock Coit, who worked as a fire hand with Knickerbocker Engine Company #5 in the 1850s until the time of her marriage and wore a gold number 5 on her dresses for the remainder of her life (Women in the Fire Service 2004b).

It wasn't until the twentieth century that a few departments began to recruit women actively to serve as volunteers, including the Los Angeles Fire Department in 1912, which faced a shortage of male volunteers in the daytime and looked to women to fill the gap. A few years later, Captain Marie Stack was put in charge of the Los Angeles Fire Department's first all-woman brigade, with three such brigades being formed that decade in Los Angeles (ibid.). Although women's service was still rare in the twentieth century, out of necessity women served as volunteers during World War II while men served in the military. In 1967, several women in the small Texas town of Woodbine created the Woodbine Ladies Fire Department. The nearest fire department was ten miles away and they were worried about the risk of brushfires. The Woodbine women raised money from bake sales and raffles to buy a 1942 Ford pumper and received fire training from the U.S. Forest Service. They served for 11 years, eventually growing to 23 members (ibid.).

The first woman to be paid as a professional firefighter was Sandra Forcier, who was hired as a public safety officer—a combination police officer and firefighter—by the city of Winston-Salem, North Carolina, on July 1, 1973. Four years later, she was moved into a fire-only position and worked until 2001 in Winston-Salem as Battalion Chief Sandra Waldron. Currently, the International Association of Women in Fire & Emergency Services estimates that more than 150 women serve as district chiefs, battalion chiefs, division chiefs, and assistant chiefs throughout the United States. They also claim that as of February 2005, "there were at least 24 career-level or combination (i.e., with some career and some volunteer personnel) fire agencies in the U.S whose top-level chief was a woman" (ibid.).

Women still face many obstacles to full participation in this career because firefighting is still viewed as a quintessentially male job. Women in firefighting confront societal constraints over men's and women's roles and perceived capabilities and must deal in some cases with sexual harassment and skepticism about their competence as firefighters. The 2008 Cornell study surveyed almost 675 firefighters and interviewed 175 female firefighters to assess the challenges that women face. When women are actually hired, the study found "that 85 percent interviewed reported that they were treated differently; 80 percent said that they were issued ill-fitting equipment, 37 percent reported that their gender creates barriers to career advancement; 50 percent felt shunned or socially isolated; and 37 percent were verbally harassed" (Lang 2008). Women also face institutional barriers, such as fire stations built only to accommodate one sex in sleeping, changing and bathing facilities, and a lack of protective gear and uniforms designed to fit women's bodies.

Yet many women have served nobly in this profession, including most recently as fire professionals and rescue workers dealing with the September 11, 2001, terrorist attacks in New York City. Their stories are told in the book *Women at Ground Zero*, by Susan Hagen and Mary Caruba. ■

---

dealing with domestic violence issues (NCWP 2003). Rape victims might also feel more comfortable dealing with female police officers, as indicated by the positive relationship between the number of policewomen in a department and the number of rape reports and arrests for rape offenders. Using data from the 1990s, Nicholson-Crotty and Meier (2002) estimate that increasing the numbers of women in police departments by around 5 percent would result in an almost 12 percent increase in the number of reported sexual assaults (20). Bringing more women into the police ranks can be beneficial for all officers and the community at large. Although slow, some progress is being made for women even at the top levels. In 2007, for example, Cathy Lanier was named Chief of the Metropolitan Police for the District of Columbia and women have recently served as police commissioners in cities as large as San Francisco, Boston, and Detroit.

Whether as police officers, school superintendents, city managers, or a myriad of other positions in public administration, women have the potential to influence public policy at the local and city levels in many ways. Although much public policy is established at the state and federal levels, local bureaucrats sometimes have the discretion to implement these policies and interpret regulations in ways that have gendered implications. Although women have made inroads in terms of staff positions in local and city governments, they still lag behind in many areas, particularly in leadership roles.

WOMEN IN NONGOVERNMENTAL ORGANIZATIONS AND THE BUSINESS SECTOR

Women's involvement in local policy and politics is not limited to their roles as elected officials or as bureaucrats. In fact, women's activism is perhaps strongest in nongovernmental organizations and in grassroots politics, in which women often become involved in community issues through more informal networks of friends, kinship, and the neighborhood. Indeed, as Chapter 2 notes, women such as Jane Addams led local social reform movements despite being disenfranchised from the political system. Often, such involvement stems from women's concerns as mothers and a need to improve their children's lives, whether that means seeking government assistance with poverty or job training or cleaning up polluted environments. Women's activism at the local level is sometimes geared toward the business community as well, with women leading the movement to unionize for greater rights and protections or to litigate against sexual discrimination and harassment in the workplace. This section examines women's political activism outside the mainstream government channels at the grassroots and looks at women and business, as women face many of the same challenges in industry as they do in politics.

Women at the Grassroots

Much local political activism in communities is done by poor or working-class women. Yet too often, scholars who study the women's movement overlook poor women's efforts to gain a better life for themselves and their families, whether their efforts involve addressing environmental concerns, a lack of day care or good-paying jobs, or domestic violence, instead focusing on the efforts of middle-class or educated white women to affect public policy (Bookman and Morgen 1988; Boris 2002). But fighting for domestic rights such as welfare, as noted sociologists Frances Fox Piven and Richard Cloward have argued, means fighting for public rights (Piven and Cloward 1997). The efforts of poor, often minority women, in these struggles have important dimensions that broaden our understanding of politics as "an attempt to change the social and economic institutions that embody the basic power relations in our society" (Bookman and Morgen 1988, 4).

For African-American women, the black church has long provided an opportunity for political involvement, including during the civil rights movement, when black women—although excluded from formal leadership positions as activists—often served as "bridge leaders" between social movements and local communities (Robnett 1998). But Latina women have not traditionally had organizations of their own from which to base community activism. Latina women are not typically found in the normal channels of political and social activism at the community level, which is not meant to imply that Latinas do not have a political consciousness of their own or that their ideas of politics are the same as Latino men. Carol

Hardy-Fanta (1993, 1997) studies Latina political activism in Boston. She finds that Latina women—like many women—have a blurred perception between the private and public dimensions, in which their roles as mothers play heavily. For these Latina women, similar to African-American women during the civil rights movement, politics consists of helping others and providing support, serving as "connectors" linking the Latino community to city hall informally. Yet many Latinas continue to struggle with poverty issues, bilingual education, and achieving greater rights for undocumented Hispanic workers and are often hesitant to enter the more traditional realms of politics due to language and other racist and cultural barriers (Benmayor and Torreullas 1997).

Racial conflicts are often at the heart of community organizing, with women at the forefront of combating racism as well as sexism. However, it is important to recognize that not all women activists root their community involvement in progressive causes. Julia Wrigley (1998) writes a fascinating case study of white working-class women engaged in the struggle against school busing in Boston, forced on Boston residents in the 1970s after federal Judge Arthur Garrity's decision to desegregate the public schools by busing black students into predominantly white schools and white students into predominantly black schools in two of Boston's poorest communities. Garrity believed that the Boston school board, composed of all white elected officials, had deliberately underfunded black schools in Boston. Upon litigation in the federal courts when the school board refused to increase its spending on such schools, Garrity ruled that forced busing was the only way to ensure equal protection for African-American students. Garrity's decision, however, caused shock waves in the local communities, particularly in white neighborhoods. The antibusing forces organized ROAR—Restore Our Alienated Rights—that was led by white women who arranged school protests and boycotts, distributed flyers, made public statements, and put pressure on state and national politicians to stop busing. That women emerged as leaders of the movement, however, was somewhat surprising in a city dominated by male involvement in politics. Yet Wrigley argues that it was the "intense separation of women's and men's activities and daily lives in Boston that allowed women to take early command of the anti-busing movement" (253). In other words, education was viewed as a mother's domain, and activists, such as this one, linked their involvement directly to their maternal roles: "I always say it's like a lioness in her den. You know, these are my children. The father, I'm sure, feels that way, but the mother had a little more time. The fathers were out working . . ." (261). ROAR engaged in mass demonstrations called "Mother's Marches." These demonstrations—which were often raucous events and staged in illegal areas—allowed women to act outside the "appropriate" norms for femininity, and local police were hesitant to do much about them. Ultimately, Garrity's ruling held for more than two decades, and with ROAR unable to stop court-ordered busing, many white working-class parents fled to the suburbs or sent their students to parochial schools instead.

Maternity has also served as a political impetus in the environmental movement. As Temma Kaplan (1997) writes in *Crazy for Democracy: Women in Grassroots Movements*, "when toxic pollution or expulsion from their homes threatens their communities, certain women will take action according to female consciousness, confronting authorities to preserve life" (6). One of the most well-known grassroots campaigns dealing with the environment took place in Love Canal, a lower-middle-class neighborhood in Niagara Falls, New York. In 1956, low-cost housing was built for blue-collar workers in Love Canal—a canal that was filled in after the city had used the area for a landfill for more than 50 years. From 1947 to 1952, the Hooker Chemical Company, which was located in the area and produced pesticides and plastics, dumped more than 80 different chemicals into the canal, unbeknownst to homeowners (Kaplan 1997). In the 1970s, women who lived in Love Canal began to notice that women in the area were far more likely to suffer from frequent miscarriages and have higher rates of disabled children. For example, in 14 pregnancies that occurred during one year (1979–1980), only two resulted in able-bodied infants. Many home-owners also found black sludge filling in their basements and under swimming pools. Yet local officials decried such evidence as anecdotal, referring to the women activists as "hysterical housewives" (Kaplan 1997, 20). This propelled the women to form Love Canal Homeowners Association, which pestered government officials at local and state meetings and even lobbied the Democratic National Convention in August 1980, raising national attention about their plight. The women activists deliberately chose a strategy that portrayed them as helpless mothers, all the while growing stronger. Eventually, the group persuaded the Carter administration in Washington to sign an agreement with the state of New York to allocate $15 million for the purchase of Local Canal homes, which at that point were uninhabitable (ibid.).

Environmental causes continue to concern women activists at the grassroots. In recent years, local women have been at the vanguard of the environmental racism movement, which seeks to combat the placement of locally undesirable land uses (LULUs) in poor and economically depressed neighborhoods (Prindeville and Bretting 1998). (For another local issue often dominated by women activists at the grassroots level, see Box 6.2, *Women's Struggle Against Domestic Violence*.)

Women are also active in labor relations at the local level, although most think of labor politics as a man's domain. In fact, women make up a growing percentage of union membership according to the AFL-CIO, which reports that two out of five union members today are women (AFL-CIO 2004). In the past, women led the struggle against big business in rural areas such as Pike County in eastern Kentucky, where in the 1970s female hospital workers such as housekeepers, nurses' aides, cooks, and clerical workers engaged

Women's Struggle Against Domestic Violence

The first shelter for victims of domestic violence opened in California in 1964, which precipitated a movement to open such shelters nationwide and to recognize domestic violence as a serious problem during the next decade.[33] By 1979, more than 250 shelters had opened their doors in local communities,[34] in part as a response to the development of local Commissions on the Status of Women, which were formed by local governments to identify problems faced by women in their communities. Battered women and rape were issues that ranked high in importance for these commissions to tackle.[35] There was a recognition that the traditional institutions of the community—the law, the church, and the medical profession—were not effective in dealing with the problems caused by spousal and partner abuse.

Researcher Anne Wurr documents one attempt by the women in Santa Clara County, California, to combat domestic violence through their formation of the Mid-Peninsula Support Network for Battered Women in 1978, which was a response to a finding by the county's Commission on the Status of Women that an urgent need existed for battered women's services in the area (Wurr 1984). In Santa Clara, women not only spearheaded the opening of several shelters, but they also worked to educate women's organizations such as local NOW chapters and child advocacy groups about their efforts. In addition, they lobbied members of the county council and placed pressure on local law enforcement agencies to institute new policies and training for police officers to deal with women who were victims of spousal abuse through the efforts of a subcommittee of the local bar association that was geared at domestic violence. These women activists also worked hard to get more women appointed to local commissions and boards that addressed domestic issues.

Yet despite such local activism, domestic violence did not become a national mainstream concern until the 1990s, in part because of the sensationalism surrounding the murder of Nicole Brown Simpson—herself the victim of domestic violence at the hands of her ex-husband O.J. Simpson, who was later found not guilty of her murder in a riveting, televised trial. Feminists such as Amy Richards and Jennifer Baumgardner argue that while the Simpson trial did alert the consciousness of the nation to the issue of domestic violence, it had the unfortunate effect of ignoring "the grassroots organization that has named its reality and pioneered its treatment." (ibid, 60).

Domestic violence remains a problem, as the February 2009 incident involving the popular singer Rihanna, who was beaten by her boyfriend, fellow singer Chris Brown, indicates. The Rihanna case has brought renewed attention to this often-overlooked crime. Today it is estimated that one in four women faces at least one physical assault in her lifetime (NCADV n.d.). Yet only one in seven cases of domestic violence is ever reported to law enforcement. Such cases number more than 2 million per year, according to the FBI Uniform Crime Report (ibid). In 2002, women reported more than 2 million

(Continued)

> **BOX 6.2 (CONTINUED)**
>
> assaults by their partner or ex-partner. Although the criminal justice system initially condoned a man's right to exercise violence in his home in his attempts to discipline his family, attitudes about domestic violence among law enforcement officials have changed (Johnson 2002). Judges, prosecutors, and police officers now view domestic violence as the serious crime it is, no doubt in part to the organizing efforts of women at the grassroots to raise the profile of this issue. In 2008, Senator Arlen Specter and then-Senator Joe Biden introduced the National Domestic Violence Volunteer Attorney Network Act, which would have directed the Justice Department to establish a domestic violence volunteer attorney network to represent domestic violence victims and to establish a Domestic Violence Legal Advisory Task Force; however, while the legislation made it out of committee, it was not voted upon by Congress (Congressional Research Service 2009). Supporters are hopeful that such legislation could be passed in the 111th Congress. ■

in a strike after owners of the Pikesville Methodist Hospital—one of the largest employers in the area—did little to address their concerns about heavy and erratic work schedules, lack of job security, and poor pay (Maggard 1998). More than 200 women strikers waged a picket line for 28 months and used a slogan that tapped into the class differences found between struggling workers and hospital owners: "We're fighting millionaires!" (ibid.). The women faced a business culture that viewed their employment as supplementary to men's earnings at the time, which meant that their work at the hospital was undervalued. After a protracted legal battle, the strikers were successful in 1980 when an appeals court refused to hear a final appeal by the hospital. The hospital was forced to reinstate the workers and compensate them for their losses.

Women workers, especially in poor communities, face new challenges as we begin the twenty-first century, particularly as they relate to the outsourcing of jobs overseas and in cheaper locales. Women are disproportionately more likely than men to hold part-time, subcontracted work that is often the only type available after factories and manufacturing jobs leave town (Weinbaum 1997). In 1988, General Electric (GE) waged a large-scale campaign against attempts by factory workers to unionize a large warehouse in rural Morristown, Tennessee, which was successful as workers rejected the union. One week later, however, GE executives suddenly closed the warehouse, moving to the next county and hiring subcontracted workers at almost half the price of what they paid workers in Morristown. Finding that they could only find new jobs through temporary agencies, women formed the grassroots organization Citizens Against Temporary Services (CATS). Although unsuccessful in a sex and age discrimination suit filed against the company (after their first lawyer withdrew, they could not afford a new one), they were successful in getting the state government to revoke GE's job training grants because it is illegal in Tennessee to train workers for jobs from which other workers have been laid off (ibid.). Years later, CATS tried to get the state legislature to pass a bill that would define temporary work and regulate abuses of long-term temporary workers, but to no avail. Despite these setbacks, CATS has transformed previously apolitical women into engaged citizens and has become involved in other sorts of political movements in the area, including issues of environmental justice. As Weinbaum (1997) notes, CATS's example teaches that "women are taking on the most important and overwhelming political and economic issues facing the nation and resisting traditional categories, fighting the political elites, educating their communities and leading a movement" (Weinbaum 1997, 337).

Women in Business

Circumstances for women in the workforce may only change when more women become better represented at the management levels of private industry. How do women fare in the business sector? In terms of leadership positions—not too well. Although women make up nearly half the workforce, they are still underrepresented in the professional world, particularly in business management. According to the Equal Employment Opportunity Commission, the percentage of women officials and managers in the private sector increased from just under 30 percent in 1990 to 37.2 percent in 2007 (EEOC 2007). At the same time, the EEOC reports that women make up 79 percent of office and clerical workers in 2007. Women managers are overrepresented in certain industries, too, such as health care, and are vastly underrepresented in others, such as manufacturing.

Part of the problem may stem from getting women interested in careers in business in the first place. According to a survey of U.S. business schools, women earned 35.5 percent of MBAs in 2007; by contrast, their rates of graduation from law school are much higher (Catalyst 2009a). Research conducted by the Kellogg School of Business at the University of Michigan and Catalyst, a nonprofit research and advisory group that works to advance women in business, finds that women may not be as motivated to attend business school as compared with men because they more often lack confidence in their math abilities (45 percent of women compared with 25 percent of men), are less likely to be motivated by money to enter business (41 percent to 27 percent), and see few female role models in the business world and among business school faculty (56 percent to 39 percent) (Alsop 2001). However, upon graduating, the vast majority of both women and men M.B.A.'s saw their experiences in business school as overwhelmingly positive.

One industry in which women have a long way to go is finance. The EEOC finds that women remain underrepresented on Wall Street, making up less than one-third of investment banking officials and managers (EEOC 2008a). Although their representation is best among professional occupations within the industry, defined as accountants, research analysts, and statisticians, female representation is lowest on the sales side of the industry, which is often the most lucrative, where they make up less than 19 percent of salespeople (EEOC 2008b).

Women still struggle with a glass ceiling when it comes to being named as chief executive officers (CEOs) of companies. In 2009, just 15 women headed the top *Fortune 500* companies (Catalyst 2009b), which was at least an improvement from 2003, when only eight women headed such companies (Jones 2003). Yet among career executives who aspire to become CEOs, there is no difference between men and women, with women executives who have children living with them just as likely to want the top jobs in their companies as women who do not have children (Catalyst 2004b). A 2004 survey of career executives by Catalyst found that women reported an enduring set of "cultural barriers" to their advancement that men did not have to face, such as "gender-based stereotypes, exclusion from informal networks, lack of role models, and an inhospitable corporate culture" (ibid.). Yet when women do become CEOs and senior executives, their performances are typically strong. Another Catalyst study found that companies with a higher proportion of female senior executives financially outperform companies with lower proportions of women (Catalyst 2004a).

Women who own their own businesses may have the most control over their destinies in the private sector. According to the Center for Women's Business Research, in 2008-2009, 40 percent of privately held firms are women-owned, although just one in five firms with revenue of $1 million or more is woman-owned (Women's Business Research Center 2009). Despite their minority numbers in business ownership, there is reason for optimism. By the late 1990s, women were starting their own businesses at twice the rate of men (Palley 2001). And owning a business is what often leads many people to interact with local politics as business owners become involved with their local chambers of commerce or seek to have a voice in zoning and regulatory policies that affect their companies.

CONCLUSION

At the local level of government, women are making an impact as elected officials, bureaucrats, and activists in nongovernmental organizations. Yet women at this level do not always act in ways that differ greatly from their male counterparts, whether as mayors, city managers, or elected officials. Part of the reason that relatively few gender differences are found in local politics could be related to the demands and limits found in local governance. For instance, budgetary concerns are an overriding burden on all types of local government, whether located in rural, suburban, or city areas. Such financial worries often proscribe the ability of women to pursue public policies that they might otherwise follow, such as those that might give greater assistance to women and families in need. Also, handling the day-to-day functions of local governments, such as determining zoning requirements, handing out licenses, or picking up the garbage, has few, if any, gender components.

Despite these limitations, however, there are still a few ways that gender does become a factor in local politics. For example, one theme that emerges when examining the behavior of women and men elected officials, bureaucrats, and grassroots activists is the priority that women place on communication. Females involved in all sorts of local politics routinely stress the importance of bringing different voices to the political table, perhaps because for so many years their voices were excluded. Women officials and activists at the local level are also more likely than men to notice the strain their positions or activism places on their family lives. For example, recall the comments of female city managers who put off having children because they believed their careers were incompatible with having a family at home. The importance of communication to women and their struggles with the work/family balance extend to other local arenas that have their own political dimensions, such as business and education.

Women who do choose to become active in local politics, however, are not monolithic. At the national and state levels, the majority of women tend to be Democrats and tend to have more liberal views than men. This chapter demonstrates that the same cannot necessarily be said about women in local politics. For example, as Chapter 5 reveals as well, women school board candidates are much more likely to be Republicans than they are Democrats. Moreover, although women's involvement at the grassroots level is often felt in progressive or liberal causes, the case involving mothers against busing in Boston shows that many conservative women choose to get active in local politics as well.

REFERENCES

Adams, Kathy L. 2004. "Encouraged or Discouraged? Women Teacher Leaders Becoming Principals." *The Clearing House* 77, no. 5:209–212.

AFL-CIO. 2004. "Facts about Working Women." www.aflcio.org/yourjobeconomy/women/factsaboutworkingwomen.cfm.

Alozie, Nicholas O., and Lynne L. Manganaro. 1993. "Women's Council Representation: Measurement Implications for Public Policy." *Political Research Quarterly* 46, no. 2:383–398.

Alsop, Ronald. 2001. "Women See Few Role Models in Business School Faculties." *Wall Street Journal* (25 July): 1B.

American Association of State Colleges and Universities. 2009. Press Release. "Buffalo State College CEO Muriel Howard Appointed President of American Association of State Colleges and Universities." www.aascu.org/media/media_releases/release09march31.htm. Accessed May 3, 2009.

American Association of University Women. 1992. *How Schools Shortchange Girls: The AAUW Report, A Study of Major Findings on Girls and Education.* Researched by the Wellesley College Center for Research on Women. Washington, D.C.: The American Association of University Women Foundation.

————. 1998. "Gender Gaps: Where Schools Still Fail Our Children." Executive Summary. www.aauw.org/research/GGES.pdf.

American Council on Education. 2007. Press Release. "College Presidents Aging and Holding Jobs Longer According to a New Report on the College Presidency from the American Council of Education."/www.acenet.edu/AM/Template.cfm?Section=Search&template=/CM/HTMLDisplay.cfm&ContentID=20430. Accessed on May 3, 2009.

Antolini, Denise. 1984. "Women in Local Government: An Overview." *Political Women: Current Roles in State and Local Government*, ed. Janet A. Flammang. Beverly Hills: Sage Publications.

Arizona Women's Political Caucus (AWPC). 2004. *Facts: Women in Public Office in 2004.* www.azstarnet.com/nonprofit/awpc/facts.html.

Bailey, Margo. 2004. Interview by Melissa Deckman. July 13. Chestertown, MD.

Battered Women's Shelter." pp. 221–241 in Political Women: Current Roles in State and Local Government, ed. Janet A. Flammang. Beverly Hills: Sage.

Baumgardner, Jennifer, and Amy Richards. 2000. *Manifesta: Young Women, Feminism, and the Future.* New York: Farrar, Strauss, and Giroux.

Benmayor, Rina, and Rosa M. Torreullas. 1997. "Education, Cultural Rights, and Citizenship." pp. 187–204 in *Women Transforming Politics: An Alternative Reader*, ed. Cathy J. Cohen, Kathleen B. Jones, and Joan C. Tronto. New York: New York University Press.

Blanchard, Paul D. 1977. "Women in Public Education: The Impact of Female School Board Members." *Journal of Humanics* 4:64–69.

Bookman, Ann, and Sandra Morgen. 1988. *Women and the Politics of Empowerment.* Philadelphia: Temple University Press.

Boris, Eileen. 2002. "On Grassroots Organizing, Poor Women's Movements, and the Intellectual as Activist." *Journal of Women's History* 14, no. 2:140–142.

Bowman, Ann O'M., and Richard C. Kearney. 1999. *State and Local Government.* Boston: Houghton Mifflin.

Brown, Clyde, Neil R. Heighberger, and Peter A. Shocket. 1993. "Gender-Based Differences in Perceptions of Male and Female City Council Candidates." *Women & Politics* 13, no. 1:1–17.

Browning, Rufus P., Dale Rogers Marshall, and David H. Tabb. 1984. *Protest Is Not Enough: The Struggle of Blacks and Hispanics for Equality in Urban Politics.* Berkeley: University of California Press.

Bullock, Charles S. III, and Susan A. MacManus. 1991. "Municipal Electoral Structure and the Election of Councilwomen." *Journal of Politics* 53, no. 1:75–89.

Burheide, Catherine White. 2000. "The Changing Government Workforce in State and Localities: 1990–1997." A Report of the Center for Women and Government, University of Albany, State University of New York.

Bystrom, Diane. n.d. "From Voting to Running for Political Office: The Role of Women in Midwestern Politics." Carrie Chapman Center for Women and Politics. http://web2.iastate.edu/~cccatt/midwestwomen.htm.

Campbell, Colin. 2004. "Gender Tensions Aggravate Strain on Government." *Atlanta-Journal Constitution* (March 21): 3E.

Catalyst. 2004a. Press Release. "New Catalyst Study Finds Female Executives Are Just as Likely as Male Colleagues to Aspire to CEO Job." 24 June. www.catalystwomen.org/press_room/press_releases/2004wmicl.pdf.

———. 2004b. Press Release. "New Catalyst Study Reveals Financial Performance Is Higher for Companies with More Women at the Top." www.catalystwomen.org/press_room/press_releases/2004Fin_Per.pdf.

———. 2009a. "Women M.B.A.s." www.catalyst.org/publication/250/women-mbas. Accessed May 5, 2009.

———. 2009b. "Women CEOs of the Fortune 1000." www.catalyst.org/publication/322/women-ceos-of-the-fortune-1000. Accessed May 5, 2009.

Center for American Women and Politics. 1992. *Women in State Legislatures.* www.cawp.rutgers.edu/Facts/StLegHistory/stleg92.pdf.

———. 2009. Fast Facts. "Women Mayors in U.S. Cities 2009." January. www.cawp.rutgers.edu/fast_facts/levels_of_office/Local-WomenMayors/php.

City of Atlanta Online. n.d. "Meet the Mayor: Atlanta Mayor Shirley Franklin." www.atlantaga.gov/Mayor/Meet.aspx. Accessed on 15 April, 2009.

Congressional Research Service. 2009. "S. 1515: National Domestic Violence Volunteer Attorney Network Act." www.govtrack.us/congress/bill.xpd?bill=s110-1515&tab=summary. Accessed May 5, 2009.

Crow, Barbara A. 1997. "Relative Privilege? Reconsidering White Women's Participation in Municipal Politics." pp. 435–446 in *Women Transforming Politics: An Alternative Reader*, ed. Cathy J. Cohen, Kathleen B. Jones, and Joan C. Tronto. New York: New York University Press.

Czubaj, Camilla Anne. 2002. "An Analysis of School Board Members." *Education* 122, no.3:615–618.

Darcy, Robert, Susan Welch, and Janet Clark. 1994. *Women, Elections & Representation*, 2nd ed. Lincoln: University of Nebraska Press.

Deckman, Melissa. 2004. "Women Running Locally: How Gender Affects School Board Elections." Article Abstract. *PS: Political Science & Politics* 36, no. 1: 61–62. Full article available as part of the E-Symposium "An Open Boundaries Workshop: Women and Politics in Comparative Perspective." *PSOnline.* January 2004. www.apsanet.org.

———. 2006. "Women at the School Board Level: Ideology, Party and Policy Concerns." *Journal of Women, Politics, and Public Policy.* 28(1):87–117.

Donahue, Jesse. 1997. "It Doesn't Matter: Some Cautionary Findings about Sex and Representation from School Committee Conversations." *Policy Studies Journal* 25, no.4:630–648.

———. 1999. "The Non Representation of Gender: School Committee Members and Gender Equity." *Women & Politics* 20, no. 3:65–81.

Equal Employment Opportunity Commission. 2001. *Job Patterns for Minorities and Women in State and Local Government.*

———. 2005. "Job Patterns for Men and Women in State and Local Governments, 2005." www.eeoc.gov/stats/jobpat_eeo4/2005/index.html

———. 2007. "Indicators Over Time." www.eeoc.gov/stats/jobpat/2007/indicators.htm. Accessed April 24, 2009.

———. 2008a. "Job Patterns for Minorities and Women in Private Industry, 2006, Security, Commodity Contracts & Like Activity." www.eeoc.gov/stats/jobpat/2006/nac3/523.html. Accessed May 5, 2009.

_____. 2008b. "Job Patterns for Minorities and Women in Private Industry, 2006, Investment Banking and Securities Dealing." www.eeoc.gov/stats/jobpat/2006/nac5/52311.html. Accessed May 5, 2009.

Flammang, Janet. 1985. "Female Officials in the Feminist Capital: The Case of Santa Clara County." *Western Political Quarterly* 38, no. 1:94–118.

Fox, Richard L., and Robert Schuhmann. 1999. "Gender and Local Government: A Comparison of Women and Men City Managers." *Public Administration Review* 59, no. 3:231–242.

_____. 2000. "Gender and the Role of City Manager." *Social Science Quarterly* 81, no. 20:604–621.

Gaddy, Barbara B., T. William Hall, and Robert J. Marzano. 1996. *School Wars: Resolving Our Conflicts Over Religion and Values*. San Francisco: Jossey-Bass Publishers.

Gardiner, Mary E., Ernestine Enomoto, and Margaret Grogran. 2000. *Coloring Outside the Lines: Mentoring Women in School Leadership*. Albany: SUNY Press.

"GenderGap in Government." 2004. www.gendergap.com/governme.htm.

Glass, Thomas E. 2000. "Where are all the Women Superintendents?" *The School Administrator*. June. www.aasa.org/publications/saarticledetail.cfm?ItemNumber=4046. Accessed on May 3, 2009.

Gruberg, Martin. 1968. *Women in American Politics: An Assessment and Sourcebook*. Oshkosh: Academia Press.

Gurwitt, Rob. 2004. "How to Win Friends and Repair a City." *Governing* (April): 2–5.

Hagen, Susan, and Mary Caruba. 2002. *Women at Ground Zero: Stories of Courage and Compassion*. Indianapolis: Alpha Books.

Hardy-Fanta, Carol. 1993. *Latina Politics, Latino Politics: Gender, Culture, and Political Participation in Boston*. Philadelphia: Temple University Press.

_____. 1997. "Latina Women and Political Consciousness: *La Chispa Que Prende.*" pp. 223–237 in *Women Transforming Politics: An Alternative Reader*, ed. Cathy J. Cohen, Kathleen B. Jones, and Joan C. Tronto. New York: New York University Press.

Hardy-Fanta, Carol, Pei-te Lien, Dianne M. Pinderhughes, and Christine Marie, Sierra. 2006. "Gender, Race, and Descriptive Representation in the United States: Findings from the Gender and Multicultural Leadership Project." *Journal of Women, Politics & Policy* 28, no. 3,4:7–42.

Hassett, Wendy L. 2004. "Career Advancement Choices of Female Managers in U.S. Local Governments." pp. 133–152 in *Gender and Women in Comparative Perspective*, ed. Heidi Gottfried and Laura R. Reese. Lanham: Lexington Books.

"Henpecked Kansans: Males endanger Beer, Vote complaining women into Office." 1937. *Literary Digest* 123 (24 April):7.

Herrick, Rebekah, and Susan Welch. 1992. "The Impact of At-Large Elections on the Representation of Black and White Women." *National Political Science Review* no. 3:62–77.

Hess, Frederick. 2002. *School Boards at the Dawn of the 21st Century*. Alexandria, VA: American School Boards Association.

Holloway, John H. 2000. "Pathways to the Principalship." *Educational Leadership* 57, no. 8:84–85.

Holman, Mirya R. 2008. "Sex, Race, and Representation in the City: A Cross-Sectional Analysis of Female and Minority Representation in U.S. Municipalities." Paper Presented at the Women & Politics Institute at American University Conference:

"Adams EnGENDERING Theories of Difference and Commonality: Women and Political Leadership in an Era of Identity Politics." Washington, D.C. April.

International Association of Women in Fire & Emergency Services. 2008. "Frequently Asked Questions." www.i-women.org/questions.php. Accessedon May 4, 2009.

International City/County Management Association. 2001. *Municipal Form of Government Survey*. Washington, D.C.

Johnson, Richard. 2002. "Changing Atttitudes About Domestic Violence." *Law & Order 50*, no. 4: 60–65.

Jones, Del. 2003. "2003: Year of the Woman among the 'Fortune' 500?" *USA Today* (31 December). www.usatoday.com/money/companies/management/2003-12-30-womenceos_x.htm.

Kaplan, Temma. 1997. *Crazy for Democracy: Women in Grassroots Movements*. New York: Routledge.

Karnig, Albert, and B. Oliver Walter. 1976. "Election of Women to City Councils." *Social Science Quarterly 56*, no. 4:604–613.

Kerr, Brinck, Will Miller, and Margaret Reid. 2002. "Sex-Based Occupational Segregation in U.S. State Bureaucracies, 1987–1997." *Public Administration Review*. 62, no. 4:412–423.

Lang, Susan. 2008. "Women Firefighters Can Take the Heat, but too Few Firehouses Give Them the Chance, Study Finds." *Cornell Chronicle Online*. May 5. www.news.cornell.edu/stories/May08/firefighters.women.sl.html. Accessed on May 4, 2009.

Lipsky, Michael. 1992. "Street-Level Bureaucracy: The Critical Role of Street-Level Bureaucrats." In *Classics of Public Administration*, 3rd ed., ed. Jay M. Shafritz and Albert C. Hyde. Belmont: Wadsworth Publishing Co. Reprinted from *Street Level Bureaucracy: Dilemmas of the Individual in Public Services*, 1980.

MacManus, Susan A. 1999. "The Resurgent City Councils." pp. 166–193 in *American State and Local Politics*, ed. Ronald E. Weber and Paul Brace. New York: Chatham House.

MacManus, Susan A., and Charles S. Bullock. 1993. "Women and Racial/Ethnic Minorities in Mayoral and Council Positions." *The Municipal Yearbook*. Washington: International City/County Management Association, 70–84.

Maggard, Sally Ward. 1998. "We're Fighting Millionaires! The Clash of Gender and Class in Appalachian Women's Union Organizing." pp. 289–306 in *No Middle Ground: Women and Radical Protest*, ed. Kathleen Blee. New York: New York University Press.

Maharaj, Nicole. 2004. U.S. Conference of Mayors Press Release. "Women Mayors Chair Mayor Shelia Young Brings More Structure to Group." www.usmayors.org (9 February).

Mankiller, Wilma, and Michael Wallis. 1993. *Mankiller: A Chief and Her People*. NewYork: St. Martin's Press

Manning, Richard D. 1988. "How Three Women Took Over Missoula County and the Gender Factor Became an Edge." *Governing* (May): 1–7.

Manzo, Kathleen Kennedy. 2001. "Report: Female Presidents Juggle More, Earn Less." *Black Issues in Higher Education* 18, no. 22:12–14.

McCabe, Donna Hagen. 2001. "Metaphorical Descriptions of the Role of Women School Superintendents." *Education* 121, no. 4:690–704.

McCoy, Melanie. 1992. "Gender or Ethnicity: What Makes a Difference? A Study of Women Tribal Leaders." *Women & Politics* 12, no. 3: 57–68.

Meier, Kenneth and Vicky M. Wilkins. 2002. " Gender Differences in Agency Head Salaries: The Case of Public Education." *Public Administration Review* 62, no. 4:405–411.

Merritt, Sharyne. 1980. "Sex Differences in Role Behavior and Policy Orientations of Suburban Officeholders: The Effect of Women's Employment." pp. 115–129 in *Women in Local Politics*, ed. Debra W. Stewart. Metuchen: Scarecrow Press.

Mezey, Susan Gluck. 1978. "Support for Women's Rights Policy: An Analysis of Local Politicians." *American Politics Quarterly* 6, no. 4:485–497.

Milgram, Donna. 2002. "Recruiting Women to Policing: Practical Strategies That Work." *The Police Chief Magazine* (April): 23–29.

Miller, Bruce G. 1994. "Women and Tribal Politics: Is There a Gender Gap in Indian Elections?" *American Indian Quarterly* 18, no. 1:25–42.

Montjoy, Robert, and Douglas J. Watson. 1995. "A Case for Reinterpreted Dichotomy of Politics and Administration as a Professional Standard in Council-Manager Government." *Public Administration Review* 55, no. 3:231–239.

Moore, Margaret. 2009. Personal Interview by Melissa Deckman, by phone. May 5.

Mullins, Carolyn. 1972. "The Plight of the Board Woman." *American School Board Journal* 159 (February): 27–30.

National Association of Counties. 2003. "A Brief Overview of County Government." Washington, D.C.: National Association of Counties.

National Center for Women and Policing (NCWP). 2002. Report. "Equality Denied: The Status of Women in Policing: 2001" (April).

_____. 2003. Report. "Hiring and Retaining More Women: The Advantages to Law Enforcement Agencies" (Spring).

National Coalition Against Domestic Violence. 2003. "Poll Finds Domestic Violence Is Women's Main Concern." www.ncadv.org/press_release.html;

National Coalition Against Domestic Violence (NCADV). n.d. "Domestic Violence Facts." http://www.ncadv.org/resources/FactSheets_221/html. Accessed May 5, 2009.

National League of Cities. 2003a. Research Brief on America's Cities. "The Faces of America's City Councils: America's City Councils in Profile." www.nlc.org.

_____. 2003b. Research Brief on America's Cities. "Serving on City Councils: America's City Councils in Profile. Part II." www.nlc.org.

National Public Radio. 2004. "Profile: Atlanta to Replace Its Sewer System, Which May Cost $3.2 billion." All Things Considered. (31 March): 2.

National Volunteer Fire Council. 2003. Fact Sheet. www.nvfc.org/pdf/2003_fact_sheet.pdf.

National Women's History Project. www.letswrap.com/LetsWRAP/Spring98/natlhist.htm.

Nicholson-Crotty, Jill, and Kenneth J. Meier. 2002. "Gender, Representative Bureaucracy, and Law Enforcement: The Case of Sexual Assault." Paper prepared for the 2002 American Political Science Association's Annual Meeting.

Palley, Marian Lief. 2001. "Women's Policy Leadership in the United States." *PS: Political Science & Politics* 34, no. 2:247–250.

Pennington, Bill. 2004. "Title IX Trickles Down to Girls of Generation Z." *New York Times* (29 June):D1.

Piven, Frances Fox, and Richard A. Cloward. 1997. *The Breaking of the American Social Compact*. New York: The New Press.

Polisar, Joseph, and Donna Milgram. 1998. "Recruiting, Integrating, and Retaining Women Police Officers: Strategies That Work." *The Police Chief Magazine* (October): 42–50.

Prindeville, Diane-Michele. 2002. "Women's Evolving Role in Tribal Politics: Native Women Leaders in 21 Southwestern Indian Nations." www.cawp.rutger.edu/fast_facts/women_of_color/documents/TribalPolitics_Prindeville.pdf

Prindeville, Diane-Michele, and John G. Bretting. 1998. "Indigenous Women Activists and Political Participation: The Case of Environmental Justice." *Women & Politics* 19, no. 1:39–58.

Prindeville, Diane-Michele, and Teresa Braley Gomez. 1999. "American Indian Women Leaders, Public Policy, and the Importance of Gender and Ethnic Identity." *Women & Politics* 20, no. 2: 17–32.

Renner, Teri. 2001. "The Local Government Profession at Century's End." pp. 35–36 in *The Municipal Yearbook*. Washington: International City/County Management Association.

Robnett, Belinda. 1998. "African American Women in the Civil Rights Movement: Spontaneity and Emotion in Social Movement Theory." pp. 65–95. in *No Middle Ground: Women and Radical Protest*, ed. Kathleen Blee. New York: New York University Press.

Rosener, Judy B. 1995. *America's Competitive Secret: Utilizing Women as a Management Strategy*. New York: Oxford University Press.

Ross, Bernard H., and Myron A. Levine. 2001. *Urban Power: Politics in Metropolitan America*, 6th ed. Itasca: F.E. Peacock Publishers, Inc.

Saltzstein, Grace Hall. 1986. "Female Mayors and Women in Municipal Jobs." *American Journal of Political Science* 30, no. 1:140–164.

Schlozman, Kay Lehman, Nancy Burns, Sidney Verba, and Jesse Donahue. 1995. "Gender and Citizen Participation: Is There a Different Voice?" *American Journal of Political Science* 39, no. 2:267–293.

Schoenberger, Chana R., 2003. "Frankly Speaking." *Forbes*. (3 February): 171(3): 46–47.

Schumaker, Paul, and Nancy Elizabeth Burns. 1988. "Gender Cleavages and the Resolution of Local Policy Issues." *American Journal of Political Science* 32, no. 4:1070–1095.

Seklecki, Richard and Rebecca Paynich. 2007. "A National Survey of Female Police Officers." *Police Practice and Research* 8, no. 1:17–30.

Shipp, Bill. 2004. "Madam Mayor to the Rescue." *Georgia Trend*. 19, no. 8: 17–23

Sierra, Christine. 2009. Interview with Melissa Deckman by phone. April 21.

Snyder, Tamar. 2008. "Male Call: Recruiting More Men to Teach Elementary School." *Edutopia*. April 28. www.edutopia.org/male-teacher-shortage. Accessed on May 3, 2009.

Stewart, Debra. 1980. *The Women's Movement in Community Politics in the U.S. The Role of Local Commissions on the Status of Women*. New York: Pergamon Press.

Svara, James. 1990. *Official Leadership in the City: Patterns of Conflict and Cooperation*. New York: Oxford University Press.

Symborksi, Lee. 1996. "Why Are There So Few Women Managers?" *Public Management* (December): 11–16.

Thomas, Sue. 1998. "Introduction." Pp. 1–14 in *Women and Elective Office: Past, Present, and Future*, ed. Sue Thomas and Clyde Wilcox. New York: Oxford University Press.

Ulbig, Stacy. 2007. "Gendering Municipal Government: Female Descriptive Representation and Feelings of Political Trust." *Social Science Quarterly*. 88, no. 5:1106–1123.

U.S. Census Bureau. 2007. "Government Units in 2007." *U.S. Census of Governments* (July). Washington, D.C.: Department of Commerce.

U.S. Census Bureau. 2002. "Federal, State, and Local Governments: 2002 Census of Governments." www.census.gov/govs/www/cog2002.html

U.S. Department of Labor. 2002. "Facts on Working Women" (November). www.dol .gov/wb/factsheets/wbo02.htm.

Watson, Douglas J., and Wendy L. Hassett. 2004. "Career Paths of City Managers in America's Largest Council-Manager Cities." *Public Administration Review* 64, no. 2:192–200.

Weber, Ronald E., and Paul Brace. 1999. "States and Localities Transformed." pp. 1–20 in *American State and Local Politics: Directions for the 20th Century*, ed. Ronald E. Weber and Paul Brace. New York: Chatham House Press.

Weikart, Lynne A, Greg Chen, Daniel W. Williams, and Haris Hromic. 2006. "The Democratic Sex: Gender Differences and the Exercise of Power." *Journal of Women, Politics & Policy* 28, no. 1: 119–139.

Weinbaum, Eve. 1997. "Transforming Democracy: Rural Women and Labor Resistance." pp. 324–339 in *Women Transforming Politics: An Alternative Reader*, ed. Cathy J. Cohen, Kathleen B. Jones, and Joan C. Tronto. New York: New York University Press.

Welch, Susan, and Albert K. Karnig. 1979. "Correlates of Female Office Holding in City Politics." *Journal of Politics* 41, no. 2:478–491.

Wolverton, Mimi. 1999. "The School Superintendency: Male Bastion or Equal Opportunity?" *Advancing Women in Leadership Journal*. www.advancingwomen.com/ awl/spring99/Wolverton/wolver.html.

Women in the Fire Service, Inc. 2004. "Women in Firefighting: A History." www. wfsi.org.

Women in the Fire Service. 2004a. "Women Firefighters: Information and Issues." www.wfsi.org.

Women in the Fire Service. 2004b. "Women in Firefighting: A History." www.wfsi.org.

"Women Rise to the Top of Police Ranks." 2004. (27 May). www.cnn.com/2004/US/ Northeast/05/27/top/cops.ap.

Women's Business Research Center. 2009. "Key Facts about Women-Owned Businesses." www.womensbusinessresearchcenter.org/research/keyfacts/. Accessed on May 5, 2009.

Wood, Barbara. 1994. "Profile: A Woman's Place—In City Hall." PM. *Public Management* 76, no. 5:26–29.

Wrigley, Julia. 1998. "From Housewives to Activists: Women and the Division of Political Labor in the Boston Antibusing Movement." pp. 251–288 in *No Middle Group: Women and Radical Protest*, ed. Kathleen Bree. New York: New York University Press.

Wurr, Anne. 1984. "Community Responses to Violence Against Women: The Case of a Battered Women's Shelter." *In Political Women: Current Roles in State and Local Government*, ed. Janet A. Flammang. Beverly Hills: Sage.

Women in Congress and the State Legislatures

I t is an historic moment for the Congress, and an historic moment for the women of this country. It is a moment for which we have waited over 200 years. Never losing faith, we waited through the many years of struggle to achieve our rights. But women weren't just waiting; women were working. Never losing faith, we worked to redeem the promise of America, that all men and women are created equal. For our daughters and granddaughters, today we have broken the marble ceiling. For our daughters and our granddaughters, the sky is the limit, anything is possible for them. –Speaker of the House Nancy Pelosi (D-CA) January 4, 2007, Congressional Record p. H4–H5.

Nancy Pelosi's ascendancy to Speaker of the House, the most powerful position in the U.S. House of Representatives, reflects the great strides that women have made in gaining representation in Congress and the ranks of party leadership. Pelosi herself emphasized the significance of her election as a role model for young women aspiring to political leadership and as a policymaker attuned to the needs and interests of women. In the days leading up to her official election as Speaker, Pelosi sponsored a tea for women in which she promised that "America's working women, women working at home, whatever they choose to do, they have a friend in the Capitol of the United States." (Fiore and Daunt 2007). During her acceptance speech when she officially received the gavel as Speaker, Pelosi spoke of breaking the marble ceiling. She emphasized her role as legislative leader and as a mother and grandmother. Signaling the importance of women and children to her legislative agenda and the historic nature of her election, upon the conclusion of her speech, Pelosi invited all the children in the audience to come up and touch the gavel (Marcus 2007).

While the significance of Pelosi's rise to the Speakership cannot be underestimated, women and minorities still remain underrepresented in Congress and the state legislatures in comparison to their numbers in the U.S. population. For example, in 2010, women hold only 16.8 percent (73) of the seats in the House of Representatives,[1] 17 percent (17) of the seats in the Senate, and 24.4 percent (1,799) of the seats in the state legislatures (Center for American Women and Politics 2010a, 2010b) (see also Table 7.1). Further, when compared to other democratic countries, the United States lags behind in terms of women's representation in national legislative bodies.

In this chapter we look at the history of women's integration into the United States Congress and the 50 state legislatures. We also examine the similarities and differences in male and female legislators' policy activities and

TABLE 7.1

Minority Women in Congress and the State Legislatures 2010

	African Americans	Hispanics	Asian Americans	Native Americans
House of Representatives	13*	6**	3***	0
Senate	0	0	0	0
State Legislatures	230****	74	33	13

*This number includes the nonvoting delegate from Washington, D.C., Eleanor Holmes Norton Women make up 13 of the 41 African Americans serving in the House. Only one African-American woman has ever served in the Senate. Carol Moseley Braun (D-IL), was elected to the Senate in 1992. She lost her bid for reelection and later ran unsuccessfully for the Democratic presidential nomination in 2004.
**Women constitute 6 of the 28 Hispanic members serving in the House of Representatives. This number includes one male nonvoting delegate from Puerto Rico. Among the Hispanic members of the House are the first sisters to serve simultaneously in the House of Representatives, Linda Sanchez (D) and Loretta Sanchez (D) of California. There are also two brothers, Lincoln Diaz-Balart and Mario Diaz-Balart (R) of Florida. No Hispanic woman has ever served in the U.S. Senate. However, there is one Hispanic man serving in the U.S. Senate, Robert Menendez (D-NJ). President Barack Obama appointed two Hispanic members of Congress to serve in his cabinet. Representative Hilda Solis (D-CA) became Secretary of Labor and Senator Ken Salazar (D-CO) serves as Secretary of the Interior.
***Women constitute three of the ten Asian Americans serving in the House of Representatives. This number includes two male nonvoting delegates. No Asian-American woman has ever served in the U.S. Senate. However, there are two Asian-American men representing Hawaii: Democrats Daniel Inouye and Daniel Akaka.
****The 350 women of color serving in the state legislatures constitute 19.5 percent of the women in state legislatures today and 4.7 percent of all state legislators. All but 20 of these women are Democrats.

Source: Center for American Women and Politics, 2010c. "Fact Sheet: Women of Color in Elective Office 2010"; New Brunswick: Center for American Women and Politics, Rutgers, The State University of New Jersey. Giroux, Greg. 2009. "A New Democratic Demographic." CQ Weekly April 20 908–913. Manning, Jennifer E. 2010. "Membership of the 111th Congress: A Profile" Congressional Research Service February 4.

---

[1]This number excludes three Democratic nonvoting delegates representing Guam, the Virgin Islands, and Washington, D.C.

their leadership styles. We discuss the factors in the political environment that influence the ability and willingness of female legislators to work for policy changes on behalf of different groups of women.

WOMEN'S REPRESENTATION IN DEMOCRATIC LEGISLATIVE BODIES ACROSS THE WORLD

Table 7.2 highlights the percentage of women serving in the lower houses of the national legislatures of democratic countries around the world. The table demonstrates that the United States ranks quite low in women's representation

TABLE 7.2

Women's Representation in the Lower or Single House of the National Legislature in Selected Democratic Countries Around the World

Country	Percentage of Women
Sweden	46.4%
Netherlands	42.0
Finland	40.0
Norway	39.6
Argentina	38.5
Belgium	38.0
Denmark	38.0
Spain	36.6
New Zealand	33.6
Germany	32.8
Switzerland	29.0
Austria	27.9
Mexico	27.6
Australia	27.3
Canada	22.1
Italy	21.3
United Kingdom	19.5
Israel	19.2
France	18.9
United States of America	16.8
Greece	17.3
Ireland	13.9
Japan	11.3

Source: Interparliamentary Union. 2010. "Women in National Parliaments: World Classification." www.ipu.org/wmn-e/classif.htm. Data are percentages reported by countries as of February 28, 2010.

compared to other democracies. There are several factors that contribute to this ranking. First, the electoral structure in the United States presents a major barrier to the advancement of women in office. Incumbents enjoy reelection rates approaching 90 percent in a typical election year and most incumbents are men (Jacobson 2008). Second, the United States relies on single-member districts where voters choose a single candidate rather than multiple candidates. By contrast, countries such as Sweden, Denmark, and the Netherlands have electoral systems that encourage broader representation for groups. These countries utilize proportional representation in which political parties are awarded legislative seats based on the percentage of the vote they garner in the election and where voters have the option of selecting more than one candidate in multimember districts (Norris 2003; Paxton and Hughes 2007; Krook 2009).

Additionally, to enhance electoral opportunities for women, some established and new democracies have adopted statutory mechanisms (such as gender quotas) reserving a minimum number of seats for women, or mandates that require parties to reserve a certain number of seats on their party list for women. The success of these laws depends on where women are ranked within the party lists and the severity of the sanctions for noncompliance (Inglehart and Norris 2003; Paxton and Hughes 2007; Krook 2009). A couple of examples illustrate the point. In 1991, Argentina adopted a gender quota law that required all parties contesting seats in the Chamber of Deputies to submit lists including a minimum of 30 percent women. Additionally, the law required that women be placed throughout the list, not clustered near the bottom. Party lists that did not comply with the law were rejected and the party was not allowed to compete in the district's election. Following the implementation of the law, the representation of women in the Chamber of Deputies rose from 4.6 percent in 1991 to 21.3 percent in 1993. Conversely, in 2000, France adopted a parity law that required parties to include 50 percent women in their lists or risk the loss of a percentage of their state funding. Although the law improved representation at the municipal level, in the 2002 election to the French National Assembly, women's representation rose by only 1.4 percent. This poor result was due to the fact that parties concentrated women in seats that could not be won or accepted the insubstantial financial penalty for noncompliance. As a result, women's representation in the French National Assembly continues to grow at a slow pace (Inglehart and Norris 2003; Paxton and Hughes 2007; Krook 2009).

More common than statutory quotas, many European, Scandinavian, and Latin American parties, particularly those on the left, have adopted voluntary gender quotas that are not prescribed by law but are adopted within party rules. Yet scholars find that these quotas are a facilitating condition and the representation of women is more likely to advance in countries where electoral mechanisms coexist with political cultures in which the public holds more egalitarian views on gender roles and women's leadership. Additionally, the parties of the left that adopt gender quotas are already the parties that are most likely to accept women candidates (Inglehart and Norris 2003; Paxton and Hughes 2007; Krook 2009).

WOMEN IN CONGRESS AND STATE LEGISLATURES: A HISTORICAL PERSPECTIVE

The first women elected to state legislatures in the United States came from the western states that were the first to grant women suffrage. Women state legislators from Wyoming, Utah, Colorado, and Idaho were often elected with women's votes, as women voters often made up 40 to 50 percent of voter turnout in those states. In 1894, three women were elected to the Colorado House of Representatives: Clara Cressingham, Carrie C. Holly, and Francis Klock. In 1896, Martha Hughes Cannon, a doctor and woman's suffrage activist, became the first woman elected to a state senate when she beat several candidates including her husband, Angus, in an at-large election for the Utah State Senate (Center for American Women and Politics 2004; Dolan 2004).

The greatest expansion in the number of women serving in state legislatures occurred after the passage of the Nineteenth Amendment granted women the vote, between 1920 and 1925. Women who ran for office in these early years faced numerous obstacles from voters, parties, and even the state itself as they had to fight to overturn provisions in state constitutions that only men could serve in the legislature (Dolan 2004). Once in office, these women entered a male bastion that was not accustomed to the presence of women. When Ida Sammis became one of two women to serve in the New York State Assembly in 1918, it was said that her "first unofficial act was to take her brass spittoon—each member of the assembly was allocated one—and polish it to a brilliant shine. She filled it with flowers and placed it on her desk" (Andersen 1996). By 1930, there were 149 women serving in state legislatures across the country. Women's representation across the states ebbed and flowed as social attitudes about women's participation in the public sphere changed with more support for electing women during periods of social and economic prosperity and less during times of national crisis. Thus, the number of women serving in state legislatures decreased during the years of the Great Depression, increased during World War II, declined in the postwar 1950s as Americans sought a return to traditional values, and increased again after the Korean War (Werner 1968; Dolan 2004).

The percentage of women serving in state legislatures grew rapidly through the 1970s and 1980s, increasing from less than 6 percent in 1973 to more than 13 percent in 1983 as more women gained the educational and occupational qualifications associated with a run for office. By 1993 women made up 21 percent of the membership of state legislatures. However, in the decade from 1994 to 2004 women's representation stagnated hovering around 22 percent. In 2010 women hold 24.4 percent of the seats in the state legislatures (Center for American Women and Politics 2010a; Wilcox and Norrander 2005).

How do we explain why women's progress has slowed so dramatically? As alluded to earlier, one set of barriers is structural. The incumbency advantage and the high cost of campaigns makes it difficult for new groups to make progress (Jacobson 2008). Additionally, the elimination of multimember districts by many states, and the adoption of term limits present further

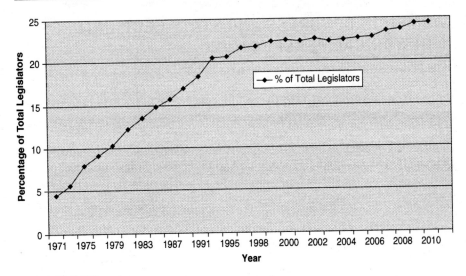

FIGURE 7.1
Progress of Women in State Legislatures Since 1970

Source: Center for American Women and Politics, Eagleton Institute of Politics at Rutgers, The State University of New Jersey.

obstacles. Most state legislators are elected in single-member districts where voters select a single candidate to represent them. In multimember districts, more than one candidate is elected to represent citizens of a district and, in those cases, voters and parties often seek balance by spreading their votes across gender and racial groups (Darcy, Welch, and Clark 1994). Term limits might provide a path to reduce the incumbency advantage and allow new groups, including women, to gain access to office. However, particularly in the lower houses of legislatures, the number of women who are running for office has not kept pace with the number of women who are being kicked out when they reach their term limit. This occurs when not enough women are running for office, either because there are not enough women in the pipeline who are willing to run for office or because the parties are not recruiting enough women to run (Carroll and Jenkins 2001; Wilcox and Norrander 2005). (see Chapter 5 for further discussion of the reasons there are fewer female than male candidates).

Another factor that has contributed to the stagnation of women's representation is the changing partisan dynamics in the country. Throughout the 1990s and early 2000s the Republican Party made gains at all levels of elective office. By 2002, the formerly solidly Democratic South had moved toward the Republicans, and the Republican Party controlled more state legislative seats than the Democrats for the first time since the 1950s (Jacobson 2008; Davidson, Oleszek, and Lee 2009). For most of the twentieth century Republicans did a better job of electing women to public office than did Democrats (Cox 1996; Werner 1968; Wilcox and Norrander 2005). Indeed, in a study of candidate recruitment to state legislatures, Sanbonmatsu (2002, 2003) finds that when Democrats have been the majority party in a legislature they have recruited fewer women candidates. However, in the 1980s and 1990s, the Republican Party included a growing and active socially conservative base that may be less receptive to electing women candidates (Palmer and Simon 2008; Elder 2008). Thus, Republican women did not share in the party's gains. Instead the number of Republican women winning seats as a proportion of all Republicans remained stagnant or declined (Carroll 2002a; Dolan 2004; Wilcox and Norrander 2005; Palmer and Simon 2001; Elder 2008). In fact, after the 2004 elections in which President George W. Bush was re-elected and Republicans expanded their numbers in Congress and the state legislatures, the number of Republican women serving in state legislatures declined from 640 to 607 whereas the number of Democratic women legislators increased from 1,006 to 1,037. In 2010 there are more than twice as many Democratic women in the state legislatures than Republican women, as there are 1,266 Democratic female state legislators and only 519 Republican women legislators (Center for the American Woman and Politics 2010a).

The changing partisan landscape also helps explain the trends in women's representation across the states. Table 7.3 lists the states with the highest and lowest percentages of women in their legislatures. There are more women serving in legislatures in the northeastern and western states which have been trending Democratic and fewer women in the mid-Atlantic and southern states which have a more conservative political culture. In 2010, New Hampshire had the most women in its state legislature (37.5 percent) while South Carolina lagged farthest behind with women comprising only 10 percent of its state legislature (Center for American Women and Politics 2010a).

TABLE 7.3

Women's Representation in the State Legislatures

The Top Ten		The Bottom Ten	
State	Percentage of Women	State	Percentage of Women
New Hampshire	37.5%	Wyoming	16.7%
Vermont	37.2	West Virginia	16.4
Colorado	37	North Dakota	16.3
Minnesota	34.8	Kentucky	15.9
Hawaii	32.9	Louisiana	15.3
Washington	32.7	Pennsylvania	14.6
Nevada	31.7	Mississippi	14.4
Connecticut	31.6	Alabama	12.9
Arizona	31.1	Oklahoma	11.4
Maryland	30.9	South Carolina	10

Source: Center for American Women and Politics. 2010a. "Fact Sheet: Women in State Legislatures 2010." New Brunswick: Center for American Women and Politics, Rutgers, The State University of New Jersey.

Beyond these broad partisan trends, we have limited understanding of why some states elect more women than others. However, there are some important factors that contribute to the disparity. Scholars have found that states with larger numbers of women in the workforce and more women in professional jobs have more women in their legislatures because the eligibility pool—the number of women who have backgrounds that traditionally lead people to consider a political career—is larger in these states. There are also more female legislators in states with more Democratic and liberal voters, as liberal voters tend to have more egalitarian attitudes about gender roles. More women serve in part-time legislatures in comparison to full-time bodies, and women are less likely to serve in those states where campaigns for the legislature are the most expensive. However, the impact of the high cost of a race is mitigated in those areas where state parties recruit and provide financial support for their women candidates (Wilcox and Norrander 2005).

THE ADVANCEMENT OF WOMEN IN CONGRESS

In 1916 Jeannette Rankin (R-MT) became the first woman elected to Congress, and she ultimately went on to serve two terms (1917–1919 and 1941–1943). A political activist who worked for social justice, Rankin had traveled the country working for women's suffrage and peace and against child labor and poverty in America's cities. In her campaign for Congress, Rankin expressed her desire to act as an advocate for women and children. She once noted that the country spent $300,000 per year to study hog fodder but only $30,000 per year to study the needs of children. She asserted, "If the hogs of the nation are ten times more important than the children, it is high time that we [women] made our influence felt." Asked why a woman should be elected to Congress, she answered, "There are hundreds of men to take care of the nation's tariff and foreign policy and irrigation projects. But there isn't a single woman to look after the nation's greatest asset: its children." As a member of Congress, she worked for the national women's suffrage amendment, against child labor, and for programs to improve mothers' and children's health. However, she is best known as the only member of Congress who voted against both World War I and World War II (Kaptur 1996).

Rankin's path to office was unique since most of the small number of women who served in Congress as late as the 1960s came to office as widows (see also Chapter 5). After the death of a politician, political parties often turned to the spouse who had name recognition and the sympathy of the voters but who did not have larger political ambitions. The widow would serve one or two terms until the party decided who the next representative would be or a candidate emerged, thus avoiding internal party strife. In fact the first woman to be seated in the U.S. Senate, Rebecca Latimer Felton (D-GA), served only one day. At 87 years old, she was appointed by the governor of Georgia to replace Senator Tom Watson after he died in office. She convinced the newly elected senator, Walter George, to delay taking the oath of office so that she could be seated and make a speech on the Senate floor. Felton was followed in the Senate by Hattie Carraway (D-AR) who replaced her deceased husband in 1931 and won election in her own right in 1932, serving until 1945 (Kaptur 1996). From 1916 to 1940, 54 percent of women who served in the House succeeded their husbands and from 1941 to 1964, 37 percent of women serving were widows. After 1964, the number of widows in office fell to 15 percent (Gertzog 1995; Dolan 2004). Today this method of gaining election is quite rare.

Several female members who began their service as widows went on to have more accomplished careers in Congress than did their husbands. Perhaps the most famous is Senator Margaret Chase Smith (R-ME) who was first elected to the House of Representatives after the death of her husband in 1940. She then became the first woman elected in her own right to the U.S. Senate in 1948 and served there for an additional 24 years until she was defeated in the 1972 election. She is most well known for her Declaration of Conscience speech in which she was the first Republican to come out against the communist witch-hunt conducted by Senator Joe McCarthy (R-WI) in the 1950s. Numerous careers and lives were ruined by his unsubstantiated accusations and televised hearings in which he searched for communists in government and society. In 1964, Smith became the first woman to seek her party's presidential nomination, receiving 205,690 votes nationally and winning 27 delegates at the Republican National Convention. She spent only $25 on her campaign in the first primary state, New Hampshire, but her campaign practice of handing out recipes and muffins on the campaign trail and posing for photos while cooking gained so much publicity that Republican candidate Nelson Rockefeller countered by distributing his fudge recipe (Kaptur 1996). Current Maine Senator Susan Collins credits Smith with inspiring her to run for public office. On a high school trip to Washington, D.C., Smith brought Collins into her office and spoke to her for several hours about her Senate career. Today Collins holds Smith's seat in the Senate (Mikulski et al. 2001).

Another widow who achieved great success in her own congressional career was Cardiss Collins (D-IL). The longest-serving black woman in Congress, Collins served her Chicago area district from 1973 to 1997, and for ten of those years she was the only black woman in Congress. During her service, she chaired the Congressional Black Caucus and held important committee positions as the first black woman to chair a subcommittee of the powerful Energy and Commerce Committee as well as the first black woman to become ranking member of a full Committee, the Government Reform and Oversight Committee. Throughout her career, Collins worked to advance legislation to help minorities and women, including legislation to prevent discrimination against minorities by mortgage insurance companies, to expand health insurance and medical services for women and minorities, to create an Office of Minority Health in the National Institutes of Health, and to advance gender equity in college sports (Kaptur 1996).

By the 1970s, most women serving in Congress were professional politicians elected in their own right. However, their occupational backgrounds and paths to politics continued to differ from that of men. For example, women were more likely than men to have begun their political careers as community activists spurred to activism for or against a particular local project or as members of the PTA, the local school board, or other community groups (see also Chapter 5). For example, Senator Barbara Mikulski (D-MD), a former social worker, entered the political arena when she got involved in the fight to stop a highway project in her East Baltimore neighborhood. Similarly, when Patty Murray (D-WA) went to the state capitol to lobby against the elimination of a preschool program, a legislator dismissed her by saying "you can't make a difference. You're just a mom in tennis shoes." In response Murray organized a statewide parents' effort to revive the program. She was later elected to the school board and the Washington state Senate. When Murray ran for her first term in the U.S. Senate, her campaign slogan was "just a mom in tennis shoes" (Mikulski et al. 2001).

The career backgrounds of women members have always been more diverse than those of men. For example, between 1968 and 1990, the majority of men in Congress (60 percent) had careers in business and law. Although women also entered politics through this path, 20 percent of elected women were educators, 10 percent were administrators, 12 percent were public officials, and 6 percent were social workers or homemakers. Women were also more likely to have held administrative positions in the public sector and to list their former elected positions as their occupation.

Today the educational and occupational backgrounds of male and female members of Congress continue to converge. However, elected women are older and more likely to wait until their children are grown before running for office (Burrell 1994; Dodson 1997; Dolan 2004). Speaker of the House Nancy Pelosi (D-CA) had been heavily involved in Democratic politics as a party fund-raiser and activist, chairing the California Democrat Party in the 1980s. However, she waited until her five children were grown before she first ran for the House of Representatives in a special election in 1987, at the age of 47 (Sandalow 2008). Today there are more women with young children serving in Congress than ever before (Cadei and Hunter 2009).

The 1992 "Year of the Woman" elections marked the most significant numerical increase in women's slow but steady advancement in representation in Congress. That year, congressional redistricting and a series of scandals, including the House banking scandal that exposed members for overdrafting their official checking accounts, put the public in the mood for a change in leadership and spurred an unusually large number of retirements among sitting members of Congress. With an increase in the number of open seats, the obstacle of incumbency advantage was reduced and more women ran in competitive races. In addition to the increased opportunities presented by the electoral structure, the political climate favored female candidates as the presidential election focused on the crisis in health care and other compassion issues that voters tend to associate with female candidates. Gender itself and women's under-representation in government became an election issue as the Senate hearings for Supreme Court Justice nominee Clarence Thomas focused on accusations of sexual harassment. The spectacle of Anita Hill being questioned by an all-male Judiciary committee prompted women across the country to run for Congress (Burrell 1994; Wilcox 1994; Dolan 2001; Swers 2002).

However, a closer look at women's advancement demonstrates that 1992 was the year of the Democratic woman. In fact, the number of Democratic women in Congress rose from 22 in the 102nd Congress to 40 in the 103rd Congress, while only four more Republican women were elected to the 103rd Congress, bringing their numbers in the House of Representatives from 10 to 14 (Center for American Women and Politics 2010b). Since the 1994 Republican Revolution, Democratic women continue to make up a larger proportion of their caucus than do Republican women. At the opening of the 111th Congress (2009–2010) there were 56 Democratic and only 17 Republican women serving in the House of Representatives and 13 Democratic and 4 Republican women in the Senate. (These numbers do not include the three female nonvoting delegates from Washington, D.C., Guam, and the Virgin Islands) (Center for American Women and Politics 2010b) (see Figure 7.2). Like in the state legislatures, the number of Republican women increased only marginally when Republicans controlled Congress. While Republicans made

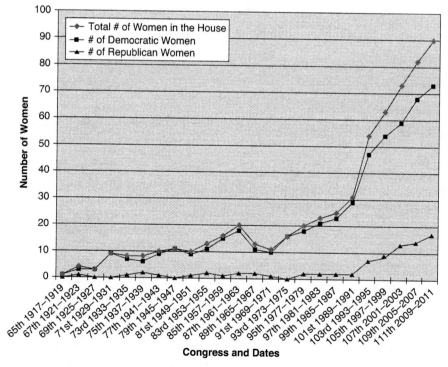

FIGURE 7.2
The Progress of Women in the House of Representatives

Source: Center for American Women and Politics, Eagleton Institute of Politics at Rutgers, The State University of New Jersey.

great gains in the South in the 1990s, the conservative political cultures of these states make them among the least likely to elect women (Elder 2008; Dolan 2004). A number of Republican women lost their seats when the Democrats regained control of Congress in 2006. Many of these Republican women were ideological moderates who served in electorally competitive swing districts, and were defeated by Democratic challengers.

Within the Democratic caucus, the continued advancement in the numbers of Democratic women is attributed to the support of the more liberal Democratic primary voters as well as financial support from the Democratic Party and from EMILY's List, a major PAC that supports pro-choice Democratic women. Furthermore, African-American and Hispanic women who are almost all Democrats, make up a larger proportion of the seats held by minority legislators in comparison to the proportion of seats held by white women in comparison to white men. Finally, Democratic women actually constitute a majority of the California Democratic delegation, the largest Democratic delegation in Congress. As we shall see below, the power of Democratic women and the California delegation helped propel Nancy Pelosi to the Speakership (Elder 2008; Palmer and Simon 2008; Giroux 2009; Lovely 2009; Rosenthal 2008).

WOMEN IN CONGRESS AND STATE LEGISLATURES: A DISTINCTIVE IMPACT ON POLICY?

A long-standing debate in political science concerns whether minority groups need their own representatives in the legislature to guarantee the representation of their interests. The debate is often summarized as whether the election of descriptive representatives, or members from a particular group in society, will yield better substantive representation for the interests of that group in politics. In her classic work, *The Concept of Representation* (1967), Hanna Pitkin characterizes descriptive representatives as individuals who mirror certain social characteristics of their constituents such as race, class, or sex, whereas *substantive representation* refers to the ability of the representative to act for the interests of the represented. Pitkin discounts the need for electing descriptive representatives to achieve substantive representation of constituent interests and asserts that the representative's descriptive characteristics will only be relevant if they affect the representative's actual actions and decisions. More recently, feminist scholars have argued that increasing the descriptive representation of women in legislatures is a necessary but not sufficient condition for achieving the substantive representation of women's interests (Phillips 1991, 1995, 1998; Mansbridge 1999; Dovi 2002). Political theorist Jane Mansbridge (1999) has outlined several reasons that the election of minority group members will improve the representation of group interests. According to Mansbridge, minority and women representatives will:

1. Build trust allowing policies to gain legitimacy in the eyes of minority group members in cases where there exists a history of discrimination and distrust between the majority and minority group.
2. Represent the views of their group at the policymaking table.

3. Bring new issues to the agenda that have not been adequately addressed by the majority.
4. Pursue the vigorous level of advocacy that members of a group bring to their own concerns.
5. Be viewed as speaking with more moral authority on issues that disproportionately affect women and minorities.
6. Serve as role models encouraging more women and minorities to see themselves as potential candidates and legislators.

As more women gained election to Congress and the state legislatures, scholars began to investigate whether female representatives differed from their male colleagues in their policy priorities and legislative activities. Early studies of women in state legislatures in the 1970s found differences in the attitudes and behavior of female legislators but few differences in their policy proposals. In comparison to their male counterparts, female state legislators held more liberal attitudes than men on such issues as support for an ERA, public funding of day care, and the liberalization of abortion laws. However, when asked to rank their policy priorities they were not significantly different from those of their male colleagues. These studies also noted that women had difficulty integrating into male-dominated legislative institutions. The fact that these women did not translate their attitudes into policy priorities has been attributed to the fact that the lack of acceptance of women in the political arena made these women unwilling to risk their standing in the legislature to pursue issues that were not viewed as legitimate by their male colleagues. Further evidence of the difficulty women faced in integrating into state legislatures in the 1970s is demonstrated by the fact that women were concentrated on committees that dealt with social welfare issues, particularly health, education, and welfare committees, and were not well represented on more powerful committees such as those dealing with taxing and budgeting issues. In comparison to men, female legislators also concentrated more energy on constituent service, a role that was compatible with their backgrounds in community service and with public expectations about women's roles. However, they reported lower levels of participation than men on other policy-oriented activities including attending committee hearings, speaking in committee and on the floor, meeting with lobbyists, and bargaining with fellow legislators. The female state legislators of the 1970s also reported lower levels of political ambition, meaning they were less likely to view politics as a career or aspire to higher office (Kirkpatrick 1974; Diamond 1977; Thomas 1994; Cammisa and Reingold 2004).

Since the 1980s, as the role of women in the public sphere became more accepted and the career backgrounds of male and female candidates began to converge, women became full participants in the legislative process by serving on the entire range of committees and gaining leadership positions (Dodson and Carroll 1991; Thomas 1994; Carey, Niemi, and Powell 1998). As women became more fully integrated into the state legislatures, scholars found clear differences in both policy attitudes and legislative activity.

With regard to their representational roles, female legislators in Congress and the state legislatures view women as a distinctive part of their constituency and feel a special responsibility to advocate for their interests (Reingold 1992,

2000; Thomas 1997; Carroll 2002b). In their policy activity, women are more likely to consider women's issues a priority than are their male colleagues. Studies of bill sponsorship and cosponsorship demonstrate that women offer more bills on issues related to women, children, and families. This includes feminist or women's rights bills that promote role equity or role change for women such as bills concerning family leave, equal pay, sexual harassment, and reproductive rights. Female legislators also offer more initiatives on the social welfare issues that underlie the gender gap among voters such as health care and education (Gelb and Palley 1996; Saint-Germain 1989; Dodson and Carroll 1991; Thomas 1994; Tamerius 1995; Bratton and Haynie 1999; Reingold 2000; Wolbrecht 2000, 2002; Swers 2002; Poggione 2004; Bratton 2005; Dodson 2006). Thus, women are clearly bringing women's issues to the legislative agenda.

In their committee activity and on the floor, women utilize their positions to advocate for women's concerns. Congressional studies of policies ranging from welfare reform to violence against women and abortion indicate that women use their positions on key committees and within their party leadership to ensure that women's interests are included in legislation and to prevent the legislation from faltering at key points in the process. For example, during the development of welfare reform in the early 1990s, women in the Republican and Democratic Party who served on the House Ways and Means Committee and held positions in party leadership were pivotal in getting Congress to include child support enforcement and more funding for child care to support working mothers in the final bill (Casey and Carroll 1998; Norton 2002; Swers 2002; Dodson 2006; Johnson, Duerst-Lahti and Norton 2007).

Analyses of floor speeches indicate that women act as vigorous advocates for women's interests. Women draw on their moral authority as women by referring to themselves as parents, mothers, and grandmothers. They are more likely to discuss the impact of policies on children and other underrepresented groups (Shogan 2001; Levy, Tien, and Aved 2002; Cramer Walsh 2002; Norton 2002; Swers 2002). There is some evidence that women have influenced the way that men view and discuss women's issues. For example, in a study of congressional debate on abortion since the 1970s, Levy, Tien, and Aved (2002) found that over time, women have moved the debate from one that emphasizes the morality of abortion to one that increasingly includes a focus on the health of the pregnant woman.

In sum, female legislators clearly prioritize women's interests in their work. Women perceive themselves as representatives of women and women's interests. They have introduced more initiatives concerning women, children, and families to the legislative agenda and they act as vigorous advocates for these interests in committee and on the floor. These findings reflect general trends in legislative behavior.

There are numerous factors that affect whether an individual female legislator perceives herself as an advocate for women's interests and whether she has the ability to pursue these preferences in the legislative process. We turn now to the important political and institutional constraints that shape legislators choices about what policies to champion.

Several congresswomen from the 111th Congress gathered for an event hosted by Women's Policy, Inc.

Party, Ideology, and Constituent Interests

Party affiliation, ideology, and constituent opinion are among the most important predictors of how representatives behave. In recent years the Democratic and Republican Parties have become more ideologically homogeneous and further polarized from each other. As the formerly solid South moved away from the Democratic Party and liberal Northeastern Republicans left the Republican Party, commentators began referring to red states and blue states to represent the ideological divides in the country (Jacobson 2008).

Roll-call vote studies in Congress demonstrate that party unity among Republicans and Democrats is at a historic high and most roll-call votes can be predicted by knowing a member's party affiliation (Poole and Rosenthal 1997; Davidson, Oleszek, and Lee 2009). In this partisan atmosphere, it is hard to see how gender might have an independent effect on legislative behavior. Indeed, studies that examine whether women are more liberal than men in their voting behavior have had mixed results. However, analyses of roll call voting on women's issues such as abortion and family leave demonstrate that women are more liberal on these issues than their male colleagues (Leader 1977; Francovic 1977; Gehlen 1977; Welch 1985; Burrell 1994; Dolan 1997; Norton 1999; Swers 1998, 2002; Frederick 2009).

Even greater differences have been found at other stages of the legislative process. For example, numerous studies show that women are more likely to sponsor bills on women's issues even after accounting for the legislator's party affiliation, ideology, constituency effects, and committee position (Dodson and

Carroll 1991; Thomas 1994; Tamerius 1995; Bratton and Haynie 1999; Reingold 2000; Wolbrecht 2000, 2002; Norton 2002; Swers 2002; Poggione 2004; Bratton 2005; Dodson 2006). Thus, the voters in a congressional or state legislative district have a general ideological view on issues. However, a legislator has wide discretion in choosing which specific policies to champion as long as they fall within the spectrum of policy views that his or her constituents can support. One would not expect a representative of a conservative district to support liberalized abortion laws. However, the member may advocate for increased funding for women's health research or programs to combat violence against women.

Since the Democratic Party is the party currently most associated with women's rights issues, Democratic women tend to be the most active advocates for legislation on women's issues. Additionally, women who consider themselves to be feminists tend to be the most committed to advancing policy initiatives related to women's interests. These women are also more likely to engage in mentoring activities targeted at bringing more women into political office (Dolan and Ford 1995; Dodson and Carroll 1991; Dodson et al. 1995; Wolbrecht 2000, 2002; Norton 2002; Swers 2002; Dodson 2006).

The political calculations for Republican women are more complicated. For Democratic women, particularly liberal Democrats, Democratic voters generally support policies to advance women's rights. On the other hand, Republican women take more risks when they choose to advocate for women's issues because many of these policies conflict with the views of social conservatives, an important constituency within the Republican Party. If Republican women advocate for women's rights legislation they could alienate Republican Party colleagues and risk losing their support on other issues important to the legislator's constituency. Yet roll-call vote analysis shows that most of the gender differences in vote studies on women's issues are driven by the votes of moderate Republican women who are liberal on social issues and conservative on fiscal issues (Swers 2002; Dodson 2006).

As the parties have become more polarized, the ranks of moderate Republicans have dwindled. Today's Republican women are being elected from the more conservative areas of the South and West while many moderate Republican women who represented Northeastern states were defeated or retired in the 2006 and 2008 elections (Palmer and Simon 2008; Elder 2008). Recent studies at the state and national level indicate that the ideological views and voting patterns of Republican women are becoming more conservative and converging with the views of Republican men (CAWP 2001; Carroll 2002a; Frederick 2009, 2010).

Future research needs to develop a better understanding of whether and how conservative women engage women's issues. Do they perceive themselves as champions of women's interests and engage with those causes such as women's health that are consistent with their ideology? Do they deny the existence of women's issues or do they engage with and champion these issues from a conservative or anti-feminist point of view?

Early research by Swers and Larson (2005) found that Republican women engaged women's issues from one of three perspectives. First, the socially conservative woman champions causes from her perspective as a wife and mother. Thus, she will fervently champion a pro-life position on abortion as both a mother and a protector of children. She also believes that women have a distinctive perspective to bring to the table and will champion causes ranging from tax cuts to women's health if they are perceived as being in the interest of women. Other conservative Republican women explicitly deny the existence of women's issues and reject the idea that their gender does or should impact their legislative behavior. Within this group of Republicans, there are also women who accept the idea of women's issues but maintain that these issues are not of interest to her or her district constituency. Finally, a smaller group of moderate Republican women describe themselves as feminists. These women, who often hail from districts with a large contingent of Democratic voters, use their support for women's issues to court women voters and to distinguish themselves as independent from the Republican Party (Swers and Larson 2005).

Finally, as legislators seek to reflect the views of their constituency and their own ideological beliefs, they also want to advance the electoral fortunes of their own party. In this era of tight electoral competition, women represent a key swing voting group that both Republican and Democrats want to court in their efforts to become the majority party in Congress and across the state legislatures. Therefore, the leadership of both parties utilizes female legislators as spokespersons for the party's position on women's issues. For example, Republican women are often asked to speak at press conferences and on the House and Senate floor to defend the party against charges that it is unfriendly to women's interests or to explain how Republican policies will help women. Republican women hold press conferences to explain how small business tax cuts benefit women since women-owned businesses are one of the fastest growing group's of small business owners. Pro-life Republican women are asked to speak on the floor when abortion is being debated to demonstrate that not all women are pro-choice and that Republicans are not anti-women. Similarly, Democratic women organize public events and coordinate floor speeches to demonstrate that the Democratic Party is protecting the interests of women while arguing that the Republican Party is opposed to the advancement of women's rights (Swers 2002; Dodson 2006).

Race, Ethnicity, and Social Class

Beyond party affiliations, women also differ from each other by race, ethnicity, and social class. Scholars are only beginning to examine the impact of intersectionality or overlapping social identities on the policy activities of legislators. Early research on race and ethnicity indicates that the legislative priorities of minority women are impacted by their racial, ethnic, and gender identities. At the congressional level Hawkesworth (2003) found that African-American and Hispanic Democratic women were united in their opposition to welfare reform and used their floor time to speak against the stereotyping of welfare mothers as irresponsible, poor minority women. By contrast minority men and white women in the Democratic Party split their votes on the welfare reform bill. Thus, minority women felt a greater responsibility to advocate for the interests of their poor minority women constituents than did minority men and white women (see also Garcia Bedolla, Tate, and Wong 2005; Barrett 1995). Similarly, Dodson (2006) finds that when Bill Clinton became President in 1992, abortion rights supporters hoped to achieve legislative victories after 12 years of Republican control of the Presidency. She notes that white women focused their attention on the Freedom of Choice Act, a bill that would codify the right to abortion granted by *Roe v. Wade*. By contrast, minority women were more committed to overturning the Hyde amendment, which prevents federal Medicaid dollars from being used to fund abortions. These minority women placed a priority on facilitating access to abortion services for their poor and often minority constituents rather than codifying the abstract right (Dodson 2006; Dodson et al. 1995). As more women from diverse backgrounds are elected to Congress and the state legislatures, researchers will continue to examine how the overlapping identities of race and gender influence members' policy priorities and the type of coalitions they build to support their initiatives.

Institutional Position

Beyond party affiliation and the prevailing political context, the ability of members to advocate for women's issues depends on their position in the institution. Legislatures are hierarchical institutions in which an individual's power depends on his or her level of seniority, committee position, and status as a member of the majority or minority party. Regardless of the promises legislators make in campaigns, if one does not have a seat at the table where decisions are made one cannot influence the content and shape of the legislation (Hall 1996; Swers 2002; Cox and McCubbins 2005; Davidson, Oleszek, and Lee 2009).

Being a member of the majority party is one of the most important determinants of a member's influence. The majority party controls the agenda in Congress and the state legislatures. Majority party leaders determine what proposals will be included in bills and which bills will be considered on the floor. Majority party members chair the committees and determine what issues the committee will consider. In a study of women in Congress, Swers (2002) found that the legislative priorities of women were strongly affected by whether they were in the majority or the minority party. Thus, Republican women were more active on feminist issues when they were in the minority party. As minority party members, these women were only expected to vote in favor of the feminist bills that the Democratic majority brought to the floor. When they were in the majority, promoting feminist legislation meant going against the policy convictions of other majority party members and important interest groups that support the party. In this situation, Republican women put more of their political capital at risk by supporting feminist causes as these causes were not likely to be taken up by the Republican majority. Swers also found that congresswomen, both Democrats and Republicans, were more active on social welfare issues such as health care and education only when their party controlled the majority. This is because social welfare issues constitute a major fault line between the two parties. When their party controlled the majority, women had access to the legislative agenda and were more motivated to offer proposals on these issues because as majority party members they were now more likely to have an impact on the direction of policy in these areas (see also Dodson 2006).

In addition to majority party status, seniority and committee position are important determinants of a legislator's influence within the institution. In the House of Representatives, members have the most influence over policies that fall under the jurisdiction of their committees. This is because most policies are first formulated in committee. By holding hearings to draw attention to issues and drafting legislation, committee leaders and rank and file members decide what issues will be important and what policy ideas will get attention and be forwarded to the full House for consideration. Although committee position is less important in the Senate, committee members in the Senate still have more influence on policy than those senators who do not serve on the committee of jurisdiction (Hall 1996; Sinclair 1989; Swers 2002).

Research shows that women do bring a different perspective to their committee work and are more likely than men to advocate for policies to help women, children, and families (Swers 2002; Norton 1995, 2002; Dodson et al. 1995; Dodson 1998, 2006). However, seats and leadership positions on the most prestigious committees such as Appropriations, the committee that determines how to allocate government funds across various programs, and Ways and Means, the tax-writing committee, are generally awarded to more senior members. Since most of the women elected to Congress were elected since 1992, women are only now gaining the levels of seniority necessary to become committee leaders and wield more influence over policy. Thus, Norton (2002) found that although women were always active on issues related to reproductive rights, until women began to gain seats on Appropriations and other committees with jurisdiction over the issue in the 1990s, they could talk about it but had no influence on the outcome. In a study of the 103rd and 104th Congresses, Dodson (2006) noted that women who served on key committees made sure that the Violence Against Women Act moved through the legislative process and did not get stalled at the many points in the process where bills are killed. Similarly, the efforts of women serving on the House Appropriations Committee ensured that funding for women's health research was greatly expanded in an era when Congress was tightening the budget and cutting funding for many popular programs (Dodson 2006; Swers 2002). Most recently women were key players in the passage of the Lilly Ledbetter Fair Pay Act, a law that makes it easier for women to file pay discrimination lawsuits (Murray 2009). Carolyn Maloney (D-NY) used her position as a senior member of the House Oversight and Government Reform Committee to push legislation through the House of Representatives that would grant paid parental leave to federal employees. If the legislation becomes law this would be the first federally mandated paid leave, as the Family and Medical Leave Act guarantees workers up to 12 weeks of leave but it is unpaid (Davidson 2009).

Critical Mass and Policy Influence

To achieve their policy goals, legislators must build coalitions and find allies. This fact has led scholars to question whether the number of women serving in a legislature influences whether individual legislators will emerge as champions of women's issues. Drawing on the theories of Rosabeth Moss Kanter (1977) concerning the impact of sex ratios on group behavior in corporate settings, scholars argue that when women constitute a small minority of legislators they will be treated as tokens that represent their group, as symbols rather than as individuals. Feeling pressure to conform to male norms, these women will not feel comfortable representing and advocating for the concerns of women. Once these women constitute a "critical mass," at least 20 to 30 percent, they will feel more comfortable pursuing policy preferences based on gender (see also Chapter 8).

Research on state legislatures has found some evidence to support the idea that legislative activity on women's issues increases as the proportion of women in the legislature increases. However, there are not clear threshold effects. For example, in her study of bill sponsorship and passage in the Arizona legislature, Saint-Germain (1989) found that women's activity on behalf of women's interests, such as health care and education, increased as the number of women in the legislature increased. Similarly, in a study of 12 state legislatures in the 1980s, Thomas (1994) found that in states where the proportion of women in the legislature reached 20 percent, women were more likely to give priority to bills concerning women, children, and families and were more successful in passing these bills into law. In a study of abortion policy, Berkman and O'Connor (1993) found that committees that included greater numbers of Democratic women were most successful in blocking restrictive abortion laws such as requirements for parental consent. At the congressional level, MacDonald and O'Brien (2008) find that between 1973 and 2003 congresswomen sponsored more bills on feminist and social welfare issues as the proportion of women in the House increased.

Yet, other scholars have questioned the value of critical mass arguing that women behave more distinctively when they are few in number and feel the responsibility for representing their group. For example, Crowley (2004) found that in state legislatures with few women, the female members played a pivotal role in passing child support legislation. Bratton (2005) found that women in heavily male dominated legislatures sponsored more women's issues legislation, and in some states sex differences in bill sponsorship diminished, as the legislature became more gender balanced. Additionally, Kathlene (1994) argued that there might be a backlash against women as they increase their numbers in the legislature. In her study of hearings in the Colorado legislature, she found that as the number of women on a committee increased, the male members of the committee became more aggressive. As a result, female committee members entered the debate later, spoke less often than their male colleagues did, and interrupted witnesses less frequently than their male counterparts. Still others note that the focus on numbers ignores the legislator's position within the institution and the level of influence he or she wields. Therefore, Childs and Krook (2006) suggest a focus on the emergence of critical actors who influence policy debates rather than critical mass (see also Grey 2006; Dahlerup 2006; Beckwtih 2007).

Although the impact of the proportion of women in the legislature remains unclear, scholars agree that the presence of a women's caucus (a legislative organization that brings together representatives who share a common policy interest) increases the amount of attention given to women's issues by providing a forum to discuss common interests and a network of allies to enlist as supporters of a bill (Thomas 1994; Dodson and Carroll 1991; CAWP 2001; Gertzog 2004). The Congressional Caucus for Women's Issues was founded in 1977 to serve as a resource for information on women's issues and an advocate for women's rights. Since its founding, the caucus has included Democratic and Republican women and therefore requires bipartisan agreement on its agenda. As a result, the caucus generally avoids highly controversial issues like abortion. The caucus reached the height of its influence during the 103rd Congress (1993–1994), when caucus members pushed through a set of bills that created the Office of Women's Health at the National Institutes of Health and increased funding for several diseases related to women's health. Still the caucus is dominated by Democrats, and the Republican Party views it as a group tied to Democratic interest groups. Indeed, when Republicans gained the majority in 1994, one of their first acts was to abolish funding for Legislative Service Organizations like the Congressional Caucus for Women's Issues and the Congressional Black Caucus. The loss of dedicated staff reduced the power of caucuses. However, today the Congressional Caucus for Women's Issues still crafts legislation and acts as a forum where women can promote legislation and seek cosponsors and allies on initiatives (Gertzog 2004; Dodson 2006).

Gender and Institutional Norms

All institutions reflect the preferences and norms of the dominant group, and legislators who want to see their policy ideas enacted into law must understand and conform to the accepted rules and practices of the legislature. However, the standard operating procedures and accepted practices within legislatures are both raced and gendered (Acker 1992; Kenney 1996; Duerst-Lahti 2002; Hawkesworth 2003; Rosenthal 1998). The need to adapt to and negotiate these standards sets up additional hurdles for gaining acceptance within the institution.

Anecdotal and interview-based evidence from state legislative and congressional research indicates that women and minorities report feeling that they have to work harder to prove themselves. Moreover, the female and minority members are more likely to perceive the existence of these separate standards than are their majority group colleagues (Hawkesworth 2003; Thomas 1994; Kenney 1996). For example, Swers (2007) finds that staffers for female members felt that Democratic women Senators had to work harder than ideologically similar male colleagues to prove themselves on defense issues and they believed they were taken less seriously by Pentagon officials. Additionally, an analysis of Senator's appearances on the five major Sunday talk shows in 2002 and 2003 demonstrated that women needed to achieve leadership positions on defense-related committees and within the party before they were viewed as experts and invited to talk about defense issues on the Sunday shows. By contrast, credentials did not play as significant a role in the appearances by male senators. While male senators who led important committees dominated the Sunday talk shows, other male senators who had not achieved leadership positions on foreign policy were also invited to speak on defense issues.[2]

Hawkesworth (2003) finds that minority women serving in the Democratic controlled 103rd Congress and the Republican controlled 104th Congress felt marginalized by white male and female colleagues. Regardless of their level of seniority, these minority women believed that their policy proposals were more likely to be ignored and their knowledge discounted by majority group members (see Smooth 2008, for similar findings in state legislatures). Uncovering the gender and race based norms within a legislature is a very difficult task but these norms have very real consequences for members' legislative power.

Women in Leadership

Party leaders and committee chairs are the most powerful members of the legislature, wielding many formal and informal powers. Committee chairs craft the policy agenda for their committees. They decide on which issues they want to hold hearings and also draft legislative proposals. They generally lead the effort to pass bills that come to the floor under their committee's jurisdiction and are usually involved in negotiating these issues with the other chamber and the executive branch (the President at the national level and the Governor for state legislators) (Hall 1996; Davidson, Oleszek, and Lee 2009). The top party leaders formulate the legislative agenda by deciding what proposals their respective parties will support and oppose. The leaders craft the party's message and serve as the major spokespersons for the party's platform in the media. Party leaders in Congress, particularly the majority party leaders, are routinely involved in the final stages of negotiating policy with the President. Party leaders in the state legislature bargain with the governor over policy details (Rhode 1991; Cox and McCubbins 2005; Davidson, Oleszek, and Lee 2009).

At the state level, women have served on and chaired the full range of committees. Early research on women in state legislatures in the 1970s and

---

[2]The five major talk shows included NBC's *Meet the Press*, ABC's *This Week*, CBS's *Face the Nation*, FOX *News Sunday*, and CNN *Late Edition with Wolf Blitzer*. In a series of studies tracking guest appearances on the Sunday talk shows by women media pundits, elected officials, government appointees, and foreign officials, researchers found that women were less likely to appear on Sunday talk shows than men. Additionally, women had fewer repeat appearances on these shows, shorter segments, and were more likely to appear in later portions of the show, rather than as the headline guests (The White House Project 2001, 2002, 2005).

1980s found that women were more likely to be assigned to committees dealing with women's issues such as health, education, and welfare. Women were less likely to be assigned to prestige committees dealing with business, taxes, and finance. These finding suggest that the party leaders in the 1970s were tracking women to women's issues committee assignments and were not placing women on prestigious committees (Kirkpatrick 1974; Diamond 1977; Thomas 1994; Carroll 2008).

More recent research on the committee assignments of women in state legislatures in the 1990s and 2000s indicates that women are now assigned to the full range of committees including the prestige committees that deal with tax and finance issues (Dolan and Ford 1997; Carroll 2008). While women and men are now generally equally represented on all committees, Carroll (2008) finds that women are still more likely to serve on committees dealing with education and health care. African-American and Latina women are particularly likely to serve on these committees. However, women's greater representation on health and education committees reflects their stronger interest in these issues rather than an effort by party leaders to channel women towards these committees and away from prestige assignments (Carroll 2008; Fraga et al 2008).

Beyond committee assignments, numerous studies find differences in the leadership styles of male and female state legislative committee chairs, suggesting that women adopt more egalitarian leadership styles that value consensus and collaboration whereas men adopt more authoritative styles that emphasize competition and conflict (Kathlene 1994, 1995; Thomas 1994; Rosenthal 1997, 1998, 2000; Carey, Niemi, and Powell 1998; Reingold 2000). However, Rosenthal (1998) notes that the female style of leadership is less prevalent in the legislatures that are more professionalized, meaning those that employ more staff, pay higher salaries, and meet for larger portions of the year. Thus, as more legislatures become professionalized, women may not continue expressing a different style of leadership.

At the congressional level, women have only recently gained the seniority to become committee chairs. Like in the state legislatures, the women who entered Congress in the early years of the feminist movement faced discrimination in their assignments. In her autobiography, Bella Abzug complained that among the 13 women serving in Congress when she came to the House in 1971, five women were assigned to the Education and Labor Committee but none of the women held assignments on the powerful Rules, Armed Services, or Judiciary Committees (Carroll 2008) (see Profile 7.1 for a discussion of the discrimination Shirley Chisholm experienced in the committee assignment process as the first black woman elected to Congress). In his study of the history of women in Congress, Gertzog (1995) notes that before the mid-1960s, women were given less prestigious committee assignments and were more likely to be assigned to committees dealing with women's issues such as Education and Labor. However, by the 1980s and 1990s women were gaining representation on the full range of committees. While women were more likely than men to be placed on committees dealing with issues such as education, aging, and health care, women were just as likely to achieve prestige assignments as men (Gertzog 1995).

PROFILES OF POLITICAL INFLUENCE

Shirley Chisholm, First Black Woman in Congress (1969–1983)

Elected in 1968, Shirley Chisholm became the first black woman to serve in Congress. In that year, Chisholm was one of only ten women and nine African Americans in Congress. A former teacher and child-care center director, she won her first election in her Brooklyn district with the campaign slogan "Unbought and Unbossed." This motto guided her career as she sought to serve the interests of groups that often go unheard, including the poor, children, women, and minorities. She was not afraid to challenge the political establishment. Upon election to Congress, she protested her assignment to the Agriculture Committee by objecting to her committee assignment on the floor of the House of Representatives. Rather than punishing her, Chisholm's actions led the leadership to move her from that committee to the Veterans' Affairs Committee. Satisfied with the result of her protest, she remarked, "There are a lot more veterans in my [Brooklyn, NY] district than there are trees" (Kaptur 1996).

Throughout her congressional career Chisholm challenged the establishment. She called the seniority system that guides the advancement of members of Congress to positions of power on committees, the "senility system" that left control of Congress to "a handful of old men." Yet while she criticized existing power structures, she managed to avoid alienating her colleagues and was able to advance first to her desired assignment to the Education and Labor Committee and later to the powerful Rules Committee. By 1972, Chisholm decided to take her message of change nationally and she became the first woman and the first African American to run for the Democratic nomination for president (see also Chapter 8). Although many of the male members of the Congressional Black Caucus actively opposed her candidacy, Chisholm was on the primary ballot in 12 states. Garnering less than 3 percent of the primary vote, she won 151 delegate votes at the Democratic National Convention. Recently, Carol Moseley Braun (D-IL), the first African-American woman elected to the U.S. Senate (1993–1999), followed in Chisholm's footsteps by running for the Democratic nomination in the 2004 presidential election. However, Moseley Braun withdrew her candidacy before any primary votes were cast.

Chisholm retired from Congress in 1982, following the 1980 election of Ronald Reagan and the corresponding rightward shift in national politics and decline in public support for the antipoverty programs that Chisholm had championed. An activist in both the civil rights and women's rights movements throughout her 14-year career in Congress, Chisholm reached out to women, minorities, the working class, the elderly, and young voters. She died at age 80 on January 1, 2005 (Kaptur 1996; Benenson 2005). ■

Today women have achieved the seniority necessary to gain leadership positions as committee and subcommittee chairs. In the 111th Congress (2009–2010), four women serve as committee chairs in the House of Representatives. Louise Slaughter (D-NY) chairs the Rules Committee, which acts in concert with the party leadership to decide which bills will be brought to the floor and what rules will guide the amendment and debate process. Nydia Velazquez (D-NY) chairs the Small Business Committee, Zoe Lofgren (D-CA) chairs the House Standards of Official Conduct Committee, which investigates ethics complaints against members, and Carolyn Maloney (D-NY) chairs the House-Senate Joint Economic Committee (CQ Staff 2009).

In the Senate, there are four female committee chairs. Barbara Boxer (D-CA) chairs the Environment and Public Works Committee, Blanche Lincoln (D-AR) chairs the Agriculture Committee, and Dianne Feinstein (D-CA) chairs the Select Committee on Intelligence, an important committee in a period of heightened concern over terrorism and national security. Mary Landrieu (D-LA) chairs the Small Business Committee and Olympia Snowe (R-ME) serves as its ranking member, making it the first committee where women hold the top two positions. The ranking member leads the minority party contingent on the committee and takes the lead in negotiating policy changes supported by the minority party. All four of the Republican women serving in the 111th Senate are ranking members on full committees. In addition to Snowe at Small Business, Kay Bailey Hutchison (R-TX) is ranking member on the Commerce, Science, and Transportation Committee, Lisa Murkowski (R-AK) serves as ranking member on the Energy and Natural Resources Committee, and Susan Collins (R-ME) is ranking member on the Homeland Security and Governmental Affairs Committee (CQ Staff 2009; Hagstrom 2009). During the 108th and 109th Congresses (2003–2007), when Republicans controlled the Senate, Collins chaired the committee. She led the effort in the Senate to draft the intelligence reform bill that implemented the recommendations of the 9/11 Commission for reforming American intelligence to better respond to terrorist and other national security threats (CQ Staff 2005). To date, no woman in the House or Senate has chaired the most prestigious money committees such as Appropriations, which decides how to allocate funds across the various government agencies and programs, or the Ways and Means Committee in the House and the Finance Committee in the Senate, which both have control over tax issues.

Perhaps the most historic development for women in Congress was Nancy Pelosi's elevation to Speaker after the 2006 elections. The election of Pelosi as Speaker of the House marks the first time a woman has become the leader of her party and the institution in either House of Congress. Pelosi's rise to the Speakership reflects the complicated and competitive nature of party politics. With the exception of Margaret Chase Smith (R-NH) who served as Republican Conference Chair in the 90th and 91st Congresses (1967–1972), before the 2000 elections no woman had risen higher than secretary or vice chair of the party conference, a lower level leadership position that works with the conference chair to craft the party message and conduct voter outreach. Viewed by many as the women's position in leadership, very few of the women who have held the post have advanced further in the leadership ranks (Rosenthal 2008; Peters and Rosenthal 2010). Today in the 111th Congress (2009–2010), Cathy McMorris Rodgers (R-WA) serves as Conference Vice Chairwoman in the House. In the Senate, Patty Murray (D-WA) is the Democratic Conference Secretary and Lisa Murkowski (R-AK) serves as vice chair of the Republican Conference (CQ Staff 2009; Isenstadt 2009).

Recognizing that there would be little hope for advancement if she ran for conference vice chair, Nancy Pelosi decided to jump into a leadership race at the highest ranks and before the position came open in order to head off any rivals. At the time, Democrats were in the minority and Pelosi decided to assume they would win back the majority in the 2000 elections allowing then party leader Richard Gephardt (D-MO) to become Speaker of the House and the whip, David Bonior (D-MI) to move up to party leader. Pelosi announced that she would run for party whip. The whip is the chief vote counter, responsible for planning legislative strategy and finding ways to encourage party members to vote with their party on policy. While Democrats did not win the majority in 2000, party whip David Bonior (D-MI) decided to retire to run for Governor and Pelosi entered the race to replace him, running against Steny Hoyer (D-MD). Because of her strong support among Democratic women, the California delegation, and fellow Appropriations Committee members Pelosi won the race. When asked about gender, Pelosi said she did not ask people to vote for her because she was a woman but she did believe that women constitute an important voting constituency for the Democrats and so she advocated the importance of having different voices present at the leadership table where the important decisions are made (Sandalow 2008). When Gephardt (D-MO) stepped down as party leader to run for the 2004 Presidential nomination, Pelosi was elected party leader and was elevated to Speaker after the Democrats regained the majority in the 2006 elections (Sandalow 2008; Rosenthal 2008; Peters and Rosenthal 2010).

In contrast to the Democratic Party, the culture of the Republican Party is less open to claims of the importance of demographic diversity in leadership. Moreover, women make up a much smaller proportion of the Republican Party caucus in comparison to the number of women in the Democratic caucus. Therefore, Republican women cannot leverage their numbers to enhance the power of individual women (Evans 2005; Swers and Larson 2005; Rosenthal 2008). Still individual women have emerged as important leaders in the Republican Party. Most recently, Deborah Pryce (R-OH) served as Republican Conference Chair in the 108th and 109th Congresses (2003–2007) and Senator Kay Bailey Hutchison chaired the Republican Policy Committee in the Senate in the 110th Congress (2007–2009). Women in both parties have also led their party's campaign committees, which recruit and raise funds for candidates in the elections. Patty Murray (D-WA) held that post for the Democrats in the run up to the 2002 elections and Nita Lowey (D-NY) was campaign committee chair for the House Democrats in the same year. Recently, Elizabeth Dole (R-NC) led the Senate Republican Campaign Committee in the 2006 elections, but no Republican woman has ever held this position on the House side (Rosenthal 2008; Swers and Larson 2005).

Following Nancy Pelosi's rise to the Speakership, the media and scholars have asked whether gender affects her leadership style. Pelosi speaks openly about the influence of her gender on her priorities. She often refers to herself as a mother of five and grandmother of six. This mantra has a dual purpose, as she wants to send the message that the needs of women and children are a priority for her but she also wants to counteract efforts by her political opponents to paint her as a San Francisco liberal whose policy views and values are outside the mainstream (Sandalow 2008; Rosenthal 2008; Peters and Rosenthal 2010; Swers and Larson 2005). After the election of President Barack Obama, Pelosi renewed her commitment to issues related to women and children. She played a key role in the decision to pass the Lilly Ledbetter Fair Pay Act as the first piece of legislation passed into law in the 111th Congress (Halloran 2009). She also pushed through an expansion of the State Children's Health Insurance

When Nancy Pelosi (D-CA) became the first female Speaker of the House, she invited all of the children in the audience to come up and touch the gavel.

Program (SCHIP), which provides health insurance to low-income children whose family incomes are above the poverty threshold necessary to qualify for Medicaid (Pear 2009). Pelosi led the fight to pass President Obama's comprehensive health care reform bill. Many of the President's advisors and Senate leader Harry Reid (D-NV) believed that the President should have scaled back his health plan after the election of Scott Brown (R-MA) to replace the liberal lion Senator Ted Kennedy (D-MA) caused Democrats to lose their filibuster proof majority in the Senate. Pelosi pushed Obama to pursue comprehensive reform and she brokered a deal to resolve the concerns of pro-life Democrats while keeping the support of her pro-choice colleagues (Bzdek 2010).

While studies of women in leadership emphasize women's roles as consensus builders (Rosenthal 1998; Kathlene 1994), Pelosi clearly has a very partisan leadership style. She prefers to sharpen the Democratic Party's message and highlight its differences with the Republican Party rather than compromising on legislation (Peters and Rosenthal 2010; Rosenthal 2008; Sandalow 2008; Swers and Larson 2005; Cochran and Martinez 2003). However, within the Democratic caucus Pelosi is viewed as a consensus builder who tries to take care of the needs of the various factions of the Democratic caucus. While Pelosi's own ideological views are in line with the progressive wing of the caucus, she takes care to consult with the more moderate and conservative Democrats, placing these members on key committees and as advisors within the leadership ranks (Peters and Rosenthal 2010; Rosenthal 2008; Sandalow 2008; Swers and Larson 2005). As one staffer notes, "Pelosi is a consensus builder; on liberal things she acts as a facilitator organizing and working behind the scenes but she does not act as the public face because she knows she has to take care of the whole caucus" (Swers and Larson 2005). Pelosi is a prodigious fund-raiser and a consummate inside player who knows how to broker deals among factions within her party. She is less skilled at the outside game of media relations and has been criticized as having a wooden speaking style and a tendency to stick to and repeat a set of talking points (Sandalow 2008; Peters and Rosenthal 2010).

As Speaker, Pelosi has also tried to expand opportunities for other women and minorities in the Democratic caucus. As one staffer explained, "Pelosi is into having the caucus look like America" (Swers and Larson 2005). Women, particularly those from her home state of California, are among Pelosi's closest advisors. She appointed Rosa DeLauro (D-CT) to serve as one of the co-chairs of the Steering and Policy Committee that determines all members' committee assignments. Pelosi herself has had more influence on committee assignments than past speakers, using her clout to move away from a strict seniority based system to spread prestigious committee seats to women, minorities, conservative Democrats and newly elected members (Peters and Rosenthal 2010; Rosenthal 2008; Sandalow 2008; Swers and Larson 2005). For example, when the House of Representatives created the Homeland Security Committee in 2002, as part of a response to the terrorist attacks of September 2001, the Republican majority assigned the relevant chairs of committees that historically had jurisdiction over various homeland security issues because these chairmen were concerned about protecting their legislative turf. Rather than assigning the corresponding ranking members, Pelosi, who was minority leader at the time, placed diverse faces on the committee that would represent the range of viewpoints and backgrounds in the Democratic caucus including African Americans, Hispanics, women, and conservative Democrats (Swers and Larson 2005). Comparing the distribution of women on committees before and after Pelosi became party leader 108th Congress, Peters and Rosenthal (2010) find that while women had less seniority overall in the 110th Congress compared to the 107th Congress, women now held more prestigious positions within the committee structure. The fact that the number of women in the Democratic Party rose from 41 in the 107th Congress to 52 in the 110th Congress does not explain women's increased power. Indeed, between the 107th and 110th Congresses, the number of female committee chairs rose from 2 to 4. The number of women holding subcommittee leadership posts increased by one-third rising from 15 to 20 women. Women increased their presence on prestige committees like Ways and Means and Energy and Commerce and the number of subcommittees that included three or more Democratic women rose from 18 in the 107th Congress to 34 in the 110th Congress (Peters and Rosenthal 2010).

CONCLUSION

Although the number of women in Congress and the state legislatures remains far below their numbers in the population, women have steadily increased their representation in the nation's legislatures over time. Across the states women's progress varies with such factors as the number of women in the workforce, the political culture of the state, the professionalization of the legislature, and the commitment of the parties to recruit women candidates. In Congress, the largest increase in women's representation occurred after the 1992 "Year of the Woman" elections, and women have continued to make steady but slow gains since that time.

Despite their small numbers, women clearly pursue different policy priorities than men do, focusing more of their efforts on the advocacy of policies that help women, children, and families. Some scholars find that women have different leadership styles than men emphasizing cooperation and consensus over competition and conflict. Yet there is also great diversity among female legislators as their legislative activities are shaped by their regional constituencies, party affiliation, ideology, and race. Women are now gaining the seniority necessary to enter the ranks of committee and party leadership. In 2006 Nancy Pelosi became Speaker of the House, the highest-ranking leadership post in Congress. Early analyses of her Speakership indicate that her gender does influence her policy priorities and leadership style. As women increase their numbers in Congress and the state legislatures and continue to advance onto important committees, they will achieve more success in their efforts to advance a distinctive agenda.

REFERENCES

Acker, Joan. 1992. "Gendered Institution: From Sex Roles to Gendered Institutions." *Contemporary Sociology* 21:565–569.

Andersen, Kristi, 1996. *After Suffrage: Women in Partisan and Electoral Politics Before the New Deal.* Chicago: University of Chicago Press.

Barrett, Edith. 1995. "The Policy Priorities of African-American Women in State Legislatures." *Legislative Studies Quarterly* 20:223–247.

Beckwith, Karen. 2007. "Numbers and Newness: The Descriptive and Substantive Representation of Women." *Canadian Journal of Political Science* 40:27–49.

Benenson, Bob. 2005. "Former Rep. Shirley Chisholm Remembered for Opening Doors for Minorities and Women." *CQ Weekly* (10 January): 81.

Berkman, Michael B., and Robert E. O'Connor. 1993. "Do Women Legislators Matter? Female Legislators and State Abortion Policy." *American Politics Quarterly* 21:102–124.

Bratton, Kathleen A. 2005. "Critical Mass Theory Revisited: The Behavior and Success of Token Women in State Legislatures." *Politics & Gender* 1, no. 1:97–125.

Bratton, Kathleen A., and Kerry L. Haynie. 1999. "Agenda Setting and Legislative Success in State Legislatures: The Effects of Gender and Race." *The Journal of Politics* 61:658–679.

Burrell, Barbara C. 1994. *A Woman's Place Is in the House: Campaigning for Congress in the Feminist Era.* Ann Arbor: University of Michigan Press.

Bzdek, Vince. 2010. "Why did health-care reform pass? Nancy Pelosi was in charge." *Washington Post* (28 March): B1.

Cadei, Emily and Kathleen Hunter. 2009. "Political Gender Bias Remains Alive and Well." *CQ Weekly* (2 March): 459–461.

Cammisa, Anne Marie and Beth Reingold. 2004. "Women in State Legislatures and State Legislative Research: Beyond Sameness and Difference." *State Politics and Policy Quarterly* 4:181–210.

Carey, John M., Richard G. Niemi, and Lynda W. Powell. 1998. "Are Women State Legislators Different?" In *Women and Elective Office: Past, Present, and Future*, ed. Sue Thomas and Clyde Wilcox. New York: Oxford University Press.

Carroll Susan J. "Committee Assignments: Discrimination or Choice?" In *Legislative Women: Getting Elected, Getting Ahead.* Ed. Beth Reingold Boulder: Lynne Rienner Publishers.

_____. 2002a. "Partisan Dynamics of the Gender Gap Among State Legislators." *Spectrum: The Journal of State Government* (Fall): 18–21.

_____. 2002b. "Representing Women: Congresswomen's Perception of Their Representational Roles." In *Women Transforming Congress*, ed. Cindy Simon Rosenthal. Norman: University of Oklahoma Press.

Carroll Susan J., and Krista Jenkins. 2001. "Unrealized Opportunity? Term Limits and the Representation of Women in State Legislatures." *Women and Politics* 23, no. 4:1–30.

Casey, Kathleen, and Susan J. Carroll. 1998. "Wyoming Wolves and Dead-Beat Dads: The Impact of Women Members of Congress on Welfare Reform." A paper presented at the Annual Meeting of the American Political Science Association.

Center for American Women and Politics. 2001. "Women State Legislators: Past, Present, and Future." New Brunswick: Center for American Women and Politics, Rutgers, The State University of New Jersey.

————. 2004. "Firsts for Women in U.S. Politics." New Brunswick: Center for American Women and Politics, Rutgers, The State University of New Jersey.

————. 2010a. "Fact Sheet: Women in State Legislatures 2010." New Brunswick: Center for American Women and Politics, Rutgers, The State University of New Jersey.

————. 2010b. "Fact Sheet: Women in the U.S. Congress 2010." New Brunswick: Center for American Women and Politics, Rutgers, The State University of New Jersey.

————. 2010c. "Fact Sheet: Women of Color in Elective Office 2010." New Brunswick: Center for American Women and Politics, Rutgers, The State University of New Jersey.

Childs, Sarah and Mona Lena Krook. 2006. "Should Feminists Give Up on Critical Mass? A Contingent Yes." *Politics & Gender* (2):522–530

Cochran, John, and Gebe Martinez. 2003. "Democrats Still Upbeat Despite Losses on Big Bills." *CQ Weekly* (13 December): 3066–3068.

Cox, Gary W., and Matthew D. McCubbins. 2005. *Setting the Agenda: Responsible Party Government in the U.S. House of Representatives.* New York: Cambridge University Press.

Cox, Elizabeth M. 1996. *Women State and Territorial Legislators, 1895–1995: A State-by-State Analysis with Rosters of 6,000 Women.* Jefferson, NC: McFarland.

CQ Staff. 2005. *CQ's Politics in America 2006: The 109th Congress.* ed. Jackie Koszczuk and H. Amy Stern. Washington D.C.: CQ Press.

————. 2009. "Special Report: CQ's Committee Guide." *CQ Weekly* (13 April): 839–871.

Cramer Walsh, Katherine. 2002. "Resonating to Be Heard: Gendered Debate on the Floor of the House." In *Women Transforming Congress,* ed. Cindy Simon Rosenthal. Norman: University of Oklahoma Press.

Crowley, Jocelyn Elise. 2004. "When Tokens Matter." *Legislative Studies Quarterly* 29:109–136.

Dahlerup, Drude. 2006. "The Story of the Theory of Critical Mass." *Politics & Gender* (2):511–522.

Darcy, R., Susan Welch, and Janet Clark. 1994. *Women, Elections, and Representation,* 2nd ed. Lincoln: University of Nebraska Press.

Davidson, Joe. 2009. "Parental Leave Passes Committee as Foe Foresees Families Stocking Up on Kids." *Washington Post* (7 May):

Davidson, Roger H., Walter J. Oleszek, and Frances E. Lee. 2009. *Congress and its Members* 12th Edition. Washington D.C.: CQ Press.

Diamond, Irene. 1977. *Sex Roles in the State House.* New Haven: Yale University Press.

Dodson, Debra L. 1997. "Change and Continuity in the Relationship Between Private Responsibilities and Public Officeholding: The More Things Change, the More They Stay the Same." *Policy Studies Journal* 25:569–584.

————. 1998. "Representing Women's Interests in the U.S. House of Representatives." In *Women and Elective Office: Past, Present, and Future,* ed. Sue Thomas and Clyde Wilcox. New York: Oxford University Press.

————. 2006. *The Impact of Women in Congress.* New York: Oxford University Press.

Dodson, Debra L., and Susan Carroll. 1991. *Reshaping the Agenda: Women in State Legislatures.* New Brunswick: Center for American Women and Politics, Rutgers, State University of New Jersey.

Dodson, Debra L. et al. 1995. *Voices, Views, Votes: The Impact of Women in the 103rd Congress.* New Brunswick: Center for American Women and Politics, Rutgers, State University of New Jersey.

Dolan, Julie. 1997. "Support for Women's Interests in the 103rd Congress: The Distinct Impact of Congressional Women." *Women & Politics* 18:81–94.

Dolan, Kathleen. 2001. "Electoral Context, Issues, and Voting for Women in the 1990s." *Women & Politics* 23, no. 1–2:21–36.

_____. 2004. *Voting for Women: How the Public Evaluates Women Candidates.* Boulder: Westview Press.

Dolan, Kathleen, and Lynne Ford. 1997. "Change and Continuity Among Women State Legislators: Evidence from Three Decades." *Political Research Quarterly* 50: 137–151.

_____. 1995. "Women in the State Legislatures: Feminist Identity and Legislative Behaviors." *American Politics Quarterly* 23:96–108.

Dovi, Suzanne. 2002. "Preferable Descriptive Representatives: Or Will Just Any Woman, Black, or Latino Do?" *American Political Science Review* 96:745–754.

Duerst-Lahti, Georgia. 2002. "Knowing Congress as a Gendered Institution: Manliness and the Implications of Women in Congress." In *Women Transforming Congress,* ed. Cindy Simon Rosenthal. Norman: University of Oklahoma Press.

Elder, Laurel. 2008. "Whither Republican Women: The Growing Partisan Gap Among Women in Congress." *The Forum* 6: Issue 1, Article 13.

Evans, Jocelyn Jones. 2005. *Women, Partisanship, and the Congress.* New York: Palgrave MacMillan.

Fiore, Faye and Tina Daunt. 2007. "Pelosi Shows She's the Head of Her Party." *Los Angeles Times* (4 January): A1.

Fraga, Luis Ricardo, Valerie Martinez-Ebers, Linda Lopez, and Ricardo Ramirez. 2008. "Representing Gender and Ethnicity: Strategic Intersectionality." In *Legislative Women: Getting Elected, Getting Ahead.* Ed. Beth Reingold Boulder: Lynne Rienner Publishers.

Francovic, Kathleen. 1977. "Sex and Voting in the U.S. House of Representatives: 1961–1975." *American Politics Quarterly* 5:515–530.

Frederick, Brian. 2009. "Are Female House Members Still More Liberal in a Polarized Era? The Conditional Nature of the Relationship Between Descriptive and Substantive Representation." *Congress and the Presidency* 36:181–202.

_____. Forthcoming (2010) "Gender and Patterns of Roll Call Voting in the U.S. Senate." *Congress and the Presidency.*

Garcia Bedolla, Lisa, Katherine Tate, and Janelle Wong. 2005. "Indelible Effects: The Impact of Women of Color in the U.S. Congress." In *Women and Elective Office,* 2nd ed., ed. Sue Thomas and Clyde Wilcox. New York: Oxford University Press.

Gehlen, Freida. 1977. "Women Members of Congress: A Distinctive Role." In *A Portrait of Marginality: The Political Behavior of the American Woman,* eds. Marianne Githens and Jewell Prestage. New York: McKay Co.

Gelb, Joyce and Marian Lief Palley. 1996. *Women and Public Policies: Reassessing Gender Politics.* Charlottesville, VA: University Press of Virginia.

Gertzog, Irwin. 1995. *Congressional Women: Their Recruitment, Integration, and Behavior,* 2nd ed. Westport, CT: Praeger Publishers.

———. 2004. *Women and Power on Capitol Hill: Reconstructing the Congressional Women's Caucus.* Boulder: Lynne Rienner.

Giroux, Greg. 2009. "A New Democratic Demographic." *CQ Weekly* (20 April): 908–913.

Grey, Sandra. 2006. "Numbers and Beyond: The Relevance of Critical Mass in Gender Research." *Politics & Gender* (2):492–502.

Hagstrom, Jerry. 2009. "Ag Panel Now Land of Lincoln." *National Journal* (3 October): 19.

Hall, Richard. 1996. *Participation in Congress.* New Haven: Yale University Press.

Halloran, Liz. 2009. "House Approves Bills To Fight Gender Wage Gap." *NPR.org* January 9, 2009.

Hawkesworth, Mary. 2003. "Congressional Enactments of Race-Gender: Toward a Theory of Raced-Gendered Institutions." *American Political Science Review* 97:529–550.

Inglehart, Ronald, and Pippa Norris. 2003. *Rising Tide: Gender Equality and Cultural Change.* New York: Cambridge University Press.

Isenstadt, Alex. 2009. "John Thune, Lisa Murkowski Ascend in Senate GOP Leadership." *Politico* (26 June).

Jacobson, Gary. 2008. *The Politics of Congressional Elections,* 7th Edition. New York: Longman.

Johnson, Cathy Marie, Georgia Duerst-Lahti, and Noelle H. Norton. 2007. *Creating Gender: The Sexual Politics of Welfare Policy.* Boulder: Lynne Rienner.

Kanter, Rosabeth Moss. 1977. "Some Effects of Proportions on Group Life: Skewed Sex Ratios and Responses to Token Women." *American Journal of Sociology* 82:965–990.

Kaptur, Marcy. 1996. *Women of Congress: A Twentieth-Century Odyssey.* Washington, D.C.: Congressional Quarterly.

Kathlene, Lynn. 1994. "Power and Influence of State Legislative Policymaking: The Interaction of Gender and Position in Committee Hearing Debates." *American Political Science Review* 88:560–576.

———. 1995. "Alternative Views of Crime: Legislative Policymaking in Gendered Terms." *Journal of Politics* 57:696–723.

Kenney, Sally J. 1996. "New Research on Gendered Political Institutions." *Political Research Quarterly* 49:445–466.

Kirkpatrick, Jeane. 1974. *Political Woman.* New York: Basic Books.

Koch, Jeffrey. 2002. "Gender Stereotypes and Citizen Impressions of House Candidates Ideological Orientations." *American Journal of Political Science* 46:453–462.

Krook, Mona Lena. 2009. *Quotas for Women in Politics: Gender and Candidate Selection Reform Worldwide* New York: Oxford University Press.

Lawless, Jennifer L. and Pearson, Kathryn. 2008. "Competing in Congressional Primaries." In *Legislative Women: Getting Elected, Getting Ahead.* Ed. Beth Reingold Boulder: Lynne Rienner Publishers.

Leader, Shelah Gilbert. 1977. "The Policy Impact of Elected Women Officials." In *The Impact of the Electoral Process,* eds. Joseph Cooper and Louis Maisel. Beverly Hills: Sage Publications.

Levy, Dena, Charles Tien, and Rachelle Aved. 2002. "Do Differences Matter? Women Members of Congress and the Hyde Amendment." *Women & Politics* 23, no. 1/2:105–127.

Lovely, Erika. 2009. "GOP Women: A Minority in a Minority." *Politico* (10 May).

MacDonald Jason A. and Erin E. O'Brien. 2008. "Quasi-Experimental Design, Constituency, and Advancing Women's Interests: 'Critically' Reexamining the Influence of Gender on Substantive Representation" Presented at the Annual Meeting of the American Political Science Association Boston: MA.

Manning, Jennifer E. 2010. "Membership of the 111th Congress: A Profile" *Congressional Research Service* (4 February).

Mansbridge, Jane. 1999. "Should Blacks Represent Blacks and Women Represent Women? A Contingent 'Yes.'" *Journal of Politics* 61:628–657.

Marcus, Ruth. 2007. "Grandma with a Gavel." *Washington Post* (10 January):A13.

Mikulski, Barbara, Kay Bailey Hutchison, Dianne Feinstein, Barbara Boxer, Patty Murray, Olympia Snowe, Susan Collins, Mary Landrieu, and Blanche L. Lincoln with Catherine Whitney. 2001. *Nine and Counting: The Women of the Senate.* New York: Harper Collins Publshers.

Murray, Shailagh. 2009. "Fair-Wage Bill Clears the Senate." *Washington Post* (23 January).

Norton, Noelle H. 1995. "Women, It's Not Enough to be Elected: Committee Position Makes a Difference." In *Gender Power, Leadership, and Governance*, ed. Georgia Duerst-Lahti and Rita Mae Kelly. Ann Arbor: University of Michigan Press.

_____. 1999. "Committee Influence Over Controversial Policy: The Reproductive Policy Case." *Policy Studies Journal* 27:203–216.

_____. 2002. "Transforming Congress from the Inside: Women in Committee." In *Women Transforming Congress*, ed. Cindy Simon Rosenthal. Norman: University of Oklahoma Press.

Palmer, Barbara, and Dennis Simon. 2001. "The Political Glass Ceiling: Gender, Strategy, and Incumbency in U.S. House Elections, 1976–1998." *Women & Politics* 23, no. 1–2:59–78.

_____. 2008. *Breaking the Political Glass Ceiling: Women and Congressional Elections* 2nd Edition. New York: Routledge.

Paxton, Pamela and Melanie M. Hughes. 2007. *Women, Politics, and Power: A Global Perspective*. Thousand Oaks, CA: Pine Forge Press.

Pear, Robert. 2009. "House Votes to Expand Children's Health Care." *New York Times* (15 January): .

Peters, Jr. Ronald M. and Cindy Simon Rosenthal. 2010. *Speaker Nancy Pelosi and the New American Politics*. Oxford University Press.

Poggione, Sarah. 2004. "Exploring Gender Differences in State Legislators' Policy Preferences." *Political Research Quarterly* 57:305–314.

Phillips, Anne. 1991. *Engendering Democracy*. University Park: The Pennsylvania State University Press.

_____. 1995. *The Politics of Presence*. Oxford: Oxford University Press.

_____. 1998. "Democracy and Representation: Or, Why Should it Matter Who our Representatives Are?" In, *Feminism and Politics*, ed. Anne Phillips. New York: Oxford University Press.

Pitkin, Hanna Fenichel. 1967. *The Concept of Representation*. Berkeley: University of California Press.

Poole, Keith T., and Howard Rosenthal. 1997. *Congress: A Political-Economic History of Roll Call Voting*. New York: Oxford University Press.

Reingold, Beth. 1992. "Concepts of Representation Among Female and Male State Legislators." *Legislative Studies Quarterly* 17:509–537.

_____. 2000. *Representing Women: Sex, Gender, and Legislative Behavior in Arizona and California*. Chapel Hill: University of North Carolina Press.

Rhode, David W. 1991. *Parties and Leaders in the Postreform House*. Chicago: University of Chicago Press.

Rosenthal, Cindy Simon. 1997. "A View of Their Own: Women's Committee Leadership Styles and State Legislatures." *Policy Studies Journal* 25:585–600.

———. 1998. *When Women Lead: Integrative Leadership in State Legislatures.* New York: Oxford University Press.

———. 2000. "Gender Styles in State Legislative Committees: Raising Their Voices in Resolving Conflict." *Women & Politics* 21:21–45.

———. 2008. "Climbing Higher: Opportunities and Obstacles within the Party System." In *Legislative Women: Getting Elected, Getting Ahead.* Ed. Beth Reingold Boulder: Lynne Rienner Publishers.

Saint-Germain, Michelle A. 1989. "Does Their Difference Make a Difference? The Impact of Women on Public Policy in the Arizona Legislature." *Social Science Quarterly* 70:956–968.

Sanbonmatsu, Kira. 2002. "Political Parties and the Recruitment of Women to State Legislatures." *Journal of Politics* 64:791–809.

———. 2003. "Candidate Recruitment and Women's Election to the State Legislatures." Report prepared for the Center for American Women and Politics, Eagleton Institute of Politics, Rutgers, the State University of New Jersey.

Sandalow, Marc. 2008. *Madam Speaker: Nancy Pelosi's Life, Times, and Rise to Power.* New York: Modern Times.

Shogan, Colleen J. 2001. "Speaking Out: An Analysis of Democratic and Republican Women-Invoked Rhetoric of the 105th Congress." *Women & Politics* 23: 129–146.

Sinclair, Barbara. 1989. *The Transformation of the U.S. Senate.* Baltimore: Johns Hopkins University Press.

Smooth, Wendy. 2008. "Gender, Race, and the Exercise of Power and Influence." In *Legislative Women: Getting Elected, Getting Ahead.* Ed. Beth Reingold Boulder: Lynne Rienner Publishers.

Swers, Michele L. 1998. "Are Congresswomen More Likely to Vote for Women's Issue Bills Than Their Male Colleagues?" *Legislative Studies Quarterly* 23:435–448.

———. 2002. *The Difference Women Make: The Policy Impact of Women in Congress.* Chicago: University of Chicago Press.

———. 2007. "Building a Reputation on National Security: The Impact of Stereotypes Related to Gender and Military Experience." *Legislative Studies Quarterly* 32: 559–596.

———. 2008. "Policy Leadership Beyond "Women's" Issues" In *Legislative Women: Getting Elected, Getting Ahead.* Ed. Beth Reingold Boulder: Lynne Rienner Publishers.

Swers, Michele, and Carin Larson. 2005. "Women and Congress: Do They Act as Advocates for Women's Issues?" In *Women and Elective Office: Past, Present, and Future,* 2nd ed., ed. Sue Thomas and Clyde Wilcox. New York: Oxford University Press.

Tamerius, Karin L. 1995. "Sex, Gender, and Leadership in the Representation of Women." In *Gender Power, Leadership, and Governance,* ed. Georgia Duerst-Lahti and Rita Mae Kelly. Ann Arbor: University of Michigan Press.

The White House Project. 2001. "Who's Talking Now: An Analysis of Sunday Morning Talk Shows." New York: The White House Project.

———. 2002. "Who's Still Talking." New York: The White House Project.

———. 2005. "Who's Talking Now: A Follow Up Analysis of Guest Appearances by Women on the Sunday Morning Talk Shows." New York: The White House Project.

Thomas, Sue. 1994. *How Women Legislate.* New York: Oxford University Press.

———. 1997. "Why Gender Matters: The Perceptions of Women Officeholders." *Women & Politics* 17:27–53.

Welch, Susan. 1985. "Are Women More Liberal Than Men in the U.S. Congress?" *Legislative Studies Quarterly* 10:125–134.

Werner, Emmy E. 1968. "Women in the State Legislatures." *Western Political Quarterly* 21:40–50.

Wilcox, Clyde. 1994. "Why Was 1992 the 'Year of the Woman'? Explaining Women's Gains in 1992." In *The Year of the Woman: Myths and Realities*, ed. Elizabeth Adell Cook, Sue Thomas, and Clyde Wilcox. Boulder, CO: Westview Press.

Wilcox, Clyde, and Barbara Norrander. 2005. "Change and Continuity in the Geography of Women Legislators." In *Women and Elective Office*, 2nd ed., ed. Sue Thomas and Clyde Wilcox. New York: Oxford University Press.

Wolbrecht, Christina. 2000. *The Politics of Women's Rights: Parties, Positions, and Change*. Princeton: Princeton University Press.

_____. 2002. "Female Legislators and the Women's Rights Agenda." In *Women Transforming Congress*, ed. Cindy Simon Rosenthal. Norman: University of Oklahoma Press.

Women in the Executive Branch

When Senator Hillary Clinton announced her candidacy for the United States' presidency in January of 2007, she became the most viable female candidate ever to run for the office. While numerous other women preceded her in a quest for the Oval Office, no other woman had ever kicked off her campaign with such a commanding lead over her party opponents in both public opinion polls and campaign dollars. When Governor Sarah Palin was announced as John McCain's vice presidential running mate in August of 2008, she also made history, but did so as the first Republican woman to run for the vice presidency. Virtually overnight, she was launched from relative obscurity as Alaska's Governor to the biggest news story of the day.

When all the dust settled on November 5, 2008, neither Clinton nor Palin emerged victorious. Clinton conceded the Democratic nomination to Barack Obama months earlier in June of 2008, and Obama went on to defeat John McCain and Sarah Palin in the general election, thereby becoming the first African-American president in the history of the United States.

In losing their respective elections, both Clinton and Palin joined a relatively short list of women who have campaigned unsuccessfully for a seat in the White House. In the history of the United States, not a single woman has ever served as president or vice president. In fact, the United States lags behind many other countries in the world that have elected one or more women to their highest executive office. As of 2010, women have served as national leaders in a total of 57 different countries.[1]

Despite the fact that very few women have campaigned for president or vice president in the United States, a growing number of women continue to gain executive experience by serving as governors, lieutenant governors, and other high-ranking government executives. More and more women are assuming leadership positions in federal, state and local governments, amassing experience that will serve them well if they decide to run for the nation's top job in the future.

---

[1]Data through 2007 collected from Farida Jalalzai, 2008. "Women Rule: Shattering the Glass Ceiling." *Politics & Gender* 4(2):205–231. Data from 2008–2010 accessed through Worldwide Guide to Women in Leadership, at www.guide2womenleaders.com.

Who are these women? What do we know about them? This chapter examines women in the executive branch of government, both at the federal and state levels.[2] The chapter is divided into two parts. In the first part, we pay particular attention to the presidential and vice presidential candidacies of Hillary Clinton and Sarah Palin as well as some of their notable female predecessors. We also examine women who have served as governors and in other statewide elected positions. Because many additional women receive executive positions through presidential and gubernatorial appointments, we cover them as well.

The second part of the chapter focuses on the impact of these executive women. Do they bring different perspectives and priorities to the table? Are government outputs qualitatively different because of their presence? Do women have the same opportunities to exercise power as their male colleagues, or do they find themselves in relatively less influential positions?

WOMEN AS PRESIDENTIAL AND VICE PRESIDENTIAL CANDIDATES

The unsuccessful candidacies of Hillary Clinton and Sarah Palin in 2008 remind us that no woman has ever served as president or vice president of the United States. Before Clinton, at least 20 other women ran for the U.S. presidency. The very first candidate was Victoria Claflin Woodhull, a women's rights advocate who ran under the banner of the Equal Rights Party in 1872, nearly 50 years before women had the right to vote. Belva Lockwood also ran as a candidate for the Equal Rights Party in 1884 before becoming the first woman to practice before the U.S. Supreme Court some four years later (CAWP 2003). More recently, former Congresswoman Cynthia McKinney ran as the Green Party nominee in 2008, along with her female running mate, Rosa Clemente ("Green Party Picks Slate" 2008). In 2004, Carol Moseley Braun, a former Senator from the state of Illinois, threw her hat into the ring for the Democratic nomination, and in the 2000 election, Elizabeth Dole ran for the Republican nomination. Both Moseley Braun and Dole withdrew from the race before the primaries and caucuses got underway.

Even fewer women have run as vice presidential candidates. Before Sarah Palin, Geraldine Ferraro made history in 1984 when Democrat Walter Mondale selected her as his running mate. Various other women have sought out the vice presidential nomination, without success. For example, former Wyoming Governor Nellie Tayloe Ross campaigned for the nomination in 1928 and received 31 votes at the Democratic National Convention (Braden 1996, 32). She was followed some 44 years later by Sissy Farenthold, a state legislator from the state of Texas. Feminist activist Gloria Steinem nominated her at the Democratic National Convention in 1972, and Farenthold took second place in the balloting with a total of 400 votes.

---

[2]See Chapter 6 for discussion of executive women at the local level.

CANDIDATE FOR REELECTION AS
GOVERNOR OF WYOMING

Nellie Tayloe Ross, Governor of Wyoming from 1925 to 1927, was the first woman to serve as a governor in the United States (CAWP 2009b).

At least three additional women have run as vice presidential candidates from minor parties: Rosa Clemente, Ezola Foster, and Winona LaDuke. Rosa Clemente, an African-American hip-hop artist, was part of the first all-female, all African-American presidential ticket when she joined forces with Cynthia McKinney on the Green party ticket in 2008. Ezola Foster became the first African-American woman to run for the vice presidency when she was tapped by conservative commentator Pat Buchanan in 2000 to run under the banner of the Reform Party. Winona LaDuke made history as the first Native-American woman to run for the vice presidency when she ran on the Green Party ticket alongside Ralph Nader in both 1996 and 2000 (see *Profiles of Political Influence*).

Because no woman has ever been elected as president or vice president in the United States, we focus our attention on the women who have campaigned for these positions.

▶ PROFILES OF POLITICAL INFLUENCE

Political Pioneer: Ezola Foster

Conservative African American Ezola Foster was the vice presidential candidate on Pat Buchanan's Reform Party ticket in 2000. An author, former teacher, and conservative activist, Foster's political views have spanned a wide spectrum in her career. She spent 17 years as a Democrat, 19 as a Republican, and a few as an Independent before following Buchanan to the Reform Party. She was raised in Louisiana and Texas and attended Texas Southern University for her undergraduate education. She moved to Los Angeles in 1960 and took a job in a law office. Married to former truck driver Chuck Foster, she is a member of the conservative John Birch Society. In 1963 she began teaching typing classes in the Los Angeles public school system. She is the author of the 1995 book *What's Right for All Americans* and is widely regarded as a troublemaker who enjoys publicity.

According to Buchanan, "She has stood up for flag and family, God and country, her whole life" (Recio 2000). Her positions are newsworthy because she is a conservative and outspoken minority. Her hard-line rhetoric has often put her at odds with other minorities. For example, in 1994 Foster supported the highly controversial Proposition 187 in California that aimed at cutting state aid to immigrants. Working at Bell High School with a nearly 90 percent Hispanic student body, Foster was not exactly the most popular teacher in school for her public stands against education and benefits for immigrants.

In the 2000 election, the Buchanan/Foster ticket received 448,895 votes, or 0.42 percent of the total vote in the 2000 election. (FEC 2000). ■

Presidential Candidates

On January 20, 2007, Hillary Clinton announced to the American public that she was forming a presidential exploratory committee. Sitting comfortably on a couch in her home in Washington, D.C., Clinton asked viewers to begin a conversation with her about the problems facing Americans. As she said, "Let's talk. Let's chat. Let's start a dialogue about your ideas and mine" (Clinton 2007). In doing so, she immediately became the most viable female candidate ever to run for the U.S. presidency. Not only did Democratic voters prefer her by a margin of nearly 2-1 over Barack Obama, her closest competitor for the nomination, but she also matched up very well in the general election against Republican hopefuls such as John McCain, Mitt Romney and Rudy Guiliani (Polling Report 2008b; Polling the Nations 2007). In fact, it seemed to many that she was the inevitable Democratic nominee.

Eighteen months, 50 states, and nearly $230 million later, Hillary Clinton conceded the Democratic nomination to Barack Obama, the first African

◥ PROFILES OF POLITICAL INFLUENCE

Political Pioneer: Winona LaDuke

Native American rights activist, author, journalist, lecturer, and two-time vice presidential candidate, Winona LaDuke was recently selected by *Time* magazine as one of 50 promising young leaders (Biema 2003). LaDuke was the Green Party vice presidential candidate in both the 1996 and 2000 elections. The Nader/LaDuke ticket had a substantial impact on the 2000 presidential elections, garnering 2,882,955 popular votes, or 2.74 percent of total votes cast (FEC 2000).

LaDuke was admittedly reluctant to enter electoral politics. She discloses that prior to 1996 she was part of the "largest political party in America: the 50 percent of people who don't vote" (Scott 2000). Although she was incredibly "political," she, like so many other Americans, felt disenfranchised by a two-party system. She initially refused the offer to join the ticket in 1996 but later with Nader's urging and insistence that sometimes private citizens must become public ones, LaDuke joined the effort. In her 2000 nomination acceptance speech, she said, "I am not inclined toward electoral politics. Yet I am impacted by public policy. I am interested in reframing the debate on the issues of this society" (LaDuke 2000).

LaDuke is a member of the Minnesota band of the Anishinaabe (also known as the Ojibwe/Chippewa) and currently lives on the White Earth reservation in Minnesota. She grew up in East Los Angeles and later in Ashland, Oregon. After graduating from Harvard in 1982 with a degree in economics, she immediately engaged herself in Native Americans' rights issues. She was instrumental in the successful struggle against the James Bay hydroelectric development project in Canada. She founded the White Earth Recovery Project, a major effort to regain lands promised to the Anishinaabe people by an 1867 federal treaty. LaDuke used grants and a $20,000 human rights prize from Reebok to launch the recovery project. She is the leader of the Indigenous Women's Network and has spoken at the United Nations on numerous occasions. She is also a former board member of Greenpeace USA. An accomplished writer, LaDuke has published numerous articles and two books, *Last Standing Woman* in 1997 and *All Our Relations: Native Struggles for Land and Life* in 1999. ■

American to win a major party nomination for the U.S. presidency. Despite her loss, her candidacy was truly groundbreaking and demonstrated that a woman could indeed run credibly for the office of the president. In the next few pages, we examine her historic run for the presidency and compare and contrast her candidacy with those of some of the women who preceded her in their pursuit of the White House (see also Chapter 5 for additional information about her candidacy).

Hillary Clinton is the first and only woman in the United States to begin her presidential campaign as the front-runner seeking her party's nomination.

When she formally declared her presidential candidacy in January of 2007, Hillary Clinton's double digit lead over her Democratic rivals in public opinion polls led many to predict that she was the inevitable Democratic nominee.

Elizabeth Dole ran for the Republican nomination for president in 1999 and was then considered the most viable woman ever to run for the presidency. Dole was well known to the American public, having served as Secretary of Transportation under President Reagan and Secretary of Labor under President George H.W. Bush and as a White House aide in the administrations of Lyndon B. Johnson, Richard Nixon, and Ronald Reagan (Watson and Gordon 2003b). She served for eight years as president of the Red Cross before she announced her own candidacy in January 1999. George W. Bush was clearly the hands-down favorite among Republican voters in 1999, but public opinion polls regularly showed Dole in second place. Until she dropped out of the race in October of 1999, Dole was running ahead of all of the other Republican candidates, including Senator John McCain, businessman Steve Forbes, and former Vice President Dan Quayle, her closest competitors. Similarly, Dole did well in presidential trial heats. When likely voters were asked for whom they would vote if the presidential election pitted Elizabeth Dole against Vice President Al Gore, Dole routinely received more support than did Gore (Moore 1999; Newport 1999; Polling Report 2000).

Soon after announcing her presidential candidacy, Hillary Clinton connects with support-ers at a campaign rally in Des Moines, Iowa.

Dole withdrew from the race in October of 1999, citing her difficulties in raising money. While she raised more money than had any other female presidential candidate at that time ($4.7 million) she noted that frontrunner George W. Bush had raised over $60 million and that Steve Forbes had unlimited personal resources to spend in the race (Seelye 1999). Eight years later, Hillary Clinton shattered Dole's record by raising a staggering $221 million for her campaign. In comparison, Barack Obama raised over $366 million through the primary campaign and an additional $379 million for the general election campaign, becoming the first presidential candidate to refuse public campaign finance in the general election (Open Secrets 2008).

Senator Clinton's fund-raising prowess enabled her to compete in all 50 states' primaries and caucuses, amassing more votes and national convention delegates than had any of her female predecessors. When she won the New Hampshire primary in January 2008, edging out Barack Obama by two points (39 percent to 37 percent), she became the first woman to win a major party's presidential primary for the purpose of delegate selection (CAWP 2008). Hillary Clinton also secured far more presidential primary election votes than did any other female presidential candidate in U.S. history. Approximately 18 million voters cast ballots for Clinton during the first six months of 2008, propelling her to victory in 20 different states (Real Clear Politics 2008). Prior to Clinton, Republican Senator Margaret Chase Smith held the record for most presidential primary election votes. Competing in five state primaries in 1964, Smith received over 200,000 votes before eventually dropping out of the race

(CAWP 2003; Kaptur 1996). And if Michigan voters are included in the popular vote count,[3] Clinton also received more popular votes in the nominating process than any of her competitors, including Barack Obama, who also received close to 18 million votes. When Clinton gave her concession speech in June 2008, she made reference to her historic support, saying "Although we weren't able to shatter that highest, hardest glass ceiling this time, thanks to you, it's got about 18 million cracks in it" (Milbank 2008).

When the Democratic National Convention got underway in Denver in August of 2008, Clinton had amassed a total of 1,896 delegates, more than had any other female presidential candidate in U.S. history. But with 2,118 delegates necessary to win the Democratic nomination, Clinton fell short. In the end, the nomination was decided by superdelegates, members of the Democratic Party who are automatically included as delegates to the national convention by virtue of their standing in the party. Neither Clinton nor Obama had enough regular delegates to win the nomination, but Obama had more support among the superdelegates and they ultimately delivered the nomination to him. As many explained, their vote was influenced by a number of considerations: Senator Obama had won the majority of primary votes in their home state, he had won more primary contests nationwide than did Clinton, or that they thought he would be a stronger candidate to take on Republican nominee John McCain in the fall (Welna 2008).

In contrast with Clinton, the vast majority of women who have run for the U.S. presidency dropped out long before their party's nominating conventions and very few of them earned any delegates along the way. Shirley Chisholm, a sitting congresswoman from New York, became the first Democratic and African-American woman to run for the office when she competed for the 1972 Democratic presidential nomination. She ran in state primaries in 12 states, and secured 151 delegates at the Democratic National Convention before dropping out of the race (Cannon 1999; Clift and Brazaitis 2000). Some sources report that Chisholm was the first woman to win a major party presidential primary election, noting that she defeated North Carolina Governor Terry Sanford with 67 percent of the vote in New Jersey's Democratic primary. While she did win the popular vote in the state, it was in a non-binding presidential preference contest and so Chisholm was not awarded any delegates in the contest. Rather, Senator George McGovern beat former Vice President Hubert Humphrey in the delegate selection primary, and so most recognize him as the rightful winner of the New Jersey primary (CAWP 2008). On the Republican side, Senator Margaret Chase Smith ran in 1964 and made history as the first woman to have her name appear on a major party ballot at

---

[3]Some counts do not include Michigan. Senator Barack Obama took his name off the ballot after the Democratic National Committee stripped the state of its delegates for violating party rules by scheduling its primary too early in the campaign schedule. Hillary Clinton kept her name on the ballot and received over 300,000 votes in Michigan. In May of 2008, the DNC reinstated all of Michigan's delegates, but gave each of them only half of a vote.

a nominating convention. She dropped out after the first round of ballots (Cannon 1999; Watson 2003).

Clinton's campaign for the U.S. presidency is significant for a number of additional reasons. First, her candidacy marked the first time that a former First Lady ran for the presidency in the United States. While spousal succession is not unheard of in many other countries, it usually occurs immediately following the removal or death of a sitting president or prime minister. In the United States, the sitting vice president assumes the office if the president is removed or becomes unable to carry out his or her duties and responsibilities. Thus, first ladies have no line of succession to the office of the presidency in the United States but must campaign for the office like all other candidates. Hillary Clinton was the first do so. She had already made history seven years earlier when she campaigned for a U.S. Senate seat in the state of New York while simultaneously serving as the nation's first lady. Never before had a first lady done such a thing. She ended up winning the Senate seat in 2000 and was re-elected to her seat in 2006.

Second, Clinton's candidacy called into question a great deal of scholarship that finds female candidates have a tough time convincing the public that they are tough enough for the job and they have what it takes to be the commander-in-chief for the United States (see also Chapter 5). According to Jennifer Lawless (2004), in a post 9/11 world, "[c]itizens prefer men's leadership traits and characteristics, deem men more competent at legislating around

John McCain surprised many when he introduced Alaska Governor Sarah Palin as his running mate, making her the first Republican woman to run for vice president.

issues of national security and military crises, and contend that men are superior to women at addressing the new obstacles generated by the events of September 11, 2001 (p. 480)." Accordingly, Lawless argues that it is difficult for any female presidential candidate to persevere in a political climate dominated by foreign policy concerns. But Clinton had no such problems in 2008. Democratic voters gave her higher marks than all of her male primary opponents for her ability to be commander-in-chief, for her toughness, and for her overall strength and leadership (*Washington Post*-ABC Poll 2008).

While Hillary Clinton was preceded by more than 20 other women in her quest for the presidency, she clearly achieved more than had all of her predecessors and demonstrated that women can be serious contenders for the presidency. Although Clinton's unique standing as a former first lady should caution us about generalizing too broadly from her experience, her historic candidacy challenged the conventional wisdom about women's foreign policy abilities and likely opened the door a little bit wider for future female presidential candidates. As of this writing, Sarah Palin has indicated that she might run for the presidency in 2012, and Condoleezza Rice is frequently mentioned as a presidential possibility. Time will tell whether or not Clinton's candidacy really did make 18 million cracks in the highest, hardest glass ceiling.

Vice Presidential Candidates

On August 29, 2008, Republican presidential candidate John McCain made history by announcing Alaska Governor Sarah Palin as his vice presidential pick, the first Republican woman to run for the position. Palin was following in the footsteps of Geraldine Ferraro, who some 24 years earlier became the first female vice presidential candidate on a major party ticket when Democratic presidential candidate Walter Mondale selected her as his running mate in 1984.

The announcement of Governor Palin came as a surprise to many, who were expecting McCain to pick either Minnesota Governor Tim Pawlenty, or Mitt Romney, one of McCain's rivals for the Republican nomination and a former Governor of Massachusetts. In fact, when McCain announced Palin as his running mate, 7 out of 10 Americans had never heard of her or did not know enough to have an opinion about her (Gallup Poll 2008a). Over the next 10 weeks of the campaign, the American public learned a great deal about Governor Palin.

Coming on the heels of Hillary Clinton's historic candidacy, the McCain campaign clearly hoped that the selection of Palin would energize and attract female voters to the ticket, especially those who were disappointed by Hillary's eventual loss to Obama. In this respect, the selection of Palin was quite similar to Walter Mondale's pick of Geraldine Ferraro in 1984. Ferraro was similarly expected to help Mondale capitalize on the newly discovered gender gap by appealing to women (see more in Chapter 3), something that proved elusive for the campaign. Reagan ended up capturing 56 percent of the women's vote, 10 percent more than he had in the 1980 elections (Baird 2008).

When Palin was announced at a campaign rally in Ohio, she made reference to both Ferraro and Clinton in her comments, essentially suggesting she would pick up where Clinton left off. As she said, "I can't begin this great effort without honoring the achievements of Geraldine Ferraro in 1984, and, of course, Senator Hillary Clinton, who showed such determination and grace in her presidential campaign. It was rightly noted . . . that Hillary left 18 million cracks in the highest, hardest glass ceiling in America. But it turns out the women of America aren't finished yet, and we can shatter that glass ceiling once and for all" (Barnes and Shear 2008).

As retold by *Newsweek*, one of McCain's senior advisers confirmed that part of the strategy in selecting Palin was "to attract female voters and exploit a 'great opportunity' to pull in Clinton supporters" (Baird 2008). In their calculations, presenting Palin as a working mom who understood the concerns and values of other women would likely resonate with undecided women. And did they ever. In story after story, many women explained that they liked Palin because they could relate to her, because she was an average mom who just happened to be the Governor of Alaska. One working mother said of Palin, "She justifies what we do every day . . . Sarah just energizes us and got us out here because she does what we do, she lives like we do" (Fisher 2008). A female college student echoed her comments, saying "I love that she is a mother, wife and a politician. That's very admirable. She's not a career politician who's been affected by the Washington games" (Merida 2008).

Beyond her potential appeal to female voters, Palin seemed to be a logical choice for vice president for additional reasons. First, McCain hoped to counter Senator Obama's message of hope and change by suggesting that McCain was the candidate more likely to bring change to Washington. As a maverick who often bucked his party, McCain stressed his own record as a reformer who did the right thing, even in the face of party opposition. Governor Palin, too, had a history of challenging her own party. Most famously, she mounted a primary challenge to sitting Republican Governor Frank Murkowski in 2006, campaigning on a message that she would root out corruption and bring much needed reform to politics in Alaska. She handily defeated Murkowski in the primary and then went on to defeat former Democratic Governor Tony Knowles in the general election (Barnes and Shear 2008).

Second, Palin could more effectively claim to be an agent of change than McCain. Because women are outsiders to politics, voters tend to believe that female candidates are better at bringing change to government than are men. And Palin highlighted her outsider status on the campaign trail, explaining "I don't have 30 years of political experience under my belt but that's a good thing. I've never been part of a good-ol'-boys club" (Grunwald and Newton-Small 2008). McCain had been a fixture in Washington for more than two decades, so Palin looked far more like the face of change than did he.

Third, the campaign also hoped that Palin would energize the Republican base of socially conservative voters, many of whom had serious misgivings about McCain's credentials as a social conservative. On this score, Palin proved enormously successful. Her appearances on the campaign trail resulted in McCain receiving far larger audiences than was usual. One campaign adviser estimated that audiences were about 12 times larger after Palin joined the ticket (Baird 2008). Palin clearly struck a chord with many conservative voters, who were ecstatic that she was selected to join McCain on the Republican ticket. Not surprisingly, Republican voters evinced much greater enthusiasm about voting for McCain after Palin joined the ticket (Gallup Poll 2008b).

Palin's addition to the campaign appeared to pay immediate dividends. In the few days following her announcement, the McCain campaign received a boost of $7 million in campaign contributions ("McCain Pick . . ." 2008). Similarly, Palin's addition to the ticket coincided with increased support among white women for McCain. Before Palin, some polls estimated that John McCain led Barack Obama among white women by 5 points (44 percent to 39 percent). After Palin, the majority of white women said they planned to vote for McCain, and the gap between McCain and Obama increased to 16 percent (53 percent for McCain, 37 percent for Obama) (Baird 2008). In the end, 53 percent of white women voted for the McCain-Palin ticket, but the overall women's vote went to Obama (CNN 2008). And while journalists ran many stories highlighting female Clinton supporters switching their allegiance to McCain after Palin was added polling data suggest that only about 15 percent did so (CNN 2008).

But while Palin clearly energized the base and appealed to many women, her star began to fade as the campaign wore on. After her rousing and well-received acceptance speech at the Republican convention, the McCain campaign cloistered her away and refused members of the media access to her for almost two weeks. The campaign publicly declared that they were doing so to protect Palin from the "cycle of piranhas called the news media" (Kornblut 2008), and would not begin to offer press avails until journalists showed proper respect and deference. Their stated reason for the outrage was the media coverage Palin's family received on the eve of the Republican convention. Hoping to quell rumors that Palin's four-month old infant was actually the biological child of her 17-year old unmarried daughter Bristol, the campaign put out a statement indicating that Bristol was pregnant, that she planned to keep the baby and wed the father. All of this happened the night before the Republican National Convention was supposed to get underway. But, in an unfortunate turn of events for the Republicans, Hurricane Gustav was bearing down on New Orleans, Louisiana, a city that had suffered devastating Hurricane Katrina almost exactly four years prior. In deference to the people of New Orleans, the Republicans essentially cancelled the first day of the convention. When Gustav turned out to be less dangerous than weather forecasters had originally predicted, and with no proceedings to report from the convention floor, the media seized upon the story of Bristol's pregnancy.

Palin eventually made herself available to the press through a series of lengthy and high profile interviews with Charles Gibson of ABC News, Sean Hannity of FOX News, and Katie Couric of CBS. Her performance in these interviews, especially those with Gibson and Couric, clearly did not live up to the hype created by her convention speech. To many, she seemed unprepared and rehearsed and polling data began to show declining voter confidence in her ability to handle the job. For example, between late September and early November, a CNN poll of likely voters recorded a 10-point drop in the percentage of people who thought Palin had the personality and leadership qualities a president should have (47 percent to 37 percent). For McCain, Obama, and Biden, these numbers all increased or remained the same over the same period of time. Similarly, the percentage of likely voters who said Palin's addition to the Republican ticket made them more likely to vote for McCain declined over time (Polling Report 2008a).

After McCain was defeated in November, some of his campaign aides began divulging dirt about Governor Palin, not so subtly suggesting that she was a disastrous pick who doomed his candidacy (Kurtz 2008). Yet political scientists agree that vice presidential candidates rarely influence the outcome of presidential elections. And considering how effective Palin was in energizing socially conservative voters, and recognizing that a larger share of white women probably voted for McCain because of Palin, it's possible that McCain would have lost by even a larger margin without her on the ballot. Palin's ultimate impact on McCain's electoral fortunes has not been studied in detail, but scholars will examine this question in the future, giving us a clearer sense of her contributions to the campaign.

In July of 2009, in a controversial move, Palin resigned her position as Alaska's Governor, surprising and puzzling many. In her farewell speech, Palin told the audience that she did not need the title of Governor to work for them, and that she could spare them a lame-duck legislative session by leaving office in the midst of her term (Daly 2009). She also complained about the continued media scrutiny surrounding her family. Others noted that Palin faced mounting legal bills to fight 20 ethics charges brought against her in her role as Governor of Alaska, and noted that her favorability numbers were slipping. Some speculate that she resigned to begin planning a presidential campaign for 2012, but she has not yet divulged her plans.

GOVERNORS AND LIEUTENANT GOVERNORS

A total of 31 women have served as their states' governors (see Appendix D for a full listing of all women governors).[4] In 2009, seven women governors held office at the same time. Although this may seem a small number, the United

---

[4]All but five of these women were elected in their own right. These five women became governor by virtue of their position in the state hierarchy coupled with the death or resignation of the sitting governor. These women include Vesta Roy (R-NH), state Senate president in New Hampshire, who served for seven days after incumbent Hugh Gallen died in office; Secretary of State Rose Mofford (D-AZ) took over after Evan Mecham was impeached and convicted while in office; Lieutenant Governor Nancy Hollister (R-OH) served for an 11-day interim after sitting Governor George Voinovich won a U.S. Senate seat and before Ohio's next governor, Bob Taft, had been sworn into office; Lieutenant Governor Jane Swift assumed the governorship of Massachusetts when sitting Governor Argeo Paul Cellucci resigned to become ambassador to Canada, and Secretary of State Jan Brewer (R-AZ) assumed the governorship when Governor Janet Napolitano resigned to serve as President Obama's Secretary of Homeland Security.

States did not witness more than two female governors holding office at the same time until the late 1980s. Female candidates for governor have become more common recently, and women constituted nearly a third of all general election gubernatorial candidates for all of the midterm and presidential election years throughout the years of 2000–2008.[5]

The state of Arizona leads the nation, having selected three different women to serve as governor over the last twelve years. In fact, the voters of Arizona have not elected a male governor since 1991. Even so, Arizona has never witnessed a gubernatorial race in which two women squared off against one another. Democrat Janet Napolitano became the first woman in the United States to succeed another female governor when she was elected to replace Republican Jane Dee Hull in 2002. Napolitano and Hull did not compete against one another, though, as Arizona state law prohibits governors from serving more than two consecutive terms. When Napolitano resigned to become President Obama's Secretary of Homeland Security in 2009, she was succeeded by another woman, Jan Brewer. As Secretary of State, Brewer received the appointment through constitutional succession. Four additional states share the distinction of having elected or appointed at least two different women to serve as governors: Texas, Kansas, Connecticut, and Washington.

While Arizona has not yet witnessed a gubernatorial contest pitting two female candidates against one another, there have been two such races in the United States (see *Paths to Power* for details). The first one occurred in 1986 when Republican Kay Orr faced Democrat Helen Boosalis in the State of Nebraska. Orr won the race, becoming the first Republican woman elected as a U. S. governor (Weir 1999). Sixteen years later, Republican Linda Lingle defeated Democrat Mazie Hirono in Hawaii's gubernatorial race and became the first woman elected governor for the state ("In the 50th State" 2002).

The first three female governors in the United States achieved their positions by way of their connections with their husbands, who had previously served as governors. The very first woman to hold this position was Nellie Tayloe Ross, a Democrat from Wyoming. After her husband fell ill and died while serving as governor, the Democratic Party in Wyoming approached Ross and asked her to run in his stead. She was their unanimous choice and agreed to run to continue the work her husband had started. She went on to win a special election to fill his seat and ended up winning by more than 8,000 votes, no small feat for a state that was then and continues to be strongly Republican (Scharff 1995). Two years later, she lost her reelection bid to serve a second term. In retrospect, she lamented that she should have done more to court the women's vote. Wyoming became the first territory in the country to grant full female suffrage (in 1869),[6] but Ross explained that she was wary of making her gender a focus of the campaign and did little to reach out to women's organizations (Scharff 1995).

---

[5]Data compiled by authors using CAWP's "Past Candidate and Election Information." Available online at www.cawp.rutgers.edu/fast_facts/elections/past_election_info.php

[6]Wyoming did not become a state until 1890.

PATHS TO POWER

History in the Making: Female versus Female Governor's Races

Only twice in the history of the United States have two major party female candidates squared off against one another in a governor's race: once in Nebraska in 1986 and 16 years later in the state of Hawaii. In both instances, the races were highly competitive, featured two well-qualified and politically experienced women, and ended with the Republican candidate winning.

Nebraska 1986. The first female Republican governor ever elected, former State Treasurer Kay Orr beat Democrat Helen Boosalis, a former mayor and head of the Nebraska Department on Aging in the nation's very first female versus female governor's race. Both candidates were seasoned political veterans with years of political experience and polls indicated a very tight race up until the end. Orr ended up winning with 53 percent of the vote (Robbins 1986a, 1986b; CAWP 2004a).

Hawaii 2002. With the retirement of Governor Benjamin Cayetano, the fourth consecutive Democratic governor elected in the state of Hawaii, two experienced and well-positioned women set their sights on the governor's job. Republican Linda Lingle began her political career on the island of Maui, starting on the county council and eventually serving two terms as mayor. She mounted a very competitive challenge to Governor Cayetano in 1998, losing by less than 5,000 votes. Democrat Mazie Hirono, lieutenant governor under Cayetano, also served seven terms in Hawaii's House of Representatives before running. The race drew national attention, with former President Clinton stumping for Hirono and Environmental Protection Agency Administrator Christine Todd Whitman doing the same for Lingle. Lingle outspent Hirono by a 3:1 ratio and squeaked out a victory with 51 percent of the vote. In doing so, she became Hawaii's first female governor and the state's first Republican governor since 1962 ("In the 50th state" 2002). ∎

In the very same electoral cycle, Texas elected Miriam "Ma" Ferguson as its first female governor. Nellie Ross enjoys the distinction of being the very first female governor in the United States only because she was inaugurated some 15 days before Mrs. Ferguson. Ferguson succeeded her husband Governor Jim Ferguson into office, who was prohibited from running for his old seat because he had been impeached, convicted, and removed from office for corruption (Sallee 1996). "Ma" Ferguson and her political allies emphasized her virtues as a traditional, wholesome woman and many photos showed her "peeling peaches, feeding chickens, or standing by a mule on the family farm wearing long traditional skirts, often in calico or gingham" (Sallee 1996, x). The Fergusons had opposed female suffrage on the grounds that women's greatest contributions to society were in the home. Accordingly, the candidacy of "Ma" Ferguson emphasized her virtues as a feminine, traditional woman, as someone who would largely serve as a stand-in while Jim Ferguson ran the show behind the scenes.

The third woman elected governor was Lurleen Burns Wallace. Again, her husband preceded her in office and she ran to take his place since Alabama state law prohibited him from serving two consecutive terms as governor. In a strange twist of fate, Lurleen Wallace was hospitalized with a cancerous tumor while in office and her husband effectively took over all her official responsibilities during and after the hospitalization. When she died, sitting Lieutenant Governor Albert Brewer succeeded her (Stineman 1980).

For both women and men, the office of lieutenant governor is the most common stepping-stone to the office of the governor. Usually elected on the same ticket as the governor,[7] the position of lieutenant governor provides its occupant with statewide visibility and responsibility for succeeding the governor if he or she dies, resigns, or otherwise vacates the position. Approximately one out of every three women governors ever elected in the United States has served previously as a lieutenant governor.

WOMEN AS PRESIDENTIAL AND GUBERNATORIAL APPOINTEES

Although elected office provides one route to executive positions in the federal and state governments, far more women receive executive positions through either presidential or gubernatorial appointment. Who are these women? How do they receive their appointments? Where do they serve?

Upon assuming office, incoming presidents are charged with appointing thousands of individuals to work throughout the executive branch of government and assist them in fulfilling the constitutional responsibility to "faithfully execute the laws of the Nation" (Pfiffner 1996). According to the latest version of the *Plum Book*, the federal government's listing of the top policymaking positions in the federal government, President Barack Obama was responsible for making approximately 7,000 appointments to federal positions when he took office in January 2009. Many of these positions are fairly routine, however, and only about 1,000 of them actually require Senate confirmation (Garcia 1997).

The most high-profile federal executive branch appointments go to the members of the president's cabinet, at minimum composed of the vice president and the heads of the 15 executive departments. Most presidents also bestow additional positions with cabinet rank. For example, President Obama's cabinet includes the White House chief of staff, the administrator of

---

[7]Whereas 24 states elect the governor and lieutenant governor on the same ticket, 19 states elect these positions separately, and 7 states do not have a lieutenant governor (Council of State Governments 2002, Table 4.1,145–146).

the Environmental Protection Agency, the director of the Office of Management and Budget, the chair of the Council of Economic Advisers, the U.S. trade representative, and the U.S. Ambassador to the United Nations (www. whitehouse.gov/administration/cabinet/). Soon after taking office, one-third of Obama's cabinet was composed of women, the highest percentage for any president in history.

In the history of the United States, a total of 40 women have served in federal cabinet-level positions (see Appendix E for full listing) (CAWP 2009c). On the whole, Democratic presidents have a slightly better record of appointing women to their cabinets than do Republicans. Among the 40 women who have held cabinet positions, 58 percent were appointed by Democratic presidents and 42 percent were appointed by Republican presidents. President Clinton leads the pack by having appointed 13 women to cabinet-level positions during his eight-year tenure. President George W. Bush comes in second, having appointed eight women to cabinet-level positions during his two terms in office. As of this writing, President Obama has appointed seven women to his cabinet. Besides these three presidents, no other president has appointed more than four women to such high-ranking executive positions (CAWP 2009c).

At the state level, women constitute about 32 percent of all executive department heads (CWG 2008). On the whole, there is evidence that Democratic governors appoint greater numbers of women to top positions than do Republicans (Riccucci and Saidel 2001), but the differences are small.

In presidential cabinets, the most frequently held position for female appointees is Secretary of Labor. Seven different women have served in this position, including the first woman appointed to a presidential cabinet, Frances Perkins, and the first Asian-American woman to serve as a cabinet secretary, Elaine Chao. Frances Perkins was appointed by Franklin Delano Roosevelt in 1933 and holds the record among female appointees for longest tenure in office, serving over 12 years under Roosevelt. Elaine Chao was tapped by President George W. Bush to head the Labor Department and came to the position with experience in both Reagan and George Bush Sr.'s administrations. In addition to appointing Chao, George W. Bush also appointed the first female Secretaries of Agriculture and Interior (Ann Veneman and Gail Norton). William Jefferson Clinton made history when he selected Janet Reno as the nation's first female Attorney General and Madeleine Albright as the first female Secretary of State. Until then, no women had ever served in the president's inner cabinet, which is composed of the heads of the Treasury, State, Defense, and Justice Departments (Borrelli 2002). President Obama appointed Janet Napolitano as the first woman to head the Department of Homeland Security in 2009 and also appointed Hillary Clinton, his chief rival for the Democratic nomination, as the third female Secretary of State in the United States. At the time of this writing, not a single woman has ever served or been nominated to the other two inner cabinet positions or to head the Department of Veterans' Affairs (CAWP 2009c).

In addition to the top cabinet positions, presidents and governors appoint many more individuals to work closely with them, such as a press secretary, communications director, and a variety of policy advisers. At the state level, more women have found access to executive staff positions through this route than through appointment as a department head. In 2007, nearly half (42 percent) of all top advisers on gubernatorial staffs were women (CWG 2008).

President Obama has appointed women to nearly a third of the top White House staff positions.[8] In addition, he has appointed more African-American women to positions of power than have any of his predecessors. At the top of the list of powerful black women in the White House is senior adviser Valerie Jarret. By most accounts, Jarrett is the most powerful woman in the Obama White House. As a long-time friend and mentor to both the president and Michele Obama, Jarrett has access to both, a common gauge of influence in Washington, D.C. Her official title is assistant to the president for intergovernmental affairs and public liaison, but colleagues inside the White House suggest that her close relationship to the president gives her greater influence than this title suggests (Fletcher 2009). Other prominent African-American women include Melody Barnes, the Director of the Domestic Policy Council and Susan Rice, Ambassador to the United Nations.

Obama also appointed Elena Kagan as his Solicitor General, the first woman to hold the position on a permanent basis. Before Kagan was confirmed for the position, she had most recently served as the first female Dean of Harvard Law School (Schworm 2009). As of this writing, it is too early to tell if any of these women are particularly influential. In May 2010, Obama nominated Kagan to the Supreme Court to fill the vacancy of retiring Justice John Paul Stevens. When this book went to press, her confirmation hearings were getting underway.

During his eight years in office, George W. Bush also drew heavily on the expertise of women, appointing "more women to positions of power and influence than any president in history" (Brant 2001). At the beginning of his first term, nearly half of Bush's top presidential advisers were women (Brant 2001; Walsh 2001). These were not low-ranking women but women who had a seat at the table and enjoyed tremendous access to the president. A few examples illustrate the point.

Karen Hughes served as counselor to the president for the first year and a half of George W. Bush's first term. After working as the executive director of the Texas Republican Party for a few years, she began working for Bush in 1994 when he ran for governor of Texas. After he won, she served for the next six years as his press secretary, both on the presidential campaign trail and while governor of Texas. She was named counselor to the president when Bush took over the presidency (Cottle 1999; Walsh 2001), and clearly exercised a great deal of influence in the White House. During her tenure, Hughes was described as the "most powerful female staffer in West Wing history" (Walsh 2001). Hughes is credited with coming up with the phrase "compassionate conservative" to sell the Bush candidacy, and Bush reportedly sought her advice on just about everything (Burka 1999; Cottle 1999). As a testament to Bush's confidence and trust in her, the day before he was inaugurated he reportedly told a number of his senior staff

---

[8]We thank James King and James Riddlesperger for sharing these data with us.

President Barack Obama with senior adviser Valerie Jarrett, one of the president's closest and reportedly most influential advisors

members that he did not want any important decisions made without Hughes in the room (Suskind 2002). After about 15 months on the job, Hughes announced her resignation in April 2002 in order to spend more time with her family (Borger 2002). But she returned to Washington about three years later for a post in the State Department where she led the Bush administration's public diplomacy efforts. From this post, she was charged with shoring up the U.S. image and promoting American democratic values worldwide (Baker 2005).

Also appointed by George W. Bush, Condoleezza Rice is the second woman and first African-American woman to hold the position of Secretary of State. She came to this position with notable federal government experience under her belt, most recently serving as the first female National Security Adviser under George W. Bush from 2001 to 2005.[9] She also served in

---

[9]Colin Powell was the first African American to hold the position. He was appointed national security adviser in 1988 under Ronald Reagan.

George H. W. Bush's administration as an expert on Soviet affairs under Bush's national security adviser Brent Scowcroft (Dowd 2000). She joined the George W. Bush campaign in 1999 as his chief foreign policy adviser (Felix 2002) and was soon thereafter described as "the most-influential black woman in the history of U.S. government" (Ray 2001). She was the first person to get a hold of President Bush when the first airplane hit the World Trade Center on September 11, 2001, and thereafter took on a more visible role for the administration, behaving as White House spokesperson by conducting press briefings and continually updating the public about the war on terrorism (Felix 2002).

An extraordinarily accomplished woman, Rice grew up in segregated Birmingham, Alabama, and lost a schoolmate in the high-profile Sixth Avenue Baptist Church bombing of 1963 (Dowd 2000). Her family moved to Denver, Colorado, when she was 14 years old and she spent most of the next 12 years living there, receiving her bachelor's degree in political science and a Ph.D. in international studies from the University of Denver by 1981. While at the University of Denver, she studied under former Secretary of State Madeleine Albright's father, Joseph Korbel, a mentor whom Rice refers to as one of the most important people in her life (Felix 2002). After graduating, she began teaching political science at Stanford University and eventually was appointed provost of Stanford, becoming the youngest person ever to hold the job (38 years old) as well as the first woman and African American to do so (Felix 2002).

Below cabinet secretaries and close staff members, presidents and governors make additional appointments to lower-level positions, often referred to as subcabinet positions. Since President Nixon, each presidential administration typically has improved upon the record of its predecessor when it comes to the percentage of women appointed to these positions. The exceptions to the pattern are both Republican presidents—Ronald Reagan and George W. Bush. That is, Reagan appointed fewer women than did Jimmy Carter, and George W. Bush appointed fewer women in his first term than did Bill Clinton (Martin 1991; Tessier 2002). The number of women appointed to governors' administrations has similarly increased over time (CWG 2008).

Regardless of party, presidents tend to appoint proportionally more women to independent agencies, regulatory commissions, and government boards than to cabinet departments (Garcia 1989, 1993, 1997). However, these positions are typically considered more distant from the president's agenda and provide fewer opportunities for influencing policy (Borrelli 2002). Further, female appointees typically find themselves in more subordinate positions within the federal executive hierarchy than do their male counterparts. Rather than being cabinet secretaries or assistant secretaries, women are likely to be found in much lower-level executive positions, such as undersecretaries or agency heads for midlevel agencies (Garcia 1993, 1997). Finally, presidents typically appoint proportionally more women at the beginning of their administrations, when the public and press are focused on these appointees and the likelihood of receiving positive press coverage increases (Borrelli 2002; Martin 1989). After demonstrating their commitment to diversity while the public is watching, midterm and replacement appointees tend to be more heavily skewed toward men. George W. Bush is a perfect example of this trend. After winning initial acclaim for being the first president to make white men a minority in his cabinet ("Are Women Better Leaders?" 2001), Bush ultimately selected women for just 26 percent of his appointees in his first term (WAP 2005). While Obama has received positive press coverage for selecting so many women to serve in his Cabinet and White House, time will tell whether or not he continues to appoint women in similar numbers throughout his tenure.

STATEWIDE ELECTED EXECUTIVES

The offices of president and vice president are the only elected positions in the federal government. But in state governments, a number of executives attain positions through popular election. Most states elect an average of six statewide executive branch officials (Fox and Oxley 2003; Beyle and Dalton 1981). In addition to the positions of governor and lieutenant governor,[10] the most common statewide executive positions are attorney general, secretary of state, and treasurer (Council of State Governments 2002).

Women have been steadily increasing their share of statewide elective executive positions over the past decade. As Figure 8.1 shows, women held fewer than 15 percent of all statewide executive positions until the early 1990s, and then their numbers began increasing more dramatically (see Figure 8.2 for breakdown by type of office). After reaching a peak of nearly 28 percent of all of these positions in 2001, slightly fewer women have been elected in recent years. The overall increase in the numbers of women serving corresponds with the increase in numbers of women seeking out and running for executive statewide positions. According to Fox and Oxley (2003), women candidates contested only about 20 percent of statewide executive offices before the 1990s but increased their share to almost 40 percent of those races during the 1990s. With more women running for these offices, it is not particularly surprising that more of them are winning their races and stepping into these positions.

How do women reach these positions? What do they have in common? Although there is currently very little research on this matter, we do know a few things about them. First, women are far more likely to run for statewide positions that are considered "feminine" rather than "masculine" (Fox and Oxley 2003). That is, women candidates are far less common in races for

---

[10]The position of lieutenant governor varies slightly from state to state but is generally the office second in command to the governor. Seven states do not have lieutenant governors: Arizona, Maine, New Hampshire, New Jersey, Oregon, West Virginia, and Wyoming (Council of State Governments 2002). Governors and lieutenant governors run on the same ticket (and so hail from the same party) in 24 states, whereas 19 states use separate elections for the two positions. This means that sometimes the governor and lieutenant governor are from different parties. One such example is the state of California. After sitting Democratic governor Gray Davis was recalled by the voters in 2003, Republican Arnold Schwarzenegger won a special election to replace Davis. Also running to replace Davis was sitting Democratic Lieutenant Governor Cruz Bustamante. After losing to Schwarzenegger, Bustamante retained his position as the state's lieutenant governor.

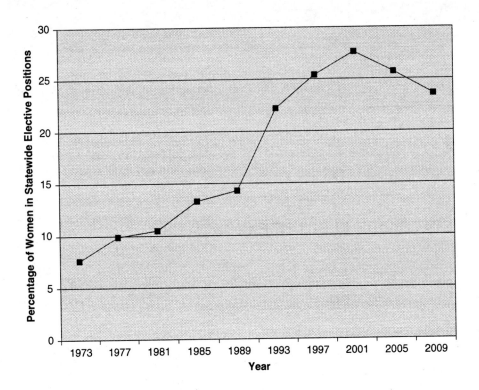

FIGURE 8.1
Women in Statewide Elective Executive Positions, 1970–2009

Source: Center for American Women and Politics, Eagleton Institute of Politics at Rutgers, The State University of New Jersey.

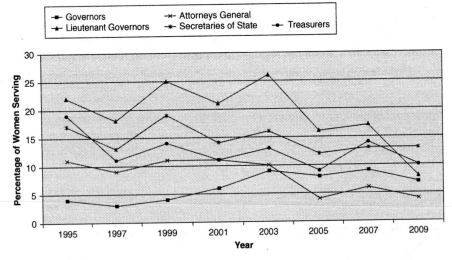

FIGURE 8.2
Women in Statewide Elected Positions, 1995–2009

Source: Data collected by authors from the Center for American Women and Politics, *State by State Facts*, 2009; *Women in Statewide Elective Executive Office*, 2009.

masculine offices such as attorney general, treasurer, auditor, tax commissioner, or agriculture commissioner than they are in races for feminine or neutral offices such as superintendent of public education, secretary of state, or labor commissioner. As such, we should not expect to see a large increase in the share of women serving in these types of offices until more women run. Second, women are more likely to run for statewide office outside of the South, in states where the Republican Party is dominant and where other women have previously won elective office (Fox and Oxley 2003).

While statewide executive women's gains have been fairly recent, women have been getting themselves elected to these positions for over 100 years. In fact, many women in the western states won seats as statewide executives before national female suffrage became the law of the land in 1920. The very first woman to serve in statewide elective office was Laura J. Eisenuth, a Democrat elected in 1893 as the North Dakota superintendent of public instruction. North Dakota did not grant female suffrage until 1917, meaning that Eisenuth was elected more than two decades before she could vote for herself. She served two years before being replaced by Emma J. Bates, the second woman in the country to win elective statewide office (CAWP 2009a). The states of Wyoming, Idaho, Colorado, and North Dakota all elected three or more women to the position of superintendent of public instruction before 1920, and every one of these states except North Dakota passed full female suffrage before the turn of the century (Wyoming in 1890, Idaho in 1896, and Colorado in 1893). Twenty-one women were elected female superintendents of public education before the U.S. Constitution was amended to enfranchise women, and this was the only position women held until New Mexican Soledad Chacon was elected as the first female secretary of state in 1923. Most of these pioneering women served as the only female statewide officials for their states. Today, more than three-quarters of the states have witnessed multiple women serving in statewide positions at the same time.[11]

More women have served as secretary of state than in any other statewide executive position. Since Chacon was first elected in 1923, an additional 111 women have served as secretary of state in 29 different states (see *Profiles of Political Influence*). New Mexico leads all states, having elected 18 different women to the position, South Dakota comes in second with 15 different women, and Connecticut has elected 13 different women to the post. As of 2010, women are better represented in the Secretary of State's office than in any other statewide executive position, and twelve women currently serve in this position.

---

[11]States that have never seen more than one executive woman in elected office at any given time include Alaska, Florida, Maryland, Mississippi, New Hampshire, New Jersey, New York, South Carolina, Tennessee, Virginia, and West Virginia. For a number of these states, women's failure to capture more than one statewide elective position simply reflects that very few such positions are available. For example, New Jersey, New Hampshire, and Tennessee elect only one executive official, the governor; Alaska selects only a governor and lieutenant governor, and Virginia elects a governor, lieutenant governor and attorney general. This explanation does not hold for the remainder of the states (Florida, Maryland, Mississippi, South Carolina, and West Virginia), as they hold an average of eight statewide positions, two more than the national average.

PROFILES OF POLITICAL INFLUENCE

Political Pioneer: Vikki Buckley

Elected Colorado's secretary of state in 1994, Victoria "Vikki" Buckley does not fit the profile of a traditional female politician. Lacking a college degree or previous political campaign experience, Buckley became the first black woman elected to statewide office in Colorado history when she won her 1994 election bid with 57 percent of the state vote. She is the very first Republican African-American woman elected to statewide office throughout the entire country.

Buckley got her start in public service in 1974 as a clerk in the Colorado secretary of state's office and steadily rose through the ranks of the office for the next 21 years. She decided to run for the position of secretary of state when her boss, sitting Secretary of State Natalie Meyer, decided not to seek reelection to the post. Having spent the past 21 years working in the secretary of state's office, Buckley emphasized her knowledge and experience on the campaign trail. She told her campaign manager, "I don't know politics, but I know that office inside and out." (Germer 1995). In the end, voters decided her knowledge of the office was sufficient and elected her to serve.

Republicans at the state and national levels embraced Buckley because of her minority status and the fact that when she talked about welfare reform she was speaking from experience. When most conservatives shied away, Buckley volunteered to give the opening address at the National Rifle Association's annual convention in Denver just two weeks after the Columbine High School tragedy, stressing that hatred, not the availability of guns, was the problem (Massaro 1999). Buckley was an important part of the Republican National Committee's (RNC) plan to diversify the image of the Republican Party by moving away from solely an "old" and "white" demographic. A mother of three grown children from different fathers, Buckley represented a new face of the Republican Party, although she did prohibit the RNC from using her picture in a brochure targeting other minorities (Buckley 1999). She did not want to be perceived as a token black female Republican.

Tragically, not long after being reelected secretary of state for a second term in 1998, Buckley died of congestive heart failure at age 51. ■

CAREER EXECUTIVE POSITIONS IN THE FEDERAL AND STATE GOVERNMENTS

Finally, the federal government and all state governments employ thousands more individuals throughout their civil service systems. Rather than being popularly elected or appointed by the president or governor, these positions are typically apportioned through competitive examination or other merit-based systems. At the very top of the federal career system is the Senior Executive Service (SES), an elite cadre of approximately 7,000 top-ranking

◤ PROFILES OF POLITICAL INFLUENCE

Political Pioneer: March Fong Eu

Born in the backroom of a hand wash laundry business in Oakland, California, March Fong Eu consistently overcame adversity to become California's first female secretary of state and the state's first Asian-American constitutional officer. Eu left her post as secretary of state after 20 years of service when the Clinton administration tapped her to serve as ambassador to Micronesia in 1994. After serving for eight years as ambassador, she decided to run again for her former job (Rodriguez 2001). Among a crowded Democratic primary field, Ambassador Eu finished second to Kevin Shelley, who went on to win the seat in the general election. Although she was 79 years old when she announced her candidacy, 633,369 California voters cast their ballots for her in the Democratic primary (California Secretary of State 2002).

As the only Asian American in her high school in Richmond, California, she became a cheerleader, editor of the paper, and president of the honor society. Overcoming poverty, Eu received her B.A. from U.C. Berkeley and a master's degree from Mills College. While raising two young children and working full time as a dental hygienist, she received her Ph.D. in education from Stanford. Her first elected office was a seat on the Alameda Board of Education. In 1966, she successfully ran for the California State Assembly. She is known for her sometimes zany tactics as a politician and candidate on the campaign trail. In 1969, from her position as an assemblywoman, she smashed a porcelain toilet with a sledgehammer on the steps of the state capitol to protest pay toilets in public buildings. It became an early women's issue, as urinals for men could not be locked. Governor Reagan signed her bill outlawing public pay toilets in 1974 (Rodriguez 2001).

After four terms in the state legislature, she was elected secretary of state in 1974. Re-elected by huge margins in 1978, 1982, 1986 and 1990, Eu earned support and respect from both sides of the aisle for maintaining California's tradition of fair elections (ibid.). ■

career executives. These individuals typically spend most of their careers working for the federal government, and by the time they reach the SES they have amassed an average of over 20 years of continuous working experience in the federal government (Brezina and Tanner 1991; Dolan 2000a). They sit at the very top of the career bureaucracy and work closely with presidential appointees to implement the president's program and policy decisions. At the time of this writing, women constitute 28 percent of federal SES members (U.S. OPM 2009).

The states likewise have their share of high-ranking career executives who work alongside gubernatorial appointees to carry out state programs as well as gubernatorial priorities. State-by-state variation makes it much more difficult to pinpoint the numbers of women serving in such positions.

Summary: Women in Executive Positions

As this section makes clear, women can be found in a variety of executive branch positions in the United States. Although no woman has ever been elected president or vice president, women are steadily increasing their numbers in many other executive positions, providing them with valuable experience to run for the highest office in the land. They serve as governors and lieutenant governors, as statewide elected executives, and in numerous statewide and federally appointed posts. As high-ranking executives, women are well poised to contribute to governance in the United States. The next section questions whether or not women's representation in executive positions matters.

DO WOMEN MAKE A DIFFERENCE? THEIR POLICY AND POLITICAL IMPACT

Does it matter whether or not women populate the uppermost echelons of government bureaucracies? Will policy decisions be made differently because of their presence? Will the government agenda be noticeably altered with greater numbers of women serving in executive branch positions? More specifically, will policy be more attuned to the needs and perspectives of women in the population as women increasingly occupy executive leadership positions in federal and state governments?

According to some scholars, the answer is yes. Representative bureaucracy theory stresses the importance of having a government that "looks like America" because it is assumed that such a government will more effectively represent the wishes and demands of an increasingly diverse American populace (Naff 2001; Selden 1997). The theory stresses that individuals' life experiences vary according to their sex, race, ethnic background, age, and other immutable personal characteristics. If women's experiences differ from men's, even in the slightest of ways, the theory posits that women will bring different talents to bear on public matters, and government outcomes will be noticeably different. Former Governor Madeleine Kunin expresses it well:

> More women in public life may not immediately turn swords into plowshares, but women do bring a different and diverse set of life experiences to the process—and for democracy to be truly representative, it is only just that we [women] be equally represented.   (Kunin 1987, 212)

And according to Kunin, women not only bring different issues to the table, but they also place these issues higher on their list of priorities. As Kunin again explains,

> My political priorities stemmed from various experiences and observations, and they expressed the totality of who I was and how I had lived my life. In that respect I was no different from any other politician. Each one of us extracts policies from the mosaic of our lives. The distinction was that I ended up with a somewhat altered list of priorities than my

male counterparts. I claimed no exclusive hold on any of the "women's issues" on my agenda, such as protecting the right to a legal abortion and advocating for children; a number of male governors espoused the same causes. What was distinct, however, was the intensity with which I pursued certain of them. (Kunin 1994, 363)

As a woman who had stayed home to raise a family for many years before getting her start in politics, Kunin explained that she simply brought a different set of skills to governing than did many of her male colleagues. The late Governor Ann Richards similarly stressed that women bring their own experiences to bear on their public roles and emphasized how women's perspectives change government decision-making:

I hope we all accepted long ago that women and men are different . . . The most sympathetic and sensitive of our men friends, no matter how hard he tries, cannot hear with a woman's ear or process information through a woman's experience . . . The experience is different. The perspective is different. The knowing is different. We see it many ways in our society now—and I see it often in policy deliberations . . . When I am part of a meeting . . . the nature of the discussion changes, because I am a woman. . . . (quoted in Dow and Tonn 1993, 294)

As these two examples suggest, women's presence in high-ranking executive positions affects the nature of public discourse and government decision making. If women and men have different attitudes, forged by different socialization experiences in their lifetimes, then we might expect their behavior to be informed by these attitudes and for policymaking to reflect their different perspectives. Does any evidence suggest as much? The next section examines executive women's contributions to governance, focusing particularly on the ways in which their attitudes shape decision making.

POLICY ATTITUDES AND POLITICAL IMPACT

Perhaps the most visible way in which female executives have left a unique impact on policy is through their commitment to making the workplace more accessible and friendly to other working women. There are numerous examples of executive women hiring record numbers of women to work in their administrations or staffs. When Elizabeth Dole became Secretary of Transportation under President Ronald Reagan, she set out to increase the numbers of women working in the department. As she explains,

Transportation of course is very much still a male-dominated area. . . . I asked when I got there, "How many women do we have in our work force?" and I was told 19 percent were female. (Quoted in Romney and Harrison 1988, 132–133)

She promptly set up a program to recruit more women and ended up increasing women's representation to 23 percent during her four-year tenure

(Romney and Harrison 1988). She was not the first female cabinet secretary to make recruiting women a priority: the very first female cabinet secretary, Frances Perkins, is credited with opening the doors of the Labor Department to greater numbers of women while Juanita Kreps (Commerce), Patricia Roberts Harris (HUD, HHS), and Shirley Hufstedler (Education) actively sought out female employees during their time in office under Jimmy Carter (Hartmann 1989; Martin 1997; Stanwick and Kleeman 1983; Stineman 1980).

Women governors have also used their appointment powers to bring more women into government positions (Riccucci and Saidel 2001). Nearly half of Ann Richards' appointments went to women, 40 percent of Governor Kunin's appointments in her second term were filled with women, Governor Granholm has been credited with appointing the most diverse cabinet in Michigan history, and Governors Barbara Roberts and Christine Todd Whitman similarly earned recognition for their records in appointing women (Cook 1991; Kunin 1994; Mayhead and Marshall 2000; State of Michigan 2003; Weir 1999). And studies suggest that appointed women, in turn, actively recruit women to fill positions in their own departments and agencies (Carroll and Geiger-Parker 1983a, 1983b; Carroll 1987; Stanwick and Kleeman 1983).

Additional evidence suggests that women executives are more sensitive to the needs of women in the workplace. While Elizabeth Dole was secretary of the Department of Transportation, senior officials got together and decided to create an on-site day care facility so that parents could bring their children to work and spend time with them at lunch (Romney and Harrison 1988). Other research indicates that female executives are more likely than men to support family friendly workplace reforms such as child care, pay equity, family leave, job sharing, and flexible working schedules (Carroll 1987; Carroll and Geiger-Parker 1983a, 1983b; Dolan 2000b; Dolan 2004; Hale and Branch 1992; Hale, Kelly, Burgess, and Shapiro 1987; Hale, Kelly, and Burgess 1989; Havens and Healy 1991; Kawar 1989; Stanley 1989). They are simply better positioned to understand the challenges working women face trying to balance work and family lives.

Female executives also use their positions to bring attention to the needs and concerns of women and to alter public policy to reflect a wider range of opinions and perspectives. While governor of Arizona, Jane Dee Hull issued an executive order mandating that state agencies formally solicit quotes from women-owned businesses when accepting bids for contracts over $25,000 with the state of Arizona (Executive Order 2000–4). Appointed as the first woman to head the National Institutes of Health (NIH), Director Bernadine Healy advocated women's health issues from the beginning of her tenure and proposed an NIH $625 million study that would include 150,000 women to study breast cancer, osteoporosis, and heart disease (Schroeder and Snowe 1994). Two months after taking office as the first female Secretary of State, Madeleine Albright instructed U.S. diplomats to make "the furtherance of women's rights a central priority of American foreign policy" (Lippman 1997). In her very first meeting with leaders from the Persian Gulf states, Albright led the charge herself, suggesting that women's rights be on the agenda for their next meeting (Gross 2003). While Bonnie Campbell was running for the position of attorney general of Iowa, she was stalked on the campaign trail. After she was elected attorney general, she parlayed her experience into legislative action by writing and supporting one of the nation's first antistalking laws ("*Time*'s 25 Most Influential Americans" 1997). In the neighboring state of Minnesota, former lieutenant governor Joanell Dyrstad also took the lead on antistalking legislation and similarly saw it passed into law during her tenure (Young and Ankeny 2000). Former Reagan appointee Amoretta Hoeber kept women's needs in mind while serving at the Department of Defense in the 1980s. At one point during her tenure, the army was planning to purchase new combat boots and put together a test group to try out the new boots before purchasing them for the entire army. As Hoeber pointed out, however, the test group contained only men. She argued for including women in the test group, emphasizing that women's feet are different than men's, and she believes that women's inclusion in the group made a difference in the boots that were ultimately chosen (McGlen and Sarkees 1993).

As these examples illustrate, executive women often bring new issues to the agenda, use their positions to advance and bring attention to women's issues, and contribute unique perspectives to American governance. But the fact that many executive women appear more sensitive to women's issues does not necessarily guarantee that these issues will take front and center during their tenures. The next section discusses some of the challenges and constraints often faced by executive women on the job.

CONSTRAINTS ON WOMEN'S POWER

The preceding stories attest to the ways in which executive women in government bring women's issues to the table. Yet various scholars argue that because women and men typically hold different types of executive positions, women's ability to exercise influence and power may be constrained. We examine some of these theories here.

First, women tend to work in different types of agencies and departments than do men. As two scholars explain it, "the more consistent an agency's function with feminine stereotypes, the more likely women are to advance in leadership positions. The more consistent an agency's function with masculine stereotypes, the greater the predominance of men in leadership posts" (Duerst-Lahti and Kelly 1995, 29). We find female executives most often in organizations dealing with stereotypically feminine issues, such as health, social services, and education, whereas men are more likely to be concentrated in agencies with masculine foci, such as budgeting, defense, foreign affairs, and law enforcement (Bullard and Wright 1993; Carroll and Geiger-Parker 1983a, Center for Women in Government 1999; Duerst-Lahti and Kelly 1995; Kleeman 1987; Martin 1989; Newman 1995; Riccucci and Saidel 1997; Saidel and Riccucci 1996; Wright, Cho, and Chai 2002).

We can see these patterns among the women who have served as U.S. cabinet secretaries. Many women have served as secretary of Health and Human Services whereas none has ever headed the Department of Defense. These placements may simply reflect the sexes' different occupational choices and areas of interest, may be a result of gender socialization and stereotyping, or may reflect subtle discrimination against women who try to establish themselves in traditionally masculine domains.

Second, Meredith Newman (1995) argues that not only do women find themselves more often in stereotypically feminine issue areas, but that these positions provide relatively less discretion and influence on the job. As she explains, some executive positions afford greater autonomy, flexibility, and power than do others. Although women are by no means always stuck at the low-influence end of the continuum, they are more likely than men to be found there (but see also Dolan 2004). This is apparent when we look at women elected to statewide executive positions. Although women have had the most historical success in winning elections as treasurers and secretaries of State, Beyle and Dalton (1981) argue that these two positions are the least powerful among the range of statewide positions.

Third, other scholars theorize that women's status as tokens or newcomers effectively constrains their power by placing unique performance pressures on them that make it more difficult to have an impact. Over 30 years ago, Rosabeth Moss Kanter (1977) highlighted the difficulties faced by token female in the workplace. She argues that when women are few and far between in an organization, or when they comprise 15 percent or less of the whole, they are regarded as "tokens" and face all sorts of performance pressures. These women are highly visible, their differences from men are exaggerated, and their behavior is often perceived as typical for all women.

For executive women, the pressures of being a token may be especially acute. For one, executive positions are often more highly visible than are legislative or judicial positions. Political executives usually sit at the apex of some hierarchy and are looked to as the top official in charge of their respective organizations: head of the state, head of a large government department or agency, and so on. Such positioning is likely to invite increased attention and publicity for both men and women. But being a woman in such a position further heightens this attention. Positions such as governor, attorney general, and cabinet secretary tend to conjure up images of male politicians. When women achieve these positions, the public often has difficulties in reconciling their images of power with a female face. As Madeleine Kunin explains it,

> In conversation, when I was introduced, I noticed that people didn't hear the word "Governor" before my name. They smiled and nodded, as they would to anyone who had just joined the circle, and promptly resumed their conversation. They had not heard the word "Governor" because their eyes had not prepared them for it. This woman, experience told them, is at best an adjunct to power, a wife, an aide, or a hanger-on. Their eyes did not allow the possibility that she might be the source. . . . The reactions weren't prompted by deliberate gender bias, but conditioned by years of accumulated information as deeply ingrained as the genetic code; men were governors and women were not. (1994, 349–350)

Other executive women have reported similar experiences, noting that the public often assumed that their husbands or male aides were in charge (Braden 1996; Kunin 1994; Young and Ankeny 2000).

In addition, the general public typically assumes that women's stereotypical strengths are better suited for legislative arenas than executive positions (Barbara Lee Family Foundation 2001; Rosenwasser and Seale 1988). When the public thinks of a successful executive, it typically lists qualities like strength, aggression, decisiveness, and ability to get things done. But the public typically gives women credit for being compassionate, sensitive, and cooperative (Kahn 1996). The end result is that women in executive positions often work against public stereotypes that give them less credit than they would a similarly situated male.

Getting noticed is rarely a problem. To the contrary, high-ranking executive women are so visible that everything they do is subjected to heightened scrutiny. Because women politicians are anomalies, they cannot simply blend into the woodwork and toil away anonymously. Others are constantly watching their behavior to see if they behave as expected or contrary to stereotypical presumptions. Many political women describe the increased attention their status as women in a man's world brings. When Carla Anderson was undergoing Senate confirmation hearings after being nominated by President Ford as only the third woman ever to serve as a U.S. cabinet secretary, Senator William Proxmire (D-WI) indirectly challenged her qualifications for the job, suggesting that her status as a woman rather than her qualifications got her the nomination (Stineman 1980). Her previous government experience was in the Justice Department, not in the Department of Housing and Urban Development that she was nominated to head. Nonetheless, it is doubtful that Senator Proxmire would have raised the same objection if a male candidate with similar experience had been nominated in her stead. This is par for the course, according to MaryAnne Borrelli (2002), who argues that women nominees are often presumed less competent during Senate confirmation hearings than are men.

In practice, heightened visibility often means that token women are presumed to speak for and reflect the strengths and weaknesses of all women. Many executive women have explained that they were cognizant of the fact that they would be held up as a standard by which all future executive women would be judged. The very first female governor, Nellie Tayloe Ross, remarked that if elected, she would conduct her administration so "that it might never be said that women were unfitted (sic) for executive office" (Scharff 1995, 93). Some 60 years later, Madeleine Kunin acknowledged the same pressures:

> I knew that as a political woman I was seen as being responsible for the actions of all women. . . . The performance of outsiders must demonstrate not only that we are just as good as those who have a historic territorial claim, but that we may well be better. For too long we have feared that if one woman, one black, one Jew, or one Hispanic makes a mistake, we will all be punished. (Kunin 1994, 185–186)

After losing her bid to be the first female vice president in the United States, Geraldine Ferraro voiced a similar frustration: "It is a sorry fact in this country that the defeat of one woman is often read as a judgment on all women" (quoted in Watson and Gordon 2003c).

Some women suggest that their status as tokens had positive ramifications, though. For example, former Governor Ann Richards likened her status as a female governor to that of a two-headed cow. Because female governors are still relatively uncommon, Richards claimed that her uniqueness got her noticed and even opened a few doors for her: "Some people are willing to let me into their office just because they want to see the genuine article" (quoted in Cook 1991). When Fran Ulmer, former lieutenant governor and gubernatorial candidate in Alaska in 2002, ran in her first mayoral election, she acknowledged that her status as the only woman in the race worked to her advantage. While all of the male candidates tried to differentiate themselves from the others, she stood out from the pack by virtue of her gender (Romney and Harrison 1988).

If women feel constrained in their actions when they are perceived as tokens, it stands to reason that their leadership styles may be a function of their unique status as outsiders (see Deutchman 1996; Kanter 1977). According to Kanter (1977), organizational structures and context, rather than gender, influence one's behavior on the job. If women appear to employ different leadership strategies or have different conceptions of power than their male colleagues, such may be interpreted as a consequence of their particular work environment, not their gender. If women are greatly outnumbered and perceive that their minority status has negative implications on their ability to get the job done, do they try to open up the process for other outsiders? Take special pains to include others who might have previously been excluded? Employ power-to rather than power-over leadership? The next section examines these questions in more detail.

POWER AND LEADERSHIP STYLE

Much scholarship suggests that women in powerful executive positions employ different leadership styles than do men. Time and again, women explain power as a tool for getting things done, rather than a goal in and of itself. According to Jeane Kirkpatrick, the first woman to serve as the U.S. Ambassador to the United Nations,

> [W]omen who get to high places in politics don't *need* power in the way that some of the men who hang in and compete do. I don't mean "fire in the belly.". . . I think needing power is something different. "Fire in the belly" is about anything that you care deeply about. It's not necessarily the drive to succeed and to reach the top—it may be any one of a hundred other things that one cares about. I don't know why . . . but I think, for whatever reasons, there are fewer women who seem to need power than there are men.   (quoted in Romney and Harrison 1988, 160)

Former U.S. Cabinet Secretary Patricia Roberts Harris explained her relationship to power in similar terms: "You might say I have always wanted to be Number One, but I wanted power solely to help the poor and disadvantaged" (quoted in Stineman 1980, 63). Elizabeth Dole suggests that "A lot of women think power is almost a dirty word. I'd like to get them to see it depends on what you use power for. You can use it to do good things. You can't get anything done if you don't have a place at the table" (quoted in Clift and Brazaitis 2000, 154).

Many scholars find additional evidence that women executives emphasize consensus, collaboration, and empowerment, a form of leadership that has been labeled "feminine leadership" instead of masculine or "power over" leadership that stresses competition, command and control, an emphasis on individual accomplishment, and hierarchy (Eagly and Johnson 1990; Edlund 1992; Helgesen 1990; Reingold 1996; Rosener 1990).

Do political executive women lean toward consensus and collaboration? Are they more likely to use their power to empower others, and bring outsiders into government decision-making? A recent study of male and female governors finds that women are more likely than men to express an empowerment motivation in their positions (Barth and Ferguson 2002). Similarly, various scholars studying the rhetoric of former Governor Ann Richards (D-TX) conclude that her speaking style and rhetoric were very much geared toward empowering others, especially women (Dow and Tonn 1993; Kaml 2000). According to these scholars, Richards used public speaking occasions to draw connections with her audience, to encourage them to connect their experiences as average citizens with hers, and to draw on their own instincts in judging politicians and the political process. They characterize her rhetoric as particularly feminine because she focuses on empowering others rather than boosting her own profile.

Former Secretary of State Madeleine Albright similarly suggests that consensus comes more easily for women and that women have a more difficult time with confrontation, but she acknowledges that the job sometimes necessitates as much.

Men are capable of having strong personal disagreements or arguments about a subject and then walk out of a room and go and play golf or have a drink or something. And I think women do take it more personally. And I don't think we like to have face-to-face confrontations, but I sure learned that it was essential to state my views very clearly and not care whether I was liked or not. And it took me a while to learn it. But I think others will testify to the fact that I did learn it. (Gross 2003)

Other evidence suggests that many female governors adopt a consensus style of leadership (Barbara Lee Family Foundation 2001; Current Biography 1987; Kunin 1994; Sheeler 2000). Former New Jersey Governor Christine Todd Whitman's speeches are peppered with references to government decision making being an open process, based on consensus (Sheeler 2000). She credits her style to growing up on a farm, where people need to work cooperatively to get things done, and points out that others criticize her for too much consensus building (Beard 1996). Former Governor Jane Dee Hull agrees that consensus is part of women's repertoire more often than it is for men: "Women tend to want to put people around the table and talk. Men order things, like ordering dinner" (Clift and Brazaitis 2000, 283).

But not all executive women lead by consensus. In fact, research on women and men in both state and federal executive positions finds that women do not necessarily have any special claims to using consensus-based leadership styles (Bayes 1991; Duerst-Lahti and Kelly 1995). And Condoleezza Rice, Secretary of State under George W. Bush, explains that her approach is more hierarchical than consensus based:

> [Nor do I] believe you can do everything by consensus. At the Pentagon, I learned that if you seek consensus you get a third of a tank, a third of a plane, and a third of an aircraft carrier. If you don't drive the process from the top, you get across-the-board cuts and everyone gets weaker. (quoted in Dowd 2000, 102)

CONCLUSION

Women have certainly come a long way since Victoria Woodhull made her historic bid for the U.S. presidency in 1872. Although not a single woman has yet succeeded in winning a major party nomination for the presidency, Hillary Clinton came extraordinarily close to doing so in 2008. Sarah Palin also came closer to the presidency than has any other woman since Geraldine Ferraro in 1984. We will likely continue to see more women running for the presidency and vice presidency as more and more women are gaining experience in the governor's mansions, the most common springboard to the presidency.

Outside of the governor's mansions, women continue to increase their presence in other executive positions. Women began running for statewide elective office well over a hundred years ago, but it is only fairly recently that women have made substantial gains into these positions. Women have done fairly well in securing positions as lieutenant governors, and historical patterns lead us to believe that some of these women will eventually succeed in moving up to the governor's mansion. Women likewise are securing more prominent and influential positions in governors' and presidential cabinets. President Obama's White House includes a number of high-ranking women.

Will it matter if a woman is elected president of the United States? Although it is entirely speculative at this point, the evidence presented in this chapter suggests that it will. For starters, she will likely be more attentive to the needs and perspectives of women. This hardly means that she will campaign solely on women's issues but that such issues will resonate more strongly with her than they would with a similarly situated male candidate. History suggests that she would appoint more women to her administration than her predecessors, but whether these gains would be substantially greater than if a male were in her place is not entirely clear. By virtue of being the first female president, she would undoubtedly face heightened pressures to succeed, to make sure that no one could say that women were unfit to govern. Finally, the most difficult question to answer is how she would exercise power from the highest elected office in the country. Although a decent amount of research suggests that women's leadership styles lean toward collaboration and consensus, it is difficult to assess how a woman elected to the office of the U.S. presidency would behave. Have women lagged behind men because their leadership styles differ? Would a woman have to adopt a masculine leadership style to have a chance of becoming president? Only the future will tell.

REFERENCES

"Are Women Better Leaders?" 2001. *U.S. News and World Report*. 130, no. 4:10.

Baird, Julia. 2008. "From Seneca Falls to . . . Sarah Palin?" *Newsweek* (22 September). Accessed online at www.newsweek.com/id/158893.

Baker, Peter. 2005. "Karen Hughes to Work on the World's View of U.S." *Washington Post* (12 March): A3.

Barbara Lee Family Foundation. 2001. *Keys to the Governor's Office: Unlock the Door: The Guide for Women Running for Governor*. Brookline, MA: The Barbara Lee Family Foundation.

Barnes, Robert, and Michael D. Shear. 2008. "McCain Picks Alaska Governor; Palin First Woman on GOP Ticket." *Washington Post* (30 August): A1.

Barth, Jay, and Margaret R. Ferguson. 2002. "Gender and Gubernatorial Personality." *Women & Politics* 24, no. 1:63–82.

Bayes, Jane. 1991. "Women in Public Administration in the United States." *Women & Politics* 11, no. 3:85–109.

Beard, Patricia. 1996. *Growing Up Republican: Christine Whitman: The Politics of Character*. New York: Harper Collins.

Beyle, Thad L., and Robert Dalton. 1981. "Appointment Power: Does It Belong to the Governor?" *State Government* 54, no. 1:2–12.

Borger, Gloria. 2002. "Exiting on Her Own Terms." *U.S. News and World Report* (6 May): 24.

Borrelli, MaryAnne. 2002. *The President's Cabinet: Gender, Power, and Representation*. Boulder, CO: Lynne Rienner Publishers.

Braden, Maria. 1996. *Women Politicians and the Media*. Lexington, KY: University of Kentucky Press.

Brant, Martha. 2001. "Bush's 'Power Puff Girls': The New Team Boasts a Record Number of Top Female Aides." *Newsweek* (7 May): 36.

Brezina, Joan Turek, and Lucretia Dewey Tanner. 1991. "Top Men and Women View Public Service." *The Bureaucrat* 20 (Fall): 29–32.

Bullard, Angela M., and Deil S. Wright. 1993. "Circumventing the Glass Ceiling: Women Executives in American State Governments." *Public Administration Review* 53, no. 3:189–202.

Burka, Paul. 1999. "Karen Hughes." *Texas Monthly* 27, no. 9:127+.

California Secretary of State. 2002. "Statement of Vote: 2002 Primary Election." Accessed at www.sos.ca.gov/elections/sov/2002_primary/sos.pdf.

Cannon, Carl M. 1999. "You Go, Girls: Growing Support for Women Presidential Candidates." *National Journal* 31, no. 30:2142.

Carroll, Susan J. 1987. "Women in State Cabinets: Status and Prospects." *Journal of State Government* 60, no. 5:204–208.

Carroll, Susan J., and Barbara Geiger-Parker. 1983a. *Women Appointed to State Government: A Comparison with All State Appointees*. New Brunswick, NJ: Center for American Women and Politics.

———. 1983b. *Women Appointed to the Carter Administration: A Comparison with Men*. Rutgers, NJ: Center for American Women and Politics.

Center for American Women and Politics (CAWP) 2003. *Women Presidential and Vice Presidential Candidates*. New Brunswick, NJ: Center for American Women and Politics, Eagleton Institute of Politics, Rutgers University.

———. 2004a. *Women Candidates for Governor: 1970–2004*. New Brunswick, NJ: Center for American Women and Politics, Eagleton Institute of Politics, Rutgers University.

_____. 2004b. *Women Lieutenant Governors: 1940–2004*. New Brunswick, NJ: Center for American Women and Politics, Eagleton Institute of Politics, Rutgers University.

_____. 2008. *The 2008 Presidential Campaign of Hillary Rodham Clinton*. New Brunswick, NJ: Center for American Women and Politics, Eagleton Institute of Politics, Rutgers University. Accessed online at www.cawp.rutgers.edu/fast_facts/elections/preswatch_clinton.php.

_____. 2009a. *State by State Information*. Accessed online at www.cawp.rutgers.edu/fast_facts/resources/state_fact_sheet.php.

_____. 2009b. *Statewide Elective Executive Women 2009*. New Brunswick, NJ: Center for American Women and Politics, Eagleton Institute of Politics, Rutgers University.

_____. 2009c. *Women Appointed to Presidential Cabinets*. New Brunswick, NJ: Center for American Women and Politics, Eagleton Institute of Politics, Rutgers University.

Center for Women in Government. (CWG). 1999. *Appointed Policy Makers in State Government: Trend Analysis*. Albany, NY: Center for Women in Government.

_____. 2008. *Appointed Policy Makers in State Government: Glass Ceiling in Gubernatorial Appointments, 1997–2007*. Albany, NY: Center for Women in Government.

Clift, Eleanor, and Tom Brazaitis. 2000. *Madam President: Shattering the Last Glass Ceiling*. New York: Scribner.

Clinton, Hillary. 2007. "I'm In." You Tube video of Clinton's announcement of developing presidential exploratory committee. Accessed online at www.youtube.com/watch?v=SJuRQZ2ZGTs

CNN Exit Polls. 2008. Accessed online at www.cnn.com/ELECTION/2008/results/polls/#val=USP00p3.

Coalition for Women's Appointments (CWA). 1992. "Purposes and Policies." Washington, D.C.: National Women's Political Caucus.

_____. 1993. "Project Report." Washington, D.C.: National Women's Political Caucus.

Cook, Alison. 1991. "Lone Star: Popular Ann Richards May Be Too Popular for Her Own Good." *New York Times Magazine* (7 February) 22–27+.

Cottle, Michelle. 1999. "The Woman Behind George W.'s Iron Bubble: The Enforcer. *The New Republic* (29 November): 20.

Council of State Governments. 2002. *Book of the States*. Lexington, KY: Council of State Governments.

Current Biography Yearbook. 1987. "Madeleine May Kunin," ed. Charles Moritz. New York: The H.W. Wilson Company. pp. 228–331.

Daly, Matthew. 2009. "Sarah Palin Steps Down as Alaska Governor." *Washington Post* (27 July).

Deutchman, Iva Ellen. 1996. "Feminist Theory and the Politics of Empowerment." In *Women in Politics: Outsiders or Insiders?* 2nd ed., ed. Lois Lovelace Duke. Englewood Cliffs, NJ: Prentice Hall.

Dolan, Julie. 2000a. "Influencing Policy at the Top of the Federal Bureaucracy: A Comparison of Career and Political Senior Executives." *Public Administration Review* 60, no. 6:573–581.

_____. 2000b. "The Senior Executive Service: Gender, Attitudes and Representative Bureaucracy." *Journal of Public Administration Research and Theory* 10, no. 3:513–529.

_____. 2004. "Gender Equity: Illusion or Reality for Men and Women in the Federal Executive Service?" *Public Administration Review* 64, no. 3:299–308.

Dow, Bonnie J., and Mari Boor Tonn. 1993. "'Feminine Styles' and Political Judgment in the Rhetoric of Ann Richards." *Quarterly Journal of Speech* 79:286–302.

Dowd, Ann Reilly. 2000. "Is There Anything This Woman Can't Do?" *George* 5:86–91.

Duerst-Lahti, Georgia, and Rita Mae Kelly, ed. 1995. *Gender Power, Leadership, and Governance*. Ann Arbor: University of Michigan Press.

Eagly, Alice H., and Blair T. Johnson. 1990. "Gender and Leadership Style: A Meta-Analysis." *Psychological Bulletin* 108, no. 2:233–256.

Edlund, Carol J. 1992. "Humanizing the Workplace: Incorporating Feminine Leadership." pp. 75–88 in *Public Management in an Interconnected World: Essays in the Minnowbrook Tradition*, ed. Mary Timney Bailey and Richard T. Mayer. Westport, CT: Greenwood Press.

FEC. 2000. Presidential Popular Vote Summary. www.fec.gov/pubrec/fe2000/prespop.htm.

Felix, Antonia. 2002. *Condi: The Condoleezza Rice Story.* New York: Newmarket Press.

Fisher, Marc. 2008. "For Working Moms, 'Flawed' Palin is the Perfect Choice." *Washington Post* (11 September): B1.

Fletcher, Michael A. 2009. "High-Powered and Low-Key; Washington Observes The Influence of Obama Adviser Valerie Jarrett." *Washington Post* (15 March): A1.

Fox, Richard L., and Zoe M. Oxley. 2003. "Gender-Stereotyping in State Executive Elections: Candidate Selection and Success." *Journal of Politics* 65, no. 3:833–850.

Gallup Poll. 2008a. "Palin Unknown to Most Americans." August 30th. Accessed online at www.gallup.com/poll/109951/Palin-Unknown-Most-Americans.aspx.

Gallup Poll. 2008b. "Republicans' Enthusiasm Jumps After Convention." September 8th. Accessed online at www.gallup.com/poll/110107/Republicans-Enthusiasm-Jumps-After-Convention.aspx.

Garcia, Rogelio. 1989. *Women Nominated and Appointed to Full-Time Civilian Positions by President Reagan.* CRS Report 89–236 GOV. Washington, DC: Congressional Research Service.

———. 1993. *Women Nominated and Appointed to Full-Time Civilian Positions by President George Bush.* CRS Report 93–542 GOV. Washington, DC: Congressional Research Service.

———. 1997. *Women Nominated by President Clinton to Full-Time Positions Requiring Senate Confirmation, 1993–1996.* CRS Report 94–272 GOV. Washington, D.C.: Congressional Research Service.

Germer, Fawn. 1995. "Vikki Buckley's Climb." *Rocky Mountain News/Sunday Magazine* (12 February).

"Green Party Picks Slate." 2008. *Washington Post* (13 July): A6.

Gross, Terry. 2003. "Madeleine Albright on Her New Book 'Madam Secretary'." Fresh Air, National Public Radio. (September 16), 2003. WHYY.

Grunwald, Michael, and Jay Newton-Small (2008). "Why McCain Picked Palin." *Newsweek* (29 August). Accessed online at www.time.com/time/politics/article/0,8599,1837510,00.html.

Hale, Mary M., and M. Frances Branch. 1992, "Policy Preferences in Workplace Reform," in *Women and Men of the States*, ed. Mary E. Guy. Armonk, NY: ME Sharpe.

Hale, Mary M., Rita Mae Kelly, and Jayne Burgess: 1989. "Women in the Arizona Executive Branch of Government," in *Gender, Bureaucracy, and Democracy: Careers and Opportunity in the Public Sector*, ed. Mary M. Hale and Rita Mae Kelly. Westport, CT: Greenwood Press.

Hale, Mary M., Rita Mae Kelly, Jayne Burgess, and Rhonda Shapiro. 1987. "Women in the Executive Branch of Government," in *Women and the Arizona Political Process*, ed. Rita Mae Kelly. Lanham, MD: University Press of America.

Hartmann, Susan M. 1989. *From Margin to Mainstream: American Women in Politics Since 1960.* Philadelphia: Temple University Press.

Havens, Catherine M., and Lynne M. Healy. 1991. "Cabinet-Level Appointees in Connecticut: Women Making a Difference," in *Gender and Policymaking: Studies of Women in Office*, ed. Deba L. Dodson. New Brunswick, NJ: Center for American Women and Politics.

Helgesen, Sally. 1990. *The Female Advantage: Women's Ways of Leadership*. New York: Doubleday.

"In the 50th State, the End of the Democrats 40-Year Reign." 2002. *New York Times* (7 November): B8.

Jalalzai, Farida. 2008. "Women Rule: Shattering the Glass Ceiling." *Politics & Gender* 4(2):205–231.

Kahn, Kim Fridkin. 1996. *The Political Consequences of Being a Woman*. New York: Columbia University Press.

Kaml, Shannon Skarphol. 2000. "The Fusion of Populist and Feminine Styles in the Rhetoric of Ann Richards." In *Navigating Boundaries: The Rhetoric of Women Governors*, ed. Brenda DeVore Marshall and Molly A. Mayhead. Westport, CT: Praeger Publishers.

Kanter, Rosabeth Moss. 1977. *Men and Women of the Corporation*. New York: Basic Books, Inc.

Kaptur, Marcy. 1996. *Women of Congress: A Twentieth-Century Odyssey*. Washington, DC: Congressional Quarterly Inc.

Kawar, Amal. 1989. "Women in the Executive Branch." In *Gender, Bureaucracy, and Democracy: Careers and Opportunity in the Public Sector*, ed. Mary M. Hale and Rita Mae Kelly. Westport, CT: Greenwood Press.

Kleeman, Katherine E. 1987. "Women in State Government: Looking Back, Looking Ahead." *Journal of State Government* 60, no. 5:199–203.

Kornblut, Anne. 2008. "Palin to Give Interview to ABC This Week." *Washington Post* (8 September): A2.

Kunin, Madeleine. 1987. "Lessons from One Woman's Career." *Journal of State Government* 60, no. 5:209–213.

Kunin, Madeleine. 1994. *Living a Political Life: One of America's First Women Governors Tells Her Story*. New York: Alfred A. Knopf.

Kurtz, Howard. 2008. "After Taking Some Shots, She Fires Back; Palin Aims at Detractors in Remaking Her Image." *Washington Post* (13 November): C1.

LaDuke, Winona. 2000. "Acceptance Speech for Nomination." www.votenader.com/laduke_acceptance.html.

Lawless, Jennifer L. 2004. "Women, War and Winning Elections: Gender Stereotyping in the Post-September 11th Era." *Political Research Quarterly* 57(3):479–490.

Lippman, Thomas W. 1997. "State Department Seeks Gains for Women: Albright Is Stressing Rights Concerns in Foreign Policy Agenda." *Washington Post* (25 March): A1.

Martin, Janet M. 1989. "The Recruitment of Women to Cabinet and Subcabinet Posts." *Western Political Quarterly* 42, no. 1:161–172.

_____. 1991. "An Examination of Executive Branch Appointments in the Reagan Administration by Background and Gender." *Western Political Quarterly* 44, no. 1:173–184.

_____. 1997. "Women Who Govern: The President's Appointments." In *The Other Elites: Women, Politics and Power in the Executive Branch*, ed. MaryAnne Borelli and Janet Martin. Boulder, CO: Lynne Rienner Publishers.

Massaro, Gary. 1999. "Vikki Buckley Loses Biggest Battle." *Rocky Mountain News* (15 July).

Mayhead, Molly A., and Brenda DeVore Marshall. 2000. "Re-visioning and Re-framing Political Boundaries: Barbara Roberts' Response to Oregon's Budget Crisis." In *Navigating Boundaries: The Rhetoric of Women Governors*, ed. Brenda DeVore Marshall and Molly A. Mayhead. Westport, CT: Praeger Publishers.

"McCain Pick Appears to Bring in $7 Million." 2008. *Washington Post* (31 August): A13.

McGlen, Nancy E., and Meredith Reid Sarkees. 1993. *Women in Foreign Policy: The Insiders*. New York: Routledge.

Merida, Kevin. 2008. "She's the Star the GOP Hitched its Bandwagon To." *Washington Post* (11 September): C1.

Milbank, Dana. 2008. "A Thank-You for 18 Million Cracks in the Glass Ceiling." *Washington Post* (8 June): A1.

Moore, David W. 1999. "Gore Trails Bush, Dole in Trial Heat." Gallup Poll, March 17th. Accessed online at www.gallup.com/poll/4015/Gore-Trails-Bush-Dole-Trial-Heat.aspx.

Naff, Katherine C. 2001. *To Look Like America: Dismantling Barriers for Women and Minorities in Government.* Boulder, CO: Westview Press.

National Governors Association. 2003. *Past Governors.* Accessed online at www.nga.org/governors/1,1169,C_PAST_GOV,00.html. Washington, D.C.: National Governors Association.

Newman, Meredith Ann. 1995. "The Gendered Nature of Lowi's Typology; or, Who Would Guess You Could Find Gender Here?" pp. 141–166 in *Gender Power, Leadership, and Governance,* ed. Georgia Duerst-Lahti and Rita Mae Kelly. Ann Arbor: University of Michigan Press.

Newport, Frank. 1999. "Dole Unable to Pull Republican Voters Away from Front-Runner Bush." Gallup Poll, October 20th. Accessed online at www.gallup.com/poll/3526/Dole-Unable-Pull-Republican-Voters-Away-from-Frontrunner-Bush.aspx

Open Secrets. 2008. "Banking on Becoming President." Accessed online at www.opensecrets.org/pres08/index.php

Pfiffner, James P. 1996. *The Strategic Presidency: Hitting the Ground Running,* 2nd ed. Lawrence, KS: University Press of Kansas.

Polling Report. 2000. "White House 2000: Republicans." Accessed online at www.pollingreport.com/wh2rep.htm.

Polling Report. 2008a. "Campaign 2008." Accessed online at www.pollingreport.com/wh08.htm.

Polling Report. 2008b. "White House 2008: Democratic Nomination." Accessed online at www.pollingreport.com/wh08dem.htm.

Ray, Diana. 2001. "Bush's Cabinet Has Diverse Experience." *Insight* (15–22 January): 8.

Real Clear Politics. 2008. "2008 Democratic Popular Vote." Accessed online at www.realclearpolitics.com/epolls/2008/president/democratic_vote_count.html

Recio, Maria. 2000. "Buchanan Taps Black Woman as No. 2." *The Record* (12 August).

Reingold, Beth. 1996. "Conflict and Cooperation: Legislative Strategies and Concepts of Power among Female and Male State Legislators." *Journal of Politics* 58, no. 2:464–485.

Riccucci, Norma M., and Judith R. Saidel. 1997. "The Representativeness of State-Level Bureaucratic Leaders: A Missing Piece of the Representative Bureaucracy Puzzle." *Public Administration Review* 57, no. 5:423–430.

———. 2001. "The Demographics of Gubernatorial Appointees: Toward an Explanation of Variation." *Policy Studies Journal* 29, no. 1:11–22.

Robbins, William. 1986a. "Nebraska Gubernatorial Bid: It's Woman Against Woman." *New York Times* (15 May): A22.

———. 1986b. "The Political Campaign: Nebraska Race Called Nearly Neck and Neck." *New York Times* (30 October): B14.

Rodriguez, Emelyn. 2001. "The Comeback Kid." *California Journal* (15 May).

Romney, Ronna, and Beppie Harrison. 1988. *Momentum: Women in American Politics Now.* New York: Crown Publishers.

Rosener, Judy. 1990. "Ways Women Lead." *Harvard Business Review* 68, no. 6:119–125.

Rosenwasser, Shirley M., and Jana Seale. 1988. "Attitudes toward a Hypothetical Male or Female Presidential Candidate. A Research Note." *Political Psychology* 9, no. 4:591–598.

Saidel, Judith R., and Norma M. Riccucci. 1996. *Appointed Policy Makers in State Government: The National Profile.* Albany, NY: Center for Women in Government.

Sallee, Shelley. 1996. "'The Woman of It': Governor Miriam Ferguson's 1924 Election." *Southwestern Historical Quarterly* 100, no. 1:1–16.

Scharff, Virginia. 1995. "Feminism, Femininity, and Power: Nellie Tayloe Ross and the Woman Politician's Dilemma." *Frontiers* 15, no. 3:87–106.

Schroeder, Patricia, and Olympia Snowe. 1994. "The Politics of Women's Health." In *The American Woman: 1994–95,* ed. Cynthia Costello and Anne J. Stone. New York: W.W. Norton & Company.

Scott, Cynthia. 2000. "Why Winona Runs." *Minnesota Women's Press* online (16 August).

Selden, Sally Coleman. 1997. *The Promise of Representative Bureaucracy: Diversity and Responsiveness in a Government Agency.* Armonk, NY: M.E. Sharpe.

Seelye, Katharine Q. 1999. "Low on Cash, Dole Withdraws from G.O.P. Race." *New York Times* (21 October): A1.

Sheeler, Krista Horn. 2000. "Christine Todd Whitman and the Ideology of the New Jersey Governorship." In *Navigating Boundaries: The Rhetoric of Women Governors,* ed. Brenda DeVore Marshall and Molly A. Mayhead. Westport, CT: Praeger Publishers.

Stanley, Jeanie R. 1989. "Women in the Texas Executive Branch of Government." In *Gender, Bureaucracy, and Democracy: Careers and Opportunity in the Public Sector,* ed. Mary M. Hale and Rita Mae Kelly. Westport, CT: Greenwood Press.

Stanwick, Kathy A., and Katherine E. Kleeman. 1983. *Women Make a Difference.* New Brunswick, NJ: Center for American Women and Politics.

State of Michigan. 2003. "Governor Appoints Cabinet That Reflects One Michigan." Accessed online at www.michigan.gov/gov/0,1607,7-168-21984-60731—,00.html. Release date February 3, 2003. State of Michigan.

Stineman, Esther. 1980. *American Political Women: Contemporary and Historical Profiles.* Littleton, CO: Libraries Unlimited, Inc.

Suskind, Ron. 2002. "Mrs. Hughes Takes Her Leave." *Esquire* 138, no. 1:100+.

Tessier, Marie. 2002. "Women at the Top: Window Dressing or Policy Makers?" *Ms.* 12, no. 4:8–10.

"*Time*'s 25 Most Influential Americans." 1997. *Time* 149, no. 16:40–62.

United States Office of Personnel Management. 2009. *Senior Executive Service: Facts and Figures.* Accessed online at www.opm.gov/ses/facts_and_figures/demographics.asp.

Van Biema, David. 2003. "Tomorrow." *Time* (5 December): 48.

"Vikki Buckley 1947–1999." 1999. Editorial, *Rocky Mountain News* (15 July).

Walsh, Kenneth T. 2001. "A Prime Seat at the Table." *U.S. News and World Report* 130, no. 17:25.

Watson, Robert P. 2003. "Introduction: The White House as Ultimate Prize." In *Anticipating Madam President,* ed. Robert P. Watson and Ann Gordon. Boulder, CO: Lynne Rienner Publishers.

Watson, Robert P., and Ann Gordon, eds. 2003a. *Anticipating Madam President.* Boulder, CO: Lynne Rienner Publishers.

Watson, Robert P., and Ann Gordon. 2003b. "Profile: Elizabeth Dole, Executive Leadership." In *Anticipating Madam President,* ed. Robert P. Watson and Ann Gordon. Boulder, CO: Lynne Rienner Publishers.

———. 2003c. "Profile: Geraldine Ferraro, Media Coverage of History in the Making." In *Anticipating Madam President,* ed. by Robert P. Watson and Ann Gordon. Boulder, CO: Lynne Rienner Publishers.

Welna, David. 2008. "Hundreds of Superdelegates Remain Undecided." *National Public Radio* (28 April).

Weir, Sara J. 1999. "The Feminist Face of State Executive Leadership: Women as Governors." In *Women in Politics: Outsiders or Insiders?* 3rd ed., ed. Lois Duke Whitaker. Upper Saddle River, NJ: Prentice Hall.

Women's Appointment Project (WAP). 2005. "National Women's Political Caucus Launches 2005 Women's Appointment Project." Accessed online at www.appointwomen.org/news.htm (cached).

Worldwide Guide to Women in Leadership. 2010. Accessed online at www.guide2womenleaders.com.

Wright, Deil S., Chung-Lae Cho, and Yoo-Sund Chai. 2002. "Top-Level State Administrators: Changing Characteristics and Qualities." pp. 370–375, tables in *The Book of the States*. Lexington, KY: Council of State Governments.

Young, Billie, and Nancy Ankeny. 2000. *Minnesota Women in Politics: Stories of the Journey*. St. Cloud, MN: North Star Press.

Women in the Judiciary

When most people picture a judge in their minds, it is likely that they see an older white male, whether kindly or stern, in a black robe, seated behind a tall bench in a courtroom. On television, we occasionally see women or people of color serving as judges, such as Judge Judy. But white men are the images that most people conjure up when they think of a typical jurist. In fact, as judicial scholars Elaine Martin and Barry Pyle (2002) point out, the description of state judges in a leading textbook on the judiciary conforms to this stereotype. In *Judicial Process in America*, Carp and Stidman (1998) describe state judges as being:

> . . . [H]omegrown fellows who are moderately conservative and staunchly committed to the status quo. They believe in the basic values and traditions of the legal and political communities from which they come. State judges, then, [have], the distinction of being local boys who made good.   (260)

Indeed, the most recent data show that most judges, both at the federal and state levels of government, are still white males. However, in the past few decades, the judiciary has experienced a marked increase in diversity in terms of gender and race.

This chapter concentrates on women in the judiciary. How many women currently serve as judges nationwide? Does their behavior differ from that of male jurists? Does the presence of females on certain courts, such as appellate courts and state courts of last resort, alter the behavior of male judges? Ultimately, how important is it that women serve in this branch of government?

Before examining how gender affects judicial decision making, this chapter takes a look at the history of women in the judiciary. Before women could become judges, however, they had to become attorneys. Studying attorneys is important given their substantial impact on politics. For instance, lawyers are disproportionately represented in the ranks of elected legislators at most levels of government (O'Connor 1988). This chapter begins with a focus on the history of women lawyers, their current status in the legal profession, and the discrimination that female attorneys sometimes face in their work.

Next, the chapter takes a look at the first women to serve as judges, both at the state and federal levels. Among other notable women, the chapter pays special attention to Sandra Day O'Connor and Ruth Bader Ginsburg—the first two women to be appointed to the highest court in the land, the United States Supreme Court. In May 2010, President Barack Obama sought to change the gender balance on the Supreme Court once again by nominating U.S. Solicitor General and former Harvard Law School Dean Elena Kagan as his pick to replace the retiring justice John Paul Stevens. In August 2009, U.S. Appellate Court Judge Sonia Sotomayor became the third woman—and first Hispanic— to be named to the Supreme Court in wake of the retirement of Justice David Souter. Although there is little research yet on Sotomayor's decision-making style, her appointment to the Court was not without controversy (at least among conservative lawmakers). The current status of women in the federal and state judiciary will also be examined.

As the number of women judges has grown, so has speculation as to their impact on the legal process. The chapter examines what legal theorists say about women's potential impact as jurists. Here the work of Carol Gilligan is explored in some detail. Next, the chapter examines if these theories about the potential impact of women in the judiciary have actually played out. What have political scientists found with respect to the decision making of women judges compared with their male counterparts? Does gender actually make a difference on the bench?

Finally, this chapter examines how gender—particularly gender bias— affects courtroom administration. First, however, the role of the courts in American politics—and how gender interplays with them—is addressed.

WHY THE COURTS ARE IMPORTANT

Although different than the legislative and branches executive, the courts hold an important place in our political system. The judiciary handles a variety of disputes between two parties—whether those parties are private citizens or the government, or the dispute under question is civil or criminal in nature. One result is that the courts play a significant role in the lives of everyday Americans, as they provide one of the most frequent contacts between people and their governments, particularly at the state and local levels (Hurwitz and Lanier 2003).

The decisions made by the judiciary in facing such conflicts often have important gender dimensions. For example, at the local level, in divorce cases that involve minor children, judges sometimes have to decide who should receive custody of children or whether a spouse should receive child support and/or alimony payments. To take another example, local judges must decide in domestic violence cases whether a restraining order should be imposed on the alleged aggressor against the victim. Judicial decision making in both child custody and domestic violence cases has the potential to affect women's (and men's) daily lives dramatically.

Verdicts made by the courts, especially when one of the parties involved is the government, can also have important political and policy ramifications. Nowhere is this more evident than at the United States Supreme Court. The job of the Supreme Court is to maintain national supremacy in the law by ensuring uniformity in the interpretation of national laws. One way that it does so is to examine the constitutionality of acts of Congress or, more frequently, state legislation. For example, if a state legislature passes a law that places certain limits on a woman's ability to obtain an abortion, the United States Supreme Court may decide to hear challenges to the law to decide if it violates liberties or guarantees provided in the U.S. Constitution. However, few such challenges make it all of the way to the Supreme Court. Given the limited ability of the Supreme Court to review most cases involving state legislation, the lower federal courts and state supreme courts have also come to play an important role in determining public policy.

In recognition of the increasing role of courts in policymaking, interest groups and citizens often turn to the courts—both federal and state—when the legislative process is not accessible or does not produce desired results. In that vein, the courts are often viewed as the institution that protects the rights of minorities. For instance, the civil rights movement in the twentieth century used litigation as a strategy to advance its cause when many state legislatures, especially in the segregated South, refused to consider its claims. The best-known example of the results of such a litigation strategy is *Brown v. Board of Education*, in which the Supreme Court in 1954 ruled that state education systems that segregated students by race were inherently unequal according to the Fourteenth Amendment's guarantee of equal protection under the law. By doing so, the Supreme Court ruled that racial segregation in public educational institutions by state or local government is unconstitutional.

Women have also turned to the courts to expand their rights (O'Connor 1980). In the late 1960s and 1970s, Congress passed several pieces of legislation that banned sex discrimination in the workplace and in higher education. Given that determining what constitutes discriminatory behavior can be nebulous at times, various women (often with the backing of women's legal and political organizations) have often been compelled to bring their individual cases regarding discrimination before the courts. For example, in 1996 the Supreme Court heard a case involving the state of Virginia and its state-sponsored military academy, the Virginia Military Institute (VMI), which had for its long history excluded women from attending. Although the state of Virginia established an ROTC program at a nearby women's college to address concerns about VMI's discriminatory practices, the Supreme Court ruled in *United States v. Virginia et al.* (1996) that this "sister" program was not sufficient. Instead, it declared that all categorical exclusion of women from state-funded colleges was unconstitutional.

While women and other minorities have often sought relief in the courts for their grievances, the judiciary is restricted in its ability to make policy compared with the legislative or executive branches. Unlike legislators or administrators, for example, judges cannot make decisions that will affect policy unless a case appears before them in their dockets. Also, unlike legislators who run for office with the clear intent of crafting legislation based on their own ideas and opinions about public policy, judges are often circumscribed from such behavior by the norms of their profession. Judges are expected to be impartial and detached from the cases that they hear, relying on evidence in a case before making a decision. Judges are also constrained by the nature of law. As Martin and Pyle (2000) note: "The law itself, statutes and precedents, the facts of the case, the requirements of evidence, the possibility of being overturned on appeal, even the nature of the adversarial system, all restrict the freedom of judicial discretion" (1211).

Yet many who study the courts also acknowledge that the act of adjudication is potentially influenced by the personal characteristics of judges. It is in this capacity that the gender of judges could potentially make a difference in judicial decision making. As research in political science finds that women differ from men politically, both in terms of their activism and their attitudes (see, for example, Darcy, Welch, and Clark 1994; Burns, Schlozman, and Verba 2001), many scholars and political observers believe that women judges will differ in important ways from men judges. Proponents of increasing the presence of women on the bench argue that it is only fair to have a judiciary that is made up of both men and women. They contend that recruiting representatives with more diverse backgrounds and experiences to the bench would result in a judiciary that would be a fairer institution—one that would more effectively use the talents of all citizens (Goldman 1979; Bratton and Spill 2002).

Indeed, this line of reasoning came to more public prominence during the Supreme Court confirmation hearings of Sonia Sotomayor, who was confirmed in August 2009. As a U.S. appellate judge in 2001, Sotomayor once said in a speech addressing the role that her background played in her jurisprudence, "I would hope that a wise Latina woman with the richness of her experiences would more often than not reach a better conclusion than a white male who hasn't lived that life" (quoted in Baker and Zeleny 2009, A1). The comment sparked much debate among pundits and lawmakers on both sides of the aisle. For example, former U.S. House Speaker Newt Gingrich stated that the speech indicated that Sotomayor was a "Latina woman racist," although he later backtracked from such language. Most conservatives expressed concern that the statement, combined with her previous ties with left-leaning Hispanic advocacy groups that actively promoted affirmative action policies, indicated that she would let her personal bias influence her judicial decision making. President Barack Obama defended his nominee, stating that while she may have used a poor choice of words to express her beliefs, in essence, what was clear from her statement was that "she was simply saying that her life experiences will give her information about the struggles and hardships that people are going through— that will make her a good judge" (quoted in Kirkpatrick 2009, A1).

Sotomayor also sought to diffuse the controversy over those specific words, saying in her testimony at the hearings for her confirmation that the words were "a rhetorical flourish that fell flat" and that they had been misinterpreted (quoted in Baker and Lewis 2009, A1). She said "it was bad because

In May 2009, President Barack Obama nominated Sonia Sotomayor, the third woman—and first Latina—to serve on the U.S. Supreme Court

it left an impression that life experiences command a result in a case. But that's clearly not what I do as a judge" (ibid.). Sotomayor was confirmed by the U.S. Senate, notwithstanding her "wise Latina" remarks, and one person was especially pleased with the result—Justice Ruth Bader Ginsburg, who remarked shortly before Sotomayor's confirmation hearings were set to begin that being the lone female on the Supreme Court "just doesn't look right in the year 2009" (quoted in Bazelon 2009, 22).

HISTORY OF WOMEN IN THE LEGAL PROFESSION AND JUDICIARY

Women Lawyers

The first known woman to practice law in the United States was Margaret Brent in the Maryland colonies, who arrived at St. Mary's Parish from Great Britain in 1638 (Morello 1986). She was a cousin of Sir George Calvert, Lord Baltimore—who founded and named the state of Maryland in 1630—and came from a wealthy landowning family. Once here, she amassed a large real estate holding in her own right and, being unmarried, was able to keep and manage it. Holding land was a prerogative for political power in the colonies, and Brent amassed much of it. She was an accomplished litigator, having been involved in 124 court cases during an eight-year period, with records indicating that she was referred to as "gentleman Margaret Brent" while in court sessions (ibid.). She was so well connected and politically savvy that she was appointed as counsel to the governor, Lord Leonard Calvert (son of George), and later served as the administrator of his estate upon his death. Although she made an unsuccessful plea to have her own voting rights (as other landowners enjoyed at that time), she continued to handle the estate of Lord Calvert and never married. Other records indicate that a number of other women, although not attorneys, also argued their cases in the early days of the nation, such as Lucy Terry Prince—a free black woman who was the first woman to have ever addressed the Supreme Court in 1795 (ibid.).

Women such as Margaret Brent and Lucy Terry Prince were few and far between, however. As America changed from a colony to an independent nation, society's rules became more formalized, and restrictions on race and sex prevented women and minorities from practicing law and holding most professions. However, several changes led to the emergence of some women practicing law. First, women became active in the abolitionist, and later suffrage, cause, which no doubt showed them that they had capabilities outside of the home. Second, the expansion of the country westward meant that women were able to forgo many of society's more formal conventions in the East and South as their skills and services were needed in frontier life. Many, if not most, colleges in the West were coeducational from the outset. In fact, the first known woman to practice law as a profession did so in Iowa in 1869—then considered a pioneer state. In February 1869, *The Chicago Legal News* reported a story about Mrs. Mary E. Magoon of North English, Iowa, describing her as a "very successful" jury lawyer (Morello 1986, 11). The first woman to become officially recognized as an attorney who gained admission to a state bar also hailed from Iowa in 1869: Belle Babb Mansfield. In her history on women attorneys, Karen Berger Morello (1986) says that Mansfield was able to attend Iowa Wesleyan College due to the slumping enrollments brought on by the Civil War. Upon graduation, she joined her brother's law firm and began to study or "read" the law, as it was common for many attorneys to be trained this way instead of attending law school (O'Connor 1988). She went on to become an active suffragette and a professor of history, later becoming dean of DePauw's School of Music and Art.

Another notable woman in legal history is Myra Colby Bradwell, who took and passed the 1869 Chicago bar exam. However, the State of Illinois declined to admit her to the bar, which she challenged first at the state supreme court (where she lost) and then at the United States Supreme Court, where her attorneys charged that Bradwell was unconstitutionally denied the right to practice law because of the Fourteenth Amendment's guarantee that states provide equal protection under the law to its citizens. In *Bradwell v. Illinois* (1873), the U.S. Supreme Court ruled 8 to 1 against Bradwell's petition—ruling that the Fourteenth Amendment did not secure the right to be admitted to a bar since "admission to the bar of any state was not one of the privileges or immunities of U.S. citizenship" (O'Connor and Clark 1999, 266). History better remembers, however, the famous concurrent opinion written by Justice Joseph Bradley, viewed by many as a blow to the cause of women's rights:

> The civil law, as well as nature herself, has always recognized a wide difference in the respective spheres and destinies of man and woman. Man is, and should be, woman's protector and defender. The natural and proper timidity and delicacy which belongs to the female sex evidently unfits her for many of the occupations of civil life. The constitution of the family organization, which is founded in the divine ordinance, as well as in the nature of things, indicates the domestic sphere as that which properly belongs to the domain and functions of womanhood . . . So firmly fixed was this sentiment in the founders of the common law that it became a maxim of the system of jurisprudence that a woman had no legal existence separate from her husband.   (83 U.S. 130 at 140–142, 1873)

Luckily for Myra Colby Bradwell, and the women who followed her, the state legislature changed the law and allowed women to be admitted to the bar in Illinois in 1882, the year before her case was heard by the Supreme Court. However, the Supreme Court's unwillingness to grant women the legal right to practice law meant that women would be "engaged in a state-by-state struggle for admission to their individual bars" (Morello 1986, 22). Georgia became the last state in the union to allow women admission to the bar in 1916 (O'Connor 1988).

Although some states did allow women to practice law in the late nineteenth century, their numbers were still quite small, prompting a group of women in Michigan to found the first national organization for women lawyers, known as the Equity Club in 1886. The Equity Club had 32 members, both women lawyers and law students, who corresponded with each other for four years in a series of letters (Drachman 1993). Club members wrote about everything from professional matters to courtroom etiquette for female attorneys (for instance, should they wear bonnets in the court?) to work and family balance issues. For example, there was a disagreement among members as to whether or not it was appropriate to marry or to forgo marriage for a professional career. About half of the members did in fact marry, including eight who were married to lawyers and who practiced with them (ibid.). Among the members of the Equity Club was Belva Lockwood, who was the first woman admitted to practice before the United States Supreme Court. Although Lockwood graduated from National University Law School (now part of George Washington University) in 1873, it was not until Congress passed the "Lockwood" bill in 1879 that women were allowed admittance to the federal bar (Morello 1986). When the Equity Club disbanded in 1890, just 208 women were practicing attorneys, according to the U.S. Census Bureau (Drachman 1993).

Women's numbers in the legal profession grew slowly through the twentieth century as more law schools admitted women as students. Part of the explanation is due to the large growth in the number of law schools and law students in the United States, as fewer people read the law as apprentices in

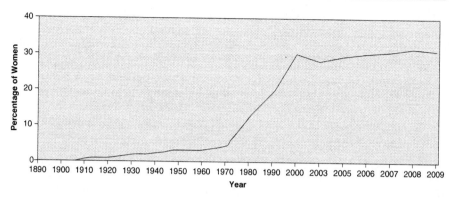

FIGURE 9.1

Percentage of Women in the Legal Profession 1890–2009

Source: U.S. Department of Commerce, Bureau of the Census, *Statistical Abstracts.*

law offices to become attorneys (O'Connor 1988). Yet relatively few women chose to become attorneys until well into the 1970s and 1980s (see Figure 9.1). More recent data from the American Bar Association estimates that in 2007, 30.7 percent of lawyers in the United States were female (ABA 2007).

Prior to the 1970s, most women who practiced law typically worked in the government or specialized in family law. One study found that in 1970, 37 percent of all female lawyers worked for the federal government (O'Connor 1988). This changed with the advent of the women's movement in the late 1960s and 1970s, as more women were inspired to seek professional degrees, resulting in a spike in law school applications. Moreover, similar to what occurred during the Civil War a century before, the war in Vietnam left law schools deprived of male students, making them more receptive of women applicants (Hermann and Kelly 1988). Additionally, many women were aided in this endeavor by the passage of the federal antidiscrimination law, which forbids sex discrimination in employment and education. According to the American Bar Association (ABA), women made up just 9.4 percent of law students in 1971. A decade later, in 1981, women's ranks in law schools grew to 35.8 percent (ABA 1998). The most current data show that women now make up approximately half (49 percent) of all law school students (ABA 2004).

Women Lawyers Today

Although women have reached parity with men in terms of law school enrollment, they still make up far less of the percentage of practicing attorneys. In 2007, roughly 33 percent of attorneys were female (U.S. Census Bureau 2007). In 2000, the ABA reported that women were still slightly more likely than men to work in government (11 percent compared with 7 percent, respectively), but that the vast majority of both women (71 percent) and men (75 percent) attorneys worked in private practice (ABA 2000). Today, although women make up almost 33 percent of lawyers, their numbers as leaders in the legal profession are disproportionately low. For example, women make up only 18 percent of partner in law firms nationwide (ABA 2007). Although 36 percent of faculty at law schools are women, just 21 percent of deans of law schools are women; moreover, women make up just 27 percent of tenured faculty in law schools (ibid.).

Women attorneys are also more likely to leave law firms in greater numbers and earlier in their careers than men (Wellington 2003). They leave, in part, because they are less likely to make partners than their male counterparts. A key barrier to women's success at law firms is the work/family balance, as women lawyer are more likely than men lawyers to say such constraints inhibit their success. Equally important, say women attorneys, is a lack of mentoring and access to informal support networks (ibid., O'Connor 2007.)

Women lawyers also make less money than their male counterparts (Hagan 1990; ABA 2000). The ABA reports that in 2007, the annual median salary of women lawyers was just 70 percent of men's annual median salary (ABA 2007). In part, this is likely due to women's tendency to work slightly fewer hours than men, especially those women who are also mothers (Chambers 1989). Yet one study found that more than a quarter of income disparity between female and male lawyers can be attributed to gender discrimination (Hagan 1990).

Gender discrimination is not just manifested in income disparities between women and men lawyers. In one study of Pittsburgh attorneys, women were far more likely than men to report bias in their treatment when it came to interacting with other attorneys, judges, court employees, and fellow co-workers (Coontz 1995). For example, women were much more likely to report that they were asked questions about their private lives, such as whether they had or planned to have children, during job interviews. Other women reported being treated differently in the courtroom by male judges. For example, one woman reported that a judge admonished her once for being "shrill" (ibid.). In some cases, women attorneys are still not free from being typecast in stereotypical ways or from assumptions about family responsibilities that are gender based (ibid.).

Despite such stereotypes and assumptions often faced by female attorneys, women have made much progress in the profession. With more women making up the ranks of attorneys, more women are now eligible to serve as judges. Before examining the current makeup of the judiciary by gender, we will take a look at women who pioneered as the first jurists in the nation.

Women Judges: A History

History records indicate the first woman to serve as a jurist was Esther Morris, who in 1869 became a part-time justice of the peace in Wyoming at the South Pass Mining Camp (Hermann and Kelly 1988). In 1886, Carrie Burnham Kilgore (the first female graduate of the University of Pennsylvania Law School) was appointed a master in chancery (essentially, the administrative head of the court), making her the first woman to serve in a state judiciary (O'Connor 2000). The first elected woman judge was Catherine McCullough, who became a justice of the peace in Evanston, Illinois, in 1907 (Hermann and Kelly 1988).

In the early twentieth century, a few women were appointed to specialized courts, which had limited jurisdictions (Morrison 2002). For example, Georgia Bullock served on the Los Angeles Women's Court, which began in 1914 (Cook 1993). The court was developed during the Progressive Era, with the idea being that such a specialized court would help "fallen" women to learn and conform to the cultural gender role norms of the day if they were given special and separate treatment from male defendants. Judge Bullock believed that it was her duty as a judge on this court to help rather than merely punish women for small offenses, in hopes of reclaiming such women to society. Moreover, it was a duty that she believed was specially required of women at the time, remarking at the end of her first session: "The salvation of women must be through women" (Cook 1993, 146). Bullock later parlayed her experience on the women's court, along with the many connections she had made with various women's organizations of the day, to an appointment as a municipal judge in California in 1926 and then won election to the superior court in Los Angeles in 1932—a seat that she held for 25 years (Cook 1993).

The first woman to be appointed to the federal bench was Florence Allen, who in 1934 was nominated to the U.S. Court of Appeals (Sixth district) after having served 11 years on the Ohio Supreme Court (see *Profiles of Political Influence, Florence Allen, First Federal Judge*). The next woman appointed to the federal bench was Burnita Shelton Matthews, appointed to the District Court for the District of Columbia by President Truman in 1949. She was the first woman to serve as a federal trial court judge. An active suffragist, Matthews attended classes at National University (now George Washington University) while working in the Veterans' Administration. Upon her graduation in 1920, she could not find work in any law firm, so she began her own practice in Washington, D.C. (Ginsburg and Brill 1995). She also worked as counsel to the National Woman's Party, the suffragist organization founded by Alice Paul that later introduced the original text for the ERA. Upon announcement of her selection to the federal bench, one fellow judge was reported to have said, "Mrs. Matthews would make a good judge, [but there's] just one thing wrong; she's a woman" (ibid., 285). To show her faith in her fellow women, Matthews would only hire women as her law clerks (ibid.).

It was not until the 1960s that additional women were appointed to the federal bench, including Sarah Hughes, by President John F. Kennedy in 1961 (Mezey 2000). A close friend of Vice President Lyndon Johnson, it was Hughes who swore in Johnson as president following Kennedy's assassination. Shirley Mount Hufstedler was appointed by President Johnson in 1968 to the U.S. Court of Appeals for the Ninth Circuit. She is perhaps best known, however, as being the first Secretary of Education, after President Carter

PROFILES OF POLITICAL INFLUENCE

Florence Allen, First Federal Judge

The first woman to be appointed to the federal courts, Florence Allen grew up in rural Utah where her father was a surveyor for a mining company. A professor of Latin and Greek as well, Clarence Allen became Utah's first congressman while Florence was a young teenager. Florence went to live with her grandfather in Ohio at that time, attending a boarding school where he was headmaster. She entered college at the age of 16 at Ohio Western Reserve University, where she was elected class president and was an avid pianist. After spending time attending a music conservatory in Berlin, where she also worked as a music reporter and critic, she turned her attention to law school, attending Chicago University, where she was the only woman student in a class of about a hundred in 1909 (Ginsburg and Brill 1995). After finishing second in her class the first semester, she wrote that she was "amused to be visited at my work in the library by various young men who congratulated me and then told me I had a masculine mind" (Allen 1965, 24). She later transferred to New York University to complete her legal education, having been drawn to do work with the New York League for the Protection of Immigrants (Allen 1965).

Upon graduation, Allen was an active suffragist, organizing women in her home state of Ohio and delivering speeches on behalf of Carrie Chapman Catt and others. She successfully argued a suffrage case in front of the Ohio Supreme Court, although the bill that was later drafted in 1917 to allow women the right to vote in Ohio (which she helped to write) was rejected by voters in a referendum. In 1919, she was appointed as assistant county prosecutor in Cuyahoga County, Ohio, and when women were franchised in 1920, she ran for judge for the court of common pleas, which she won (ibid.). However, she soon refused an assignment as a judge in a newly created divorce division of the court, as she was not only more interested in criminal law but felt unqualified to judge divorce cases as an unmarried woman. Her refusal of the appointment brought her acclaim, as did her attitude that it was important to have women serve as judges. As Allen herself wrote, "When women of intelligence recognize their share in and their responsibility for the courts, a powerful moral backing is secured for the administration of justice" (Allen 1965, 48). Allen parlayed this popularity into a successful election onto the Ohio Supreme Court.

After 11 years on the Ohio Supreme Court, she was appointed by Franklin Delano Roosevelt to the Sixth Circuit Court of Appeals in 1934—a decision that was not supported by several male members of the circuit. Allen writes in her memoirs that when her appointment to the court was announced, one of her fellow judges "went to bed for two days" (Allen 1965, 95). She quickly won her

PROFILES OF POLITICAL INFLUENCE (CONTINUED)

colleagues' admiration, however, with her conscientious work. She garnered national attention as the author of the three-judge panel ruling that the federal government's actions in erecting dams and reservoirs in the Tennessee Valley Authority was constitutional. The United States Supreme Court later affirmed her judgment (Ginsburg and Brill 1995). Her actions in the case brought her to the attention of Eleanor Roosevelt, who advocated in one of her newspaper columns that Allen should be nominated to the Supreme Court. After retiring from the court of appeals, Allen became active in the International Bar Association and the International Federation of Women Lawyers (Allen 1965). ■

enlisted her to be the head of this newly created cabinet-level department in 1979 (Ginsburg and Brill 1995). Upon Carter's defeat, Hufstedler returned to private practice.

Women Judges in More Recent Times

It was not until Jimmy Carter's administration that women began to have more than a token presence in the federal judiciary. Presidents Nixon and Ford only managed to appoint two additional women to the federal bench. But under Carter's watch, 40 women were nominated and approved, due in part to his commitment to affirmative action principles, as he specifically sought out not just qualified female judges to appoint, but individuals of color as well. Carter was willing to reach deeper into the qualified pool of potential judges to ensure that more women were selected. He did so by for-going the traditional route of judicial selection: senatorial courtesy, in which senators of the president's party from states with openings in the judiciary make recommendations to the president. Instead, Carter established merit commissions to select potential nominees that included not just senators but also state bar association members, practicing attorneys, nonlawyers, women's and minority's organizations, sitting judges, and the ABA (Martin 1987). The result was that Carter's nontraditional nominees (both females and nonwhite males) were younger and less likely to be partners in traditional law firms (ibid.). Carter was also helped in this endeavor by the creation of 152 new judgeships by Congress under the Omnibus Judgeship Act (Mezey 2000) (see Tables 9.1 and 9.2).

President Ronald Reagan did not continue Carter's affirmative action policy toward women or minorities. Compared with Carter, for whom 15.5 percent of judicial appointees were women, Reagan appointed just 7.6 percent of women as federal judges (ibid.). The reasons for this were

---

> ▶ **TABLE 9.1**
>
> **U.S. District Court Appointments by Gender for Presidents Carter Through George W. Bush**
>
> | President | Percentage of Female Judges |
> |-----------|------------------------------|
> | Carter | 14.4% |
> | Reagan | 8.3 |
> | Bush | 19.6 |
> | Clinton | 28.5 |
> | W. Bush | 20.7 |
>
> Source: The Federal Judicial Center. www.fjc.gov

varied, but many believed it was due to Reagan's emphasis on ideology in selecting judges. Because Reagan made conservatism an important factor in his decision to appoint judges, there were likely fewer potential women nominees to select. Also, Reagan abandoned the merit system put in place by Carter, reverting to the more traditional system of senatorial courtesy (Martin 1987).

Reagan's successor, George H. W. Bush, did a much better job of appointing women to the federal bench, in part because he relied less on ideological purity as a factor for appointments. Bush was also aided, as Carter had been, by the establishment of more judicial positions nationwide. Bush appointed women to more than 19 percent of federal judgeships during his one term in office (Mezey 2000).

However, President Bill Clinton has had the best record of judicial appointments in terms of women in the judiciary and was aided (like Carter and Bush before him) by the establishment of new judgeships by Congress. Making it a top priority to diversify the bench, Clinton more than doubled the number of women serving in the federal judiciary in his time in office (Palmer 2001). For his first term, 52.1 percent of his appointments were nontraditional

---

> ▶ **TABLE 9.2**
>
> **U.S. Appellate Court Appointments by Gender for Presidents Carter Through George W. Bush**
>
> | President | Percentage of Female Judges |
> |-----------|------------------------------|
> | Carter | 19.6% |
> | Reagan | 5.1 |
> | Bush | 18.9 |
> | Clinton | 32.8 |
> | G. W. Bush | 27.9 |
>
> Source: Goldman et al. (2003); Federal Judicial Center (2009).

(either female or nonwhite). Clinton named 87 women (28.5 percent) as district court appointees. The percentage of female appointees under Clinton to the circuit court or court of appeals was even higher—32.8 percent. When Clinton began office, approximately 1 in 10 federal judges was female; when he left, it was 1 in 5 (Goldman et al. 2001; Spill and Bratton 2001). Unlike Reagan, Clinton cared less about the ideology of judges and concentrated more on diversity. One result is that Clinton's nontraditional appointees (including minority men) were more likely to come from diverse backgrounds than the traditional ones. For example, they were more likely to have backgrounds in government or the state judiciary or to have prosecutorial experience than were white males (ibid.). Despite having impeccable credentials, however, one study found that under divided government, Clinton's female judicial nominees were delayed longer in their processing under the GOP Senate than were his male nominees (Hartley 2001).

President George W. Bush also had a good track record of appointing women to the bench—coming close to, but not quite matching, Clinton's numbers in terms of women. During his two terms in office, out of 327 judicial appointments, 77 (23.5 percent) were women (Federal Judicial Center 2009). As of March 2009, women currently make up 26.4 percent of active district judges and 28.7 percent of active appellate judges serving on the federal bench (ibid.).

Presidents Reagan, Clinton, and Obama share the distinction of appointing the only three women to serve on the United States Supreme Court. In 1981, keeping a promise he made while campaigning for president (in part to appeal to women voters), Reagan appointed Sandra Day O'Connor as the first female justice of the Supreme Court. In her short time as a state Supreme Court justice in Arizona, O'Connor had developed a reputation as a solid conservative on many issues that were important to the Reagan administration, especially federalism. Yet she was a moderate on issues such as abortion, which led women's organizations to support her nomination while pro-life groups opposed her (Palmer 1991; Behuniak-Long 1992). The National Association of Women Judges, which was formed in 1979 in part to advocate for the appointment of a woman to the United States Supreme Court, was also pleased with O'Connor's nomination.

In 1993, President Bill Clinton appointed Ruth Bader Ginsburg as his first nominee to the Supreme Court. At the time, Ginsburg was serving her twelfth year as an appellate judge on the federal Court of Appeals for the District of Columbia Circuit. Ginsburg was brought to Clinton's attention as a possible nominee, in part, due to the efforts of her husband Martin Ginsburg, a prominent tax attorney and law professor at Georgetown University. To help publicize his wife as a possible candidate, Martin Ginsburg began a letter-writing campaign, contacting various dignitaries and legal scholars to call or write the White House in support of Ginsburg's candidacy as a Supreme Court justice (O'Connor and Palmer 2001). Upon his wife's nomination, Martin Ginsburg told the *Washington Post:* "If there was something that I could have done to be helpful, I would have done it, because I think my wife is super, and the

President couldn't have made a better appointment than the one he just made" (O'Connor and Palmer 2001, 264).

Tale of Two Justices: Sandra Day O'Connor and Ruth Bader Ginsburg

Born in 1930, Sandra Day O'Connor grew up on the Lazy B cattle ranch on the Arizona–New Mexico border (Lane 2004). During the school year, she lived with her grandparents and attended private school in El Paso, Texas, but she returned to the ranch during the summers—where she grew up learning to ride horses and spent time with her father and his cowboys during their work, no doubt making her comfortable working and competing with men (Maveety 1996; Lane 2004). Upon graduating high school at age 16, O'Connor attended Stanford University in 1946, earning a joint B.S. in economics and law degree in a six-year program. It was at Stanford Law where she met her husband and was a classmate of former Chief Justice William Rehnquist. Despite graduating magna cum laude, the only job offer she received upon completing law school was as a legal secretary.

Instead of private practice, O'Connor sought work in the public sector upon returning with her husband to Arizona. She found work as a deputy county attorney—but only because she volunteered to work for free until a paid position opened (Lane 2004). Later, she took a leave from practicing law to raise her three small sons from 1960 to 1965. While raising her family, O'Connor was active in state Republican Party politics and in community

The first two women appointed to the Supreme Court—Sandra Day O'Connor (left) and Ruth Bader Ginsburg—served together on the Supreme Court from 1993 to 2006.

service organizations such as the Junior League. In 1965, she returned to work full time as a state assistant attorney general—a position she gained due to her political contacts—and was later appointed to a vacant seat in the state senate in 1969. Her time in the senate was successful, as she won reelection twice and was the first woman nationally to be elected as majority leader in a state senate (Maveety 1996). It is notable that during her tenure on the Supreme Court, O'Connor was the only justice on the Supreme Court with elected political experience. It was this experience, particularly as a consensus-building majority leader in a legislative body where Republicans enjoyed just a one-seat advantage—that many believe shaped her performance on the Court (ibid.). In addition to making her respectful of states' rights, O'Connor was keen on crafting compromise decisions that brought the other justices together—an important dimension to her jurisprudence as O'Connor was often the critical fifth and swing vote on many decisions (Lane 2004).

In some ways, Ruth Bader Ginsburg's personal story differs dramatically from O'Connor—but in other ways, it is very similar. Ginsburg was born in Brooklyn in 1933, and was taught by her mother to be independent and scholarly despite the gender norms that pervaded their ethnic neighborhood (Campbell 2002). Ginsburg's academic success in New York's public schools earned her a scholarship to Cornell University, where she met her husband Martin Ginsburg, whom she married in 1954 after graduating first in her class (ibid.). Ginsburg followed her husband to Harvard Law School—he had just completed his first year there—where she was one of just nine women in a law class of 500 (Ginsburg 1997).

Ginsburg excelled at Harvard, and she earned a coveted spot on the *Harvard Law Review*. Her academic performance was all the more remarkable because not only was she the mother of a young child at the time, but also in her second year, her husband developed testicular cancer. She maintained her high level of work while also taking notes for him when he missed classes and typing his papers. When Martin Ginsburg accepted a job at a New York law firm, she transferred to Columbia Law School for her final year, graduating at the top of her class. As Ginsburg recalls, no woman taught any classes while she was attending law school at Harvard or Columbia (Ginsburg 1997).

Similar to the situation faced by Sandra Day O'Connor, not a single law firm would hire Ginsburg upon her graduation, and despite recommendations from her Columbia professors, she was denied a chance to clerk with Supreme Court Justice Felix Frankfurter. She accepted a position as a clerk with a federal district court judge in New York and then went into academia, becoming a law professor at Rutgers University. She later became the first tenured woman faculty member at Columbia Law School (Ginsburg 1997).

Unlike Sandra Day O'Connor, Ginsburg did not work in the public sector nor was she involved in elected politics. Instead, in addition to becoming a notable law professor, she also was founder and general counsel to the American Civil Liberties Union's (ACLU) Women's Rights Project (Campbell 2002). While still teaching at Rutgers, and realizing that women faculty members were paid less than men, Ginsburg was part of a class action lawsuit that brought women's salaries on par with men (Ginsburg 1997). At the same time, the ACLU was beginning to hear similar complaints about discriminatory behavior from other women in different fields, and they recruited Ginsburg to help with these sex discrimination cases under the auspices of the Women's Rights Project. As part of the ACLU, Ginsburg helped in 34 cases at the Supreme Court level (Campbell 2002).

Moreover, she successfully argued five out of six such cases in front of the Supreme Court, including the pivotal 1971 *Reed v. Reed* case, which was the first decision to establish that laws that segregated on sex-based differences were "entitled to some sort of scrutiny under the Fourteenth Amendment" (O'Connor and Clark 1999, 273). In other words, this case called into question the constitutionality of statutes that allowed for gender discrimination. Given Ginsburg's successful and prodigious record as a litigator, professor, and legal scholar, she was appointed to the U.S. Court of Appeals for the District of Columbia Circuit in 1980 by Jimmy Carter.

Upon joining the Supreme Court as the second female justice, Ginsburg and O'Connor quickly became close friends, despite their ideological and partisan differences. Ginsburg is solidly in the liberal to moderate camp of the Court, whereas O'Connor leaned more to the conservative side, although she was typically the key deciding vote on a number of issues on the Court. Both women, however, shared a similar voting record when it came to issues that affected women disproportionately, such as abortion and sex discrimination. In 2006, O'Connor retired from the bench to spend time with her ailing husband, who suffers from Alzheimer's disease, although she still hears oral arguments occasionally as a substitute judge in the federal appellate courts, following in the tradition of other retired Supreme Court justices (Brust 2008). In February 2009, Ginsburg took a brief leave-of-absence to undergo pancreatic cancer surgery, which doctors deemed successful, and returned to work by the end of the month. Still, at 77 and with a previous record of colorectal cancer, many wonder if she will soon retire from the bench like O'Connor.

Despite O'Connor and Ginsburg's high profile positions, women more generally still have a long way to go in terms of representation in the judiciary. Even several years after her appointment, Ginsburg noted that she and O'Connor were sometimes confused by counsel during oral arguments. Ginsburg recounts that in 1996 the acting solicitor general three times called her Justice O'Connor. Ginsburg writes that "The National Association of Women Judges, anticipating such confusion might occur, presented Justice O'Connor and me with T-shirts the month after my appointment. Hers read: I'm Sandra, not Ruth; mine read, I'm Ruth, not Sandra" (Ginsburg 1997, 15).

But O'Connor, Ginsburg, and other female judges remain hopeful that more women will be tapped to take seats in the judiciary. As Ginsburg noted in an address to Washington University in 2001:

> Since the 1970s, Supreme Court Justices, in common with judges in other courts, have become increasingly aware of a sea change in United States society. Their still evolving enlightenment has been advanced by the briefs filed in Court, the women lawyers and jurists they nowadays routinely encounter,

and perhaps most deeply by the aspirations of the women, particularly the daughters and granddaughters, in their own families and communities. Anticipating the way it will be, the Court now has in the Justices' robing room a women's bathroom equal in size to the men's. (Ginsburg 2001, 425)

O'Connor, Ginsburg and Beyond

In the fall of 2005, President George W. Bush nominated the woman who served as his White House Counsel, Harriet Miers, to fill the spot being vacated by Sandra Day O'Connor. After much criticism from conservatives in the Republican Party, who worried that she was neither sufficiently experienced nor conservative enough for the job, Miers eventually withdrew her nomination (Halloran 2005). Bush then nominated Samuel A. Alito, Jr., to fill O'Connor's seat. He was confirmed by the U.S. Senate on January 31, 2006 (Romano and Eilperin 2006). Bush had no other opportunities to fill a Supreme Court seat during the remainder of his term, so the number of women on the Supreme Court in January 2009, when he left office, stood at one.

Women's rights activists were hopeful that President Barack Obama, once given the opportunity, would appoint another woman to the bench. That moment arrived fairly soon in his presidency, when Justice David Souter announced in April 2009 his intention to step down from the Supreme Court. In May 2009, Obama announced Judge Sonia Sotomayor to be his pick for the Supreme Court. Sotomayor, a U.S. Appellate Court judge with 17 years experience on the federal bench and a Yale Law School grad, is not only the third woman to be appointed to the Supreme Court, she is also the first Hispanic and has a compelling life story having been raised by a widowed mother in public housing in the Bronx. Her parents were originally from Puerto Rico and her father died when she was nine. Sotomayor graduated from Princeton University (on a full scholarship) *summa cum laude* in 1976 and after law school worked as a prosecutor in New York City and in private practice before her first judicial appointment by President George H.W. Bush in 1991. Her Supreme Court appointment was met (largely) with enthusiasm from both women's rights organizations and Latino groups (less so from conservative organizations). She was confirmed in August 2009, although she did not receive overwhelming support from Republican senators, many of whom stated their objections over her past support of affirmative action (see earlier discussion in this chapter under "Why the Courts are Important"). Sotomayor's appointment to the Supreme Court was also lauded by former Justice Sandra Day O'Connor:

> I am very happy that another woman is being appointed. I think that's very important. I was terribly disappointed when I retired in 2006 not to be replaced by a woman. We have to remember that slightly more than 50 percent of us in this country have two X chromosomes and I think it doesn't hurt to look at our national institutions and see women represented. I don't think two females on the Supreme Court is enough, but it is certainly better than one. (quoted in Lodge 2009)

The 2009–2010 Session of the Michigan State Supreme Court. Michigan was just one of three states, including Tennessee and Wisconsin, in which women justices outnumbered men on the state's highest court in 2009; the highest court of appeal in the District of Columbia also had a majority of women justices.

In April 2010, President Barack Obama was again given the chance to alter the makeup of the Supreme Court with the retirement announcement by Justice John Paul Stevens, who has served on the nation's highest court since his appointment by President Gerald Ford in 1975. The following month, Obama selected a second woman nominee, Elena Kagan, whom he had appointed U.S. Solicitor General in his early months in office. The U.S. Solicitor General is considered the government's top lawyer, tasked with the job of representing the United States in cases that appear before the United States Supreme Court, and hence is often referred to as the "10th Justice" given the frequency with which he or she interacts with the nation's highest court. At the time this book went to press, her confirmation hearings were set for late June 2010, and many predicted that her odds of confirmation are high given that she already was approved by the Senate in 2009 for her position with Office of the Solicitor General. If confirmed, for the first time in history, women would hold three seats on the Supreme Court.

Women in the State Judiciary

Given that the United States Supreme Court hears few appeals (typically, out of thousands of requests, the Court agrees to hear fewer than 100 annually), state courts of last resort are increasingly important when it comes to establishing public policy. How do women fare on these vital courts? According to the National Center for State Courts, as of January 2009, women currently make up 31 percent of justices serving on state courts of last resort; moreover, out of 52 such courts (Texas and Oklahoma have two such courts, divided into the supreme court and the court of criminal appeals), 19 women serve as chief justices. Historically, two courts—Michigan and Minnesota—held a majority of female justices for short time periods in the 1990s. As of January 2009, the state supreme courts in Michigan, Tennessee, Wisconsin, and the District of Columbia have a majority of female justices. Table 9.3 shows a gender breakdown of justices on state courts of last resort for 2009.

What factors determine the number of women sitting on state supreme courts? Is there a link between diversity on the bench and the type of method that the court uses to select judges? Unlike at the federal level, where judges are appointed by the president and approved by the Senate, selection of state judges varies by state—although selection generally boils down to two major methods: election and appointment (Glick 1999). In 26 states, all or most judgeships are decided by either partisan (9 states) or nonpartisan (17 states) elections. In reality, many of these elections are noncontested, with incumbents carrying an extraordinary advantage. Moreover, in many cases, incumbent judges are often

TABLE 9.3

Members of State Courts of Last Resort, by Sex as of January 1, 2009

	Percentage of Female Justices	Female Chief Justice?
Alabama	33%	Y
Alaska	20	Y
Arizona	40	Y
Arkansas	29	N
California	43	N
Colorado	43	Y
Connecticut	43	Y
Delaware	20	N
Florida	29	Y
Georgia	29	Y
Hawaii	20	N
Idaho	0	N
Illinois	29	N
Indiana	0	N
Iowa	14	Y
Kansas	29	N
Kentucky	29	N
Louisiana	43	Y

(Continued)

	Percentage of Female Justices	Female Chief Justice?
Maine	29	Y
Maryland	43	N
Massachusetts	43	Y
Michigan	57	Y
Minnesota	29	N
Mississippi	11	N
Missouri	43	Y
Montana	14	N
Nebraska	14	N
Nevada	29	N
New Hampshire	20	N
New Jersey	43	N
New Mexico	20	N
New York	43	N
North Carolina	43	Y
North Dakota	40	N
Ohio	43	N
Oklahoma Supreme Court	11	N
Oklahoma Court of Criminal Appeals	20	N
Oregon	29	N
Pennsylvania	14	N
Rhode Island	20	Y
South Carolina	20	Y
South Dakota	20	N
Tennessee	60	Y
Texas Supreme Court	11	N
Texas Court of Criminal Appeals	44	Y
Utah	40	Y
Vermont	40	N
Virginia	29	N
Washington	44	N
West Virginia	40	N
Wisconsin	57	Y
Wyoming	20	N
Total	**31**	**20**

Courts range in size from 5 to 11 members; there are a total of 349 state supreme court justices, of whom 109 are female.

Source: The National Center for State Courts. www.ncsc.org.

appointed by the governor, as vacancies on the bench frequently occur prior to elections. Thus, even in states with no appointive system, governors have a large hand in shaping the judiciary. The other states use some sort of appointment selection process. In four states, all or most judgeships are done by gubernatorial appointment, whereas two others use legislative appointment. The most popular method of judicial selection at the state level, however, is the merit selection or Missouri Plan used by 18 states. This plan involves a merit panel that makes suggestions to the governor for nominees for state judicial vacancies. Once appointed, these judges serve a trial one-year term and then face a retention election asking voters whether they should be retained in office (they face no opposition). Rarely do these appointed judges lose such retention elections.

Political scientists have examined whether the method of judicial selection at the state level—appointment or election—is related to the number of women serving on the bench at the state supreme court level and, in some cases, state appellate courts. One theory is that appointive systems in general tend to depress diversity in state courts, because such systems tend to "favor the status quo by perpetuating the dominance of elites in the judiciary, thus decreasing judicial opportunities for political minorities who may not have the conventional legal backgrounds or experience" (Hurwitz and Lanier 2001, 86). Alternatively, others argue appointive systems could be more beneficial to women because elite decision makers might be more cognizant of the need for greater diversity than voters, leading to an increase in the number of women in the judiciary (Alozie 1996; Hurwitz and Lanier 2003). While women have greatly increased their numbers on state appellate courts, irrespective of selection method, the recent work of Margaret Williams (2007) finds that the merit system actually depresses women's representation on the bench. She writes that "states using merit selection to fill the appellate judiciary, on average, see three fewer women on the appellate bench relative to similar states using partisan elections to fill the appellate bench" (1199). However, the appointment system does appear to boost gender diversity on state supreme courts in one case: when such courts are all male. Yet once women have been appointed to a vacancy in an all-male state supreme court, "the chance that a woman will be appointed to the bench drops significantly once the court achieves any degree of gender diversity" (Bratton and Spill 2002, 516).

Few studies have examined the gender dimensions of judicial campaigns among states that use elections to select state supreme court justices. However, McCarthy (2001) found that although some female judicial candidates did campaign on the theme that more women should be elected to help diversify state supreme courts in the 1980s and early 1990s, as more women have come to serve on state supreme courts by the late 1990s, the gender of the candidate rarely becomes an issue in campaigns. McCarthy's analysis of judicial campaign platforms in recent years found that candidates stress their professional experience and judicial philosophy during campaigns—not their gender (or the gender of their opponent). However, the effect that such campaign themes actually have on the outcome of elections is tenuous given the low salience of judicial campaigns.

What appears to count more than selection method when it comes to the presence of women on state courts of last resort is the number of judges on the bench, as scholars have noted a positive relationship between the size of the court and female presence on it (Alozie 1996; Hurwitz and Lanier 2003). The more seats that are available to be filled, the more opportunities women have to serve on the bench. Greater representation of women on state supreme and appellate courts has also come about because of their greater numbers in the legal profession (Williams 2007). Not surprisingly, ideology is also related to greater representation for women on courts of appeals: the more liberal the state, the more likely that women will be justices on state courts of last resort (ibid.). Moreover, women have not only increased their presence in the eligibility pool from which judges are considered, but also the criteria for eligibility have expanded in recent years. For instance, women and men state supreme court justices often take a different path to the bench, with women being more likely to serve in the public sector, whereas men are more likely to come from a private law practice. Moreover, women justices are less likely than their male counterparts to have served in elected political office (Martin and Pyle 2002). These findings suggest that the traditional eligibility pool has shifted to allow for people with more diverse backgrounds, especially women and minorities, to be considered for service on the high court.

In addition to state courts of last resort and appellate courts, all states have trial courts, of which there are approximately 11,600 judges as of 2009, and some (but not all) states have nonattorney courts, or state limited and special jurisdiction courts, which have approximately 5,100 judges (NAWJ n.d.). Such nonattorney courts handle small claims (or small dollar amount) considerations or minor issues such as traffic violations. As a result, most states that have such courts allow nonattorneys to be judges. Women's representation on such courts has grown significantly in the past three decades. Epstein (1993) estimates that in 1983, about 2 percent of trial court judges were women; Cook (1984) estimated that same year that about 8 percent of limited jurisdiction court judges were women. More than a decade later, another study found that about 10 percent of state trial court judges were women (Githens 1995). According to *The American Bench: Judges of the Nation* (2009), 26 percent of the nearly 17,000 state court judges are women in 2009, although their numbers vary tremendously from state to state. Specifically, women make up 23 percent of state general jurisdiction courts and 29 percent of state limited and special jurisdiction courts.

How do women fare when getting selected to local courts? One case study examined the process for selecting trial court judges in Baltimore, Maryland, written by Marianne Githens, a political science professor who, from 1983 to 1988, sat on a nominating commission that was responsible for recommending candidates to the governor to serve as trial and appellate court judges (Githens 1995). During her service on the commission, Githens witnessed numerous examples of gender (and racial) bias, noting that the professional credentials of white male applicants were discussed in greater detail than nontraditional applicants. While women's credentials for the job were discussed by commissioners, so, too, were their appearance and their personal life in contrast to the men under consideration. For example, one commissioner raised an issue about an unmarried mother who was applying, arguing that her appointment would send a "bad message to the public and diminish respect for the bench" (Githens 1995, 18). In many cases, Githens noted that some commissioners expressed concern about women's ability to control a courtroom because of "their small voices and stature" (ibid., 19). Despite such gender bias, the commission recommended that two-thirds of the female applicants be nominated for judgeships (though only half ended up being appointed by the governor). Githens argues that women fared better because those females who sought consideration to be judges were much more highly qualified than white males in the eligibility pool (only about one in five males was nominated from the same committee). She believes this was the case because qualified white males, in particular, had more attractive and lucrative options available to them in the private sector and were, thus, less willing to become state trial judges—indicating that gender bias may still be an indirect problem when it comes to the appointment of women to the bench. One study she cites found that in 1989, 69 percent of women judges in Maryland indicated that they were aware of gender bias in the judicial selection process (Githens 1995).

In recent years, women's representation on general jurisdiction trial courts has increased, and women's representation is positively related to the percentage of female lawyers in the state (Williams 2007). Unlike higher state courts, merit selection does not appear to be related to the number of women serving on trial court benches; however, states that use non-partisan elections have higher rates of women serving than states that use partisan elections to select judges.

Women have begun to move away from their token status on the bench in both the federal and state judiciary, regardless of whether they are appointed or elected to serve. As more women serve as judges, attention has focused on their impact in the judiciary. In what ways does it matter that more women now serve as judges? Are women judges different from their male counterparts? Does having more women on the bench translate into more representation for women's causes?

THE DIFFERENCE WOMEN JUDGES MAKE

Scholars focus on two primary questions when it comes to comparing men and women judges (Palmer 2001). First, do women judges use a different style or "voice" when it comes to legal reasoning? Second, do women judges make different decisions than men, especially when it comes to policy issues that are potentially of greater interest to women? For example, are they more sensitive to issues of sex and race discrimination?

Do Women Judges Use A "Different Voice"?

Few books in recent years have had as much of an impact on various fields in the social sciences (or have been as controversial) as Carol Gilligan's *In a Different Voice: Psychological Theory and Women's Development* (1982).

A thorough analysis of Gilligan's work is beyond the scope of this chapter, but an overview of her theory and how it could apply to the judiciary is relevant here. Gilligan's theory grapples with moral development among men and women, and how men and women often differ when it comes to speaking and thinking about moral problems and the relationship between oneself and the larger community. Through interviews about conceptions of self and morality, Gilligan found that women often thought about such problems differently than men, regardless of their age or social status. For most men, morality is viewed in terms of fairness, with a concern rooted in individual rights. For most women, caretaking rather than fairness is more important, and they tend to place greater emphasis not on the formal rules of society in deciding what is moral but more on an understanding of responsibilities that they have toward the larger community.

Gilligan argues that these conceptions of morality are rooted in childhood, as studies that focus on how girls and boys play show that when quarrels arise during games, boys are preoccupied—in a legal sense—with the rules of games, whereas girls are more tolerant in their attitudes toward the rules (Gilligan 1982). Boys care more about competition, and girls care more about cooperation. Over time, Gilligan argues that men and women begin to see larger moral problems differently. For women, she writes:

> . . . the moral problem arises from conflicting responsibilities rather than from competing rights and requires for its resolution a mode of thinking that is contextual and narrative rather than formal and abstract. This conception of morality as concerned with the activity of care centers moral development around the understanding of responsibility and relationships, just as the conception of morality as fairness ties moral development to the understanding of rights and rules.   (19)

In essence, to solve problems men seek an answer available in existing rules, whereas women seek solutions that maintain their relationships. While Gilligan notes that most people use both "moral" voices at one time or another, women and men tend to emphasize one voice much more often.

Given its emphasis on reason and decision making, legal scholars interested in the impact of gender on decision making have analyzed whether Gilligan's theory has any applicability to jurisprudence. If Gilligan is correct, then we may find that women judges reach their decisions in a different manner than do men, bringing to the bench a different perspective. For example, Suzanna Sherry has argued that women could bring to the bench a "feminine" (*not* feminist) perspective, closely linked to what in political philosophy is known as the classical republican tradition (Sherry 1986). Unlike the modern, liberal philosophy that supports the current legal system, with its emphasis on individual rights and liberties, this classical tradition is communitarian and contextual. A feminine legal paradigm, according to Sherry, would be one that emphasizes connectedness, context, and responsibility rather than autonomy or rights.

A virtual cottage industry has developed around whether this "different voice" is evident in the jurisprudence of the Supreme Court's first female justice, Sandra Day O'Connor. While O'Connor generally sided with her fellow conservatives on the High Court, her tendency to write concurring and separate opinions that rejected the reasoning of her colleagues led some scholars to speculate that she worked from a "feminine" perspective (Sherry 1986; Behuniak-Long 1992; Palmer 2001). Sherry (1986) writes that in many of her decisions, especially those regarding freedom of religion, "O'Connor often rejects bright-line rules and occasionally makes explicit her preference for contextual determinations" (ibid., 605). Sherry's legal analysis of several of O'Connor's decisions shows that, in some cases, O'Connor favored the concerns of the community over the rights of the individual. Other scholars point to her decisions in abortion cases as more evidence of O'Connor's unique feminine voice. Rather than asserting a woman's clear right to have an abortion—as feminist scholars would hope—O'Connor upheld some state restrictions on abortion, but only if they did not present an undue burden on a woman's fundamental right to seek an abortion (Sullivan and Goldzwig 1996). This "balancing-of-interests" approach to abortion is an attempt, according to some, to "circumvent the divisive polarity of her colleagues' ideologically driven tests" on the controversial issue (Maveety 1996, 33). Those who maintain that O'Connor spoke with this accommodationist, feminine voice criticized her from both sides of the spectrum: Some on the right believe she inhibited the Court's ability to form a solid conservative majority, whereas others on the left believe she undermined any potential for a more femin*ist* jurisprudence on the Court (Behuniak-Long 1992).

Still others question whether O'Connor's voice on the High Court was truly distinct, and, if so, if it was colored mainly by her gender. On 40 different equal protection cases, for example, Aliota (1995) finds that O'Connor's voice or voting pattern was not unique from fellow justices—in direct contrast to Sherry's work on O'Connor that focused on far fewer numbers of such cases. O'Connor's proclivity to disagree with her fellow conservatives, some argue, may not stem from any feminine voice but could be because she was simply less conservative in these areas (Davis 1993; Maveety 1996). Moreover, others argue that her centrist or accommodationist tendencies in some cases may have stemmed more from her political experiences as a former majority leader in the Arizona State Senate than from her gender (Maveety 1996; Palmer 2001; Lane 2004).

Extending the "different voices" theory to other judges has also yielded few corroborating findings (no such studies have been extended to Ruth Bader Ginsburg as of yet). Sue Davis (1992–1993) compared the legal reasoning of a group of women and men appellate judges from the Ninth Circuit Court of Appeals. For example, in discrimination cases, she looked for evidence that women judges, embodying a female voice according to Gilligan's theory, would be more likely to emphasize the importance of full membership in the community in their decisions, with the notion that exclusion (through discrimination) is unacceptable. Alternatively, a "male" voice in discrimination cases would show up in the decisions of judges when discrimination was discussed in terms of the "denial of personal autonomy of the victims," treating equality not in terms of connection but in terms of independence. Yet while Davis found that sometimes women do speak in a different voice in their decisions, so do men. Therefore, she found little evidence to suggest that "the presence of women judges will transform the very nature of law" (171). David Allen and Diane Wall (1993) also looked for, but failed to find, evidence of a different voice among women judges at the state supreme court level by examining whether women justices were more likely to pen dissenting decisions, which would indicate that there was a lack of common ground between women and men on the bench. Although women were somewhat more likely to write dissents than men, particularly in criminal rights and economic liberty cases, there was no pattern that suggested that women state supreme court justices consistently used different legal reasoning to decide cases—although they did find that women justices were uniformly more supportive of expanding women's rights, regardless of party.

Generally speaking, empirical studies have not gathered much evidence to verify that women judges have a different voice when it comes to legal reasoning. Why not? Gilligan's theory itself might be flawed, or may not be appropriate for application to jurisprudence. Palmer (2001) argues that failure to find a unique, different voice among women judges could be linked to socialization experiences women face in law school: Law school is structured to teach students to think about law in similar ways, and women who might otherwise wish to use any alternative approach to legal reasoning—one that is more contextual than abstract—may abandon it to become successful in their field. Moreover, once women become judges, the nature of the legal process, whereby judges "examine the facts of a legal dispute, identify the features of those facts, determine what legal principles should apply, and apply those principles to the facts" may subvert any sex-based differences (Davis 1992–1993, 151).

Empirical Studies: The Impact of Sex on Jurisprudence

One argument in support of having more women appointed or elected to the judiciary is that it would enhance women's representation in government. This argument, though, is predicated on the assumption that women judges will do a better job of "acting for" or representing other women's interests than men judges. Although some empirical evidence suggests that female legislators are more inclined to initiate or support policies that disproportionately affect women or children (see Chapter 7 on Women in Congress and the State Legislatures), can the same be said for female judges? In other words, do women judges decide cases differently from their male counterparts in such a way that the interests or rights of women are advanced? This question has less to do with the reasoning of cases—unlike those empirical studies reviewed earlier that analyzed whether Gilligan's "different voice" theory was applicable to judicial decision making—and more to do with the actual outcomes of cases. For instance, do women jurists make judgments that can be interpreted as more liberal or more conservative? Do women judges decide cases in such a way that women's rights or other minority rights are expanded? Given that women are most frequently the victims of harassment, for example, women judges may be more sympathetic to victims of sexual or employment discrimination than men judges.

Early studies found few differences among men and women judges—or found that women judges were *less* likely to make decisions that disproportionately affected the interests of women in the ways that feminists had hoped. For example, one study of local trial judges in a large northeastern city who served from 1971 through 1979 found that men and women judges did not differ with respect to conviction or sentencing behavior—with one exception (Gruhl, Spohn, and Welch 1981). Male judges were much less likely than women trial court judges to sentence women to prison, causing the authors to label their behavior as "paternalistic" (ibid.). Another study focused on men and women on the federal bench, examining 12 matched sets of judges appointed by President Carter (Walker and Barrow 1985). These judges served in the same district and were of the same race. The idea behind the study was that if differences were found between the matched pairs of judges, the likely explanation for such differences would be due to gender since they were similar in most other respects. Walker and Barrow found no real evidence that these female district court judges were more likely to "act for" other women when it came to cases involving sexual harassment, gender discrimination, maternity rights, or affirmative action. Although female district judges were more likely to be liberal on economic regulation cases, in that they deferred more often to the government's position in such cases, they were actually *less* supportive than male district judges of personal rights claims (at least in some cases).

Why did early studies find that women judges were not more likely than men judges to represent the interests of women in their decision making? On the one hand, given their minority status within the judiciary—both at the state and federal levels—there is some concern that women judges would not want to stand out or appear too different from their male counterparts. As "tokens" on the court, women judges may feel pressured to conform to a more male model of judicial behavior, causing them to act more conservatively in such cases (Martin 1993a). On the other hand, the early findings that show a lack of support among women judges for female litigants could simply be a result of having too few female judges to examine.

Later studies of women judges, which have come about as their numbers have greatly increased, have shown mixed results when it comes to gender differences among judges. One study of state supreme court justices found that women judges vote more liberally than male judges on two types of cases not necessarily associated with women's issues: obscenity and death penalty sentencing. However, those gender differences appeared only among Democratic judges, as Republican men and women of the bench tended to vote the same (Songer and Crews-Meyer 2000).

Most studies—but not all—show that women judges have been found to be more supportive of plaintiffs in employment discrimination cases (even after controlling for party) whether at the U.S. Court of Appeals (Davis, Haire, and Songer 1993; Songer, Davis, and Haire 1994) or on state supreme courts (Gryski, Main, and Dixon 1986; Allen and Wall 1993). Moreover, the presence of at least one female justice on state supreme courts results in the court being more likely to find the presence of sex discrimination in noncriminal cases (Gryski, Main, and Dixon 1986).

At the Supreme Court level, the appointment of both Sandra Day O'Connor and Ruth Bader Ginsburg led to increased support among male justices for sex discrimination cases (O'Connor and Segal 1990; Palmer 2002). Further analysis of the impact of O'Connor and Ginsburg on sex discrimination cases shows that both justices wrote a disproportionate number of majority opinions in the areas of women's rights: Between 1993 and 2000, they wrote on half of the 12 cases in this area (Palmer 2002). Even though O'Connor and Ginsburg differed with respect to many of their decisions— they usually voted together about 66 percent of the time—they voted together 90 percent of the time in favor of women's rights cases (ibid.). Indeed, some women's groups have been alarmed at the more conservative swing taken by the court with respect to women's rights since O'Connor's retirement. In 2007, the Supreme Court in *Ledbetter v. Goodyear* narrowly upheld a lower court decision that prevented women from seeking back pay over pay discrimination alleged to have occurred years earlier. In a stinging dissent, Justice Ginsburg argued that the majority was either indifferent to or failed to recognize the "insidious" way that women can be subject to pay discrimination and she called on Congress to pass legislation that would allow victims of past pay discrimination to be able to seek justice under Title VII of the Civil Rights Act (Barnes 2007). Congress did, in fact, pass such legislation, and the Lilly Ledbetter Fair Pay Act—named after the plaintiff of the Supreme Court case—was the first piece of legislation President Barack Obama signed in January 2009.

On the other hand, studies of justices on the Michigan Supreme Court, one of the few high state courts to have had a majority of women serve on its bench, find that although women justices generally do make more liberal decisions than men, on "feminist" issue cases party matters more than gender. One exception is for cases concerning divorce, in which women justices are more likely than men to support a woman's claim (Martin and Pyle 2000). Segal (2000) used the same research design employed by Walker and Barrow in their study of Carter appointees. In this case, Segal selected 13 matched gender pairs of Clinton appointees, and found, like Walker and Barrow, few gender differences among Clinton appointees. If anything, Clinton's female appointees were more likely to rule against women's claims than were his male appointees in those districts, leading Segal to conclude that Clinton's female appointees "are not inclined to support a judicial role that is particularly sensitive to the claims of various out-groups in American society" (149). Finally, one recent study of trial judges found that although younger judges and Democratic judges were more likely to find in favor of plaintiffs in sexual discrimination cases, gender was not a significant predictor in statistical models that examined such cases (Kulik, Perry, and Pepper 2003).

How do women judges themselves feel about taking on a "representative" role on behalf of women more generally? The National Association of Women

Judges conducted a survey of women judges in 1989 that asked its members their attitudes on different representative roles women judges might play (Martin 1993b). Overwhelming majorities indicated the need for more women to serve as judges (98 percent) and believed that women bring important and unique qualities to the bench. For example, three in four judges agreed that women judges "worked to heighten the sensitivity of other judges to the problems of gender bias" and that they "influence attitudes of their male colleagues toward cases involving women" (Martin 1993b, 171). Moreover, nearly three-quarters of judges felt that they had "increased their male judicial colleagues' respect for professional women" and more than half indicated that they had "made a difference in the sensitivity of their judicial colleagues to the consequences of gender discrimination"(ibid.).

Do women, then, make a difference when it comes to serving as judges? Yes and no. Clearly, female judges themselves believe that it is important to have women serving on the bench, not only because it is fair in terms of democratic theory, but also because women bring a unique view and much-needed qualities to the bench—including raising awareness about issues such as gender discrimination to their male brethren. Many studies find, in addition, that women judges are more liberal in their decision-making when it comes to some issues of greater relevance to women, such as sexual harassment. Yet other studies find little evidence that women judges decide cases differently from men. For example, there is not much indication that women judges have a unique decision-making style, or "different voice," than men when it comes to their jurisprudence. Although women can potentially make distinctive contributions in some limited areas of the law while serving on the bench, they are limited in what changes they can pursue by the constraints of the judiciary itself. More often than not, women decide cases in similar ways to men because they are socialized in law school and later in the profession to think like lawyers and judges. Judges are also constrained in their decision-making by their needs to consider precedent, the rule of law, and fact patterns in their cases. Some scholars, in fact, believe it may not be a bad thing that there are little consistent data to show that women judges routinely act differently than their male counterparts—even in sexual harassment cases. Studies that find few differences between men and women judges are an indication that most judges apply consistent standards in their decisions, regardless of gender (Kulik, Perry, and Pepper 2003). That personal characteristics such as gender take a back seat to the more relevant situational or behavioral factors in court cases can raise our confidence about judges—regardless of their gender or personal background—and about the judiciary more generally.

GENDER BIAS IN THE COURTS

The effects of having more women serving on the bench are not necessarily isolated to judicial decisions. Some scholars believe that men and women judges could potentially treat attorneys, litigants, and other court actors differently. A concern about differential treatment based on gender is especially important in the courts, as the American legal culture strives for equal treatment and fairness in the courtroom setting. Research has found that women in courtrooms at times face discriminatory treatment, often in the form of informal comments by men attorneys or judges (more often attorneys than judges), who may make remarks about the personal appearance of women actors in the court or may make sexist or demeaning remarks about women (Rosenberg et al. 1993; Stepnick and Orcutt 1996). Research has found differences in the perception of biased treatment against women courtroom participants among judges and attorneys of both genders: Women judges and attorneys are more aware of gender-biased behavior toward women in the courtroom than are men judges and attorneys (Stepnick and Orcutt 1996).

This perception of gender bias in the nation's courts has led most states to undertake Gender Bias Task Forces (spurred, in part, by the National Association of Women Judges; see *Paths to Power* box). As of 2005, only three states had not commissioned such a task force. The Federal Courts Study Committee in 1990 also examined gender bias in the federal courts. Such task forces and commissions have led to changes in court behavior and processes. Both the state and federal courts have adopted education programs to educate judges and other court personnel on the prevalence of gender bias and its negative effects in the courtroom. For example, court education programs highlight behavior on the part of male judges that may stem from unconsciously held stereotypes, such as addressing female attorneys or witnesses by their first names more often than male attorneys or witnesses (as many of the task force studies found in their research) (Jackson 1997). Other changes brought by the task force studies include the establishment of affirmative action policies in some states that have led to more hiring of women in certain court personnel positions as well as the development of both diversity training and systematic procedures that allow women (or other minorities) to lodge formal complaints about discriminatory behavior (Schafran 1993; Kearney and Sellers 1997; Jackson 1997; Selby 1999). Statutory law has even been changed in a few cases, such as in Virginia, where the Gender Bias Task Force uncovered problems in the treatment of stalking victims (who are primarily female) by the legal system. The Virginia General Assembly passed tougher antistalking measures in response to the task force findings (Roush 2001).

The effectiveness of the changes wrought by the Gender Study Task Forces is hard to measure entirely. A backlash to their findings emerged in the mid-1990s, when a small group of federal judges attacked the data—which some scholars believe is an indicator that the task forces are having a major impact (Morrison 2002). More recent research suggests that although biased behavior toward women in the courtroom has improved, it still persists to some degree. Winkle and Wedeking's (2003) study of Mississippi judges and attorneys found that while survey respondents as a whole indicated that men and women receive fair treatment in the courtroom, there is a greater perception of unfairness toward women. Both female judges and attorneys indicated that gender bias existed in greater numbers than their male counterparts. For instance, many women judges and attorneys reported "incidents of patronizing

PATHS TO POWER

National Association of Women Judges

The National Association of Women Judges (NAWJ) began in 1979, when more than 100 women judges across the nation gathered for a conference organized by California state judge Joan Dempsey Klein and Vaino Spencer, a trial court judge (Morrison 2002). Founded as a product of the feminist movement, the major goal of the bipartisan organization was to advocate for the selection of more women to the bench, in part through promoting the knowledge and history of women lawyers and judges and to use it as "an agent of change" (ibid.). Of particular concern early on was the NAWJ's effort to focus on the appointment of the first woman to the United States Supreme Court (Martin 1993b). These efforts paid off in 1981, when Sandra Day O'Connor was selected as Reagan's first appointee to the Supreme Court.

In addition to working for the appointment of more women as judges, the NAWJ supported passage of the ERA and spoke out against sex discrimination in general. More specifically, the NAWJ sought an end to discriminatory behavior against women judges, attorneys, and court personnel (ibid.). Following the lead of the State of New Jersey, which in 1983 commissioned a task force to study gender bias in the state's courts, the NAWJ established a National Task Force on Gender Bias in the Courts and developed a manual to encourage other states to conduct similar studies (Schafran 1993). According to Judge Gladys Kessler, the president of the NAWJ from 1982 to 1983, it was important for the national organization to take up the cause of gender discrimination in the courts: "As a large, national organization, we can speak out on those issues, often controversial ones such as discriminatory clubs or federal judicial appointments, that individual judges, with all their ethical restrictions, do not feel they can appropriately address" (Martin 1993b, 173).

Today, the NAWJ continues to stand for gender equality and fairness in American courts, particularly for vulnerable populations. In addition to continuing the call for an increase in the number of women and minority judges, the NAWJ also seeks to enhance their leadership potential once they arrive on the bench, according to Drucilla Stender Ramey, former executive director of the NAWJ. They do so through a variety of methods, including networking, which allows women judges the opportunity to meet with one another and to know they are not alone. As Ramey indicates, "Although the number of women judges has increased, there is still isolation for women judges in some states. The NAWJ gives women the opportunity to discuss these issues with one another and to learn from their sisters." Ramey maintains that networking is especially important for new judges, who often use their NAWJ connections to learn how to become better judges and to manage their courtrooms effectively.

The NAWJ also sponsors cutting-edge education training seminars for its members. Recent seminars have included multiday training sessions on the implications of the Human Genome Project for law, especially how such genetic advantages could affect women and other vulnerable groups in the population. For example, if women are

(Continued)

identified with having the breast cancer gene, will they be denied employment opportunities? Other topics range from the impact of international law on domestic courts to the effects of sentencing decisions on the status of immigrants. The NAWJ also offers to its members "bench books" with the findings from most of these training initiatives to educate judges further. The NAWJ also has extended its interests to helping women and minorities succeed in law firms, by sponsoring seminars aimed at attorney retention. The NAWJ in recent years has become more active in lobbying Congress on behalf of federal legislation that seeks to ensure fairness and equality in the criminal justice system and has written letters to state governors, urging them to consider the appointments of outstanding women jurists to state courts.

In the future, the NAWJ is hoping to raise its profile and to become more active in several areas. For example, in the wake of the recent murder of a state judge in Georgia and the family of a federal judge in Illinois, and the intense political debate that arose over the Terri Schiavo case, the NAWJ has taken a vocal position on the importance of judicial independence, including publishing a high-profile opinion letter in the April 6, 2005, edition of the *New York Times*. In this letter its current president, Sandra Thomas, wrote that "[i]n this overheated political environment, it is particularly irresponsible to urge retaliation against judges who, with near unanimity, made difficult decisions under the most stressful of circumstances." Ramey believes that the NAWJ is well positioned to take a more visible stand on such issues because of its strong bipartisan makeup and the diversity of its membership, which includes not only female and male members but also judges serving at the appellate, trial, and administrative law courts at the both the state and federal levels. ∎

---

comments or unwanted touches. Some one-third of female attorneys, for example, report having received, witnessed or heard remarks disrespectful of women . . . often, but not always, they attribute the untoward remark and patronizing conduct to older men" (130). Moreover, nearly half of the female attorneys in the Mississippi study indicated that they are "treated with less dignity and equality" (ibid.). Finally, a majority of women attorneys (but not women judges) believe that male experts and male attorneys are assigned "more weight" by judges and juries than females in similar roles (133). However, most attorneys and lawyers agreed that although some gender bias exists, it is largely limited and isolated. Studies that have focused on gender bias in the mediation process—either voluntary or as part of a court-ordered process—have found few differences between men and women litigants who had recently been through the mediation process; litigants, regardless of gender, report high rates of satisfaction with the process (Gordon 2002).

WOMEN AS JUDICIAL LAW CLERKS

One important position in the courtroom is that of the judicial law clerk—particularly for high-ranking courts such as the United States Supreme Court or the U.S. courts of appeals. Judicial clerkships are often an important stepping-stone for participants: individuals who serve in clerkships typically go on to serve in prestigious jobs as attorneys or in academia. Clerks for high-ranking judges develop important mentoring relationships, make critical contacts, and receive crucial recommendations as a result of their time serving with judges. Many often end up appearing before the Supreme Court to argue cases (O'Connor and Hermann 1995), although women are still far less likely to litigate Supreme Court cases than men (Sarver, Kaheny, and Szmer 2008).

How do women fare when it comes to being selected as law clerks? One survey of third-year students serving on the main law journals of the top ten law schools in the nation addressed the question of whether gender bias exists in the selection process for judicial law clerks (Rhinehart 1994). The survey found that 72 percent of respondents sought judicial clerkships—among those, 42 percent were women and 58 percent were men, with women being less likely than men overall to seek federal clerkships (ibid.). The survey found that success in attaining federal clerkships among women and men students was high, as both women (80 percent) and men (74 percent) were accepted at similar rates (remember that these are top students in the nation's highest-ranking programs). In most cases, women and men reported appropriate behavior on the parts of judges who interviewed them, although about one in five women students did find that judges asked them about their personal lives (for example, if they were married)—while no men reported such instances. In most cases, however, both female and male students believed that gender was not a factor in the judges' selection of law clerks (ibid.).

The findings from the survey are largely borne out by more recent statistics of women as law clerks. Nationally, women's ranks as law clerks have improved as more women graduate from law school—and have even surpassed the ranks of men as clerks in most cases. In its most recent national and comprehensive survey of law school graduates, the National Association of Law Placement—which tracks the career paths of law school graduates—found that 53.3 percent of all clerks were women in 2007. Women are most likely to serve as clerks to local or state judges (56.1 percent) rather than federal judges; for example, 60.8 percent of local judiciary clerks were women compared with men, while women made up 46.9 percent of clerks to the federal courts compared with men (NALP n.d.).

Dr. Stefanie Lindquist, the Thomas W. Gregory Professor of Law at the University of Texas Law School, has firsthand knowledge of being a judicial clerk. Before obtaining a Ph.D. in political science, Lindquist worked as an attorney, graduating magna cum laude from Temple University in 1988, where she served as editor in chief for *Temple Law Review* (volume 61). Lindquist served as a law clerk for Judge Anthony Scirica, U.S. Court of Appeals for the Third Circuit from 1988 to 1989, before working in the private sector in regulatory law. Lindquist sought the clerkship because she believed it "allowed for an insider view of judicial decision-making" and because the prestige of the position would help her in her future career (Lindquist 2005). Lindquist also noted that she had a positive female role model to follow: a female mentor of hers—a woman who had previously served as the chief editor of the same law review that she had headed—also sought an appellate clerkship, which later led to her selection as a Supreme Court clerk. Among her peers in law school, Lindquist did not notice that there were any gender differences with respect to the rates of acceptance for men and women in clerkships, but she did see a trend that led more of her female peers to seek an appellate clerkship (primarily because they sought careers in academia) while her male colleagues more often sought trial court clerkships, which would expose them to more experience in the courtroom.

Dr. Lindquist recalls that her time as an appellate clerk was "an invaluable experience" that allowed her to develop not only a personal relationship with a federal appellate judge but also to gain direct knowledge of the inner workings of the federal judiciary. She was especially fascinated with watching the cases she handled go through the legal process; one decision she helped write eventually landed at the United States Supreme Court. Lindquist noted that when she served in the 1988–1989 term, the gender balance at the Third Circuit was very close, although men still outnumbered women in this position. In Scirica's chambers, two out of the three clerks were women, and she did not recall any chambers in the Third Circuit that did not have at least one female clerk. She also believed that the judges were "remarkably progressive" when it came to their clerks, noticing no differential treatment. She says, "As a clerk, there were no gender issues at all; I felt completely comfortable."

The one exception in which women have not reached parity with men in terms of clerkships is at the Supreme Court level. The first woman to serve as a Supreme Court clerk was Lucille Lomen, a graduate from the University of Washington Law School who clerked for Justice William O. Douglas during World War II. Raised in Washington state, Douglas would often inquire about recent graduates from law schools on the west coast by writing deans and asking who would make outstanding law clerks. In 1944, when those deans were unable to nominate any men for consideration, Douglas indicated he would be willing to hire a woman graduate, if one was deemed "first-rate" (Ginsburg 2001). As Ruth Bader Ginsburg (2001) recounts, Douglas was pleased with Lomen's performance, describing her as "very able and very conscientious." Lomen later served as an assistant attorney general for the state of Washington before becoming counsel of corporate affairs for General Electric.

After Lomen's turn as a law clerk, subsequent women were hired only sporadically, and most justices were reluctant to hire women well into the early 1980s (from 1973 to 1980, women made up just 13 percent of Supreme Court clerks). Mark Brown's study of the clerkship selection process from 1960 to 1994, in which he compared the percentages of men clerking for the Supreme Court with the relative percentages of men at those times who attended elite law schools, served as law review editors, and clerked at the U.S. Court of Appeals, found evidence of discrimination against women (Brown 1996). For example, from 1990 through 1994, the male clerkship rate was 18 percent higher than the male enrollment rate at elite law schools (Brown 1996, 366). Deborah Jones Merritt, a law professor at the Ohio State University who clerked for Ruth Bader Ginsburg on the Appellate Court for the District of

Columbia Circuit, notes that part of the discrepancy could be linked to the fact that a Supreme Court clerkship requires relocating to Washington as well as demanding hours. She says that "women juggling family responsibilities may be less willing than men to make that commitment" (Reske 1996). Alternatively, Merritt argues that the disparity between male and female clerks might be linked to women receiving less mentoring or recommendations from law school professors or to the notion that men disproportionately make up more clerks at the appellate court level. Ninety percent of Supreme Court clerks first spend a year clerking for an appellate judge (ibid.).

In terms of hiring women clerks historically, one justice was a notable exception. *New York Times* reporter Linda Greenhouse points out that by the time he had retired in 1994, Justice Harry Blackmun, perhaps best known for penning the majority decision in *Roe v. Wade*, had "hired more female law clerks than the other sitting justices combined, and during the last 10 years on the court, a majority of his clerks were women" (Greenhouse 2005, 28). Karen Nelson Moore, now a judge on the U.S. Court of Appeals for the Sixth Circuit, was the first female clerk hired by Justice Blackmun in 1974. She remembers her time working with Blackmun fondly and recalled that "he combined a real sensitivity to women's concerns with absolutely none of the odd chivalry that some of the other justices showed to their female clerks, as opposed to their male clerks. I think he really did treat them as complete equals" ("Terms of Assessment" 1994).

Women's representation as Supreme Court law clerks improved after the appointment of Sandra Day O'Connor. From 1981 through 1997, women made up 27 percent of judicial clerks (Ginsburg 2001). And Mark Brown's data from the mid-1990s showed that Justices Breyer, Ginsburg, and O'Connor—at least through the 1996 term—had hired either an equal number or close to equal numbers of female law clerks as male clerks. The level of women represented as clerks reached an all-time high of 41 percent in the 2001–2002 term (Strauss 2003). Some feminists were alarmed during the Court's 2006–2007 session that women accounted for only 7 out of 37 possible clerkships, the lowest number of women since 1994 (Greenhouse 2006). They speculated that the retirement of Supreme Court Justice Sandra Say O'Connor might have caused the numbers to drop. However, Justices David Souter and Stephen Breyer—both of whom have had strong records of hiring women clerks—believed that the numbers were an anomaly, reflecting random variation in the application pool (ibid.). Indeed, the number of women clerks did rise again in 2007 and 2008, filling 13 clerkships each.

However, some wonder in an era in which women have reached parity with men in law school, why haven't women been equally represented at the very top of clerkships? Research suggests a mix of factors. Supreme Court clerks tend to come from a number of elite "feeder" schools and typically serve on the editorial staff of law reviews; moreover, they also tend to have prior experience clerking for certain appellate courts. In both cases, women are less represented in this initial pool of likely candidates (Kaye and Gastwirth 2008). Others speculate that women may have less ambition for the grueling task of a Supreme Court clerkship, perhaps due to family concerns, and may be less likely to have developed appropriate mentorships with law school faculty who are successful in helping potential clerks steer through the process (Benson 2007).

CONCLUSION

From the pioneering days of early women attorneys in the late 1800s, and early female judges such as Florence Allen, the first woman appointed to the federal judiciary, women have made huge strides in the legal profession. Women now make up 18 percent of federal judges, while more than one in four state supreme court justices are women. With half of all law students currently female, it is likely that more women will make their impact felt both as attorneys and as judges in this crucial third branch of government. Having more women represented as judges is important, for in the words of Ruth Bader Ginsburg, "[a] system of justice will be richer for diversity of background and experience. It will be poorer, in terms of appreciating what is at stake and the impact of its judgments, if all its members are cast from the same mold" (quoted in Martin 1993a, 126).

Although the representation of more women in the judiciary is important with respect to democratic norms, and may also inspire future generations of girls and boys by providing more diverse judges as role models, whether the inclusion of more women on the bench actually leads to the enhanced representation of women or women's interests is more debatable. For instance, although some studies show that female judges are somewhat more sympathetic to the victims of sexual or racial discrimination (who tend to be female or minority), most studies show that women and men judges largely decide cases in the same manner. Moreover, the hypothesis that women would potentially use a different, "feminine" voice in terms of their jurisprudence has not borne out. On the bench, women largely decide cases in the same way as men—which likely reflects their common legal training and the conservative nature of law itself. Some believe that the finding that gender has little effect on the way that judges make decisions actually boosts our confidence in women's ability to perform this demanding job—and supports the notion that more women should be selected to serve in the judiciary.

Although having more women on the bench may not affect legal outcomes differently, it may have an impact on the courtroom's environment. Gender bias task forces commissioned in the last few decades in court systems around the country found that women attorneys and judges were more likely than men to perceive inappropriate treatment toward women in the courtroom. Such findings have prompted education programs to raise awareness about potentially inappropriate behavior, particularly on the part of older male judges and attorneys. Moreover, many courts have established systematic procedures to allow women (and other minorities) to lodge formal complaints about any biased treatment they may receive. Gender bias task force reforms, combined with a greater leadership role for women in the courts as judges and attorneys, has likely resulted in a fairer courtroom for all parties involved.

REFERENCES

Aliota, Jilda M. 1995. "Justice O'Connor and the Equal Protection Clause: A Feminine Voice?" *Judicature* 78, no. 5:232–235.

Allen, David, and Diane Wall. 1993. "Role Orientations and Women State Supreme Court Justices." *Judicature* 7, no. 3:156–165.

Allen, Florence. 1965. *To Do Justly.* Cleveland: The Press of Western Reserve University.

Alozie, Nicholas. 1996. "Selection Methods and the Recruitment of Women to State Courts of Last Resort." *Social Science Quarterly* 77, no. 1:110–126.

American Bar Association (ABA). 1998. "American Bar Association Section of Legal Education and Admissions to the Bar, Approved Law Schools." www.abanet.org/media/factbooks/womenlaw.pdf.

———. 2000. "A Snapshot of Women in the Law in the Year 2000." ABA Commission on Women. www.abanet.org/women/snapshots.pdf.

———. 2004. "Lawyer Demographics." www.abanet.org.

———. 2007. "A Current Glance at Women in the Law." www.abanet.org/women/CurrentGlanceStatistics2007.pdf.

The American Bench: Judges of the Nation. 2009 edition. Forster-Long, Inc.

Baker, Peter and Neil A. Lewis. 2009. "Republicans Press Judge About Bias and Activism." *New York Times* (15 July): A1.

Baker, Peter and Jeff Zeleny. 2009. "Obama Chooses Hispanic Judge for Supreme Court Seat." *New York Times* (27 May): A1.

Barnes, Robert. 2007. "Over Ginsburg's Dissent, Court Limits Bias Suits." *Washington Post* (30 May): A1.

Behuniak-Long, Susan. 1992. "Justice Sandra Day O'Connor and the Power of Maternal Legal Thinking." *Review of Politics* 54, no. 3:417–444

Bazelon, Emily. 2009. "The Place of Women on the Court." *New York Times Magazine* (12 July): 22.

Benson, Christopher R. 2007. "A Renewed Call for Diversity Among Supreme Court Clerks: How a Diverse Body of Clerks Can Aid the High Court as an Institution." *Harvard BlackLetter Law Journal* 23, 23–54.

Bratton, Kathleen A., and Rorie L. Spill. 2002. "Existing Diversity and Judicial Selection: The Role of the Appointment Method in Establishing Gender Diversity in State Supreme Courts." *Social Science Quarterly* 83, no. 2:504–519.

Brown, Mark R. 1996. "Gender Discrimination in the Supreme Court's Clerkship Selection Process." *Oregon Law Review* 75:359–388.

Brust, Richard. 2008. "A Cowgirl Rides the Circuit." *ABA Journal* 94, no. 4:26–28.

Burns, Nancy E., Kay Lehman Schlozman, and Sidney Verba. 2001. *The Private Roots of Public Action: Gender, Equality, and Political Participation.* Cambridge: Harvard University Press.

Campbell, Amy Leigh. 2002. "Raising the Bar: Ruth Bader Ginsburg and the ACLU Women's Rights Project." *Texas Journal of Women and the Law* 11, no. 20:157–244.

Carp, Robert A., and Ronald Stidham. 1998. *Judicial Process in America.* 4th ed. Washington, D.C.: CQ Press.

Chambers, David. 1989. "Accommodation and Satisfaction: Women and Lawyers and the Balance of Work and Family." *Law and Social Inquiry* 14, no. 2:251–287.

Cook, Beverly Blair. 1984. "Women on the State Bench: Correlates of Access." pp. 191–218 in *Political Women: Current Roles in State and Local Government*, ed. Janet A. Flammang. Beverly Hills: Sage.

_____. 1993. "Moral Authority and Gender Difference: Georgia Bullock and the Los Angeles Women's Court." *Judicature* 77 no. 3: 144–155.

Coontz, Phyllis. 1995. "Gender Bias in the Legal Profession: Women 'See' It, Men Don't." *Women & Politics* 15, no. 2:1–22.

Darcy, R., Susan Welch, and Janet Clark. 1994. *Women, Elections & Representation*, 2nd ed. Lincoln: University of Nebraska Press.

Davis, Sue. 1992–1993. "Do Women Speak in a Different Voice? Carol Gilligan, Feminist Legal Theory, and the Ninth Circuit." *Wisconsin Women's Law Journal* 81, no. 1:143–173.

_____. 1993. "The Voice of Sandra Day O'Connor." *Judicature* 77, no. 3:134–139.

Davis, Sue, Susan Haire, and Donald R. Songer. 1993. "Voting Behavior and Gender on the U.S. Courts of Appeal." *Judicature* 77, no. 3:129–133.

Drachman, Virginia. 1993. *Women Lawyers and the Origin of Professional Identity in America*. Ann Arbor: University of Michigan Press.

Epstein, Cynthia Fuchs. 1993. *Women in Law*, 2nd ed. Urbana: University of Illinois Press.

Federal Judicial Center. 2009. Federal Judges Biographical Database. www.fjc.gov/public/home.nsf/hisj.

Gilligan, Carol. 1982. *In a Different Voice: Psychological Theory and Women's Development*. Cambridge: Harvard University Press.

Ginsburg, Ruth Bader. 1997. "Remarks on Women's Progress in the Legal Profession in the United States." *Tulsa Law Journal* 33:13–21.

_____. 2001. "The Supreme Court: A Place for Women." *Vital Speeches of the Day* 67, no. 14:420–425.

Ginsburg, Ruth Bader, and Laura W. Brill. 1995. "Address: Women in the Federal Judiciary: Three Way Pavers and the Exhilarating Change President Carter Wrought." *Fordham Law Review* 64:281–290.

Githens, Marianne. 1995. "Getting Appointed to the State Court: The Gender Dimension." *Women & Politics* 15, no. 4:1–24.

Glick, Henry R. 1999. "Courts: Politics and the Judicial Process." pp. 232–266 in *Politics in the American States: A Comparative Analysis*, 7th ed., ed. Virginia Gray, Russell L. Hanson, and Herbert Jacob. Washington, D.C.: CQ Press.

Goldman, Sheldon. 1979. "Should There Be Affirmative Action in the Judiciary?" *Judicature* 62, no. 10:488–494.

Goldman, Sheldon, Elliot Slotnick, Gerald Gryski, and Gary Zuk. 2001. "Clinton's Judges: Summing up the Legacy." *Judicature* 84, no. 5:220–254.

Goldman, Sheldon, Elliot Slotnick, Gerald Gryski, Gary Zuk, and Sara Schiavoni. 2003. "W. Bush Remaking the Judiciary: Like Father, Like Son?" *Judicature* 86, no. 6:282–309.

Gordon, Elizabeth Ellen. 2002. "What Role Does Gender Play in Mediation of Domestic Relations Cases?" *Judicature* 86, no. 3:134–143.

Greenhouse, Linda. 2005. "The Evolution of a Justice." *New York Times Magazine* (10 April): 28.

_____. 2006. "Women Suddenly Scarce Among Justices' Clerks." *New York Times* (30 August). www.nytimes.com/2006/08/30/washington/30scotus.html?ei=

Gruhl, John, Cassia Spohn, and Susan Welch. 1981. "Women as Policymakers: The Case of Trial Judges." *American Journal of Political Science* 25, no. 2:308–322.

Gryski, Gerald S., Eleanor C. Main, and William J. Dixon. 1986. "Models of State High Court Decision Making in Sex Discrimination Cases." *Journal of Politics* 48, no. 1:143–155.

Hagan, John. 1990. "The Gender Stratification of Income Inequality among Lawyers." *Social Forces* 68, no. 3:835–855.

Halloran, Liz. 2005. "One Down and One to Go." *U.S. News & World Report* 139, no. 17:45.

Hartley, Roger E. 2001. "A Look at Race, Gender, and Experience." *Judicature* 84, no. 4:191–197.

Hermann, Ria, and Rita Mae Kelly, with the assistance of Donna Langston and Julie Greenburg. 1988. "Women in the Judiciary." pp. 84–108 in *Women and the Arizona Political Process*, ed. Rita Mae Kelly. Lanham: University Press of America.

Hurwitz, Mark, and Drew Noble Lanier. 2001. "Women and Minorities on State and Federal Appellate Benches, 1985 and 1999." *Judicature* 85, no. 2:84–92.

———. 2003. "Explaining Judicial Diversity: The Differential Ability of Women and Minorities to Attain Seats on State Supreme and Appellate Courts." *State Politics & Policy Quarterly* 3, no. 4:329–352.

Jackson, Vicki C. 1997. "What Judges Can Learn from Gender Bias Task Force Studies." *Judicature* 81, no. 1:15–21, 38–39.

Kaye, David H. and Joseph L. Gastwirth. 2008. "The Disappearance that Wasn't? 'Random Variation' in the Number of Women Supreme Court Clerks." *Jurimetrics: The Journal of Law, Science, and Technology*, 48, no. 4:457–463.

Kearney, Richard C., and Holly Taylor Sellers. 1997. "Gender Bias in Court Personnel Administration." *Judicature* 81, no. 1:8–14.

Kirkpatrick, David. D. 2009. "A Judge's Focus on Race Issues May Be Hurdle." *New York Times* (30 May): A1.

Kulik, Carol T., Elissa L. Perry, and Molly B. Pepper. 2003. "Here Comes the Judge: The Influence of Judge Personal Characteristics on Federal Sexual Harassment Case Outcomes." *Law and Human Behavior* 27, no. 1:69–86.

Lane, Charles. 2004. "Courting O'Connor: Why the chief justice Isn't the Chief Justice." *Washington Post Magazine* (4 July): W10.

Lindquist, Stefanie. 2005. Personal Interview with Deckman, by phone. (11 May).

Lodge, Sally. 2009. "Q&A with Sandra Day O'Connor." *Publisher's Weekly*. (28 May). www.publishersweekly.com/article/CA6660760.html

Martin, Elaine. 1987. "Gender and the Judicial Selection: A Comparison of the Reagan and Carter Administrations." *Judicature* 71, no. 3:136–142.

———. 1993a. "Women on the Bench? A Different Voice?" *Judicature* 77, no. 3:126–128.

———. 1993b. "The Representative Role of Women Judges." *Judicature* 77, no. 3:166–173.

Martin, Elaine, and Barry Pyle. 2000. "Gender, Race, and Partisanship on the Michigan Supreme Court." *Albany Law Review* 63:1205–1236.

———. 2002. "Gender and Racial Diversification of State Supreme Courts." *Women & Politics* 24, no. 2:35–52.

Maveety, Nancy. 1996. *Justice Sandra Day O'Connor: Strategist on the Supreme Court*. Lanham: Rowman & Littlefield.

McCarthy, Megan. 2001. "Student Paper. Judicial Campaigns: What Can They Tell Us About Gender on the Bench?" *Wisconsin Women's Law Journal* 16:87–112.

Mezey, Susan Gluck. 2000. "Gender and the Federal Judiciary." pp. 205–226 in *Gender and American Politics*, ed. Sue Tolleson-Rinehart and Jyl Josephson. London: M.E. Sharpe.

Morello, Karen Berger. 1986. *The Invisible Bar: The Woman Lawyer in America: 1683 to the Present*. New York: Random House.

Morrison, Linda. 2002. "The National Association of Women Judges: Agent of Change." *Wisconsin Women's Law Journal* 17:291–320.

National Association of Law Placement (NALP). n.d. "A Demographic Profile of Judicial Clerks." www.nalp.org/jun2008demographicprofile?s=gender.

National Association of Women Judges. n.d. "2009 Representation of United States State Court Judges." www.nawj.org/us_state_court_statistics_2009.asp

O'Connor, Karen. 1980. *Women's Organizations' Use of the Courts*. Lexington: Lexington Books.

_____. 1988. "Women as Lawyers." pp. 1–8 in *Women in the Judicial Process*, ed. Beverly Cook, et al. Washington, D.C.: American Political Science Association.

O'Connor, Karen, and Patricia Clark. 1999. "Women's Rights and Legal Wrongs: The U.S. Supreme Court and Sex Discrimination." pp. 262–277 in *Women in Politics: Outsiders or Insiders?*, ed. Lois Duke Whitaker. Upper Saddle River, NJ: Prentice Hall.

O'Connor, Karen, and John R. Hermann. 1995. "U.S. Supreme Court Law Clerk Participation before the Supreme Court." *Judicature* 78, no. 5:247–252.

O'Connor, Karen, and Barbara Palmer. 2001. "The Clinton Clones: Ginsburg, Breyer, and the Clinton Legacy." *Judicature* 84, no. 5:262–273.

O'Connor, Karen, and Jeffrey Segal. 1990. "Justice Sandra Day O'Connor and the Supreme Court's Reaction to Its First Female Member." *Women & Politics* 10, no. 2:95–103.

O'Connor, Sandra Day. 2007. "Foreward." pp. xiii–xv in *Women and Leadership: The State of Play and Strategies for Change*, eds. Barbara Kellerman and Deborah L. Rhode. San Francisco, CA: Jossey-Bass.

_____. 2000. "Remarks at University of Pennsylvania Law School Sesquicentennial." Accessed online at www.law.upenn.edu/alumni/alumnijournal/Spring2001/feature1/oconnorremarks.html

Palmer, Barbara. 1991. "Feminist or Foe? Justice Sandra Day O'Connor, Title CVII Sex Discrimination, and Support for Women's Rights." *Women's Rights Law Reporter* 13, nos. 2 and 3:159–170.

_____. 2001. "Women in the American Judiciary." *Women & Politics* 23, no. 3: 89–99.

_____. 2002. "Justice Ruth Bader Ginsburg and the Supreme Court's Reaction to Its Second Member." *Women and Politics* 24, no. 1:1–23.

Reske, Henry J. 1996. "Supreme Challenge: A Law Professor Hopes Some Justices Will Correct Their Dismal Hiring Records for Women Law Clerks." *ABA Journal*. (September): 32.

Rhinehart, Lynn K. 1994. "Is There Gender Bias in the Judicial Law Clerk Selection Process?" *The Georgetown Law Journal* 83:575–602.

Romano, Lois, and Juliet Eilperin. 2006. "Republicans Were Masters in the Race to Paint Alito; Democrats' Portrayal Failed to Sway the Public." *Washington Post* (2 February): A1.

Rosenberg, Janet, Harry Perlstadt, and William R. F. Phillips. 1993. "Now That We Are Here: Discrimination, Disparagement, and Harassment at Work and the Experience of Women Lawyers." *Gender and Society* 7:415–433.

Roush, Jane Marum. 2001. "Gender Bias Task Force: Comments on Substantive Law Issues." *Washington and Lee Law Review* 58:1095–1098.

Sarver, Tammy A., Erin B. Kaheny, and John J. Szmer. 2008. "The Attorney Gender Gap in U.S. Supreme Court Litigation." *Judicature* 91, no. 5:238–251.

Schafran, Lynn Hecht. 1993. "Gender Equality in the Courts: Still on the Judicial Agenda." *Judicature* 77, no. 2:110–113.

Segal, Jennifer A. 2000. "Representative Decision Making on the Federal Bench: Clinton's District Court Appointees." *Political Research Quarterly* 53, no. 1:137–151.

Selby, Myra C. 1999. "Examining Race and Gender Bias in the Courts: A Legacy of Indifference of Opportunity." *Indiana Law Review* 32, no. 4:1167–1185.

Sherry, Suzanna. 1986. "Civic Virtue and the Feminine Voice in Constitutional Adjudication." *Virginia Law Review* 72:543–615.

Songer, Donald, Sue Davis, and Susan Haire. 1994. "A Reappraisal of Diversification in the Federal Courts: Gender Effects in the Courts of Appeals." *Journal of Politics* 56, no. 2:425–439.

Songer, Donald R. and Kelley A. Crews-Meyer. 2000. "Does Judge Gender Matter? Decision Making in State Supreme Courts." *Social Science Quarterly*, 81, no. 3: 750–762.

Spill, Rorie, and Kathleen A. Bratton. 2001. "Clinton and the Diversification of the Federal Judiciary." *Judicature* 84, no. 5:256–261.

Stepnick, Andrea, and James D. Orcutt. 1996. "Conflicting Testimony: Judges' and Attorneys' Perceptions of Gender Bias in Legal Settings." *Sex Roles* 34, no. 718: 567–579.

Strauss, Debra. 2003. "Diversity Begins at Home: Supreme Court Clerkships and Affirmative Action." *JURIST: Legal Intelligence.* http://jurist.law.pitt.edu/forum/forumnew105.php.

Sullivan, Patricia A, and Steven R. Goldzwig. 1996. "Abortion and Undue Burdens: Justice Sandra Day O'Connor and Judicial Decision-Making." *Women & Politics* 16, no. 3:27–54.

"Terms of Assessment. An ABA Journal Roundtable." 1994. *ABA Journal* 80, no. 7: 52–56.

U.S. Census Bureau. 2007. "Employed Civilians by Occupation, Sex, Race, and Hispanic Origin." www.factfinder.census.gov.

Walker, Thomas G., and Deborah J. Barrow. 1985. "The Diversification of the Federal Bench: Policy and Process Ramifications." *Journal of Politics* 47, no. 2:596–617.

Wellington, Sheila. 2003. "Women in Law: Making the Case." In *The Difference Difference Makes: Women in Leadership*, edited by Deborah Rhodes. Stanford: Stanford University Press, 90–97.

Williams, Margaret. 2007. "Women's Representation on State Trial and Appellate Courts." *Social Science Quarterly*, 88, no. 5:1192–1204.

Winkle, John W., and Justin Wedeking. 2003. "Perceptions and Experiences of Gender Fairness in Mississippi Courts." *Judicature* 87, no. 3:126–134.

APPENDIX A

"Declaration of Sentiments" and "Resolutions" Adopted by the Seneca Falls Convention of 1848

When, in the course of human events, it becomes necessary for one portion of the family of man to assume among the people of the earth a position different from that which they have hitherto occupied, but one to which the laws of nature and of nature's God entitle them, a decent respect to the opinions of mankind requires that they should declare the causes that impel them to such a course.

We hold these truths to be self-evident: that all men and women are created equal; that they are endowed by their Creator with certain inalienable rights; that among these are life, liberty, and the pursuit of happiness; that to secure these rights governments are instituted, deriving their just powers from the consent of the governed. Whenever any form of government becomes destructive of these ends, it is the right of those who suffer from it to refuse allegiance to it, and to insist upon the institution of a new government, laying its foundation on such principles, and organizing its powers in such form, as to them shall seem most likely to effect their safety and happiness. Prudence indeed will dictate that governments long established should not be changed for light and transient causes; and accordingly all experience hath shown that mankind are more disposed to suffer, while evils are sufferable, than to right themselves by abolishing the forms to which they were accustomed. But when a long train of abuses and usurpations, pursuing invariably the same object evinces a design to reduce them under absolute despotism, it is their duty to throw off such government, and to provide new guards for their future security. Such has been the patient sufferance of the women under this government, and such is now the necessity which constrains them to demand the equal station to which they are entitled.

The history of mankind is a history of repeated injuries and usurpations on the part of man toward woman, having in direct object the establishment of an absolute tyranny over her. To prove this, let facts be submitted to a candid world.

He has never permitted her to exercise her inalienable right to the elective franchise.

He has compelled her to submit to laws, in the formation of which she had no voice.

He has withheld from her rights which are given to the most ignorant and degraded men—both natives and foreigners.

Having deprived her of this first right of a citizen, the elective franchise, thereby leaving her without representation in the halls of legislation, he has oppressed her on all sides.

He has made her, if married, in the eye of the law, civilly dead.

He has taken from her all right in property, even to the wages she earns.

He has made her, morally, an irresponsible being, as she can commit many crimes with impunity, provided they be done in the presence of her husband. In the covenant of marriage, she is compelled to promise obedience to her husband, he becoming, to all intents and purposes, her master—the law giving him power to deprive her of her liberty, and to administer chastisement.

He has so framed the laws of divorce, as to what shall be the proper causes, and in case of separation, to whom the guardianship of the children shall be given, as to be wholly regardless of the happiness of women—the law, in all cases, going upon a false supposition of the supremacy of man, and giving all power into his hands.

After depriving her of all rights as a married woman, if single, and the owner of property, he has taxed her to support a government which recognizes her only when her property can be made profitable to it.

He has monopolized nearly all the profitable employments, and from those she is permitted to follow, she receives but a scanty remuneration. He closes against her all the avenues to wealth and distinction which he considers most honorable to himself. As a teacher of theology, medicine, or law, she is not known.

He has denied her the facilities for obtaining a thorough education, all colleges being closed against her.

He allows her in Church, as well as State, but a subordinate position, claiming Apostolic authority for her exclusion from the ministry, and, with some exceptions, from any public participation in the affairs of the Church.

He has created a false public sentiment by giving to the world a different code of morals for men and women, by which moral delinquencies which exclude women from society, are not only tolerated, but deemed of little account in man.

He has usurped the prerogative of Jehovah himself, claiming it as his right to assign for her a sphere of action, when that belongs to her conscience and to her God.

He has endeavored, in every way that he could, to destroy her confidence in her own powers, to lessen her self-respect, and to make her willing to lead a dependent and abject life.

Now in view of this entire disfranchisement of one-half the people of this country, their social and religious degradation—in view of the unjust laws above mentioned, pressed, and fraudulently deprived of their most sacred rights, we insist that they have immediate admission to all the rights and privileges which belong to them as citizens of the United States.

In entering upon the great work before us, we anticipate no small amount of misconception, misrepresentation, and ridicule; but we shall use every instrumentality within our power to effect our object. We shall employ agents, circulate tracts, petition the State and National legislatures, and endeavor to enlist the pulpit and the press in our behalf. We hope this Convention will be followed by a series of Conventions embracing every part of the country.

The following resolutions were discussed by Lucretia Mott, Thomas and Mary Ann McClintock, Amy Post, Catharine A. F. Stebbins, and others, and were adopted.

WHEREAS, The great precept of nature is conceded to be, that "man shall pursue his own true and substantial happiness." Blackstone in his Commentaries remarks, that this law of Nature being coeval with mankind, and dictated by God himself, is of course superior in obligation to any other. It is binding over all the globe, in all countries and at all times; no human laws are of any validity if contrary to this, and such of them as are valid, derive all their force, and all their validity, and all their authority, mediately, and immediately, from this original; therefore;

Resolved, That such laws as conflict, in any way, with the true and substantial happiness of woman, are contrary to the great precept of nature and of no validity, for this is "superior in obligation to any other."

Resolved, That all laws which prevent woman from occupying such a station in society as her conscience shall dictate, or which place her in a position inferior to that of man, are contrary to the great precept of nature, and therefore of no force or authority.

Resolved, That woman is man's equal—was intended to be so by the Creator, and the highest good of the race demands that she should be recognized as such.

Resolved, That the women of this country ought to be enlightened in regard to the laws under which they live, that they may no longer publish their degradation by declaring themselves satisfied with their present position, nor their ignorance, by asserting that they have all the rights they want.

Resolved, That inasmuch as man, while claiming for himself intellectual superiority, does accord to woman moral superiority, it is pre-eminently his duty to encourage her to speak and teach, as she has an opportunity, in all religious assemblies.

Resolved, That the same amount of virtue, delicacy, and refinement of behavior that is required of woman in the social state, should also be required of man, and the same transgressions should be visited with equal severity on both man and woman.

Resolved, That the objection of indelicacy and impropriety, which is so often brought against woman when she addresses a public audience, comes with a very ill-grace from those who encourage, by their attendance, her appearance on stage, in the concert, or in feats of the circus.

Resolved, That woman has too long rested satisfied in the circumscribed limits which corrupt customs and a perverted application of the Scriptures have marked out for her, and that it is time she should move in the enlarged sphere which her great Creator has assigned her.

Resolved, That it is the duty of the women of this country to secure themselves their sacred right to the elective franchise.

Resolved, That the equality of human rights results necessarily from the fact of the identity of the race in capabilities and responsibilities.

Resolved, therefore, That, being invested by the Creator with the same capabilities, and the same consciousness of responsibility for their exercise, it is demonstrably the right and duty of woman, equally with man, to promote every righteous cause by every righteous means; and especially in regard to the great subjects of morals and religion, it is self-evidently her right to participate with her brother in teaching them, both in private and in public, by writing and by speaking, by any instrumentalities proper to be used, and in any assemblies proper to be held; and this being a self-evident truth growing out of the divinely implanted principles of human nature, any custom or authority adverse to it, whether modern or wearing the hoary sanction of antiquity, is to be regarded as a self-evident falsehood, and at war with mankind.

At the last session Lucretia Mott offered and spoke to the following resolution:

Resolved, That the speedy success of our cause depends upon the zealous and untiring efforts of both men and women, for the overthrow of the monopoly of the pulpit, and for the securing to women an equal participation with men in the various trades, professions, and commerce.

Source: Shanley, Mary Lyndon. 1988. *Women's Rights, Feminism, and Politics in the United States.* Washington, DC: American Political Science Association.

APPENDIX B

NOW (NATIONAL ORGANIZATION FOR WOMEN) BILL OF RIGHTS

Adopted at NOW's first national conference, Washington, D.C., 1967.

I. Equal Rights Constitutional Amendment.
II. Enforce Law Banning Sex Discrimination in Employment.
III. Maternity Leave Rights in Employment and in Social Security Benefits.
IV. Tax Deduction for Home and Child Care Expenses for Working Parents.
V. Child Day Care Centers.
VI. Equal and Unsegregated Education.
VII. Equal Job Training Opportunities and Allowances for Women in Poverty.
VIII. The Right of Women to Control Their Reproductive Lives.

WE DEMAND

I. That the U.S. Congress immediately pass the Equal Rights Amendment to the Constitution to provide that "Quality of rights under the law shall not be denied or abridged by the United States or by any State on account of sex," and that such then be immediately ratified by the several States.
II. That equal employment opportunity be guaranteed to all women, as well as men, by insisting that the Equal Employment Opportunity Commission enforces the prohibitions against sex discrimination in employment under Title VII of the Civil Rights Act of 1964 with the same vigor as it enforces the prohibitions against racial discrimination.
III. That women be protected by law to ensure their rights to return to their jobs within a reasonable time after childbirth without loss of seniority or other accrued benefits, and be paid maternity leave as a form of social security and/or employee benefit.
IV. Immediate revision of tax laws to permit the deduction of home and child-care expenses for working parents.
V. That child-care facilities be established by law on the same basis as parks, libraries, and public schools, adequate to the needs of children from the pre-school years through adolescence, as a community resource to be used by all citizens from all income levels.
VI. That the right of women to be educated to their full potential equality with men be secured by Federal and State legislation, eliminating all discrimination and segregation by sex, written and unwritten, at all levels of education, including colleges, graduate and professional schools, loans and fellowships, and Federal and State training programs such as the Job Corps.
VII. The right of women in poverty to secure job training, housing, and family allowances on equal terms with men, but without prejudice to a parent's right to remain at home to care for his or her children; revision of welfare legislation and poverty programs which deny women dignity, privacy, and self-respect.

VIII. The right of women to control their own reproductive lives by removing from the penal code laws limiting access to contraceptive information and devices, and by repealing penal laws governing abortion.

Source: Shanley, Mary Lyndon. 1988. *Women's Rights, Feminism, and Politics in the United States.* Washington, D.C.: American Political Science Association. Also available in the Early Documents section of the Feminist Chronicles online at www.feminist.org/research/chronicles/early4.html.

REDSTOCKINGS MANIFESTO

I. After centuries of individual and preliminary political struggle, women are uniting to achieve their final liberation from male supremacy. Redstockings is dedicated to building this unity and winning our freedom.

II. Women are an oppressed class. Our oppression is total, affecting every facet of our lives. We are exploited as sex objects, breeders, domestic servants, and cheap labor. We are considered inferior beings, whose only purpose is to enhance men's lives. Our humanity is denied. Our prescribed behavior is enforced by the threat of physical violence.

Because we have lived so intimately with our oppressors, in isolation from each other, we have been kept from seeing our personal suffering as a political condition. This creates the illusion that a woman's relationship with her man is a matter of interplay between two unique personalities and can be worked out individually. In reality, every such relationship is a *class* relationship, and the conflicts between individual men and women are *political* conflicts that can only be solved collectively.

III. We identify the agents of our oppression as men. Male supremacy is the oldest, most basic form of domination. All other forms of exploitation and oppression (racism, capitalism, imperialism, etc.) are extensions of male supremacy: men dominate women, a few men dominate the rest. All power structures throughout history have been male-dominated and male-oriented. Men have controlled all political, economic, and cultural institutions and backed up this control with physical force. They have used their power to keep women in an inferior position. *All men* receive economic, sexual and psychological benefits from male supremacy. *All men* have oppressed women.

IV. Attempts have been made to shift the burden of responsibility from men to institutions or to women themselves. We condemn these arguments as evasions. Institutions alone do not oppress; they are merely tools of the oppressor. To blame institutions implies that men and women are equally victimized, obscures the fact that men benefit from the subordination of women, and gives men the excuse that they are forced to be oppressors. On the contrary, any man is free to renounce his superior position provided that he is willing to be treated like a woman by other men.

We also reject the idea that women consent to or are to blame for their own oppression. Women's submission is not the result of brainwashing, stupidity, or mental illness but of continual, daily pressure from men. We do not need to change ourselves, but to change men.

The most slanderous evasion of all is that women can oppress men. The basis for this illusion is the isolation of individual relationships from their political context and the tendency of men to see any legitimate challenge to their privileges as persecution.

V. We regard our personal experience, and our feelings about that experience, as the basis for an analysis of our common situation. We cannot rely on existing ideologies as they are all products of male supremacist culture. We question every generalization and accept none that are not confirmed by our experience.

Our chief task at present is to develop female class consciousness through sharing experience and publicly exposing the sexist foundation of all our institutions. Consciousness-raising is not "therapy," which implies the existence of individual solutions and falsely assumes that the male–female relationship is purely personal, but the only method by which we can ensure that our program for liberation is based on the concrete realities of our lives.

The first requirement for raising class consciousness is honesty, in private and in public, with ourselves and other women.

VI. We identify with all women. We define our best interest as that of the poorest, most brutally exploited woman.

We repudiate all economic, racial, educational, or status privileges that divide us from other women. We are determined to recognize and eliminate any prejudices we may hold against other women.

We are committed to achieving internal democracy. We will do whatever is necessary to ensure that every woman in our movement has an equal chance to participate, assume responsibility, and develop her political potential.

VII. We call on all our sisters to unite with us in struggle.

We call on men to give up their male privileges and support women's liberation in the interest of our humanity and their own.

In fighting for our liberation we will always take the side of women against their oppressors. We will not ask what is "revolutionary" or "reformist," only what is good for women.

The time for individual skirmishes has passed. This time we are going all the way.

July 7, 1969

Source: Shanley, Mary Lyndon. 1988. *Women's Rights, Feminism, and Politics in the United States*. Washington, D.C.: American Political Science Association.

APPENDIX C

Contemporary Women's Groups

Today's women's organizations vary greatly in the issues they represent, their ideological orientations, the demographic groups they appeal to, and the tactics they employ to influence the political process. Following is a listing of some of the many groups that are currently active in politics today.

Group Name	Year Founded	WebSite	Mission	Political Strategies
National Organization for Women	1966	www.now.org	Multi-issue feminist organization	Grassroots activism, lobbying, policy research, litigation
American Association of University Women	1881	www.aauw.org	Multi-issue feminist organization with a special focus on education policy as related to women from elementary school to university	Grassroots activism, lobbying, research, litigation
Feminist Majority Foundation	1987	www.feminist.org	Multi-issue feminist organization	Grassroots activism, lobbying, policy research, public education
Business and Professional Women	1919	www.bpw-foundation.org	Feminist organization seeking equity for women in the workplace	Single-issue Grassroots activism, lobbying, professional development

Group Name	Year Founded	WebSite	Mission	Political Strategies
Older Women's League	1980	www.owl-national.org	Multi-issue organization focusing on issues concerning aging women such as health care, Social Security, pension reform, and domestic violence.	Lobbying, policy research, public education
Black Women's Health Imperative	1983	www.black womenshealth .org	Single-issue research, focused on promoting optimum physical, mental, and spiritual health for black women and girls	Policy advocacy, leadership development, public and professional education
National Council of Negro Women	1935	www.ncnw .org	Organization seeking to advance the quality of life for African-American women, their families, and communities	Policy research, advocacy, professional development, community outreach (in United States and Africa)
MANA	1974	www.hermana .org	Organization focused on improving the quality of life for Latinas, their families, and communities	Leadership development, advocacy, community outreach
Latina Institute for Reproductive Health	1994	www.latina institute.org	Single-issue feminist organization focused on ensuring rights to reproductive health care for Latinas, their families, and communities	Policy research, advocacy, leadership development, community organization
National Pacific Asian American Women	1995	www.napawf .org	Multi-issue feminist organization focused on social justice for Asian and Pacific American women and girls	Grassroots activism, lobbying, public education
CODEPINK	2002	www.codepink .org	Multi-issue feminist organization focused on social justice through nonviolent action	Grassroots activism, public education

(Continued)

Group Name	Year Founded	WebSite	Mission	Political Strategies
Third Wave Foundation	2000	www.thirdwave-foundation.org	Multi-issue feminist organization focused on gender, racial, social, and economic justice regarding women ages 15–30	Financial support, public education, network of contacts and resources
National Women's Law Center	1972	www.nwlc.org	Multi-issue feminist organization focused on protecting the legal rights of women	Lobbying, litigation, public education
Institute for Women's Policy Research	1987	www.iwpr.org	Multi-issue feminist public policy research organization	Policy research
Concerned Women for America	1979	www.cwfa.org	Multi-issue conservative public policy organization with special focus on incorporating biblical principles into public policy	Lobbying, grassroots activism, public advocacy and education
Eagle Forum	1972	www.eagleforum.org	Multi-issue conservative public policy organization focused on promoting conservative and pro-family values in public policy	Lobbying, grassroots activism, public education
Independent Women's Forum	1992	www.iwf.org	Multi-issue conservative public policy organization	Lobbying, policy research, public education
Feminists for Life	1972	www.feministsforlife.org	Pro-life feminist organization	Public education and advocacy, grassroots activism
Clare Booth Luce Institute	1993	www.cblpi.org	Dual-issue organization focused on promoting conservative women's leadership and conservative choices in education K–12	Lobbying, advocacy public education, leadership, and professional development

Female Governors in the United States

Name and Party	State	Previous Officeholding Experience	Type of Race	Years Served
Nellie Tayloe Ross (D)	Wyoming	None	Open—succeeded deceased husband in special election	1925–1927
Miriam "Ma" Ferguson (D)	Texas	None	Open—ran as surrogate for husband	1925–1927, 1933–1935
Lurleen Burns Wallace (D)	Alabama	None	Open—ran in place of her husband George Wallace, who was prohibited from serving consecutive terms as governor	1967–1968
Ella Grasso (D)	Connecticut	1. Connecticut State Legislature (1952–1956) 2. Connecticut Secretary of State (1959–1970) 3. Member of U.S. House of Representatives (1971–1975)	Open	1975–1980
Dixy Lee Ray (D)	Washington	1. Chair of the U.S. Atomic Agency Commission (1973–1975)—Appointed 2. Assistant Secretary of State, U.S. State Department (1975)—Appointed	Open	1977–1981

(Continued)

Name and Party	State	Previous Officeholding Experience	Type of Race	Years Served
Vesta Roy (R)	New Hampshire	1. New Hampshire State Legislature (1973–1986)	Served for seven days after incumbent Governor Hugh Gallen died while in office	1983
Martha Layne Collins (D)	Kentucky	1. Clerk of the Kentucky Court of Appeals (statewide elective office) (1976–1980) 2. Kentucky Lieutenant Governor (1980–1983)	Open	1984–1987
Madeleine Kunin (D)	Vermont	1. Vermont State Legislature (1973–1979) 2. Vermont Lieutenant Governor (1979–1982)	Open	1985–1991
Kay Orr (R)	Nebraska	1. Nebraska State Treasurer (1981–1986)	Open	1987–1991
Rose Mofford (D)	Arizona	1. Arizona Assistant Secretary of State (1953–1975) 2. Arizona Department of Revenue, Assistant Director (1975–1977) 3. Arizona Secretary of State (1977–1988)	Appointed to fill seat after Governor Evan Mecham was impeached and convicted while in office	1988–1991
Joan Finney (D)	Kansas	1. Kansas State Treasurer (1975–1981)	Challenger	1991–1995
Ann Richards (D)	Texas	1. Travis County Commissioner (1976–1982) 2. Texas State Treasurer (1982–1990)	Open	1991–1995
Barbara Roberts (D)	Oregon	1. Oregon State Legislature (1981–1985) 2. Oregon Secretary of State (1985–1990)	Open	1991–1995

Name and Party	State	Previous Officeholding Experience	Type of Race	Years Served
Christine Todd Whitman (R)	New Jersey	1. Somerset County Board of Freeholders (1984–1988) 2. President, NJ State Board of Public Utilities (1988–1990)— Appointed	Challenger	1994–2001
Jeanne Shaheen (D)	New Hampshire	1. New Hampshire State Senate (1990–1996)	Open	1997–2003
Jane Dee Hull (R)	Arizona	1. Arizona House of Representatives (1979–1992). Majority Whip (1987–1988) Speaker of the House (1989–1992) 2. Arizona Secretary of State (1993–1997)	Appointed to fill seat after Governor J. Fife Symington resigned; was elected in 1998	1997–2003
Nancy Hollister (R)	Ohio	1. Marietta City Council member (1980–1984) 2. Mayor of Marietta (1984–1991) 3. Ohio Lieutenant Governor (1995–1998)	Served for 11 days between Governors Voinovich and Taft	1998–1999
Jane Swift (R)	Massachusetts	1. Massachusetts State Senate (1991–1997) 2. Director of Massachusetts Office of Consumer Affairs and Business Regulation (1997–1998) 3. Massachusetts Lieutenant Governor (1998–2001)	Succeeded Governor Argeo Paul Celluci when he was appointed U.S. ambassador to Canada	2001–2003
Judy Martz (R)	Montana	1. Montana Lieutenant Governor (1997–2001)	Open	2001–2005

(Continued)

Name and Party	State	Previous Officeholding Experience	Type of Race	Years Served
Ruth Ann Minner (D)	Delaware	1. Delaware State Legislature (1974–1992) 2. Delaware Lieutenant Governor (1993–2001)	Open	2001–2009
Jennifer Granholm (D)	Michigan	1. Michigan Attorney General (1998–2002)	Open	2003–present
Kathleen Sebelius (D)	Kansas	1. Kansas State Legislature (1987–1994) 2. Kansas State Insurance Commissioner (1994–1998)	Open	2003–2009
Linda Lingle (R)	Hawaii	1. Maui County Council (1980–1990) 2. Mayor of Maui (1991–1998)	Open	2003–present
Janet Napolitano (D)	Arizona	1. U.S. Assistant Attorney General (1993–1997) 2. Arizona Attorney General (1998–2002)	Open	2003–2009
Olene Walker (R)	Utah	1. Utah House of Representatives (1981–1989) 2. Utah Lieutenant Governor (1992–2003)	As sitting lieutenant governor, took office when Governor Mike Leavitt was appointed EPA Administrator by George W. Bush	2003–2005
Kathleen Blanco (D)	Louisiana	1. Louisiana State Legislature (1984–1988) 2. Louisiana Public Service Commission (1989–1995) 3. Louisiana Lieutenant Governor (1996–2003)	Open	2004–2007

Name and Party	State	Previous Officeholding Experience	Type of Race	Years Served
M. Jodi Rell (R)	Connecticut	1. Connecticut House of Representatives (1984–1994) 2. Connecticut Lieutenant Governor (1994–2004)	As sitting lieutenant governor, took office after Governor John Rowland resigned	2004–present
Christine Gregoire (D)	Washington	1. Director, Washington Department of Ecology (1988–1992) 2. Washington Attorney General (1992–2004)	Open	2005–present
Sarah Palin (R)	Alaska	1. Mayor of Wasilla (1996–2002) 2. Chair, Alaska Gas and Oil Conservation Commission (2003–2004)	Open, defeated incumbent governor in Republican primary	2007–2009
Beverly Perdue (D)	North Carolina	1. North Carolina State Legislature (1987–1999) 2. North Carolina Lieutenant Governor (2000–2009)	Open	2009–present
Jan Brewer (R)	Arizona	1 Arizona State Legislature (1983–1996) 2. Maricopa County Supervisor (1997–2002) 3. Arizona Secretary of State (2002–2008)	Succeeded sitting Governor Janet Napolitano when she resigned to serve as President Obama's Secretary of Homeland Security	2009–present

Sources: Center for American Women and Politics. 2009b. *Statewide Elective Executive Women 2009.* New Brunswick, NJ: Center for American Women and Politics, Eagleton Institute of Politics, Rutgers University; *Current Biography* (various issues); National Governor's Association, *Past Governors* (www.nga.org/governors/1,1169,C_PAST_GOV,00.html). Cox, Elizabeth M. 1996. *Women State and Territorial Legislators, 1895–1995.* Jefferson, NC: McFarland & Company, Inc.

Women Appointed to Presidential Cabinet-Level Positions

Appointee	President Who Appointed Them	Position Held	Years Served
Frances Perkins	Franklin Delano Roosevelt (D)	Secretary of Labor	1933–1945
Oveta Culp Hobby	Dwight Eisenhower (R)	Secretary of Health, Education, and Welfare	1953–1955
Carla Anderson Hills	Gerald Ford (R)	Secretary of Housing and Urban Development	1975–1977
Juanita A. Kreps	Jimmy Carter (D)	Secretary of Commerce	1977–1979
Patricia R. Harris	Jimmy Carter (D)	Secretary of Housing and Urban Development	1977–1979
Patricia R. Harris	Jimmy Carter (D)	Secretary of Health and Human Services	1979–1981
Shirley M. Hufstedler	Jimmy Carter (D)	Secretary of Education	1979–1981
Jeane J. Kirkpatrick	Ronald Reagan (R)	UN Ambassador	1981–1985
Margaret M. Heckler	Ronald Reagan (R)	Secretary of Health and Human Services	1983–1985
Elizabeth Hanford Dole	Ronald Reagan (R)	Secretary of Transportation	1983–1987
Ann Dore McLaughlin	Ronald Reagan (R)	Secretary of Labor	1989–1993
Elizabeth Hanford Dole	George H. W. Bush (R)	Secretary of Labor	1989–1991
Carla Anderson Hills	George H. W. Bush (R)	Special Trade Representative	1989–1993
Lynn Morley Martin	George H. W. Bush (R)	Secretary of Labor	1991–1993

Appointee	President Who Appointed Them	Position Held	Years Served
Barbara H. Franklin	George H. W. Bush (R)	Secretary of Commerce	1992–1993
Madeleine K. Albright	Bill Clinton (D)	UN Ambassador	1993–1997
Hazel R. O'Leary	Bill Clinton (D)	Secretary of Energy	1993–1997
Alice M. Rivlin	Bill Clinton (D)	Director, Office of Management and Budget	1994–1996
Laura D'Andrea Tyson	Bill Clinton (D)	Chair, National Economic Council	1995–1997
Janet L. Yellen	Bill Clinton (D)	Chair, National Council of Economic Advisers	1997–1999
Carol M. Browner	Bill Clinton (D)	Administrator, Environmental Protection Agency	1993–2001
Janet Reno	Bill Clinton (D)	Attorney General	1993–2001
Donna Shalala	Bill Clinton (D)	Secretary of Health and Human Services	1993–2001
Madeleine K. Albright	Bill Clinton (D)	Secretary of State	1997–2001
Aida Alvarez	Bill Clinton (D)	Administrator, Small Business Administration	1997–2001
Charlene Barshefsky	Bill Clinton (D)	U.S. Trade Representative	1997–2001
Alexis Herman	Bill Clinton (D)	Secretary of Labor	1997–2001
Janice R. Lachance	Bill Clinton (D)	Director, Office of Personnel Management	1997–2001
Christine Todd Whitman	George W. Bush (R)	Administrator, Environmental Protection Agency	2001–2003
Elaine Chao	George W. Bush (R)	Secretary of Labor	2001–2009
Gale Norton	George W. Bush (R)	Secretary of Interior	2001–2006
Condoleezza Rice	George W. Bush (R)	National Security Adviser	2001–2005
Ann Veneman	George W. Bush (R)	Secretary of Agriculture	2001–2005
Condoleezza Rice	George W. Bush (R)	Secretary of State	2005–2009
Margaret Spellings	George W. Bush (R)	Secretary of Education	2005–2009
Susan Schwab	George W. Bush (R)	U.S. Trade Representative	2006–2009
Mary E. Peters	George W. Bush (R)	Secretary of Transportation	2006–2009
Hilda Solis	Barack Obama (D)	Secretary of Labor	2009–present
Kathleen Sebelius	Barack Obama (D)	Secretary of Health and Human Services	2009–present

(Continued)

Appointee	President Who Appointed Them	Position Held	Years Served
Christina D. Romer	Barack Obama (D)	Chair, Council of Economic Advisers	2009–present
Susan E. Rice	Barack Obama (D)	U.N. Ambassador	2009–present
Janet Napolitano	Barack Obama (D)	Secretary of Homeland Security	2009–present
Lisa Jackson	Barack Obama (D)	Administrator, Environmental Protection Agency	2009–present
Hillary Rodham Clinton	Barack Obama (D)	Secretary of State	2009–present

Source: Center for American Women and Politics. 2009c. *Women Appointed to Presidential Cabinets.* New Brunswick, NJ: Eagleton Institute of Politics, Rutgers University.

PHOTO CREDITS

Chapter 2:
p. 14: Courtesy of the Library of Congress; p. 33: National Organization for Women. Photo reprinted with permission of the National Organization for Women; p. 45: Republican National Committee. Photograph provided courtesy of Ann Wagner/Republican National Committee; p. 47: Democratic National Committee, Office of Ann Lewis;

Chapter 3:
p. 70: Steve Marcus/Reuters/Landov; p. 72: Jason Reed/Landov; p. 73: Shannon Stapleton/Reuters/Landov;

Chapter 4:
p. 92: Courtesy of the Library of Congress; p. 93: Courtesy of the Library of Congress; p. 96: Courtesy of the Library of Congress; p. 108: Courtesy of *The New Yorker Magazine*/Cartoonbank.com; p. 109: Courtesy of Conde Nast/ The Cartoonbank.com; p. 113: Paul Hosefros/*The New York Times*/Redux; p. 114: CBS/Landov; p. 118: Signe Wilkinson Editorial Cartoon used with the permission of Signe Wilkinson and the Washington Post Writers Group in conjunction with the Cartoonist Group;

Chapter 5:
p. 149: Joe Raedle/Getty Images; p. 153: Daniel Gluskoter/iconSMI/Corbis; p. 169: Leslie Kossoff, LK Photo;

Chapter 6:
p. 184: Anne Leighton Massoni. All rights reserved; p. 186: AP Images; p. 212: Stephanie Sinclari/VII/AP Images;

Chapter 7:
p. 241: Courtesy of Women's Policy, Inc.; www.womenspolicy.org; p. 250: Corbis/ Bettmann; p. 253: Stephen Crowley/*The New York Times*/Redux Pictures;

Chapter 8:
p. 268: Toles ©2007 *The Washington Post*. Used by permission of Universal Uclick. All rights reserved; p. 269: Scott Olson/Getty Images; p. 272: Mark Lyons/epa/Corbis; p. 281: Alex Brandon/AP Images;

Chapter 9:
p. 307: Alex Brandon/AP images; p. 313: Courtesy of the Library of Congress; p. 317: David Hume Kennerly/Getty Images; p. 321: Photo by Doug Elbinger, courtesy of the Michigan Supreme Court.

INDEX